BRITAIN'S ELUSIVE EMPIRE IN THE MIDDLE EAST, 1900–1921

THEMES IN EUROPEAN EXPANSION: EXPLORATION,
COLONIZATION, AND THE IMPACT OF EMPIRE
(General Editor: James A. Casada)
Vol. 2

GARLAND REFERENCE LIBRARY
OF SOCIAL SCIENCE
Vol. 109

BRITAIN'S ELUSIVE EMPIRE
IN THE MIDDLE EAST, 1900–1921
An Annotated Bibliography

William J. Olson

with the assistance of
Addeane S. Caelleigh

GARLAND PUBLISHING, INC. • NEW YORK & LONDON
1982

Library of Congress Cataloging in Publication Data

Olson, William J., 1947–
   Britain's elusive empire in the Middle East, 1900–
1921.

   (Themes in European expansion : exploration, coloniza-
tion, and the impact of empire ; v. 2) (Garland
reference library of social science ; v. 109)
   Includes indexes.
    1. Near East—Foreign relations—Great Britain—
Bibliography. 2. Great Britain—Foreign relations—Near
East—Bibliography. 3. Near East—Politics and govern-
ment—Bibliography. I. Caelleigh, Addeane S. II. Title.
III. Series: Themes in European expansion ; v. 2.
IV. Series: Garland reference library of social
science ; v. 109.
Z3014.R44O47 [DS63.2.G7]   016.32741056   81-43360
ISBN 0-8240-9273-2   AACR2

Printed on acid-free, 250-year-life paper
Manufactured in the United States of America

016.32741
01 52

CONTENTS

v

114416

EDITOR'S INTRODUCTION

The timeliness of *Britain's Elusive Empire in the Middle East,
1900–1921: An Annotated Bibliography* is readily obvious. The un-
folding events of recent years in the region have served to bring
into sharp focus an area which long had languished as a little-
known backwater that the wider world generally misunderstood
or ignored. However, factors such as the growing economic clout
of the Organization of Petroleum Exporting Countries and its
Middle East–dominated membership, Iran's revolution and the
subsequent drama surrounding the American hostages, Russia's
intervention in Afghanistan's affairs, and a host of related developments have contributed to enhanced general awareness of
both the turbulent nature of politics in the Middle East and the
area's immense importance and potential for the future. With
these realizations has also come a belated awareness of how
abysmally lacking the wider world is in knowledge of and serious
scholarship on the region. Even the most basic of English-
language research tools—those that are essential to offer
would-be students guidance as they seek to make up lost
ground—are virtually nonexistent. The appearance of Dr.
Olson's volume, the second in the series "Themes in European
Expansion: Exploration, Colonization, and the Impact of Empire," marks a significant step towards redressing existing gaps
in reference literature on the Middle East.

Dr. William Olson is a budding scholar whose early endeavors show promise of a highly productive publishing career.
He did his graduate work at the University of Texas at Austin,
where he studied under the noted British imperial historian,
William Roger Louis. Upon completion of his Ph.D. in 1977
Olson held a Leverhulme Trust Research Fellowship at the University of Aberdeen for nine months. Subsequently he was
awarded a two-year post-doctoral fellowship at the University of

Sydney. While in Australia his expertise on the Middle East resulted in several appearances on national television and the publication of a series of interpretative articles on Iran and Afghanistan in *The National Times*. He is the author of several articles, including the contribution of two chapters to E. Kedouri and S. Haim (eds.), *Iran: Toward Modernity—Studies in Thought, Politics and Society* (1980). His book, *A True and Lasting Order: Anglo-Iranian Relations in World War I*, a detailed study of British attitudes and policies regarding Iran during and just after the Great War, is currently in press. The present work incorporates information garnered from all of Olson's previous researches and in a very real sense marks the full fruition of a decade of scholarly endeavor. With this impressive effort behind him, the author has now focused his research interests on the manner in which historically differing conceptualizations of science and technology produced marked cultural differences between Europe and the East.

Britian's Elusive Empire in the Middle East opens with a lengthy essay which constitutes a most useful introduction to twentieth-century British policy in the Middle East. More importantly, it sets the stage for the extensive bibliography which follows. The 664 main entries of the bibliography are carefully and critically annotated, and collectively they comprise a full guide to the principal existing sources on the subject. The author's preface explains his methods of selection and arrangement of entries, but the obvious care which has gone into formulation of the individual chapters and subheadings is deserving of special mention. This consideration, together with a full author-subject index, results in a readily understood and easily used bibliography. Additionally, Olson's inclusion of a section on theses and dissertations assures the reader of access to unpublished yet often very important research on the Middle East.

In short, this is a finely crafted bibliography which sets a high standard in the most vital areas of evaluation for such research tools—utility and comprehensiveness. Students of Middle Eastern affairs in a wide range of disciplines will find it a useful literature guide, and the author's incisive comments on his entries are certain to be of assistance to the novice and experienced scholar alike. Libraries should find it a vital source in a field that is ill-served by reference works, and certainly it forms a welcome addition to the series of which it is a part.

James A. Casada, *Series Editor*
Winthrop College

PREFACE

This project grew like Topsy. Once embarked, I realized that its tendency to expand beyond control could only be limited by imposing arbitrary standards. This means the selections, perforce, have an idiosyncratic quality. Also, I was unable to overcome certain inherent disadvantages in the library facilities available to me, since I was unable to obtain some books, and I have not included as an annotated entry any item I have not personally held in my hands. The result is shortcomings and oversights that I am painfully aware of or will be made painfully aware of by reviewers. As much as I would like to blame external forces for my errors and shortcomings, I am unable to find any scapegoats.

This work, as part of a general series on empire and imperialism, brings together monographs and articles that deal with the general and specific nature of European expansion and the reaction to it. This volume concerns British policy in the Middle East from 1900 to 1921, beginning, roughly, with the Baghdad Railway concession to the Germans, and ending with the Cairo Conference which set out the main features of Britain's post-war policy in the area. What countries actually constitute the Middle East is still a matter of debate; here, the area includes Iran, the Ottoman Empire, including Egypt and the Sudan, and the Arabian Peninsula. North Africa is not included.

I have included material that will introduce the Middle East expert to the perplexities of British and international politics, and introduce the British imperial expert to the key features of Middle Eastern history and Britain's role in that history. Such an undertaking covers a vast range of material, more than a single-volume study of this nature could hope to cover. I have, therefore, selected materials that are the best representatives of their types, and that can be used as guides for further study.

As a rule I have covered works published since the 1950's, unless an earlier work has not been superseded by later scholarship. I have also tried to select works that best illustrate the inner workings of policy formation: the clash of individuals and their constituencies, the rivalries of lobbying groups, the role of personalities, and the influence of chance and accident. I have also included works that reflect the impact of larger forces—public opinion, economic activity, and international rivalry—on policy development. Since the range of material available is extensive, I have treated some of the individual annotations as short bibliographic essays that suggest further sources, in an effort to include a wide range of material in limited space. In addition, I have included a list of reviews of many of the annotated monographs so that the reader can explore the range of comments of particular works and their place in the literature.

The concentration has been on British policy in the crucial years before and during World War I, and in the peace settlements that followed. This period marked significant changes in Middle Eastern history and in the scope and development of British policy in the area. The work is divided into two parts: the Introduction and the Bibliography. The introduction summarizes the circumstances of British interest in the Middle East and how these interests related to and were affected by regional and international conditions. The bibliography is divided into six major sections covering (1) reference tools, (2) theories of imperialism and the peculiar features of British imperialism, (3) international rivalry and its influence on British policy, (4) the nature and growth of Britain's interest in the Middle East, (5) the rise of regional nationalism and its effect on British imperial interest, and (6) an unannotated list of some recent British and American dissertations on the Middle East.

The citations always contain three and often four elements: the bibliographic information; the annotation; further references; and the reviews. In most cases I have given the American publication information, and I have tried to give the latest edition. The annotation provides a brief description of the item and its relations to others on the same subject, and usually a guide to other, similar works. The suggestions for further reference (denoted by "cf.") do not attempt to list every annotated work with related information, but give a short list of the most relevant items. They are listed in order of relevance, moving from the most directly related items to more general or distant ones. The reviews are self-explanatory, listing the abbreviated journal title (see list of abbreviations), the bibliographic information and, in most cases, the author. I have surveyed some thirty major journals, concentrating on the last fifteen years, and have used standard indexes to give as many reviews as possible, but I do not pretend that these are any more than a preliminary guide to reviews.

In the course of any work such as this one develops a list of long-suffering friends, helpful colleagues, supportive institutions, and enemies, without whose advice, aid and hindrance nothing and everything would have been accomplished. In particular I would like to acknowledge the aid and patience of Addeane S. Caelleigh, my worst critic and constant taskmaster. I would also like to thank the University of Sydney, and the History Department, particularly Professors Marjorie Jacobs and Ian Jack, for their help and support. Dr. Richard Waterhouse also deserves recompense for my many bad jokes and thanks for having read sections of the introduction. I also want to thank Dr. David Morgan of the School of Oriental and African Studies, London, for his vigil from afar, and Professors Hafez Farmayan and Wm. Roger Louis for their unwitting contributions. Finally, I want to thank my general editor, Dr. James Casada, for his help and calm assurance.

Wm. J. Olson
Sydney, Australia
August 1980

ABBREVIATIONS OF JOURNALS
CITED IN REVIEWS

AA	*American Anthropologist*
AAPSS-A	*American Academy of Political and Social Science, Annals*
AHR	*American Historical Review*
APSR	*American Political Science Review*
ARBA	*American Reference Books Annual*
BHR	*Business History Review*
BSOAS	*Bulletin of School of Oriental and African Studies* (University of London)
CH	*Church History*
CJH	*Canadian Journal of History*
CRL	*College and Research Libraries*
EcHR	*Economic History* (2nd series)
EHR	*English Historical Review*
GJ	*Geographical Journal*
H	*History*
HJ	*Historical Journal*
IJMES	*International Journal of Middle East Studies*
JAH	*Journal of American History*
JAS	*Journal of Asian Studies*
JBS	*Journal of British Studies* (U.S.)
JCH	*Journal of Contemporary History*
JEH	*Journal of Economic History*
JEL	*Journal of Economic Literature*
JICH	*Journal of Imperial and Commonwealth History*
JMH	*Journal of Modern History*
JP	*Journal of Politics*
JR	*Journal of Religion*
MEJ	*Middle East Journal*
MES	*Middle Eastern Studies*
PA	*Pacific Affairs*
PHR	*Pacific Historical Review*
PSQ	*Political Science Quarterly*
S&S	*Science and Society*
VS	*Victorian Studies*

Part I
Introduction

Britain entered World War I with no clear definition of aims other than the defeat of the enemy, with a military and political system unprepared for the war, and with a labyrinthine bureaucratic structure in the Middle East that encouraged, even necessitated, confusion and bumbling. Not until the end of the war did the British seriously consider why they were fighting, and in the process wartime confusion gave way to peacetime equivocation.

With the successful conclusion of the war, Britain possessed a variety of conquests and commitments in the Middle East. What had begun as a tentative local campaign to protect British interests and keep the Ottoman entrance into the war from developing into an anti-British Muslim crusade, had mushroomed into a sizeable effort that left Britain in occupation of the areas today comprising Iraq, Syria, Palestine, and Jordan. Before World War I the natural consequences of such a victory would have been self-evident, for annexation was one of the symbols of diplomatic or military success. Territories were acquired or bartered as symbols of good faith, of prowess, of winning. But circumstances at the end of the war made annexation impossible.

This was true partly because the scale of the war had exceeded the Allies' means for winning it, and they had to turn to non-Europeans for help. In doing so the Allies, and especially the British in the Middle East, made commitments, raised expectations and displayed weaknesses that compromised any return to pre-war diplomatic relations and assumptions. Further, the entrance of the U.S. into the war interjected Wilsonian ideology into the diplomatic process. Wilson did what the Europeans had failed to do, namely conceived a well-articulated, if not as well-defined, set of principles for why the war was being fought. In order to make America a party to the war the Allies made themselves a party to Wilson's philosophy, which committed them at least publicly to an anti-annexationist post-war policy. The Russian Revolution and the collapse of two multi-national, multi-ethnic empires (the Austro-Hungarian and the Ottoman) raised further hopes of self-determination and strengthened the opposition to pre-war di-

plomacy. The victorious French and the British empires shared
few of these sentiments.

World War I was a revolution in which the Bolshevik seizure
of power was but a scene in the drama. Post-war expectations
worldwide had changed; new concepts of order and of the need
for changes emerged. The horror of the war indicted the old
diplomacy; wartime rhetoric unleashed old furies and aroused
new expectations; and the efforts to win the war left the
major European powers physically, morally and psychologically
shattered. Furthermore the Allies had made a series of promises to local peoples that inhibited their post-war freedom
of movement, while the same local peoples had absorbed, however
incompletely, a lesson in self-reliance along with the promises
of self-determination, for it was not just the victors that
sat down to deliberate, but also all the legatees and clients
their wartime promises had enfranchised.

The delegates of the major European powers at the Peace
Conference were neither uniformly aware of nor committed to
the same high principles of peace contemplated in Wilson's
espousal of war or to the post-war diplomatic climate they
dictated. Britain, France and Italy were aware of shifts in
world opinion, but this did not mean they were prepared to accept these changes or their economic and strategic consequences.
Expectations may have changed, but the realities of international relations and power had not; nor had older styles of
diplomacy simply given way, if for no other reason than that
older-style diplomats, with their memories and conceptions,
had not simply vanished.

Diplomacy exists on a margin of doubt, on the gap in understanding between what one power intends and what another
perceives those intentions to be. It is the goal of diplomacy
to keep that margin small, to mediate the discrepancies, and
as much as possible to discover and control the other nation's
intentions. Therein lies security. But since it is generally
impossible to always know or control other states, insecurity
is an inherent feature of diplomacy. In such a mutually suspicious climate, a nation rarely will unilaterally forego ex-
ploiting an advantage at a rival's, or even a friend's, expense.
Knowing this, each nation is watchful and tries to know and
control the actions of others. In such an atmosphere the important concern is not "will another power do such-and-such"
(that is generally obscure), but "*can* they do it." Nations
tend to work on the assumption that not far behind the capacity is the opportunity, and opportunity is only a short step
from intention, and then necessity.

The British delegates to the Peace Conference were aware
of these realities. In addition, they came from a small social

elite that shared certain goals, expectations and methods.
This elite also shared a certain ethos with the elites of the
other Great Powers, as well as sharing the patterns of diplomacy shaped by that ethos in the decades before the war. The
war destroyed neither that sense of community among diplomats
nor the underlying imperatives dictated by security and insecurity. Thus, when the victorious Powers convened at Paris,
the old sat down with the new and both came away dissatisfied.
It is little wonder that the world spent the next twenty years
trying to circumvent their compromise peace that had settled
nothing because it satisfied no one.

The following essay examines the diplomatic background to
the war years and peace, first taking up the nature of imperialism that was at the heart of the struggle, and then describing British policy in the Middle East, showing in the process
how Britain won and at the same time lost an empire there.

THE IMPERIAL SETTING

Discussions of imperialism commonly begin with disclaimers
or assertions that imperialism defines nothing about the modern
world or says all. One thing is clear: as a word, "imperialism" has become a generalization representing the political
opinions of the user more than a descriptive term. For the
sake of argument it is stripped of shade and nuance, and after
this forced conversion it is treated as if it had been this
way all along and not a device for winning debates--the map
has become the territory.

The chief definition of imperialism, the most sophisticated
and the most politicized, is an economic one. The chief pro-
ponents of such an interpretation are Marxists, though there
were and are secular economic interpretations. The basic pre-
mise of economic arguments of imperialism stresses the search
for or protection of markets, raw materials and investment opportunities. The main difference between species of economic
interpretations is the degree to which they vilify this process or attribute it solely to the inherent evils of one particular system--namely, capitalism. In most cases to do this
is also to argue for an alternative economic system, and so it
is often difficult to dissociate economic interpretations from
special pleading.

Many of the alternative explanations of imperialism set
out to invalidate this or that or all economic arguments, sometimes with an alternative explanation in mind. Thus, many of

the counterarguments are their own forms of special pleading. This has produced a third set of interpretations, which says, more or less, "a plague on both your houses," and sets out either to redefine the whole process, subsuming economics and "anti-economics" in another all-embracing definition, or simply dismisses the whole argument as absurd and concentrates on the matter of facts. Thus there are definitions or non-definitions of imperialism to suit every taste.

The initial vilification of empire began with Marx, unless one wants to count the Gauls. But Marx never developed a clear definition of empire or applied even an unclear definition consistently. That was left to those who devoted their lives to explaining what Marx really meant by what he did not say. The result has been a number of definitive, if contradictory, interpretations. Chief among these were those advanced by Lenin in *Imperialism, the Highest Stage of Capitalism* (Stokes, item 076). Whether his arguments succeeded because of their inherent brilliance or because Lenin established a political authority that bolstered his claims against those of Rosa Luxemburg and Karl Kautsky, Lenin's views are central to Marxist-Leninist interpretations.

Perhaps the key non-Marxist anti-imperialist economic argument, said to have influenced Lenin, was advanced by John Hobson in *Imperialism*, published in 1902 (see Trevor Lloyd, item 065). This argument and those advanced by Marxists were reduced to historical and theoretical rubble by William Langer in an article, "A Critique of Imperialism," *Foreign Affairs* 14 (1935): 102-15 (views elaborated in his *Diplomacy of Imperialism*, item 064). The demolition was later completed by David Fieldhouse in "Imperialism: An Historiographical Revision" (item 056). As might be expected, these attacks convinced those who saw few economic imperatives in imperialism, while they inspired the believers in economic imperialism, Marxist or non-Marxist, to reinterpret their sources, proving that their subtlety had been misinterpreted by critics. This process says far more about the dialectical nature of historiography than ever it does about imperialism.

A more recent interpretation of imperialism which takes issue not with Marxist views (though it has implications for them), but with the received notions of a far older economic orthodoxy, are the views advanced by Ronald Robinson and John Gallagher (items 072, 073). Robinson and Gallagher set non-Marxist interpretations on their ears by displacing economic arguments with a subtle view stressing that the reaction of European officials to colonial pressures threatening the security of their nation's overseas interests provided the principal motive for expansion. Needless to say, these new views

have attracted their share of detractors, supporters, and re-
interpreters (see Platt, item 071).

Rather than sorting through these conflicts, assessing
right and wrong, I offer instead my own views and working assumptions on the nature of imperialism, which are central to
my arguments concerning British policy in the Middle East.
Most definitions of imperialism go wrong in their attempts
to devise monochrome explanations for multicolored events.
They define by exclusion, or in terms of what they regard as
the leading element among a variety of explanations. Naturally enough, this always offends someone else's sense of priorities. It is very much like the parable of the blind men and
the elephant, each describing the whole beast in terms of the
part he has encountered, instead of interpreting the parts as
a function of the whole. As a methodological tool, this dif-
ferentiation is useful for gross interpretation of large
amounts of data, but it would appear that in examining imperialism, the tail has ended up wagging the elephant.

The following arguments propose that there are no sharp
divisions between economic, political, psychological or moral
goals in international relations. Rather, there is a gradual
shading of these motives into one another. Economic goals are
pursued by political means and political objectives are sustained by economic motives. Only in the self-imposed regular-
ity of an argument are there neat compartments for human motivation.

The notion of imperialism used here is quite simply stated.
It is the term used to describe the process of interstate relations on an international scale, the contention being that
European exploration and expansion overseas inaugurated the
era of world history and internationalized the characteristics
of economic, political and social relations that had previously
epitomized regional, localized relations.

First, it is assumed that the aim of a political system or
nation, whether locally confined or international in scope, is
a *favorable* equilibrium: one that permits a nation to achieve
its ends without frustration or delay, and assures that what
is achieved is not ephemeral except at its own discretion.
Needless to say, such a blessed equilibrium is normally beyond
the means of any nation, and the attempt to achieve it is
fraught with difficulties because one nation's equilibrium is
often another's anathema.

The second assumption is that circumstances, although they
can be influenced by human actions, have their own momentum
apart from the aims and intentions of individuals or states,
and that their momentum limits human choices or influences
their direction. What reason and rationality did not dictate,

observed Dr. Johnson, reason cannot explain. This might be a
summary of the development of imperialism. Many causes of the
expansion of Europe and the development of empire grew from irrational or unintended circumstances outside the consideration,
control or knowledge of the principal actors or the understanding of their subsequent critics and observers. This is not an
attempt to base a theory of imperialism on the irrational in
history, or to deny the effect of deliberate policy or motive
in shaping events; but there is a case to be made for the influence of events, the limitations imposed on intentions by
habit and circumstances, the constraints of geography, knowledge and capability, and the operation of chance and the un-
anticipated in shaping the milieu within which individuals and
societies must function. What individuals and societies are
able to achieve or what they must endure is the result of this
intermingling of intention and possibility.

Weather, distance, geographical features, plagues, droughts,
storms, etc. are all environmental factors that can limit or
influence human actions regardless of human intentions. Going
further, the requirements of membership in a society, political
community, interest group, economic organization; the demands
of custom, morality and practice; in other words, the obligations imposed on individuals and nations by the systems they
participate in to regulate and sustain their lives can restrict
the type and direction of human wants and needs. The operations of such systems can be as uncontrollable, unpredictable
and elemental in their disruptive impact on intentions as the
forces of Nature. The social, political, economic and strategic forces that impelled Europe into the First World War are
an example.

Turning from these assumptions, there are three major
features of imperialism as it is used here. First, are the
consequences of disparity of power--whether economic, political, strategic, technological or organizational--between societies or nations that give one an advantage in dealing with
others. Second, is the habit of a given society or nation to
prefer its own methods and systems, its own interests and ways
of pursuing them over those of others; to distrust others; and
given the opportunity, to insist on its own rights and privileges and ways of doing things. And finally, there is every
nation's concern and search for security and stability. Three
further contributing factors complete the picture: the consequences of rivalry between societies or nations that make the
fulfilment of goals difficult or doubtful; the problems of
prestige or national self-image that can make a particular society touchy; and the effects of collaboration and resistance
in the relations between weak and powerful nations. What is

common to these various features is reciprocity, the notion
that states do not exist in isolation and that relations between states or groups of people are not solely determined by
one party; the intentions and needs of one nation cannot escape the effect of uncontrolled or unforeseen actions by others
or by events. Friction, paraphrasing from Clausewitz, is an
important element in the exercise of any system and its operation is what distinguishes reality from the ideal. All of
these features and contributing factors can be seen in regional affairs by looking at Chinese expansion and empire building
in East Asia or Muslim-Arab expansion from the Great Wall to
Seville. For the development of an international system of
state relations, we must look to European capitalism.

The major event of modern history was the growth of tightly-
knit nation-states in Europe and their spread into the world
at large, sustained by revolutionary developments in technology, economics, social organization, military and naval science, and industry that gave Europe an edge in dealing with
the world it encountered. The Europeans did not intentionally
embark on nationalism or the industrial-technological revolution because they anticipated world empire, nor did the non-
European world deliberately bask in traditionalism and decline
to facilitate European domination. But the natural willingness
to follow-up on advantages imparted a momentum to Europe that
gradually increased the disparity of power between Europe and
the rest of the world, adding a sense of the inevitable, the
right and proper; making the process, at least for the Europeans, seem part of the natural order, divinely inspired and
sustained. It was, after all, a short leap from realizing one
enjoyed particular advantages to assuming those advantages were
ordained.

In making this leap the Europeans discovered world empire.
Beginning in the 15th century European technology, expansion,
and renewing energies broke down the barriers of time and distance that had kept the various societies of the world in comparative isolation from one another. In doing so the Europeans
engendered an international economic system based on their
ideas of trade and their abilities to exploit them, and spread
a system of international relations based on European imperatives and notions. This process was gradual and uneven, en-
compassing five centuries in the case of Asia, much of its pace
depending on the relative strengths of Europe and the rest of
the world, with local ability to resist and the degree of local cooperation being important elements governing the relations between Europeans and non-Europeans. In Asia the Europeans encountered well-developed, sophisticated societies with
the power to keep the Europeans in their place, at least polit-

ically, until the 18th century; the civilizations of America,
conversely, were little able to resist and disappeared under
the weight of European interests with stunning speed given the
size of the new world and the limited resources of the old;
while the exploration and absorption of Africa had to wait on
the facilities of the 19th century.

As the Europeans pursued their interests, and the economic
and technological gap between Europe and the rest of the world
widened, the Europeans were increasingly able to insist on
their own methods and practices as the base for relations. In
the case of Asia, this insistence was retarded by Asian power
and its earliest manifestations were confined to international
trade, which from very early on was a European monopoly protected by European naval superiority. However, as the balance
of power gradually shifted in Europe's favor, the Europeans
could enlarge their position within Asian society. Again this
process was governed by the tempo of local events in response
to European pressure. Thus India, never universally organized
and prone to an indigenous chaos that invited foreign involvement, succumbed much more quickly than China, for example, or
the rest of Asia, where local political authority succeeded in
holding together a degree of unity and political solvency that
was able to retard European encroachment. But the desire to
have one's way when matched with the power to get it meant an
expanding market for European social and cultural values equal
to the expansion and protection of European trade.

Although initially confined to the regulation of international political and economic relations, increasing advantages
in power increased the scope for demanding adherence to European systems. This meant that imperialism, as it is used here,
became more than a political or economic system governing the
relations between weak and strong states; it evolved into a
social system on an international scale, and international culture based on and fortified by perceptions of European supremacy and technique.

If the European approach to the world had been uniform or
the response to Europe undifferentiated, the description of
imperialism might stop here. But there was no such neatness.
It was not a unified Europe that went overseas but a congeries
of states with individual interests. There was no rational
European system of economic, social and political organization,
only a rationalized set of guidelines and loosely shared values
that had developed after generations of struggle. This "European system" was the result of an organic compromise kept in
being by the dynamics of European relations; when the Europeans
went overseas they not only took their shared values, they also
transported their differences, animosities, fears and parochial

rivalries. The most significant consequence of this cultural export was the internationalization of European rivalries and the introduction of international considerations into those rivalries.

Because each European nation had its own goals, and circumstances varied, the form that empire took showed a diversity of individual expression. In other words, there is a difference between imperialism as an overall concept and the characteristics of individual empires, although the characteristics of individual empires are subsidiary to the concept of imperialism, and the presence and actions of rival empires contributed to the development of the overall pattern of imperialism. If a series of treaties of Trodesillas had divided the world into mutually exclusive enclaves, and if such a division had guaranteed absolutely equal returns to the interested parties along with the inescapable assurances that no one would try to capitalize on its interests to the detriment of others, then the course of world history would have been far different and perhaps more docile. But this was not the case, and no one escaped the consequences.

From virtually the beginning of the European overseas adventure, rivalry between states figured prominently. Attempts to preclude rivals, to smash trade monopolies, to poach on or ruin a rival's position were exported along with other goods, while new animosities and rivalries were imported into Europe along with the spices and treasures of Asia and America. This spirit of rivalry and the threat it posed to security permeated the international diplomatic atmosphere. For much of this period the very concept governing trade—mercantilism —was militant commerce. Contributing to this competition were the attempts of European states to use their international positions to hurt their rivals either by employing advantages gained overseas to advantage in Europe, or by hitting at the overseas interests of a rival to undercut their position in Europe. The presence of real or potential rivals introduced uncertainty into all arrangements, jeopardizing stability and security. Concern for security is a theme that threads its way throughout the history of European expansion, and the measures nations took to cope with this uncertainty on an international level were important in the development of imperialism.

Also important, but mentioned so far only in passing, was the contribution of the non-European world to the process. Two features of the relationship need to be remarked on—the collaboration of the non-European world in its own difficulties and its resistance to domination by the Europeans, processes that went hand-in-hand throughout the history of the growth of modern empires.

The non-European world did not greet the newly-arrived
Europeans as conquerors or the harbingers of civilization,
but as curiosities, or in the same spirit that took the Europeans overseas--as sources of profit or advantage. In the
case of Asia, the European presence was countenanced on restricted terms; and because the Asian states enjoyed equal or
superior power to the initial motley assortment of European
adventurers and merchants, relations were based on Asian suf-
ferance. For much of the period from the 15th to the 18th
centuries there were no formal relations between states except trade; European merchants doubled as diplomatic representatives, on occasion inventing their position or their
state, and few Asians cared to venture to Europe in the same
way as the Europeans came to Asia. States such as Turkey or
Iran recognized the superior quality of Western arms and military science and sought advice; but others, such as China,
were not so impressed, and the Japanese, after initial expe-
riments with European arms, rejected them and then slammed
the door on further contact. But imperceptibly the Europeans
expanded their trading interests and also became involved in
local politics. In the late 16th century, for example, British officers advised Shah Abbas of Iran on a war against the
Ottomans; and later a British squadron helped the same Shah
evict the Portuguese from the island of Hormuz in the Persian
Gulf. In India a similar involvement had more far-reaching
effects.
    The decline of the Moghul Empire, the involvement of the
British and others in the spreading political chaos of India,
and the consequences of subsequent Anglo-French rivalry for
predominance in India is a tale too familiar to need retell-
ing here, other than to hold up as a metaphor of the changes
in European-Asian relations and of the increasing involvement
of Europeans in Asian affairs. When this involvement and increasing contact were joined by a widening gap in economic and
technological ability in Europe's favor, it became increasingly difficult for India or other Asian states to maintain
their former posture towards Europe. By an evolutionary process the Europeans became part of the economic landscape and
gradually part of the political one as well. By some per-
versity the European states seemed to grow stronger while
Asia grew progressively weaker, in a process that was not
wholly a consequence of the interrelationship between the two.
When Asia awoke to this reality, an arousal that varied from
society to society, the process had gone on too long for Asia
to reverse; and the benefits plus the inherent pressures--the
need for markets or fear of rivals--were too much for the
Europeans to resist without a change of psychology or of the
economic, social and political realities of European life.

This, of course, was a gradual development, proceeding most rapidly in those areas where local political authority was fragmented and unable to offer sustained resistance. Thus China, Japan, Persia and the Ottoman Empire, though weak by comparison to the Europeans in the 18th and 19th centuries, were able to withstand them longer than India, where society collapsed into a confusion that at once gave the Europeans even greater advantage while sucking them into a more intimate local political involvement.

Patterns of local history gave European influence another road on which to penetrate local societies, which shared regional loyalty and cultural identity but only limited loyalty to the idea of a nation-state on European lines. In practice, political loyalty was largely motivated by self-interest and went to the power that could exact it. This explains, in part, why the Europeans benefited from local collaboration. Local political authorities sought the help of any available influence in advancing their interests, while people at large were accustomed to accepting the prevailing political order. Advantage and power gave the Europeans the ability to embarrass or destroy local political authority and thus to excite the cooperation of the ambitious and the acceptance of much of the general population. In this sense the growth of European predominance fitted into Asian traditions of rule by conquest and was therefore acceptable to or acquiesced in by large numbers of people.

But if there was collaboration there was also determined resistance. Much of this was confined to groups that stood to lose economic or political power to increasing European involvement; but as contact with Europeans spread so did resistance, especially when local customs, habits and livelihoods had to give way to European ideas. But without a system of political nationalism to coordinate and legitimize such responses throughout society, resistance remained diffuse or isolated, riven by internal struggles for power and liable to rapid disintegration. As long as this was the case, and as long as the Europeans could rely on their economic, political or military power to secure a degree of local cooperation, resistance remained an aggravation to European influence that could excite further involvement, rather than an effective force to limit it.

Collaboration and resistance contributed to the intensification of European involvement in yet another way. Not only did Europeans become embroiled in local Asian affairs, but as Europeans developed ongoing overseas interests that could be menaced by other European powers, Asians were caught up in European affairs as well. As long as one European imperial power could not be sure that a rival European power would not suborn local cooperation or incite local resistance, it could never be sure of a situation unless it controlled that situation absolutely; since that was impossible, security remained a nagging concern.

Intimately involved in this whole process was the elusive question of prestige. Deriving as it does from the complexities of national psychology and difficult to pin down definitely, it was an undeniable force in European imperialism, as it was for national, or indeed individual, self-esteem. Taken as a whole, prestige might be described as the national ego, the psychological embodiment of all that a nation or empire felt about itself, its rights and privileges, its status and its ability. Like economic or political interests, which were absorbed into the image of prestige, it could suffer from insecurity, be threatened by the actions of others. In more practical terms, in Asia in particular, it was a necessary element in maintaining influence, in rule. To a degree all government, national or imperial, is an illusion acquiesced in by the ruled and rulers. Government may be sustained by real power, but to be effective it must also be believed, have the illusion of legitimacy and power. The Chinese concept of the Mandate of Heaven is one expression of this principle; the Enlightenment concept of government as a contractual relationship is another. In both, revolution is the punishment for failure. The same held true for the expansion and maintenance of European overseas influence, especially in Asia.

The establishment and maintenance of the British Empire, for example, was a psychological triumph in its orderliness of control. The British not only had real power but large numbers of their subjects and others accepted it. British imperial literature resounds with the vocabulary of prestige, with words like "moral effect" or "pluck." As one prominent British imperialist, Frederick Lugard, summed up, if the illusion of power were penetrated the European would have to run or get his throat cut. This is one reason why the Japanese victory over Russia in 1905 was so important in Asia, because it penetrated the illusion of European invincibility. It was part of Gandhi's genius, too, that he realized that the British could not govern India if the Indians, all at once, refused to accept it. Threats to prestige could not be taken lightly and explains, perhaps, why insignificant incidents such as Denshiwai in Egypt, a perfectly normal occurrence in local terms, could elicit such an excited response by Britain; or why Field Marshall Sir Henry Wilson could argue after World War I that Irish independence would be a crack in the façade of prestige that would bring down the whole imperial edifice.

Prestige also had an international character, representing as it did a nation's face to the world. In the international system engendered by the Europeans, prestige became important as a symbol of respect and of power, and was intimately associated with national security. In a system where weakness invited presumption, where one nation was always prepared to take advantage of another, a nation had to be seen to stand up for its rights or risk losing them. But since no nation could be sure of another's intentions, and ideas of prestige could change suddenly, there was always the question of how best to maintain prestige. Thus there was always a note of anxiety and a consequent touchiness in all diplomatic relations just as there was in all relations between ruled and rulers. This defensiveness could lead to all types of activity, from expansion to forestall others, to maneuvers to frustrate opponents, to war; for failure to maintain prestige could invite the further encroachments of rivals as well as undermine the illusion of power necessary to govern.

No definition of imperialism would be complete without at least a mention of the factors that inhibited it. Ironically, there were some of the same factors that promoted it. But first it is necessary to repeat that there was a difference between the rationalized set of shared European methods of economic and political organization and the values and methods of the individual European states. In the first sense, imperialism was not ultimately inhibited, for the Europeans were successful in establishing their shared values as the operative model for international social organization. But in the second sense no single European state succeeded in making its own particular interpretations of the order of things the single, dominant form nor in completely absorbing its subject society. The physical manifestation or proof of this was the existence of various, competing empires or states and the persistence of local customs and patterns of life. On this subsidiary level a variety of factors inhibited the development of empire, as opposed to imperialism.

Chief among such inhibiting factors, of course, was equality or near-equality in power between European nations or groups of nations. Balance of power meant rivals and on an international scale as well as on a local one this meant a check to the free exercise of power and to the complete enjoyment of security. Another limiting feature was insufficient returns for the effort required to pursue hegemony. Diseases, geographic barriers and worthless land were strong arguments against or restraints on empire. Too, a nation for a variety of reasons could forego dominance, either for reasons of sentiment or because an increase in the area of control

increased the burdens beyond the available means to provide
for security. And finally, local resistance could be sufficient to restrict or deny the possibility of formal control.
This, in sketchy form, is the view taken here of both the
characteristics of imperialism and the factors that promoted
it. It is possible to convey only a suggestion of the complexity of the process as described, one that took five hundred years to develop and that went through a variety of
stages that occurred at different times in different places.
But disparity of power, ideas of cultural superiority, concern
for security and prestige as the result of rivalry, and the
consequences of collaboration and resistance, characterized
the process throughout and formed a system at once controlled
by and controlling human actions that, when placed in an international context, became what is called imperialism. In
such a system political, economic and strategic concerns as
reasons for empire meet and mingle inseparably. The phenomenon of empire and colonization was the consequence of the
internationalization of history, the establishment of a world
community. In effect, imperialism was the world order.

BRITAIN ACQUIRES A STAKE IN THE MIDDLE EAST

British presence in the Middle East has no significant
starting points, no spectacular watersheds. The British presence resulted not from any singular event, but from an evolution, a slowly accumulating British interest in and concern
for what happened in the Middle East. At some ill-defined
point that interest and concern passed a frontier into direct
action and involvement, punctuated by crises that demanded a
British response. But the nature and degree of that response
grew out of a network of commitments that had long preceded
overt action.

British presence in the Middle East did not initially
arise from causes in the Middle East, but rather developed as
a by-product of European expansion in the 17th and 18th centuries, as a consequence of the British presence in India,
and as a result of international rivalry. That Britain later
acquired sufficient local reasons for direct action in the
Middle East should not obscure the fact that the region was
not always regarded as vitally important in and of itself.

If there is any single event that rivetted British eyes
on the Middle East it was Napoleon's invasion of Egypt in
1798. Until that point the British had viewed the region with

indifference, often, as with Africa, seeing it as an inconvenient barrier on the route to India and the East. There were some efforts at trade, and a growing interest in the fate of the Ottoman Empire as the result of Russian pressures on that weakened state, but for the most part the region was insignificant in British calculations. Napoleon disturbed that complacency.

He had expansive dreams and seemed to believe that he could emulate Alexander by subduing the Middle East and then moving on India. It is a matter of speculation how seriously Napoleon regarded the venture, though he was serious enough to lead an army to the area. It is also questionable how serious a threat to India the British considered the move; but they thought enough of it to encourage local resistance and to despatch Nelson to smash the French fleet in Egypt. In any event, the real significance to Britain of Napoleon's adventure did not lie in whether he could seriously threaten India, though doubt was enough to justify precaution, but in the fact that by going to Egypt Napoleon reminded the British that rivalry between states was confined only by the limits of imagination and daring. Repeated wars in the 1700's, many of which had been fought in colonial areas as well as Europe, showed that competing powers would strike at an opponent wherever opportunity presented itself.

During the 18th century the British had employed a successful policy of colonial warfare against the French, depriving them of most of their colonial possessions in America and India; and the French, in turn, had aided the American colonists in a successful revolution against Britain. The British could not forget these pertinent facts regardless of the immediate feasibility of Napoleon's schemes in Egypt. Diplomacy and state policy must concern itself not only with what happens but with what might happen. And an unchallenged French presence in Egypt opened the door to too many unwelcome possibilities.

As a consequence the British became interested in frustrating any Napoleonic schemes in the Middle East. This involved them in supporting the Ottomans against the French, in pursuing relations with Iran to block any overland route to India, and in limited direct military involvement. The effort was successful and Napoleon returned to France, though he continued to disturb the British with glances eastward. But his departure did not abruptly end British interest in the Middle East. It retracted, but once aroused could never completely return to its old indifference, and other forces at work saw to it that even this modified indifference could not long survive.

At the same time as Napoleon provided Britain with reason
to examine interests in the Middle East, a slower but more
profound movement was underway that would ultimately be a
more convincing reason for sustained interest in the area.
In the course of the late 18th century and for more than the
first half of the 19th century, Britain gradually acquired a
firm regional base in India. With the status of a local
power the British were initiated into regional affairs. As
the British consolidated their hold in India they expanded
economically and politically not only as an imperial power
but also as a regional power. The position in India forced
the British to consider the implications of a landbased strategic policy, a fact that the seafaring British were never
truly comfortable with; and demanded that they consider the
necessity of protecting Indian economic interests as well as
the lines of communication to and from India. Since much of
India's trade was in the Middle East and the shortest routes
to India passed through it, the British had to take an interest in the area in order to protect their pre-existing commitments. (See Hoskins, item 362; and Graham, item 203.)

Efforts to protect those pre-existing commitments in turn
involved the British further in Middle Eastern affairs. Thus
slowly Britain was drawn into the area to protect local interest in order to defend India as a means of safeguarding the
empire, while the growth of regional commitments increased
the necessity for more sustained concern. The impetus came
from a variety of sources. Chief among these were: (1) concern for the security of the routes to India, which by 1870
included the Suez Canal; (2) the fate of the Ottoman Empire;
(3) the political stability of Persia and the Persian Gulf
region; and (4) the promotion and protection of Anglo-Indian
commerce. This latter motive was the smallest and least important. The most important involved the fate of the Ottoman
Empire.

The Eastern Question

The tempo of much of Britain's involvement in the Middle
East was set not by Britain but by the consequences of Ottoman weakness and the maneuvers of France, Russia, and Austria
to exploit that weakness. The so-called "Eastern Question,"
or, "what to do with the Ottoman Empire," became one of the
key features in the diplomatic history of the Middle East.
(See Anderson, item 195.) For most of the last half of the
18th century that once-dreaded Turkish power declined steadily, and the Ottomans became unable to defend their European

frontiers. Russia and Austria slowly wore the Turks down,
humiliating them in a series of wars and annexing province
after province. Internal decay, characterized by bureaucratic inefficiency, revolts, corruption and declining economic
vigor, combined with these European assaults to undermine the
stability of the Ottoman Empire. Once begun, the Ottomans,
despite efforts at reform, could not halt this process nor
prevent the Europeans from becoming directly involved in internal affairs. (See Lewis, item 477; Berkes, item 465; and
Shaw, item 481.)

Ottoman decline attracted a variety of European powers
who had different interpretations of the meaning and value of
that decline. The Russians, for example, considered themselves
the rightful heirs to Byzantium and expected to inherit Ottoman possessions, including the Straits connecting the Black
Sea and the Mediterranean. They wanted an Ottoman state too
weak to resist Russia but strong enough to keep anyone else
from annexing bits of the empire before Russia could. The
Austrians, on the other hand, did not want to be left out of
their share of Ottoman possessions, and they did not want to
see the Russians in control of the Straits or in a position
to encourage Slavic nationalism among Austria's population.
They, too, wanted a weakened Turk but one that could resist
Russia. The French and British, too, had interests to protect, and neither wanted Russian fleets loose in the Mediterranean. In the course of the 19th century they became
protectors of Ottoman integrity in order to forestall the
Russians. What all this meant, in practice, was that the
timing of the dismemberment of the Ottoman Empire, which was
an underlying feature of European interest in Ottoman affairs,
proceeded at a pace largely determined by the European powers,
who watched each other carefully to see that no one got too
much of an advantage or one for which there was no adequate
compensation in return. This wariness meant that no single
power could unilaterally remove the Ottoman Empire from the
board without risking diplomatic pressure or war--a lesson
the Russians learned only too well in the 1850's and again in
1878 (see Millman, item 207; and Jelavich, item 206)--but it
also left the Ottomans at the mercy of European diplomats
while keeping open a divisive issue between the European
powers. At one time or another in the course of the 19th
century every European power interested in Ottoman decline
would have cause to regret that weakness.

British interests in preserving the Ottoman Empire began
in the 1790's when William Pitt became concerned that Russian
pressure on the Ottoman Empire might cause the collapse of
the Turk and mean an unfortunate shift in the balance of power

in Europe, ultimately threatening British interests. Pitt
tried to organize a continental league to stop Catherine the
Great's efforts to absorb bits of the Turkish state. Pitt's
opinions about the importance of the Ottoman Empire to British
interests, however, were well in advance of his contemporaries', and while he could find continental allies, he could
not find any means of using that alliance and British power
against Russia—a perennial problem for Britain in the future.
He had to give up his policy for lack of support at home and
inability abroad; and the Turks had to give up bits of their
empire to Catherine.

In the 1830's and 1840's, though, opinion in Britain,
which had pictured the Turk as deserving of his fate and
Russia as Britain's natural ally, began to change. The expansion of Russia in Asia and attempts to absorb the Ottoman
Empire and gain access to the Mediterranean began to look more
and more like a threat to British interests in India and in
the Middle East. This process was a slow one, first convincing only a few, but developing gradually into a general Russophobia (see Gleason, item 247). The precipitating event in
arousing this British concern over Russian motives was not,
however, a consequence of Russian action but a result of British inaction and the threat posed to the Turkish Sultan by
one of his own subjects.

In the early 1830's Muhammad Ali, the ruler of the Ottoman province of Egypt and an able reformer and military leader, turned his army against the Sultan and threatened to overthrow him. The Turks sought help from Britain, Russia and
other European powers. Only the Russians, interested in maintaining a weak Ottoman state and not a powerful one headed by
Muhammad Ali, responsed positively. The British remained
aloof. As a consequence the Ottomans put themselves under
Russian protection, signing the Treaty of Hunkar Iskalesi in
1833 which allowed a Russian fleet into the Bosphorus and
permitted Russian armies within the empire. This alarmed
Lord Palmerston, the British Prime Minister. He reconsidered
Britain's diplomatic aloofness and undertook the defence of
Ottoman integrity to keep the Straits free of warships and
out of Russian hands, a practice that became a regular feature
of British foreign policy. Palmerston acted by pressuring
the Sultan to renounce Russian protection and then removed
the need for that protection by obliging Muhammad Ali to give
up his campaign and retire to Egypt. Palmerston succeeded in
defending the Sultan and British interests, but in doing so
he involved Britain directly in Ottoman internal affairs,
from which it became impossible to disengage thereafter, and
it contributed to continuing Anglo-Russian tensions.

British efforts to uphold Ottoman integrity, though, were not the only avenues by which British interests entered Ottoman internal affairs, nor were they the sole cause of Anglo-Russian tension. British economic and political interests developed in other parts of the Ottoman Empire along local lines or in response to other European imperatives that were unrelated to British attentions at the Sublime Porte. And Anglo-Russian rivalry extended across Asia, deriving from British nervousness over the potential threat to India represented by Russian territorial aggrandizement (see Gillard, item 245).

The Occupation of Egypt

Although British policy at Constantinople underwrote Ottoman territorial and political integrity, Britain developed interests in the Persian Gulf, in the Mediterranean, and in Egypt that conflicted with that very policy. This anomaly was not deliberate, but the consequence of having interests that required incongruent approaches. To protect interests in Egypt or in the Persian Gulf, various British statesmen found themselves executing a policy that undermined the very Ottoman integrity they hoped to uphold. The underlying theme in both instances was the protection of British interests, but the requirements of defence differed according to locality and on more than one occasion involved contradictory approaches. The occupation of Egypt is an excellent example.

It appears disingenuous to say that the British occupied Egypt so they would not have to, and later events seem to support the contention that British statesmen shed crocodile tears over the occupation. But statesmen are not always as in control of events as they would like to be, because situations can have a logic, a context, of their own that can force a line of action quite apart from intention. A large portion of the British occupation of Egypt resulted from just such a logic. There is a temptation in studying or in practicing diplomacy to imbue actions with more purpose than circumstances warrant. People may have all the sufficient knowledge and reasons at hand for acting, though that is rare, but they do not necessarily know or have any control over the consequences of their actions, which may be quite different from intentions. There is something to the paraphrased proposition that man proposes and history disposes when looking at the British occupation of Egypt in 1882.

British interest in Egypt had grown slowly. Even by the mid-19th century French economic investment exceeded British,

and French cultural influence predominated. Britain had only
taken a keen interest in the area when Napoleon tried to turn
it into an anti-British base, and when Muhammad Ali threatened
to overthrow the Sultan. Britain also developed an interest
in the area as part of a shorter communication route to India.
But there was no sudden rush to absorb Egypt.

There were many complex reasons for the occupation, developing out of economic and security motives, local unrest
and the long-term consequences of European involvement in
Egypt. Like other areas in the non-European world, Egypt
had at the beginning of the 19th century encountered an economically and technologically powerful Europe confident of
its own strength and sense of purpose. The non-European
response varied from area to area, but the most common reaction was emulation of those elements that seemed to give
the Europeans their power—military reforms and economic
contact with Europe. Unfortunately these efforts seldom
yielded the expected results, since the reforms disturbed internal arrangements and economic contact usually resulted in
integration into the European economic world system. While
not necessarily a bad thing in itself, such integration of
a pre-modern, non-industrial economy quite often dislocated
the local economy, undermined its rationale and forced it
into a relationship for which it was unprepared and at a
competitive disadvantage.

In Egypt's case, the reform policies of Muhammad Ali in
the first decades of the 19th century had profitable results.
Local industry developed and foreign investment, mainly
French, flowed in (see Landes, item 232). But by mid-century
the economy, forced into the European international system,
could not insulate itself from economic shocks, and the economy began to slow down. At the same time, in the 1860's and
1870's, Egypt's rulers embarked on even more ambitious development programs, such as the Suez Canal, that involved
substantial foreign loans. But the Egyptians failed to undertake necessary internal reforms to meet growing financial
and bureaucratic problems. Expenses outstripped income.
Egypt's leaders then borrowed yet more money from European
financiers, which increased indebtedness without alleviating
economic decline, until ultimately interest payments could
not be met. Nineteenth-century European economic interests
had little experience of nations going bankrupt or defaulting
on loans, but they realized that default could not only ruin
individuals but also undermine the whole international economic system, and that if one nation succeeded in evading its
financial responsibilities, others might follow. To avoid
ruin these interests appealed to their respective governments
for support when Egypt appeared on the verge of economic collapse.

The two Powers were aware of the dangers of Egyptian collapse as well, but not for the same reasons as the money interests. Both Powers worried about the strategic consequences, the British in particular being concerned for the fate of the Suez Canal, the major artery to India. To head off impending troubles, the two Powers formed a financial advisory body in 1876 to supervise Egyptian finances and guarantee the payment of Egypt's debts. Britain was yoked to the French in order to protect its interests from France, but it was not a particularly harmonious relationship.

A similar debt administration in the Ottoman Empire (see Anderson, item 212) worked reasonably well, but in Egypt the economic situation continued to deteriorate, and in 1878 the two Powers had to increase their financial supervision, this time assuming broad powers to reform the entire financial structure. While consistent with European concepts of sound fiscal management, the reforms failed to take sufficient notice of local conditions, and struck at vested interest within Egypt, as well as insulting Egyptian pride. The new controls undermined the Khedive's authority, thus weakening Egypt's native administration, while foreign reform measures annoyed the indigenous population. The result was a collapse of local government and rising local hostility to European influence, the reverse of what the two powers intended. It was, however, a familiar cycle.

Of course, at any point the British or French could have decided to do nothing. In situations where a variety of competing interests are involved, though, failure to act invites others to do so. In the international arena competing nations constantly test the capacity and determination of their rivals, and in such a climate inaction can suggest inability or unwillingness to act, leading rivals to fill the space. Also, unattended problems have a tendency to compound and then require even more effort to resolve later. These features, plus the fact that the rationale of political systems is to act, to handle problems, impelled Britain and France to resolve their problems to their greatest benefit. Ottoman or Egyptian collapse might have unleashed disruptive economic repercussions or invited Russian advances, so the British and French acted.

When Britain and France set up economic controls in Egypt they were concerned with their own projects, but their intervention had a local impact that upset their calculations of a limited control of Egyptian economic life. Contact with the West from the late 18th century had a profound effect on Egypt, as well as the rest of the non-European world, for not only were European political and economic interests injected into the area, but the force with which this was done and the sym-

bols of power and ability that accompanied it also impressed
themselves upon Egyptian minds. Political leaders and intellectuals responded by reconsidering the fundamentals of their
own society, the main object being to find the formula of
Western power so that that power could then be effectively resisted. Unfortunately experimentation with Western ideas,
while Western pressure continuously increased, undermined
Egyptian political, economic and social stability, all of
which spurred more Western involvement. But resistance to
the West never disappeared; rather it intensified as local
institutions proved incapable of holding off the West. This
ineffective resistance to Western dominance in all aspects of
Egyptian life created the next crisis for Britain and France
and led directly to the occupation.

By 1881 Egypt was in a cycle of increasing unrest. The
government was prostrate as internal discontent mounted. In
this atmosphere the Egyptian army, still proud of its record
under Muhammad Ali and regarding itself as the protector of
Egypt, moved to take control of the country under the banner
of "Egypt for Egyptians." Encouraged by visible signs of resistance, anti-foreign sentiment exploded and Egyptian mobs
attacked Europeans and European interests, burning, killing
and looting. Though the level of violence was relatively
low, the spectacle disturbed Britain and France, since each
worried that any changes in Egypt would adversely affect its
economic and strategic interests. Neither power was prepared
to accept such a threat, and they decided on military intervention to protect their interests. Although the French
pulled out at the last minute, the British went ahead, invaded
Egypt, defeated the Egyptian army, and attempted to restore
domestic order.

The British intended to subdue the dangerous anti-foreign
elements in Egypt, assure the protection of European interests,
establish a favorable, efficient political order and then
withdraw. But once in it became increasingly difficult to devise a formula for getting out again. Ironically, British
Prime Minister William Gladstone had wanted to avoid any commitments in Egypt, and while out of office he had criticized
policies that increased British interests there, arguing that
they created circumstances involving ever-expanding responsibilities. This, in fact, is what happened, and when the
crisis came it fell to Gladstone to undertake the forward
policy that he had opposed; it was either that or leave the
Egyptians to tear up their financial commitments, thereby provoking a unilateral French move, and no British government was
prepared to see the French in control of the Suez Canal. To
prevent this Britain had agreed to cooperate with the French

in a joint effort. The last-minute French withdrawal left
Britain committed to a course of action which it had to
carry through alone, though with the intention of withdrawing
as soon as circumstances allowed. Cooperative circumstances,
however, were not forthcoming.

The British did not go into Egypt with the idea of stay-
ing, but once in they discovered that Egyptian economic and
political collapse, exacerbated by the invasion, required a
degree of reform at every level of society that the Egyptians
had proved unable to effect. Without such reform the country
remained susceptible to the disorders that had initially created the crisis, and the British were unwilling to evacuate
Egypt until they had devised a formula that would make their
presence unnecessary. That formula evaded them, and the longer it did so the greater became the reasons for not finding
the formula.

In British eyes the Egyptians had demonstrated an inability to manage a modern state without assistance. In order to
ensure that the Egyptians received the necessary training,
the British became their teachers. But the more they tried
to teach the Egyptians to govern themselves, the more convinced the British became that they could not. Thus the British found sufficient local reason for remaining in Egypt; but
there were other reasons based on regional and international
considerations.

The British did try to find a way of vacating direct responsibility for Egypt. They tried to internationalize the
situation by getting European acceptance of a return of formal
Ottoman control, lost since the days of Muhammad Ali. However,
the French were annoyed over the British presence in Egypt,
which they regarded as a part of the French cultural empire,
and blocked the effort, thus guaranteeing the continuance of
a situation they abhorred. French hostility and efforts to
undermine Britain's position in Egypt and elsewhere also
forced the British to tighten their hold on Egypt to protect
the Suez Canal. Furthermore, changes in the international
situation gradually made Egypt more important in British calculations.

One of these changes was the decline of Britain's influence at Constantinople in the 1880's and 1890's. Britain had
long upheld Ottoman integrity, but resentment over Turkish
treatment of its ethnic and religious minorities, disillusion-
ment over Ottoman willingness or ability to effect meaningful
reforms, and a deterioration in Britain's ability to take effective military action to protect Turkey eroded Anglo-Ottoman
relations. The Turks, in turn, became annoyed with Britain's
pious pronouncements about the rights of Ottoman minorities,

whom the Turks regarded as subversives, and the decline in
British support for Ottoman rights. This led the Porte to
seek new protectors, among them Germany, which introduced the
Germans into the Eastern Question and further undermined
Anglo-Ottoman harmony, a deterioration the Germans were only
happy to encourage. Since the position in Egypt also meant
Britain had a firm regional base to protect its lines of com-
munications eastward, the traditional pro-Ottoman policy at
Constantinople lost much of its rationale. This did not mean
that Britain suddenly abandoned its efforts at the Porte, but
the climate and spirit of that relationship changed, making
Egypt more important in British calculations and withdrawal
more unlikely (see Robinson, item 072; and Jelavich, item
206).
    The acquisition of a position in Egypt also involved
Britain further in regional affairs. Egypt had claims to the
Sudan and until the late 1870's governed the area directly
(see Holt, item 379). A revolt in the Sudan led by a Muslim
fundamentalist ended that rule, but the claims remained and
the British as titulary rulers of Egypt found themselves with
an interest in the Sudan. Determined to minimize their commitments, however, the British at first chose to ignore the
Sudan. Then, in the late 1890's the Mahdist state in the
Sudan began to decline, while at the same time the French,
still smarting over Egypt, sent a small military mission
across Africa in the direction of the Sudan looking for an
opportunity to embarrass Britain. The British, meantime, had
developed a deep sense of commitment in Egypt and in examining potential threats to Egypt they became very sensitive
about the security of the sources of the Nile. The Nile was
Egypt's lifeline and any interference with the Nile's flow
jeopardized Egypt. To protect their position in Egypt the
British found it necessary to protect Egypt's claims to the
Sudan and the Nile. To do this Britain mounted a military
campaign that destroyed the Mahdist state, frustrated the
French mission and brought the Sudan under British control.
    By a slow process Britain found itself with ever-increas-
ing responsibilities in Egypt, with every move to protect an
existing interest creating obligations to acquire further interests that needed husbanding. This was the case in other
parts of the Middle East and was a self-sustaining feature
of Britain's presence in the area for over a hundred years.

Persia and the Persian Gulf

    British involvement in Persia grew out of three condi-
tions: the nature of Britain's position in India, Persian
decline, and Russia's steady expansion in Central Asia. Only

the first instance was of Britain's making; the other two were beyond Britain's control, and they set the pace for British involvement.

The British would have preferred to minimize their contacts with Persia and only crisis forced them to do otherwise, as when Napoleon tried to involve Persia in his schemes. Then Britain had troubled itself over Persia, sending missions in 1800 and in 1807 to counter the French. But when the French danger receded, British interest in Persia faded. For most of the 19th century this indifference was reflected by the fact that the British could not make up their minds whether relations with Persia should be the responsibility of British officials in India or in the Home Government in London. Even after the Foreign Office finally took responsibility for diplomatic relations, half the consular staff in Persia received its appointments and instructions from the Government of India; and the Persian Gulf Resident, another India civil servant based at Bushire in Iran, remained a center of diplomatic activity apart from the Foreign Office or the British Minister at Tehran. This situation reflected two realities about Britain's interest in Persia, and in much of the Middle East.

First, the main British concern in Persia was for the security of their position in India, security in the broader sense not just in strict military terms. And, second, the British were not interested in relations with Persia *per se*, but in securing circumstances favorable to their position in India. To understand this we must first suffer a brief digression.

India was not simply a fort or a commodity that needed an armed guard watching over it. It was a state, a nation, with its own traditions, its own local and regional ties, and its own economic needs. Though the British did much to alter India's circumstances to fit it into their empire, India also forced the British to adopt a local view. As long as the British intended to remain in and govern India they had to involve themselves with Indian concerns, which meant providing for internal peace and stability, securing the frontiers against enemies, and supporting local economic activities even as they were altered to suit British patterns. Because threats to the peace of the sub-continent and to India's economic well-being existed beyond the British-dominated frontier in Afghanistan, Persia and the surrounding areas, the British had to direct their attentions to these areas. In doing so they became caught up in the logic of local and regional circumstances. While British diplomacy could affect those circumstances it could not control them; and since those circumstances also created situations affecting British interests, they could not be ignored by British policy. Thus the British found themselves drawn into situations beyond their intentions or means. That some officials actively worked to enlarge the area of British responsibility should not obscure the fact that the basic intent was to restrict involvement.

For most of the first half of the 19th century the British worked to secure their position in the sub-continent, and to expand regional trade. Apart from Napoleon's fantasies and the depredations of Afghan tribes, the British did not pay too much attention to external affairs. There were more than enough reasons to confine energies to the sub-continent, where local political unrest continually jeopardized the security of Britain's existing possessions, which were not the mighty state of 1900, but a series of enclaves strung out along India's east coast like islands in an archipelago. The demands of security and the British habit of mind for orderliness, however, assured that their position in the subcontinent would be rationalized; and as long as the local threats to British interests were not strong enough to resist, that rationalization would favor Britain--the sub-continent would slowly be painted all red. In the process two things happened, or rather two incipient processes reached fruition.

First, the acquisition of an empire in India forced the British to govern India, and that meant a local administration. In all of Britain's colonial possessions the growth of local administration meant the growth of local views about policy and the nature of government. Though India after the Mutiny became virtually a department of the British government as opposed to a self-governing dominion, it nonetheless became a separate bureaucratic entity, a state within a state, with its own professional army and administration, its own traditions, interests and policies. In the course of the 19th century, British India developed its own view of the world based on a regional perspective. To defend India and to insure its prosperity, India's British rulers had to base their estimations on the local and regional circumstances that might affect India. Though the need to defend India was shared by British officials in London and in India, their respective views of defence requirements were quite often very different. Thus, British policy in the East found itself divided, or at least arrayed against itself, in any effort to achieve a common purpose. The development and execution of British policy in Persia and the Middle East must be understood against the background of this dichotomy. Furthermore, it needs to be remembered that even within the Home Government and the Government of India conflicting views existed. Recent historiography notes the phenomenon of the "official mind," of the importance of the shared views and

experiences of men in power in shaping a response to events.
The "official mind" should not obscure the fact, however,
that what is shared is a background and a common approach,
the sense of duty and a motivation to serve and solve problems. What is not shared are opinions on how best to proceed.
Bureaucracies are made up of ambitious individuals, place-
servers, brilliant or dull thinkers, conservatives, moderates,
and extremists, all competing for the right to influence or
determine policy. The policies that emerge from such a system are either compromises or the result of one individual or
group holding the upper hand. Compromises break up, however,
and advantages are temporary, opinions change and with them
policies. Government policies are as much responses to their
departmental heritage as they are to objective external circumstances. To understand British policy in the Middle East
one must appreciate their lineage.

The gradual consolidation of Britain's place in India and
the growth of a regular local bureaucracy also confirmed a
second trend. The more normal and permanent the British position became, the more time there was for officials in India
to examine the requirements for maintaining their position.
The view from India revealed a necessity to become involved
in affairs beyond India.

There was no neatness in this process as suggested by
this brief summary. There were fits and starts, retrench-
ments, bold gestures, cautious maneuvers and indecision.
When a firm policy of non-interference was in vogue there
were opinions that urged a more assertive policy; and when
assertiveness held sway it was bedevilled by nagging voices
of caution. Through it all there was never a shortage of
local officials prepared to misread their instructions, structure their reports, or create local incidents that required
their superiors to act against their intentions. Clearly,
such a situation tended to expand British interests, but as
it turned out circumstances beyond British control forced
them to become involved in affairs beyond India.

Napoleon's invasion of Egypt indicated the likely British
response to external threats--diplomatic activity and military
action. But Napoleon represented no sustained threat and he
had evoked no sustained response. In the decade following
Napoleon's retirement, however, the British discovered what
they believed was an enduring threat to their interests--
Russia. In the late 1820's the Russians humbled Iran, reducing that unfortunate country's independence, and they intruded
themselves into the internal affairs of the Ottoman Empire.
When Russian actions in the following years did nothing to
dispel this impression of threats to British interests, Anglo-

Russian rivalry began to spread across Asia. Once British officials concluded that Russia menaced British interests, a response was not far behind--thus Palmerston's forceful actions at Constantinople in the 1830's and Aberdeen's Crimean campaign in the 1850's to check Russian contagion with a good dose of British medicine. The response in Persia, however, was neither so forceful nor unambiguous.

In the early 1800's the British had pursued diplomatic relations with Persia in order to preclude Franco-Persian relations and not for any intrinsic interest in contact with Iran. Persia remained an object in British diplomacy and not the subject of it. Even though Britain had a defensive alliance with Persia--aimed at Napoleon--they did little to honor it during Persia's fateful struggle with Russia, though there was not a great deal Britain could have done. Russia's final victory in 1828, after nearly two decades of intermittent fighting, changed that situation. Gradually the British came to believe that defeat had made Persia a Russian pawn, and that the Russians intended to use Persia as a surrogate to expand Russian influence towards India. In this fashion Anglo-Russian rivalry became superimposed over local events, like a double exposure. The focal point for this rivalry became the fate of Afghanistan and of Herat, a city in western Afghanistan claimed by Persia.

On two occasions the British resorted to force to keep Herat out of Persian hands. In 1838 they occupied islands in the Persian Gulf threatening to incite local unrest against the Shah; and in 1856-57 they went to war with Persia to force the Shah to surrender Herat. The British believed that Herat and its rich surrounding farm land constituted the most likely route for an invasion of India; or if not that, at least a secure base from which to encourage and supply Afghan tribes to descend on India. Officials in India wanted neither prospect, and suspecting Persia of being a Russian tool, they pressured the Persians. They succeeded in keeping Herat out of Persian hands, but at the cost of weakening Persia further and necessitating greater involvement in Persian affairs (see Alder, item 241, and Gillard, item 245).

This involvement was by no means straightforward, for British officials were reluctant to become involved, and there was not definite consensus that such involvement was necessary. There were two main schools of thought, both wanting to defend India and both recognizing a Russian threat. Where the schools parted company was on the extent of the threat and on what to do about it. One school, most influential from the 1850's to the 1870's, argued that the Russians were far away and that any army they sent towards India would be lost trying to cross

the trackless wastes of Central Asia. This school believed
the best approach was to concentrate on consolidating the
position in India, defending a definite frontier, and letting
a hostile distance act as a buffer. The other school, most
influential after 1870, argued that the best defence was a
good offence and wanted to fix some distant point and say to
the Russians, "this far and no farther." Both policies had
serious defects.

Unfortunately for the first school, steady Russian expansion in Central Asia shrank the distance between the two
frontiers, gradually putting the Russians into better positions to menace India. As this became more apparent the
Russians began to appreciate that menacing gestures towards
India had the gratifying effect of diverting the British from
interfering with Russian policies elsewhere. This development gave weight to the forward school in Britain and India
that wanted to check the Russians at some distant point, but
unfortunately Britain lacked the means to sustain such a
policy. Furthermore Russia was not particularly vulnerable
to British diplomatic pressure in Europe or to Britain's navy,
while India was increasingly vulnerable to Russian armies.

Two courses remained open to give effect to a forward
policy—either extend Britain's control to meet the Russians,
or create a buffer zone to stop them. The first approach
meant assuming immense new burdens quite beyond Britain's
resources; and it did not solve the problem, for it did not
remove the Russian threat: it only brought it closer more
quickly. The second approach was more likely but equally
difficult, for Persia was already weakened by Russian and
British pressure, and Afghanistan was a hodge-podge of warring
tribes. A similar situation had prevailed in Central Asia
and rather than checking Russian advances the confusion on
their frontiers had encouraged it. But a buffer policy
seemed the only alternative, even though it meant being drawn
into Persian affairs.

After years of suspecting Persia of being a Russian tool,
the British became concerned for Persia's survival. Once
again this was not a concern for Persia but for how Persia
could be used to protect British interests (see Greaves, item
416). The British decided on two main efforts, similar to
their approaches to the Ottoman Empire. In the 1880's and
1890's, to bolster the Persian state, they encouraged reform
of Persia's political institutions and they sought to rehabilitate the country's sagging economy. This British interest coincided with Persian concerns for reform, although
the Persians hoped to use reforms to strengthen their country
against both Britain and Russia, and they hoped to involve
Britain in the process of reform to counterbalance the Russians.

Unfortunately for the Persians, the British would not or could not provide serious material support against Russia, and their moral support proved of little use. Unfortunately for the British their ideas of reform were unsuited to the Persian climate, and the Russians, who did not want to see Iran strengthened, worked against them (see Kazemzadeh, item 251, and Bakhash, item 502). Reforms failed, further weakening the country, undermining the government's support among the people, spreading social disorder and eventually bringing on a revolution in 1906. The failure of reforms, as in Egypt, also disillusioned the British over the prospect of Persia being able to maintain its own independence. The Russians virtually absorbed northern Iran, and to safeguard their position in Persia and the Gulf, the British increased their influence in the south. Eventually the British reached a rapprochement with Russia in 1907, establishing a virtual condominium in Persia (see Churchill, item 243).

By a process of degrees the British had been drawn deeper and deeper into Persian affairs by circumstances beyond Britain's control. A similar process saw the spread of British involvement in the Persian Gulf as well.

As with the case of Egypt and Persia, British interests in the Persian Gulf region expanded steadily throughout the 19th century in response to local, regional and international imperatives. Britain became involved in the area as early as the late 16th century, but not until it acquired a permanent position in India did involvement become significant. In the 18th century the East India Company began exploring trade possibilities with Persia and the other reparian states of the Gulf, traditional areas for Indian trade (see Kelly, item 407; Busch, item 404; and Kumar, item 409).

At this time the Arabian side of the Gulf was peopled by a number of fractious petty kingdoms that made their living from piracy, the slave trade, and smuggling. When the British began moving into the Gulf they objected to having their ships attacked by pirates. Later, in the 19th century, they would also raise objections to the slave-trade and to smuggling, and since there was no local authority to check these activities, the British took policing matters into their own hands. They put an end to piracy, suppressed the slave trade and waged a ceaseless campaign against smuggling, which was mostly in arms and ammunition that reached obstreperous tribes on India's northern frontiers. These efforts required continuing invigilation, and so Britain slowly acquired a continuing commitment in the area. The British also developed a lively trade, one that was important to India though not directly to Britain, which encouraged the British to sustain

their presence in the Gulf. In the process the British also
developed a sense of possession. They did not formally annex
any areas in the Gulf but they came to look on the area as a
British preserve. Much of the British literature on the Gulf
(including Kelly's work as late as the 1960's: see item 407)
makes much of the fact that British blood and treasure brought
peace and prosperity to the Gulf, and that this conferred
special privileges, and obligations, on Britain to protect
interests won at such cost.

The shouldering of this burden involved Britain in local
politics. The suppression of piracy and the slave-trade destroyed the staples of the local economy and produced regional
unrest. This forced the British to meddle in the politics of
the petty states in the Arabian peninsula to see to it that
local unrest did not lead to a return of piracy. The British
also established intimate relations with local rulers, committing themselves to maintaining friendly rulers in power as
a means of protecting British interests, which in turn involved the British in local disputes, and deepened Britain's
commitment to the area by engaging British prestige. The
British came to believe that even minor setbacks in getting
their way would encourage local peoples to take advantages
(not, on the whole, an unrealistic assessment). This attitude hardened in the 1890's when other European powers moved
into the Gulf to challenge the British monopoly, offering
locals a chance of playing off rivals. The Persian Gulf became the scene of efforts to exclude French, Russian, and
later German rivals.

For most of the 19th century Britain had been the sole
power in the Gulf. But in the latter part of the century
France, Russia and Germany began to move into the area. The
British could not believe that this resulted from purely economic motives or, based on their own experiences, that even
with the best intentions could the other European powers keep
economic motives from developing political consequences. They
suspected the French of looking for means of getting back at
Britain for Egypt; they knew the Russians were looking for a
warm water port; and they were learning that the Germans were
willing to exploit any situation for economic and political
advantage. The British worried that the powers would challenge their special relationships with local rulers and gradually undermine Britain's paramountcy in the Gulf. The fact
that the Persian Gulf was one of the avenues for communications between India and Britain underlay this concern, and as
with the Suez Canal the British saw a foreign presence in the
Gulf as a threat to the security of that route. As a result
they established treaty relations with the local states that

precluded relations with any third power. They also challenged
Ottoman and Persian authority in the area for fear that European powers would use Ottoman and Persian claims as surrogates
for fulfilling their own local aims, and in 1901 and 1903 they
issued public warnings to Persia and the European powers to
respect Britain's special position (see Hurewitz, item 047).

This process had the effect of involving British prestige
in the most mundane of local affairs and undermined their relations with the Turks and the Persians. Concern for prestige
could produce ludicrous incidents, as when Lord Curzon toured
the Gulf in 1899 and almost severed Anglo-Persian relations
because the local Persian representative did not accord the
honors Curzon felt he deserved. Concern for prestige could
also produce unusual competitions. One writer, only half-
jokingly, mentions that efforts of the various European powers
to show their flags in the Gulf resulted in a funnel race--
if one power sent a warship with three funnels, Britain had
to send one with four lest the natives gathered on the fore-
shore should receive a wrong impression from their poll of
smokestacks. While ridiculous in itself, this example points
up the more serious realities of rivalry, concern for security, and the pressures that can influence the formation of
policy. Policy must be made in a context, often one which
statesmen do not control and to which they must respond.

Despite Britain's efforts to keep the Gulf sacrosanct, it
could not forcibly exclude other economic interests, though it
did succeed remarkably in precluding foreign political interests. By the early 1900's France, Germany and Russia had
developed a small trade in the area, and the Germans in particular had developed local interests which they threatened
to expand with the extension of a railway to the head of the
Gulf (see Staley, item 240; and Cohen, item 394). The development of the so-called Baghdad Railway became a major concern
for Britain. In protecting their interests the British found
themselves at odds with local powers, and they had created
tensions in their relations with France and Russia, to the
extent that French animosity dogged them, and the Russian
menace nagged their every effort. When France and Russia
formed an alliance in the 1890's, Britain's security problems
compounded and forced them to reconsider their arrangements
for imperial security. At the same time a new force developed
to challenge not only Britain's position in the Middle East
but in the world, one that would hasten a realignment of Britain's diplomacy and a restructuring of imperial resources. It
would also strengthen British determination to protect their
interests in the Middle East and lead them into a deeper local
involvement in the Persian Gulf and throughout the Middle East.
The threat came from Germany.

ANGLO-GERMAN RIVALRY BEFORE WORLD WAR I

In 1898 Kaiser Wilhelm II visited Constantinople and the
Ottoman Empire, being the first and last reigning European
monarch to do so. His presence emphasized not only his anti-
quarian concerns, but the expanding interests of his state.
The Kaiser proclaimed his love of the East and his protective
concern for Islam and departed, leaving behind not a few cre-
dulous Muslims and suspicious Europeans. The Kaiser's posturing demonstrated Germany's desire for a place in the sun, but
his manner of shouldering a way into the light left the dis-
tinct impression that Germany intended to push others into
the shade. By pushing their way into the Eastern Question
the Germans added geometrically to the diplomatic complexity
of Ottoman decline and European imperial rivalry.

The three powers most affected by German expansion were
France, Russia and Great Britain, who had sought to preserve,
or rather reserve, the Ottoman Empire for their respective
interests. They each had reasons to resent and fear German
dynamism in the Middle East as well as elsewhere; and it is
not surprising that within the first decade of the 20th century these three powers, former rivals, formed a loose association with Germany in mind; and that by the second decade
of the century had allied in a war to defeat Germany.

Of the three powers, Britain had the most to lose from an
expanding Germany--the largest empire, the heaviest overseas
commitment, and predominance in trade and industry. German
industry challenged Britain's manufacturing predominance;
German economic power expanded rapidly at British expense,
or so it seemed to the British; German imperial territorial
claims threatened to upset cherished balances or to jeopardize
strategic interests; and the growth of German military power
threatened the balance of power in Europe, while the expansion
of the German navy seemed aimed at Britain's imperial lifeline.
By 1900 a growing body of opinion in Britain regarded Germany
as the chief threat to security, a conviction that became a
key element in Britain's foreign policy down to the war. It
is arguable that this fact, the shift in British diplomacy,
altered the climate of European diplomacy that helped create
the climate for the war.

Fritz Fischer and others (see item 288) argue that the
war was the result of German intentions, but it seems that
another likely contributor was the shift in the European diplomatic atmosphere, marked most significantly by British re-
alignment. The aim of this shift had an increasing anti-
German bias and resulted in confining German options, frus-

trating German intentions and isolating Germany, making its policy more strident and caustic. Rightly or wrongly, the Germans expected to build an empire in Europe and overseas, to match the states and empires built by their neighbors, at the very time the European and world situation had reached a limit in the imperial demands it could accommodate.

Within certain bounds the Germans had been successful, but at the price of three wars and a bluster only made acceptable by an effective army and Bismarck's brilliant diplomacy. But increasingly German demands impinged on a rival's vital interests, and Bismarck's heirs were not as adroit in placating the hurt feelings of Germany's victims. Germany became increasingly frustrated while her neighbors became increasingly anxious, for Germany could not be compensated without depriving other powers that became unwilling to surrender key interests in order to pacify Germany. The established powers responded by isolating Germany, and thereby made the Germans more determined to have their way, which to them meant justice. It was a recipe for disaster.

However, there was nothing preordained about Anglo-German rivalry, nor was the diplomatic revolution in the early 1900's, whereby Britain formed closer ties with two former rivals-- France and Russia--a necessarily permanent feature of the diplomatic landscape before World War I. The war has tended to fix what preceded it in the amber of inevitability, but there was nothing inexorable about Anglo-German rivalry. German diplomatic bluster, the fact that Britain could no longer face multiple enemies alone, and the presence of Germanophobes in Britain--such as Arthur Nicolson, Charles Hardinge, and Eyre Crowe--made a policy aimed at Germany likely, but it did not make it a certainty.

Two factors pushed them into rivalry. First, Britain needed to come to an understanding with some European power to help ease its imperial defence burdens. Second, Germany seemed determined to challenge Britain's world-wide position. In the late 1890's and early 1900's Anglo-German relations were not at their best, but British political and military leaders still regarded France and Russia as Britain's main security worries. These two Powers had formed an alliance in 1894 and together threatened Britain's interests in Africa, the Middle East, the Mediterranean, and across all of Asia. Though the Germans made themselves unpopular in Britain during the Boer War by open sympathy for the Boers, the Russians had posed a more serious threat by menacing India, and Britain and Russia had almost come to blows in 1904 when Russia was at war with Japan, Britain's ally. In the early 1900's Britain found itself friendless, and the war in South Africa had exposed an embarrassing unpreparedness not only to themselves but to the world. And pressures were increasing everywhere. The Americans and Japanese challenged Britain's position in the New World and in East Asia, respectively, just as French, German, Russian and Italian imperial competition increased. Furthermore, Britain's chief deterrent declined in effectiveness at the same time competition increased. Earlier in the 19th century the Royal Navy had stood between Britain and the world, but changes in naval technology and the existence of land frontiers in Asia and Africa, plus the growth of large, sophisticated armies, nullified much of Britain's primary defence. This forced the British to confront the uncomfortable fact that the empire was too spread out and vulnerable at too many points to be defended everywhere equally. One of the advantages Britain had derived from its naval supremacy and world-wide position was maneuverability, for the British had not had to decide where to defend the empire since they could protect it all. But the increased rivalry of the late 1890's and early 1900's deprived the British of this advantage, putting them in the unenviable position of having to choose where best to defend the empire. Making this choice became a strategist's nightmare.

The growing awareness of imperial vulnerability created a crisis of confidence affecting the intellectual and political leadership, producing a search for a rational base for empire and an imperial ideology, as well as an effort to produce a new breed of men to govern the empire (see Semmel, item 106; Hyam, item 090; and Shannon, item 107). Along with this mental activity, and especially after the Boer War, political leaders began to reorganize imperial institutions. There were attempts to promote a more rational imperial economic and political unity with the colonies and self-governing Dominions, reflected in the Colonial Conferences, first held in 1887 and roughly every seven years afterwards; there was an attempt to develop an overall planning and coordinating body for imperial defence--the Committee for Imperial Defence; and the army and navy underwent reorganization and re-equipment to modernize their leadership and performance (see Mansergh, item 129; Gooch, item 114; Johnson, item 123; Kendle, item 124; and Marder, item 131). But these efforts produced only partial success. Reforms ran into bureaucratic opposition, from those who stood to lose out or from those who considered any change to be for the worse; and they suffered the fate of all reform efforts, a conflict of interests. Not everyone's ideas of reform were the same and thus reforms emerged as a compromise between competing interests. This process made reform possible but it seldom made for the best possible reform.

The British realized, though, that even the best reorganization of imperial institutions and coordinated defence planning no longer permitted a unilateral defence policy, or one
based strictly on naval supremacy. But at the end of the 19th
century Britain had running disputes with France and Russia,
distant relations with Germany, the competition of Japan and
America, increasing demands on security throughout the world,
and no friends. The awareness that Britain had no real supporters coincided with the awareness that imperial defence
was beyond Britain's unaided resources, producing a reconsideration of Britain's diplomatic position, sometimes referred
to as the "end of isolation" (see Monger, item 098; Grenville,
item 085; and Howard, item 088). The demarcation of this
change was the tenure at the Foreign Office of Lord Lansdowne,
who replaced the Third Marquis of Salisbury in 1900.

Salisbury, who relished diplomacy, had an older age's confidence in Britain's power and in his personal diplomatic
abilities. He and Bismarck had been superb practitioners of
the art of diplomacy. Salisbury's successors, though competent, had neither his skill nor his confidence, and they
embarked on changes reflecting their views of new circumstances
and their realization of Britain's reduced maneuverability.

Even Salisbury had received a hint of Britain's declining
abilities, when in the 1890's the Admiralty informed him that
they could not, in the face of the Franco-Russian alliance,
use the fleet at the Straits to protect the Ottomans or British interests. This left Britain with a policy but no material support. Salisbury was disappointed but, having confidence in his own abilities, did not see the necessity of major
shifts in Britain's diplomatic posture. It was an isolated
view. Lansdowne represented those who saw the need for change,
who were not confident that they could sustain policies without material support. Since it was becoming obvious that
there were any number of areas where Britain no longer had the
resources for unilateral defence, and that Britain needed a
list of priorities of what to defend and what not to defend,
Lansdowne and others tried to make the best of things. In-
ternally this meant reorganization; externally it meant a
search for possible allies as a way of reducing demands on
Britain's overstretched resources. The true significance of
the end of isolation was not that Britain abandoned a supposed
policy of diplomatic aloofness, but in the fact that Britain
had lost the maneuverability that had made aloofness a matter
of discretion.

In the early 1900's Britain had a free field of hostile
or politically distant Powers from which to choose a possible
ally. The power least hostile to Britain was Germany, while

Russia and France were the most distant. Lansdowne made approaches to all, hoping to ease hostilities everywhere. But the French and the Russians were not particularly interested in a rapprochement, and the Germans already enjoyed tolerable relations with Britain. Furthermore, there were few points at which Anglo-German interests either coincided or clashed in a fashion to make an agreement worthwhile to either party; and the one area they did was the one area in which no compromise was possible.

Unable to make an arrangement in Europe, Lansdowne settled outstanding differences with America, thus reducing defence requirements in the New World, and concluded an alliance with Japan in 1902, both to forestall a Russo-Japanese alliance and to make it possible to withdraw naval units from East Asia for more vital areas (see Nish, item 100; and Benians, item 196). At the same time he continued to seek some accommodation with Russia, France, and Germany. France and Russia represented the greatest threat, for it was their combined fleets and Russian pressure in Asia that weighed the heaviest in Britain's strategic calculations. An agreement with Germany to balance Russia and France offered the best possibilities for easing British security problems, but the German asking price was inflated because Britain's isolation served German interests as well as an agreement would; they both, after all, shared the same potential enemies. The fact that Britain could not reach an accommodation with Germany, however, meant it continued to seek arrangements with France and Russia. Germany made a mistake in letting the British remain free agents at a time when they were seeking commitments. The Germans also made another blunder in relations with Britain—they built a navy.

Britain's empire had been built on its navy, and that navy still guarded Britain's life-line to the world, and protected the ships that carried Britain's trade around the world. Though there was an awareness after 1900 of the need to strengthen the army, the navy remained the premier concern and the basis of Britain's home and imperial defence. Changes in naval technology had wiped out Britain's absolute naval supremacy by rendering Britain's unimpeachable lead in sailing ships useless; but the British had responded with that technical skill and adaptive ability that had made them powerful. They were the first to develop and deploy in the 1890's the "dreadnought," the new-style armored battleship. Other nations followed suit, but Britain maintained a lead, at least in the absolute number of ships if not always in overall quality. However, this lead was precarious because competition was greater. Everyone started at zero, and there were more com-

petitors. Technological development also dated even the new-
est designs quickly and so there was no respite. The life of
a sailing ship had been twenty or more years; that of a new
expensive battlecruiser half that, some being dated before
they left the navy yards. Thus along with the other problems
facing Britain, the one area of traditional British supremacy
suddenly and forever became insecure. This naval vulnerability, combined with other problems, forced the British to find
friends so they could reallocate their naval resources to the
best effect, since they no longer had the ability to dominate
every area of the world simultaneously. Again, France and
Russia posed the greatest naval threat to Britain in the early
1900's, but Germany came to replace them.

The Germans were determined to build a powerful state and
empire and they succeeded marvelously, though in the process
they worried everyone else, especially France and Russia.
German military might in Europe threatened both, and the
French had actually suffered a humiliating defeat at German
hands in 1870. German development and expansion also alarmed
the British. At first Britain welcomed German industrious-
ness, but this fellow-feeling declined as German industries
and financial interests began to compete successfully, even
pushing Britain out of some areas (see Hoffman, item 226; and
Henderson, item 224). What might have been acceptable had
the Germans contented themselves with overseas trade and wor-
rying the French and Russians with their armies, was unaccept-
able when the Germans built up the full arsenal of a great
power. This meant a navy, and not just a small navy but a
modern, efficient navy capable of defending German interests
overseas, and of challenging Britain's cherished supremacy
at sea.

The Germans turned their formidable technological skill
to the creation of a great ocean-going navy just at the time
when technology had reduced Britain's naval supremacy to pulp.
And, undiplomatically, they chose a naval doctrine aimed directly at Britain. The Germans recognized Britain's naval
mastery and did not intend to compete in a ship-for-ship arms
race they could not hope to win; instead they developed the
"doctrine of risk." The idea was not to take on the numeri-
cally superior British battle-fleets but to make a collision
too risky for Britain. The Germans believed that without a
first-rate navy Britain would eventually act with impunity
to end Germany's international economic challenge and to forestall such a move, to prevent a war or a *fait accompli*, to
protect Germany's international position, the Germans needed
a strong navy that would make the British think twice about
a pre-emptive attack. A navy also increased Germany's bar-

gaining position with France and Russia, for it meant it could offer a third naval force to those rivals of Britain in the event of a war. Thus a navy seemed an ideal, a necessary investment. Coming on top of German trade rivalry and diplomatic coyness, however, the naval issue convinced Britain that Germany was becoming a definite threat. Although, so long as the French and Russians remained hostile, the increasing tensions with Germany remained only one element in Britain's diplomatic isolation.

The Germans believed that a rapprochement between Britain on the one hand, and France and Russia on the other, was in the realm of cheap fiction, a diplomatic impossibility. The Germans also believed the British needed German goodwill. These convictions meant they saw no necessity of placating the British, and made them willing to risk aggravating them. It was a serious misreading of Britain's mood, and an overly confident evaluation of diplomatic immutability. In 1904 the British defied German expectations and concluded an agreement with France over differences in Egypt and Africa that became the basis for a more far-reaching rapprochement. German diplomatic intransigence and naval development had helped channel British efforts elsewhere and their efforts had finally been rewarded. Though the 1904 settlement did not necessarily mean a permanent Anglo-French connection, the Germans helped make it possible in the first place, and their subsequent attempts to break it up only made it stronger. Since the Anglo-French détente had as part of its original rationale an underlying anti-German bias, German bullying to force the French and British apart only drove them closer together. It also convinced a growing number of British statesmen that an inevitable, irreducible rivalry existed between Britain and Germany. Though there were many who continued to regard France and particularly Russia as the main enemies, significantly, it was the anti-German group who came to predominate at the Foreign Office and in key embassies; and it was this group that enjoyed the most diplomatic success in easing Britain's security problems, their commitment to the Anglo-French entente converting it from a settlement of differences into the foundation for an enduring alignment of interests aimed at Germany. Furthermore, this group achieved the second of Germany's impossible diplomatic settlements—an Anglo-Russian rapprochement.

Anglo-Russian rivalry in Asia had become such an accepted part of international relations that the Germans might be forgiven for lacking the prescience to see that the two rivals would ever be reconciled, especially since an even more unlikely event made the rapprochement possible. The Russians,

considered irresistable, lost a war to an Asian power, considered impossible. The Germans could not have foreseen such
an outcome, but they should have been less naive about fixed
principles in international relations.

The Russians had gained considerable maneuverability in
the late 19th century by compromising Britain's. The Russians
learned that gestures towards India could be utilized to dis-
tract the British from Russian moves elsewhere (see Gillard,
item 245). They also benefited from their invulnerability to
Britain's prime weapon, the navy, for one of Russia's chief
economic problems, a lack of suitable seacoasts and ports,
was also one of its principal strategic assets. Capitalizing
on this the Russians had largely ignored Britain's anxiety
over expansion in Central Asia and pushed forward every advantage in East Asia and in the Ottoman Empire. But in doing
so they created other enemies, including the Japanese, whose
imperial ambitions the Russians treated with contempt. The
result was a war that Russia lost. This humiliating defeat
led to a revolution that weakened the government and forced
the Russians into a more conciliatory posture. They had to ·
consider the proven and only too well-developed German armies to the west, at a time when the country was prostrate,
and they were in no position to pursue an aggressive policy
against Britain. This time the Russians accepted British
overtures for a settlement, signing an agreement in August
1907 (see Churchill, item 243; and Greaves, item 248).

The Anglo-Russian Convention put aside almost a century
of Anglo-Russian rivalry in Asia. By it the Russians agreed
to recognize the paramountcy of British interests in Tibet,
Afghanistan and southern Persia, while the British recognized
Russia's special position in north Persia, an area coming increasingly under Russian control. Initially conceived and
loyally defended by Edward Grey, and especially by Arthur
Nicolson, as a means of putting an end to Russia's unrelent-
ing pressure on India, the convention became the grounds for
a broader sense of cooperation. For Britain the galvanizing
influence was the need to reduce pressures on the empire, and,
increasingly, to counter a rising German challenge. Thus, by
1907 Germany had effected its own isolation by menacing Britain, France and Russia at their most vulnerable points; and
continued diplomatic bullying only made the three more determined to keep alive their entente against Germany. This
arrangement, however, was not necessarily permanent, for it
depended on a continuing identity of interests among France,
Britain and Russia, and a continued antagonism toward Germany.

The Germans seemed prepared to continue as a source of
anxiety, but the identity of interests of the entente powers,

especially those of Britain and Russia, underwent severe
strains before World War I. The Anglo-Russian Convention was
a self-denying ordinance whereby both powers agreed to respect
the interests of the others. The British were happy to receive such a guarantee, but the Russians had agreed to it
only as an expedient. The Russian Government, whatever its
real or stated opinions, had been unable to restrain its
agents from pushing forward Russian interests during the 19th
century and almost before the ink dried on the agreement
Russian agents in Persia, and on the borders of Afghanistan
and Tibet, began violating its spirit. And as their Government recovered its confidence after the disasters of the
Russo-Japanese War and the 1905 Revolution, it too returned
to more assertive policies in Persia. The 1907 Convention
was insufficient to restrain the logic of a hundred years of
forward motion and the British lacked the physical means to
check Russia, which is one reason they had sought an agreement, hoping it would substitute for the material means to
resist. The agreement had not grown out of any fundamental
change in the relationship in Anglo-Russian relations, but
out of a temporary condition, and when that condition faded
so did the agreement.

The British struggled manfully to keep it alive, even
going so far as to sacrifice a time-honored pledge to uphold
the integrity and independence of Persia. The British were
disillusioned with Persia's ability to stand alone, which
was another reason an agreement with Russia was so attractive;
and it is the fate of states that cannot keep others from unilaterally guaranteeing their independence to suffer the loss
of that independence whenever the guarantors find their pledge
damaging to their own interests. The British did not want a
return of Anglo-Russian rivalry because they did not want to
face two potential enemies--Russia and Germany. By binding
Russia in an agreement the British reduced their defence problems in order to concentrate on Germany, and at the same
time precluded a Russo-German agreement. The Russians, after
all, had posed the most sustained, impenetrable threat to
India, and the agreement was important so long as it kept the
Russians in check. Although the convention became the foundation for an Anglo-Russian entente aimed at Germany, this
should not obscure the fact that at base it was designed to
reduce Russian pressure on British interests. While the British might be willing to go to great lengths to sustain the
agreement, it became a useless item once it lost its original
rationale, and there was no point to an agreement when the
cost of keeping it was the payment of those interests it had
been designed to protect.

At the same time as the difficulties with Russia over
Persia increased, Britain and Germany found a solution to
some of their differences in the Middle East, agreements that
might have become foundations for the general improvement of
Anglo-German relations. This settlement involved the issues
of the Baghdad Railway and membership in the Turkish Petroleum
Company (see Earle, item 219; and Kent, item 398).

The Baghdad Railway developed as an issue in the early
1900's when German interests received a concession from the
Sultan to construct a railway line to Baghdad and from there
eventually to the Persian Gulf. Like the Suez Canal, the contemplated railway had strategic as well as economic implications, and the British were disturbed by the prospect of a
German-controlled railway in an area of traditional concern.
The railway threatened to give Germany greater ability to
compete with British economic interests, such as the monopoly
on local transport or in manufactured items. It also threatened British strategic interests, for the railway in German
hands suggested the possibility that the Germans or the Turks
might use the line, secure from Britain's navy, to bring military pressure on Britain's lines of communications with India,
and on interests in Egypt, Arabia and the Persian Gulf. The
British opposed the concession but, unable to get it revoked,
they turned to seeking a share in it, insisting on absolute
control of any branch line from Baghdad to the head of the
Persian Gulf. Negotiations went well until 1903, when a combination of public pressure in Britain and an inability to
resolve certain matters of representation on the board of
control for the railway caused the British to withdraw from
the project.

British withdrawal, however, did not stop the Germans
from pushing ahead with the project. In the ensuing years
the British had to face the fact that the line would be built
with or without them. Realizing this the British returned to
negotiations, but the situation had become more complex. The
Germans were less willing to make concessions and the British
had to consider the interests of their entente partners,
France and Russia, who also expected equal representation in
the line. In 1914, however, the Ottomans and Germans accepted
that they could not realistically push the line beyond Baghdad
without British cooperation and they reached an agreement giving Britain majority control of the line running to the Gulf
(see Hurewitz, item 048, for the text of the agreement). At
the same time they reached an agreement on participation in
an oil exploration company, the Turkish Petroleum Company
(see Kent, item 398). These two agreements, reached in the
summer of 1914, eased much of the tension in Anglo-German,

Anglo-Turkish relations in the Middle East, and combined with
indications that the heat in the naval race was simmering
down, plus increasing Anglo-Russian rivalry, might have caused
a shift in British diplomacy.

But the Anglo-Russian agreement survived, for the Germans
continued to worry both Britain and Russia enough to make
them seek some basis for continuing accommodation. What this
came down to was a planned revision of the 1907 Convention.
Russian violations of the spirit of the agreement had by 1914
reached exasperating levels, even annoying Arthur Nicolson,
the staunchest adherent of the Anglo-Russian connection. The
planned revision would have resolved Anglo-Russian tensions
by a partition of Persia and a guarantee for Britain's position in the south.

Throughout the 19th century the British had repeatedly
guaranteed Persia's independence and integrity, but had done
little to back up their assurances. In fact, the British were
not willing to give more than moral support and assurances,
at least until threats to specific British interests reached
a critical level. While Persia was important to Britain as a
buffer, the British did not see the survival of the country
worth a war with Russia; thus they had done what they could
to bolster Persia with good advice. When that proved inef-
fectual they struck the bargain with Russia, hoping that the
agreement would protect India and incidentally preserve as
much of Persia's independence as remained. When by 1914 that
hope had proved no more effective than former ones, the British were prepared to sacrifice what they privately regarded
as nonexistent anyway, Persia's integrity. But in the proposed new settlement the British were prepared to back up
their position with force, for they regarded southern Persia
and the Gulf as interests worth direct and sustained force.
If the Russians had ignored this then it is quite possible
that Britain would have no longer seen Germany as the chief
threat. But no revision proved necessary, though, and the
Russian threat did not become critical. The assassinations
at Sarajevo intervened and the subsequent events in the summer of 1914 reduced that possibility to a might-have-been.

WORLD WAR I IN THE MIDDLE EAST

As much as a specialist likes to make claims for his special interest, the Middle East was not one of the most vital
areas of international rivalry before World War I. In many

ways, despite international tension and arms racing, there
was no "climate" for war, and the Middle East had provided as
many excuses for easing tensions as for provoking them. After
all, France and Britain had resolved their differences over
Egypt, the Russian and the British their differences over
Persia and Central Asia, and had gone on to use these as bases
for closer relations. By mid-1914 the British and Germans
had succeeded in reconciling some of their thorniest outstanding problems: over the construction and control of the Baghdad
Railway to the Persian Gulf and over participation in the
Turkish Petroleum Company. These agreements might have formed
the basis for a general Anglo-German rapprochement, especially
given increasing Anglo-Russian tensions over Persia. The
July Crisis, however, closed the door on that avenue.

If the Middle East was not a primary cause of World War I
nor a major theater of combat, it was, nonetheless, a significant scene of conflict where various international and local
rivalries coincided. The Allies saw their main effort in
Europe, where the enemy forces lay, and they hoped to confine
the conflict there. The Central Powers shared this idea, and
both sides expected a short war. But nations at war with one
another strike wherever the opportunity arises, and thus,
though the combatants maneuvered for quick victories in Europe,
they also prepared to strike at each other overseas. Even if
the home governments had wanted to ignore peripheral interests,
they could not ignore the possibility that the enemy would
use overseas interests to dangerous effect; nor could they
control their own representatives who did not want to be left
out of the conflict simply because duty or geography put them
in out-of-the-way places. At the same time, many small states
and peoples saw new opportunities for their own interests, a
sentiment reinforced by the fact that as the Europeans became
bogged down in the horrible stalemate in Europe they began
making promises to win the support of other states or colonial
peoples. In this fashion non-Europeans were drawn into the
struggle and the war underwent a subtle, qualitative change.
It became not just a conflict between European powers, but
between their interests and the aspirations of countless local peoples. And it made no difference which side won.

The war spread to the Middle East gradually. The Allies
hoped to keep the area neutral and aimed their diplomacy at
the only two independent local states, Persia and the Ottoman Empire. The Germans, hesitantly, sought to involve both
these countries, not believing that they could add appreci-
ably to the fighting in Europe, but hoping that by creating
a regional crisis they could flank the Russians and menace
the British in India and Egypt, forcing both powers to divert
needed men and materials from more vital theaters.

Unfortunately for the Allies, their pre-war policies had certainly not created receptive climates at the Porte or at Tehran. Both the Ottomans and Persians had suffered their most humiliating experiences at the hands of either Britain or Russia, while before the war the Germans had provided them with their main hope of counterbalancing these evil effects. The Allies tried to strike a conciliatory note, which rang discordantly after years of playing wrong notes. The Persian Government declared its official neutrality, but large numbers of German sympathizers, who hoped a German victory would release Iran from the Anglo-Russian grip, connived with many government officials and German agents to involve Persia in the war. Their activities, plus unpopular Allied countermeasures, made Persia the most violated neutral of the war after Belgium. The Ottomans, on the other hand, signed a secret agreement with Germany in August 1914, mobilized their forces and in October attacked Russian ports in the Black Sea. There was no unanimity in Turkey for joining the Germans, however; a war party, who believed in a sure German victory, took the nation into war convinced that a successful outcome would save the Empire. The actions of the Ottoman and Persian nationalists meant that the war spread to the Middle East, forcing the Allies, chiefly Britain and Russia, to act to defend their interests not only from the enemy but from each other (see Trumpener, item 340; and Sachar, item 480).

For Britain there were two wars in the Middle East: the war to defend local interests, the routes to India, and India itself; and the war to defeat Germany. The Mesopotamia and Palestine campaigns, the Arab revolt and the effort in Persia were directed towards the former goal; while the ill-fated Gallipoli campaign aimed at the latter. While these efforts shared a common area and origin--the threat to empire--they should not be confused. Nor should the war in the Middle East be dismissed as a sideshow for Britain because the main effort centered on Europe. The war for Britain was a struggle for survival as a Great Power; defeat in Europe *or* defeat overseas that deprived Britain of India and its outworks meant the end of empire. The reorganization of imperial defence had been undertaken with just this threat in mind--to handle a challenge both in Europe or overseas--and it was hoped that a choice of where to fight and where to lose would not have to be made. Britain's war in the Middle East must be understood in this context.

Although the British recognized that the spread of war to the Middle East jeopardized their interests, especially if an appeal to Islamic *jihad* (holy war) enflamed Muslims there and in India to rise against Britain, there was a degree of acci-

dent in drawing Britain into fighting in the area. Before
the war military and political authorities rejected plans for
direct involvement in the area, and when the war came the
British determined to concentrate their efforts in Europe,
only drawing up hasty plans at the last minute to cope with
potential Ottoman hostility (see Cohen, item 395). When that
hostility actually developed, the British aimed at a limited
campaign in the Persian Gulf area designed to secure and protect their local interests, among them prestige and the oil
fields in Iran. But this intention quickly ran afoul of opportunity and circumstance (see Busch, item 352; and Moberly,
item 315).

The initial British campaign in Mesopotamia, launched after the Turks attacked the Russian Black Sea ports, enjoyed
immediate success. Within a few days British forces had occupied the head of the Gulf and had taken Basra, the principal
city in southern Mesopotamia. The ease of this success suggested that further campaigning might produce even greater
rewards; and, in any event, the initial gains were vulnerable
to counter-attack and so a limited campaign was necessary to
secure more defensible terrain, and to secure the southern
approaches to Persia where the oil fields lay.

The campaign in Mesopotamia was the responsibility of the
Government of India, and though most of India's field army
had gone to Europe or East Africa, sufficient forces were
found to make a limited campaign in Mesopotamia feasible.
The ease of the initial campaign, the desire of local officials to be a part of the war, and Britain's need for victory
somewhere after months of stalemate in Europe encouraged further advances. British eyes turned towards Baghdad, the administrative center of Mesopotamia, and a seemingly easy tar-
get. The campaign in Mesopotamia and the Dardanelles offensive, both developing their momentum in 1915, offered the
prospect of knocking the Turks out of the war, flanking the
Central Powers and opening a supply route to Russia; and, for
Britain, promised security for their position in Egypt and
the Gulf. It also would have meant an end to enemy activities in Persia and the demise of the threat of a Muslim *jihad*,
all for only marginal investments of men and material. The
expectations were bold, the execution was bungled. The Gallipoli campaign ended in a humiliating withdrawal, and the
advance in Mesopotamia collapsed with the capture of 10,000
men at Kut al-Amara in April 1916. Though Britain recovered
quickly and occupied Baghdad within another year, these failures put an end to any idea of a quick solution to the problems in the Middle East.

The campaigns in the Middle East created another set of
problems for Britain, besides defeating the Ottomans, for the

war raised two very vexing questions: how to defeat the Turk; and what to do with him once he was defeated. If Britain had been alone it might have found satisfactory answers, but the British could not defeat the Ottomans singlehandedly, and any other powers involved would expect to help divide up the spoils (see Kedourie, item 333; Gottlieb, item 290; and Busch, item 352).

The fact that Britain was best able to conduct campaigns in the Middle East worried its allies. The French and the Russians were concerned that if Britain were left to fight in the area alone it would be in a position to deny their interests after the war. The Russians were concerned that they would lose their claims to Constantinople and the Straits, thus they opposed the Dardanelles campaign until they received assurances from both Britain and France in 1915 that Russia would receive the Straits after the war (see Renzi, item 325). The French, too, feared for their long-term interests in Syria and negotiated the Sykes-Picot Agreement with Britain in 1916 to secure British recognition of French claims (see Nevakivi, item 324). But neither of these agreements changed the fact that the brunt of the military effort fell to the British. To placate their allies the British had made valuable political concessions, but received little material support in return, which left them with the problem of defeating the Turks with limited resources. Faced with the dangers of losing, the British turned to subversion.

At this point, if the story is not confused enough, things became quite muddled. It is difficult to convey in a linear narrative the complexity of the actual situation. The orderly progression of sentences gives the impression of a seemingly complimentary orderliness in events pushed along by clear purposes. This was not the case. Looking back the pressure of circumstances, the urgency, is lost to us. Lost too is the simultaneity of many incidents, the need to make decisions under pressure, encapsulated for us now in papers and memoirs, with the lines of chance or conflicting purpose obscured by decisions taken and by subsequent events.

British policy in the Middle East had to respond to conflicting circumstances--internal, or subjective, and external, or objective. External circumstances included Ottoman hostility, German efforts to force Britain out of the war, the interests of the Allies, the necessities of defending British interests, and the local and regional social and political situation. Internal circumstances included the recognition of the need for some overall approach to the Middle East, and the divided nature of the policy-making machinery charged with determining that approach. Most British officials shared an estimation of the external, objective circumstances, but there was little agreement over what to do about them. (see Guinn, item 291; Rothwell, item 306; and Busch, item 352).

The Asquith Government was not particularly ready to fight a modern war. Although there was an attempt to stream-line the Cabinet in order to facilitate decision-making, in practice Cabinet members refused to accept any diminution of their pre-war privileges. The result was a lack of coordina-tion between departments, and no efficient single Cabinet body emerged for conducting the war. Instead decisions tended to proceed along their pre-war departmental lines, producing duplication and intensifying inter-departmental rivalry. Or, just as bad, a number of competing Cabinet committees created to coordinate inter-departmental relations merely added to the general fragmentation by increasing the steps in decision-making, producing busy-work and more duplication of effort but little coordinated planning. When this structure was added to the already complicated policy-making apparatus for the Middle East, one can begin to see why so much of British policy bore little relation to events; or rather, that by the time a policy emerged for handling a particular situation con-ditions had markedly changed and the process had to begin all over again, usually with similar results.

During the war, policy in the Middle East had to pass through at least four major departmental channels: the Govern-ment of India, the India Office, the Foreign Office, and the War Office, to which might be added the Admiralty. Each of these departments had its own local representatives making recommendations that struggled upwards within their respec-tive hierarchies. This meant considerable duplication and then endless hours in inter-departmental meetings trying to thrash out a compromise between the divergent goals of the various departments. These compromises often had to be re-submitted to the various departments, passing downwards in the hierarchies to local officials who vetted them for fea-sibility, opening up the whole process once more to the nu-merous lobby groups within each department, and requiring yet more inter-departmental maneuvering to iron out the new differences of opinion. An so on ... (see Busch, item 352).

Before the war the Foreign Office had enjoyed virtual in-dependence in deciding British foreign policy. In the ten years before 1914 Sir Edward Grey had been in charge of the Foreign Office, and though he had a reputation for detachment and a fondness for fishing over work, he was a keen politician and an effective Foreign Secretary, his handling of affairs receiving general approbation and limited interference from either Parliament or public opinion. During this period the mood of reform within the government that urged more coordination of imperial defence saw the Foreign Office increase its influence over policy-making for the Middle East. As international considerations gained more importance over the parochial interests of the Government of India, so India's independence in conducting its own local foreign policy declined, and the Foreign Office in conjunction with the India Office (the department of government representing India in the Home Government) took up the slack. When the foundation of British policy became the ententes with France and Russia, India objected, at least to the entente with Russia, but to no avail. The opinions of India were listened to but not necessarily heeded in London. When war came it was not unreasonable to assume that the Foreign Office would retain its dominate position, but this was not the case.

Several factors reduced the Foreign Office's independence and with it a firm direction in the formation of foreign policy. As noted above, the Asquith Cabinet made no credible attempt to streamline the government, and even though there had been considerable departmental reorganization before the war to cope with new challenges, these changes did not extend to a regular system for inter-departmental coordination, especially between the service branches (see Roskill, item 186; and Hankey, item 292). When war came this lack of coordination proved a handicap in many areas. As a consequence of a lack of control, various departments were left to decide for themselves what their role would be.

In the case of the Foreign Office, Sir Edward Grey saw a much-reduced role for his department (see Steiner, item 137; and Robbins, item 184). He believed foreign policy was irrevocably tied to the alliances with Russia and France, and thus Britain's maneuverability was severely constrained by the necessity of consulting the Allies before any decision. Furthermore, he believed that the war required the subordination of foreign policy to the requirements of the service branches. He also recognized that the rapid change of circumstances required quick, informed responses to local events and he gave his local agents more independence and say in policy. This inevitably meant that the influence of local authorities, which had been declining before the war, increased. While a legitimate response to the demands of war, the Foreign Office nevertheless lost control of the pace and a measure of its independence to its own subordinates, who flooded the Foreign Office with proposals and dire descriptions of events requiring immediate attention. The pressure of work, which expanded remorselessly, overtaxed the mental and physical stamina of Foreign Office personnel, hitting

particularly hard at Grey who was already ailing and whose
morale was at a low ebb because of the war. The Foreign Office lost its detachment and control, and the precious time
needed for thought was consumed in the mountains of work.

Compounding this was Grey's belief in the decline of the
importance of foreign policy, and the increasing tendency of
other departments, especially the service branches, to assume
more responsibility for foreign affairs. The Foreign Office
did not, however, abdicate responsibility for foreign affairs,
nor were other departments truly able to conduct their own
foreign policies; and the natural response of bureaucracies
to guard their own terrain forced the departments to consult
one another. But the lack of overall direction from the
Cabinet or anywhere else meant there was no coordinating
principle for inter-departmental consultation and no binding
conceptual basis; the coordination was *ad hoc* and decisions
were *propter hoc*. The net result was a decline in Foreign
Office influence and a corresponding loss of incisive action
in Foreign policy. A case in point involves the question of
the Arab revolt.

The question of encouraging the Arab subjects of the
Ottoman Empire to revolt had surfaced very early in the war.
Not only did such an armed revolt offer the prospect of damaging the Ottoman war effort, it also lessened the chances of
a general Muslim *jihad*. But it was one thing to consider the
idea; it was quite another to give it life. The Arabs were
divided and had given no real signs before the war of being
discontent with Ottoman rule. Furthermore no one was sure
what the Arabs might ask as the price for their cooperation,
or that Britain would be ready to pay it; and arousing Arab
hopes only to frustrate them could make matters worse by
driving them into an anti-British stance. On the other hand,
if the Arabs were interested in a revolt, ignoring them could
produce the same situation. With these various concerns in
mind the British began tentatively to explore various possibilities and they quickly discovered that there was a body
of Arab opinion hostile to Ottoman domination, and the question then became one of how to exploit this. There was little
agreement, and the divided nature of British policy-making
machinery guaranteed that disagreement compounded.

The Government of India had handled approaches to the
Arabs of the Gulf States for years and naturally felt best
able to conduct relations with Arab leaders. In addition,
India was conducting the military campaign in Mesopotamia,
a fact that gave added weight to India's opinion, at least
in military matters until the debacle at Kut al-Amara, when
the Home Government took over the war effort in Mesopotamia.

India's idea, however, was not to encourage an active role
for the Arabs, which would have involved arming and supplying
them as well as making inconvenient binding promises, but to
secure their neutrality and cooperation. Other British officials, including the Secretary for War, Lord Kitchener, and
officials at the India Office and the Foreign Office, did
not share this opinion. Even within the Indian Government
there was lack of coordination and dissent. Local Indian
agents such as Captain Shakespear and later St. John Philby
(see items 191 and 180), for example, embarrassed their superiors with their differing and forward ideas favoring an
active role for their favorite Arab, ibn Saud. The main con-
trary view, though, came from officials in Egypt and the
Sudan, the Foreign Office and elsewhere, who felt they knew
something of the Arabs. These officials, among them Ronald
Storrs, Reginald Wingate, Mark Sykes, and D.G. Hogarth, explored the possibilities of encouraging an armed Arab revolt,
and they found a likely candidate--Husayn, the Sharif of
Mecca (see Kedourie, item 346).

Husayn was a member of the Prophet's tribe and he held a
patent from the Ottomans to supervise the Holy City of Mecca.
Husayn's lineage and his prestige made him a likely candidate
to use to blunt Ottoman appeal among Muslims. The Muslims of
India looked to the Ottoman Sultan as the leader of Islam,
and the British worried that this fact might be used against
them. Therefore, they saw Husayn's anti-Ottoman stance as
an instrument to undermine the prospect of a united Islamic
upheaval aimed at Britain. Negotiations with Husayn proceeded
slowly, however. The British were unsure of his support in
the Islamic world or among other Arabs, and they did not want
to aggravate Muslim sympathies by encouraging sedition
against the Ottomans; it was bad enough being at war with
them. Nor did the British want to commit themselves to Husayn
before it became clear what he expected in return, and what
contribution he could make to the war effort. Husayn, for
his part, did not want to join a losing cause, displaying his
disloyalty to the Ottomans only to have them win. Nor did
Husayn want to commit himself until he received guarantees
from the British concerning the post-war settlement, for his
claimed leadership of an Arab nationalist movement with the
aspiration of creating an Arab state from the former Ottoman
provinces.

The Government of India particularly opposed the idea,
but the weight of opinion tended towards an agreement. The
so-called Arab Bureau in Cairo, including such figures as
T.E. Lawrence and Ronald Storrs, which began as an intelligence-
gathering agency, believed in the importance of Husayn, and

one suspects in their own importance for promoting the idea
of an Arab revolt. They received support from Mark Sykes,
who was sort of a wandering trouble-shooter and negotiator
with influential connections at the Foreign Office and with
Lord Kitchener, the Secretary for War. The Foreign Office
generally supported the scheme, but not wholeheartedly. They
wanted only limited promises to the Arabs, based solely on
performance, and they were also aware of promises to the
French that were not strictly compatible with discussions
then in progress with Husayn. Still, the prospect of an
agreement was a powerful incentive, stronger than India's
objections or the Foreign Office's caution.

But consideration and promotion of an Arab revolt had
further difficulties, chief among them Britain's alliance
with France. When preliminary negotiations began with Husayn
in mid-1915, it became clear that he had grandiose ideas going far beyond what Britain was prepared to entertain. The
British had to find a way to retain Husayn's friendship while
not appearing to frustrate his exorbitant demands. A compromise was found in obfuscation and vagueness, with promises
left deliberately ambiguous, which served both parties because it left them maneuvering room. Meanwhile the French,
whose alliance was far more crucial to Britain than any Arab
one, were nervous that Britain was planning to steal a march
on them in the Middle East while they were fighting for their
survival in Europe. To reassure the French the British, with
Russian approval, negotiated the Sykes-Picot Agreement recognizing the areas of French interest, which included some
of the areas discussed with Husayn. These promises were made
while negotiations continued with Husayn, who did not declare
against the Ottomans until June 1916 after a year of haggling.

More or less at the same time, the British were also beginning to consider what their own intentions in the former
Ottoman provinces would be after the war. After maintaining
Ottoman integrity for many years, they were now at war with
the Turks and faced with having to decide what to do about
settling the security of their interests in Ottoman territory.
It was becoming clear that Russia, France and the Arabs intended to partition the Ottoman Empire and that Britain had
to participate to protect its interests. Needless to say,
there were any number of conflicting opinions on how to
achieve this that varied according to the fluctuations of the
war. But what began to emerge was a realization that victory
in the Middle East offered Britain the chance to put its interests on secure, British-controlled terms, without foreign
interference. Since this intriguing idea ran counter to promises to the French or pledges to the Arabs, it was left to

policy-makers to strike a harmony between these conflicts or find a way out of the commitments. The trouble was, there was no harmony among the policy-makers.

India, in particular, worried about the effect on its Muslim subjects of partitioning the Ottoman Empire and opposed supporting the Arabs. At the same time, they were conducting a military campaign in Mesopotamia, were contemplating retaining the area after the war, and did not want to see British claims compromised. Officials in Egypt and London took a different view. They saw the necessity of an Arab revolt and saw no contradiction, at least during the war, between securing British interests and promises to the French and the Arabs, whose support was necessary to win. These views prevailed.

Not only were the Arabs encouraged, but promises were also made to the Jews. The British were worried that the Germans would declare their support for a Jewish homeland and thus gain an important propaganda victory, especially with the American Jews, whom the British saw as having significant influence. Led by Chaim Wiezmann, the Jews lobbied vigorously in London to sell the idea of a national home, and were rewarded with the Balfour Declaration in November 1917. With the same vagueness that allowed conflicting promises to the French and Arabs, the promises in the Declaration were ambiguous and open to interpretation.

The result was a combination of promises designed to give everybody what they wanted, or at least the impression that they were getting what they wanted, so that they could all get about the business of winning the war. With the successful conclusion of the war, however, the necessity for cooperation declined and each party found it wanted or needed more, and each reinterpreted its vague promises and rising expectations in terms of the opportunities victory offered.

POST-WAR SETTLEMENTS

The numerous wartime pledges had been made in one context, but they had to be redeemed in another. Defeat would have made them redundant; victory made them an embarrassment.

There were two new conditions in the Middle East following World War I: British troops were in direct control of most of the area, replacing the Ottomans; and local nationalist sentiment had emerged and expected self-rule. The successful campaigns in Mesopotamia and Palestine left British troops in

occupation of those areas, as well as much of Syria; and the
Armistice with Turkey in October 1918 put the Allies in control at Constantinople. British expeditions also controlled
much of Persia, and small numbers of British advisers were
in the Transcaucasus and Central Asia involved with local
struggles against the Bolsheviks. This was a unique position
for Britain. The Ottoman Empire had collapsed, the Germans
were defeated, the Russian revolution had removed a powerful
rival, the French had played little part in the Middle East,
and British troops were in actual control of most of the area.
A seemingly firm, militarily-supported, direct British control
had replaced all the old sources of insecurity. To the statesman in London who comprehended this reality, the new situation
in the Middle East offered the opportunity to put a permanent
end to Britain's security anxieties, and they determined to
do so. Unfortunately, just as they faced this brave new
world, they also faced unprecedented obstacles.

The settlement of the Middle East's fate after the war
was not entirely in British hands, despite the fact that British troops controlled most of the area. Disposition of the
former Ottoman provinces was a political, not a military
question, and the decisions were made by the assembled Allies
at the Peace Conference in Paris. The British were also
bound by certain wartime pledges to local peoples and to the
principles espoused by Wilson. They sought the best solutions
within these limits, and they also tried to nudge those boundaries in a more favorable direction. Direct control was out,
so in its place the British developed a concept of a façade
of local government with a solid inner-structure of administration dominated by British officials. This idea was legitimized by the Conference as a mandate, which recognized
the rights of the local peoples to independence, but also recognized their inability to govern themselves without a period of tutelage. If there had been no internal pressures
within these new mandates that rejected foreign domination
they might well have served as a lasting compromise, but Arab
nationalism would not accept a permanent mandate and worked
unremittingly for independence, producing riots and civil
strife in its wake.

The war had created a new atmosphere, had loosened the
binding ties of social and political order around the world,
arousing new expectations. The war itself had been a revolution, leaving a social and political confusion in its wake.
In the years following the war there were riots or upheavals
in virtually every quarter of the world--in colonial and
semi-independent areas as well as in the major imperial nations. In the years between 1918 and 1922, not counting the

upheaval in Russia, there were strikes, social upheavals, wars, or civil strife in Britain, Ireland, France, Germany, Poland, Turkey, Armenia, Central Asia, Iran, Iraq, Syria, Palestine, Egypt, Afghanistan, India, China and even isolated islands of the South Pacific. Even the political relations of the erstwhile Allies suffered severe strains and acrimonious exchanges that aggravated post-war attempts to put the world back together again.

The war itself had severely disturbed world stability, weakened the power and influence of the European states and encouraged a belief in the emergence of a new social and international order. Promises to dependent peoples to secure their cooperation or neutrality committed the Powers to changes in their relations with colonial peoples; and those people had come to expect something of these promises. The Russian Revolution and Wilson's Fourteen Points reinforced this expectation, and Allied commitment to self-determination, non-annexation and an end to secret treaties inspired new hope. Many stateless minorities saw in Wilson's declaration the chance for justice, which generally meant statehood for themselves; revolution in Russia had destroyed an imperial power, and defeat had broken up two others (the Austro-Hungarian and the Ottoman), opening new opportunities for self-determination. In such a climate it became difficult for British statesmen to follow up the advantages victory presented in the Middle East.

The question became one of how to satisfy the long-standing demands of interest and security in this new diplomatic climate. In part the search for an answer was a cynical reevaluation of wartime commitments; in part it was a sincere attempt to reconcile a maze of conflicting, vague promises with the real and expanding interests of local people, and at the same time to guarantee the security of British interests--a goal that British statesmen did not see as necessarily incompatible.

Problems in four main areas had to be dealt with: the first concerned the disposition of the Ottoman Empire in Europe and Asia Minor; the second, the disposition of the Arab provinces of the Ottoman Empire; the third, the fate of Egypt; and the fourth, the nature of Britain's future relations with Persia. Each of these major concerns had its own besetting problems, in addition to the collapse of social and political order in the wake of four years of war.

The Asiatic parts of the Ottoman Empire were up for grabs. The Russians no longer claimed a share, but no one missed them. To the long-standing French and British claims, were added Italian and Greek demands for their promised share of

Asia Minor. In eastern Anatolia the Armenians, a rebellious
and persecuted minority in the old empire, demanded a new,
independent state. The victorious Powers also had to deal
with the impotent remnants of the sultanate in Constantinople,
and with a growing Turkish nationalist force led by the former imperial general Mustafa Kemal (later Atatürk), whom the
Allies tried to ignore, but who increasingly came to represent Turkish interests. The Allies intended to create a rump
Turkish state in central Anatolia and let everyone else carve
out his own sphere. The Turkish nationalists, however, rejected this partition and waged a war to save a Turkish homeland incorporating all of Asia Minor and Constantinople. Con-
trary to Allied expectations, Mustafa Kemal mobilized an efficient army, defeated the Greeks in Smyrna, expunged Armenian
independence, and defied the French, Italians and British to
enforce their claims. The Allies could not muster the will
to confront the Turks, especially after the collapse of the
Greek army, and accepted Mustafa Kemal's *fait accompli*, but
only after three-and-a-half years of turmoil. The Allies
recognized Turkish independence in 1922 with the Treaty of
Lausanne (see Davison, item 467; Lewis, item 477; and Shaw,
item 481).

The situation in the former Arab provinces of the Ottoman
Empire was no less confusing, with Arab and Jewish nationalists and French and British imperialists all expecting to see
their expectations fulfilled. Not all these expectations
were compatible, nor was there any way of making them so.
The Jews were determined on a place in Palestine; the Arabs
were determined not to have them; the British did not want to
see the French in the area, and the French were determined to
stay there. The Arabs expected independence and British support for it, while the French wanted their share and saw in
British efforts to convince them that the Arabs did not want
French rule as an alarming reminder of Perfidious Albion.
Through the efforts to reconcile these ran charges and counter-
charges of double-dealing, lying and bad faith, all of them
true and all of them exaggerated.

To a degree the British had called Arab nationalism into
being by encouraging it during World War I with promises of
autonomy. Although a limited Arab nationalism had existed
before the war, the Ottomans had suppressed most of it; what
leadership there was existed in scattered and disunited secret societies; and nationalist sentiment itself had developed
along sectarian lines, and though claiming universalism, was
in reality parochial. Most Arabs had been content as Ottoman
subjects and not a few of the Arab nationalists had remained
loyal to the Ottomans throughout the war. The British, how-

ever, had sought out the scattered anti-Ottoman elements and
encouraged them to revolt, supported them in that revolt, and
made promises to nourish it. But the revolt itself remained
a minor movement until Allied victory legitimized it; with
the Ottomans gone Arab nationalism suddenly found its voice
(see Dawn, item 433; and Howard, item 332).

The British were somewhat shocked to find this vigorous
new sentiment and were suspicious of it, regarding it as a
short-lived enthusiasm or Arab effervescence. And they knew
these were poor conditions upon which to base either self-
government or British security. The British had promised the
Arabs independence but did not believe them capable of it.
The local experts, such as Percy Cox or Arnold Wilson, confirmed the impression that the local peoples were capable of
self-interest but not self-government. Furthermore, the British had a special interpretation of independence that stipu-
lated a special relationship for the Arabs in Anglo-Arab relations. It is essential to grasp the background ideas governing British relations with the Arabs to comprehend the
promises made to them.

Before the war the British had no direct contact with the
Arabs within the Ottoman Empire, contact with Arabs being confined to certain semi-independent Arab entities in the Persian
Gulf region. The British did not treat these Arab principal-
ities as sovereign states, but as autonomous tribes or authorities. The terms of those relations were not those of
equals, and while the British respected the Arabs they were
not prepared to let them jeopardize British interests. Thus
Britain devised a relationship in which the local rulers were
left alone to deal with local affairs, so long as those did
not affect British interests, and they took control over their
foreign affairs, leaving them the truncated independence of
the various autonomous states in India. This pattern of relationship informed Britain's approach to Husayn and the idea
of Arab independence during the war. The British wanted an
autonomous state, but one that was loyal to Britain; and they
contemplated an Arab state restricted largely to Arabia, while
Husayn and other Arab nationalists had more ambitious ideas
of incorporating the Arab provinces of the Ottoman Empire.
The British had little faith in the ability of the Arabs of
the former Ottoman provinces to govern themselves. Nor did
authorities in the Middle East or in London place much faith
in nationalism as a basis for government, regarding it as
little more than a transient passion confined to a few individuals, not all of them reputable characters. It was not entirely coincidental that these opinions coincided with the
realization that Britain had an opportunity to secure a per-

manently favorable situation in the Middle East; but it was
not purely cynicism that motivated officials in London or in
the Middle East.   They believed in the importance of orderly
government and of the dangers for local liberties, as well
as for British interests, and felt Britain could not abdicate
a responsibility for providing government and order to people
who had never enjoyed it, the Ottoman Government being counted
as nothing more than a predatory, corrupt regime (see Busch,
item 352).

The Arabs had a different understanding.   There may have
been no organized Arab nationalism before the War, and the
British may have fostered its development, but that background
did not in any way impugn its validity after the War.   Nationalism needs no pedigree, no long, colorful heritage to sustain
it.   And there had been a long-term development of a sense of
identity in the decades before the war.   Much of it had been
centered on Islam, but there had also been appeals by intellectuals to the Arabs' earlier primary place in the Middle
East before the arrival of the Turks.   While there had been
no organized nationalism in a modern sense, there was a sense
of place, commonality and shared backgrounds (see Sharabi,
item 457).   There had also been a sense of resistance, not so
much to the Ottomans but to the encroachment of the West.
The Ottoman Empire was the principal Islamic state and was
the symbolic head of Islam for most Muslims, even those in
India.   During the war some Arabs rejected the Ottomans as
their leaders, but they did not forego their sense of iden-
tification with Islam or their resistance to foreign domination.   It was that undifferentiated feeling, unleashed from
loyalty to the Islamic state of the Ottomans, that coalesced
during the war, giving Arab leaders a following, and introducing a new force into the Arab Middle East.   This new force
did not accept a limited sovereignty in which Britain controlled foreign relations and supervised internal administra-
tion--the Arabs preferred to be misruled by themselves than
governed well by foreigners.   It was a concept the British
failed to understand.

The British failed to grasp this change because they were
used to dealing with governments on formal terms or with individual power holders, not movements.   During the war they
had made promises to Husayn and invoked their own ideas of
Arab independence; they made no promises to Arab nationalism
or to its never-satisfied claims.   Approaches to the Arabs
after the war were consistent with British promises, in light
of their own interpretation of them, but these approaches were
no longer realistic.   Individuals such as Curzon, or even Sir
Percy Cox, who knew the Arabs, failed to accord nationalism

an appropriate place in their dealings with the Arabs, or
with the Turks and Persians. It was a serious conceptual error.

British officials were not complete innocents, though.
They may have missed the significance of nationalism as a
force for resisting local British policy, but they did not
misjudge their own interests. Lloyd George, for example, who
had replaced Asquith as Prime Minister in December 1916, recognized the significance of the Middle East to future British interests, and the campaign in Palestine, begun under his
encouragement, was not only an attempt to knock the Turks out
of the war, but also to put Britain in control of Palestine,
the long-recognized invasion route to Egypt. Lloyd George's
government had brought a new sense of order and purpose to
Britain's war effort, and more coordination to the execution
of British policy. While this did not suddenly replace the
cumbersome decision-making machinery in the Middle East, it
did promote more consistency in British policy. From this
grew a more clear-cut decision to retain the advantages Britain's armed forces had won in the Middle East. Based on this
the British had sought to renegotiate the Sykes-Picot Agreement
with France even before the war was over, to maneuver the
French out of claims in the Middle East. The British recognized the disadvantages of the conflicting agreements made
during the war and they tried to reduce those inconsistencies
by getting the French to give up their interests.

The British were also not ignorant of nationalist sentiments, Lloyd George himself being a partisan of the Greeks.
The British also supported the nationalist sentiments of the
Armenians, Georgians, and others at the Peace Conference. In
addition, elements within the British Government perceived the
importance of nationalist sentiment in the Middle East and
urged a policy of conciliation. The Government of India,
aware of nationalism among its own charges, particularly
urged the Home Government to make substantive concessions to
nationalists, urgings dismissed in London because they jeopardized British interests. Officials in London were also
well-aware of the surge of feelings for self-determination,
and they had enough appreciation of Arab nationalism to use
it against the Ottomans during the war and as an argument after the war to persuade the French that there was no place
for them in the Arab Middle East, though they tried to talk
the French into an interest in Armenia. They also appreciated
the importance of keeping Arab or Persian nationalists from
the Peace Conference where they might have appealed to Pres-
ident Wilson. These officials--Lloyd George, Lord Curzon and
others--were not ignorant of nationalism but what they wanted

in the Middle East was a domesticated nationalism that pla-
cated the locals while leaving Britain in control. They dismissed as inconsequential or subversive a nationalism that
ran counter to that expectation. This same expectation can
be seen in Britain's relations with its other protégé in the
Middle East--the Jews.

The British had promised the Jews their cooperation in
establishing a national home in Palestine. The British saw
it as a magnanimous gesture, and one that foreclosed on any
possibility that the Germans might make a similar move to win
international Jewish support. The British were accustomed to
disposing of territories they knew little about, and they saw
little incompatibility in promises to the Arabs and Jews
(though Balfour, the author of the declaration to the Jews,
was aware of the conflicting nature of Britain's promises:
see *British Documents on Foreign Policy* on Palestine, item
053; Ingrams, item 049; and Stein, item 531). But once again,
the British never contemplated an independent Jewish entity.
They envisaged a single state run efficiently by Britain that
accommodated Jewish claims for a homeland and Arab claims for
their own state, just as Britain administered multi-religious
areas in India. The British wanted neither a Jewish nor an
Arab presence that jeopardized British interests. In the
years after the Balfour Declaration, as the Jews in Palestine
displayed their increasingly independent spirit, one that
could not be dismissed on the grounds that the educated European Jews were not capable of self-government, the British,
especially those officials in the local administration, turned
on the Zionists, and by World War II Anglo-Jewish relations
shared little of that sense of patronizing cooperation that
had produced the Balfour Declaration (see Mossek, 529; Wasserstein, 535; and Porath, 530).

Problems with Arabs and Jews were only part of Britain's
problems, however. The British also failed in their efforts
to convince the French that the Arabs would never accept their
rule. Though the British reduced the extent of French claims,
the French retained their demands for a special place in
Lebanon and Syria and were not to be persuaded to abandon
those claims by British logic or Arab nationalism. The French
dismissed Arab sentiments for independence and disposed of
British efforts to talk them out of a role in the Middle East
with Gallic straightforwardness--their army seized Lebanon and
Syria, ejected Faysal, one of Husayn's sons, as King, and imposed a French mandate designed to teach the Arabs how to govern themselves (see Nevakivi, item 341; and Shorrock, item
267). The British had to content themselves with securing a
position in Palestine, which the French had claimed, and to

extending the area of their mandate in Iraq to the Turkish frontier in Anatolia, incorporating Mosul and Kirkuk, which were later to be major oil-producing sites--not bad compensation. Control of Palestine gave them control of the corridor to Egypt and the Suez Canal; and control of Iraq put them in a position to protect the Persian oilfields and the approaches to the Persian Gulf.

But the British were unable to convert this position into direct control. Recognizing the claims of Arab nationalists and bound by commitments to self-determination and non-annexation, they could not incorporate Palestine or Iraq into the empire, a logical outcome by pre-war standards. Instead the British created a façade of local rule that left them in virtual control. They settled the administrative fate of these areas at a conference held in Cairo in 1921. Responsibility for the areas passed from the military to a department of government, significantly the Colonial Office, normally charged with administering actual British possessions; and in 1921 the head of that department, Winston Churchill, visited the area, meeting with senior officials to work out detailed plans for administering the mandates. The program was a bureaucratic success, but like so much planned on paper, it never came to grips with local realities. There were really no administrative solutions to the local problems (see Klieman, item 198; and Busch, item 285).

The situation in Egypt and Persia was similarly unsatisfying. In both cases the British had vital interests that clashed with local ideas of independence, although the positions in the two places were very different. The British had a firm position in Egypt confirmed by 30 years of occupation. They had done much for the country, but they failed to do one very important thing--leave. The local nationalist movement had not disappeared with the occupation in 1882, but only retired for a while. The war gave it new hope and that spirit emerged after the war and demanded recognition, demanded that Britain leave. The position in Persia was dissimilar in that Britain had not controlled large parts of Persia. Before the war the British had an agreement with Russia that recognized a rump area of interest on the border of India, and they had sent punitive expeditions to southern Persia--quickly withdrawn--at various times to protect their interests against local tribes or the Persian Government. They had negotiated a web of agreements with local tribes as a means of protecting local interests and had acquired control of Persian oil, and there was a lively, if small, regional trade. But Britain had no direct control over Persia and limited indirect influence.

The Russians had dominated the north of the country, and the tighter Russian control became the less leverage Britain had with the Persians. During the war, though, that condition changed. Britain gradually became militarily involved in Iran as the Central Goverment proved incapable or unwilling to uphold its own neutrality; and when the Russians collapsed the British were drawn even deeper into the area, not only to defend it against the Turks, but to supply adventures in southern Russia as a way of keeping Russia in the war against Germany. When the war ended small numbers of British troops or British-subsidized auxiliaries occupied most of the country, and British subsidies kept the Persian Government and its only reliable military forces from financial collapse. It was this new position that British officials, mainly Lord Curzon, hoped to turn into a permanent arrangement that would, together with Britain's position in Palestine and Iraq, erect a line of buffer states across the extent of Asia and the Middle East to shield vital British interests (see Nicolson, 181). Not only was there to be a Cape-to-Cairo route, but a Cairo-to-Karachi route as well. It was a bold conception quite beyond Britain's resources.

The Egyptians, led by such nationalist leaders as Sa'd Zaghlul, refused to accept British control and showed their determination by encouraging strikes and riots. There was little the British could do to stop these—short of a draconian military response inimicable to the British concept of good government—except to negotiate a compromise. The eventual result was an agreement whereby Britain recognized Egyptian independence, though reserving control of the Suez Canal and the Sudan. The Egyptian nationalists rejected these terms in principle but accepted them in practice. British influence in Egypt remained strong in the interwar years, and reverted to direct control during World War II, as it did in Iraq, when it looked as though the Nazis would gain control of these vital areas (see Vatikiotis, item 391).

Matters proceeded differently in Persia. There the idea was never to incorporate Persia into the Empire, but to devise a special status for it, similar to the mandates, that would give the country a measure of independence while reserving essential control for Britain. The solution was the brainchild of Lord Curzon, acting Foreign Secretary, who regarded himself an expert on the area. His idea was to correct all of Persia's besetting problems by reforming Persia's administration, finances and army. With sound finances, an able bureaucracy and an efficient army, the government would be able to guarantee internal security and keep itself free of foreign domination—at least of any foreign power other

than Britain (see Nicolson, item 181; Busch, item 285; and
Olson, item 424).

   Curzon was constrained for time, however, as pressures
at home demanded a retrenchment, a reduction of Britain's
overextended commitments. This meant the elimination of the
subsidies and military presence in Iran that was largely
responsible for local order and the main basis of Britain's
influence. Curzon regretted this retrenchment but could do
nothing to stop it, so he had to devise a solution before the
time ran out. After the Persian delegation's inflated case
(demanding parts of Iraq, Turkey, and the Caucasus and Central
Asia) was rejected at the Peace Conference, he forced the
Persian Government, in power largely at his discretion, to
sign an agreement in August 1919 allowing Britain to rehabilitate the country. It gave Britain control of Persia's army
as well as virtually every other department of government.
It was a handy agreement with the added virtue of not requiring much money. But Persian nationalists, as well as Britain's Allies, France and America, denounced the agreement as
nothing more than a protectorate veiled in high-sounding intentions.

   Persian nationalists, recovering after the virtual occupation of part or all of their country during the war, would
have none of it. Curzon was contemptuous of this group, as
was every other British official except those in the Government of India, and expected no real difficulties. In this
he erred. Because of a law requiring that all foreign agreements receive the ratification of the Majlis (Persian Parliament), which had yet to be elected in a time-consuming process, the agreement languished for months waiting for approval.
In the meantime the nationalists mounted a devastating campaign against it, killing any chance of ratification. Curzon
eventually withdrew it in disgust and shortly afterwards a
nationalist coup in February 1921 toppled the existing government and ended any chance that the agreement would revive.
This new government and its successors managed to restore internal order and during the interwar years challenged the
British over their control of Persia's oilfields. The Persians continued to pursue an independent policy until World
War II when British and Russian forces, once again to forestall the Germans, invaded the country and occupied it for
the duration.

   Thus, at the end of the war, the British were unable to
capitalize on their unique position. The Turks refused to
be docile while the Allies partitioned their homeland, the
Egyptians insisted on at least a measure of independence,
the French declined to be talked out of their share in the

spoils, and the Persians rejected Curzon's tender considerations. Only in Palestine and Iraq did Britain secure a measure of direct control, and that was limited by the concept of self-determination, recognized by Britain as a principle during the war, and accepted--in part--as a necessity after the war. The British spent the interwar years trying to live with their new situation in the Middle East. It was a bitter time, filled with frustration and ill-will.

CONCLUSION

There is undoubtedly cause and effect in history, as we are assured by countless historians and politicians if we ever had any doubts. But at what point does cause become effect? Unless we consider a particular event inevitable, when and why do the causes we can trace coalesce to form that particular outcome which holds our attention? In considering an event as momentous and disturbing as world war, with complex antecedents, what spark or catalyst converted a multitude of circumstances from randomness to decision and upheaval, from peace to war? The richness of the answer, its variety, is what keeps the question fresh; the difficulty, if not the impossibility, of answering the question, is what keeps controversy alive.

In one sense this essay traces the evolution of British policy in the Middle East from 1900-1921, showing the transformation of a local interest into a presence little different from formal empire, almost as if 1900-1914 was the warm-up for the inevitable conflict of 1914-1918. In many senses it was, and the decisions, the patterns of relations, all the seen and unseen currents of human action produced the combustible atmosphere of world war. In other ways, however, this was not the case. Consider briefly just what historians would have said about the same period in which they see so many causes of war had there been no war. Released momentarily from the convictions imposed by events, we may glimpse the possibilities that might have developed had certain things not taken the course they did. It seems to me that the job of a historian, if he or she is to grasp the significance of particular circumstances, is to get a look at what the terrain was like before some occurence altered the landscape, casting shadows that distort once-familiar features.

If the historian is to understand human actions, to interpret the decisions of statesmen, for example, it is essen-

tial to capture at least a notion of the uncertainty that
they faced. This does not mean putting one's self in the
mind of the diplomats, but rather appreciating that they made
their decisions without knowing the outcomes. We know what
effects their decisions had, or think we do, and quite often
that knowledge gets in our way when we try to interpret why
they made the decisions they did.

Events in history are an alloy of accident and design, of
reaction to unintended, unexpected and unwelcome circumstances.
Clearly, people can command their circumstances, direct events
to their satisfaction, achieve what they set out to do. But
just as clearly, their actions can be abetted or frustrated
by circumstances beyond foresight or control.

This essay suggests that Britain's expansion in the
Middle East was a slow, halting progress at best, that the
course of empire was not the necessary result of design or
intention. That some individuals favored expansion and made
decisions to push forward British interests is indisputable;
that others resisted expansion is undeniable. In both cases
there were circumstances that favored or undermined the determination of the expansionists, and uncompromising realities that forced the hand of the reticent. Overall, the general trend was towards the expansion of British interests
and involvement. The weakness of the local states, the competition of other powers, the demands of local and regional
security, the pursuit of economic interests, and the ambitions of officials combined to make expansion seem both possible and, in certain circumstances, necessary. This process
reached its height at the end of World War I when, for a
brief moment, Britain held a unique position.

Left to themsleves there can be no doubt how the British
would have disposed of their conquests in the Middle East.
The natural corollary of their victory would have been annexation, and there were strong arguments for just such a
move within the government. But the British were in no position to define their own terms for settlement in the Middle
East, and had to accept a compromise compounded of promises
to local nationalists, pledges to their Allies, and world
public opinion. The mandate system, the 1919 Anglo-Persian
Agreement, and the negotiations with the Egyptian nationalists over independence all shared one characteristic--they
were compromises. The mandate system, in particular, was a
hybrid designed to bridge the gap between the demands of
local nationalists and the necessities of British security.
The post-war period was a transitional phase in international
relations marked most significantly by the emergence of the
demands of local peoples against the interests of the Great

Powers. Though Britain's war effort carried the empire to
its greatest extent, the exertions of war and the consequences of wartime promises meant that the British were unable
to realize the full benefits of their triumphs. Empire elu-
ded them.

Part II

Annotated Bibliography

CHAPTER 1
REFERENCE

Bibliographies

001. Albion, Robert G. *Naval and Maritime History: An Annotated Bibliography.* 4th edition. Trowbridge,
England: Redwood Press of David Collins, 1973. ix
+ 370 pp.

Surveys reference works, theses, monographs, periodicals, and some archives on all aspects of naval history from 1500 to 1960's. Limited largely to works in
English and concentrates on post-1900 material. The
Persian Gulf is covered in pages 181-3 and the Mediterranean in pages 110-5.
Cf. Marder, 131; Higham, 008; Bayliss, 002.

002. Bayliss, Gwyn. *Bibliographic Guide to the Two World
Wars: An Annotated Survey of English-Language Reference Materials.* New York: Bowker, 1977. xv +
578 pp.

Surveys archival sources, bibliographies and reference works, biographies and periodicals, films and
photograph collections related to the two World Wars.
Topically arranged with sub-sections that cover sources
country-by-country. Well-annotated, excellent survey
with useful author, subject and country indexes. In
addition, see S.L. Mayer and W.J. Koenig, *The Two World
Wars: A Guide to Manuscript Collections in the United
Kingdom* (London: Bowker, 1976), which surveys collections held at various repositories of public and private papers in Britain, listing them city by city, with
a brief description of contents. Also see A.G.S. Enser,
*A Subject Bibliography of the First World War: Books in
English, 1914-1978* (London: Andre Deutsch, 1979).
Cf. Higham, 008; Albion, 001; Public Records--Great
Britain, 036; Banks, 024.

003.   Besterman, Theodore. *A World Bibliography of Bibliog-*
           raphies and of Bibliographical Catalogues, Calendars,
           Abstracts, Digests, Indexes and the Like. 4th edi-
           tion. 5 volumes. Lausanne: Societas Bibliographica,
           1965-6.

       Material is arranged by subjects with a comprehensive
       author index, while entries under subject headings are
       arranged by date of publication. Gives very brief de-
       scriptive annotations. Covers an international range
       of bibliographies, though not in oriental languages.
       The Middle East is included under the heading "Asia,"
       with 20 or more entries. Each country is dealt with
       under separate headings. A supplement to this edition
       is Alice Toomey, *A World Bibliography of Bibliographies,*
       1964-1974: A List of Works Prepared by Library of Con-
       gress Printed Catalog Cards: A Decennial Supplement to
       Theodore Besterman, "A World Bibliography of Bibliog-
       raphies," 2 volumes (Totowa, N.J.: Rowman & Littlefield,
       1977); unfortunately, the usefulness of this work is
       limited by the lack of an index. In addition, see
       Bibliographic Index: A Cumulative Bibliography of Bib-
       liographies (New York: H.W. Wilson, continuing publica-
       tion), which is a yearly cumulative index beginning in
       1937. Material is arranged by subject and is for the
       aficionado of bibliographies. On Asia in particular,
       see Besterman, *A World Bibliography of Oriental Bibliog-*
       raphies, revised and updated by J.D. Pearson (Totowa,
       N.J.: Rowman & Littlefield, 1975). Material is listed
       alphabetically by country, divided into geographic re-
       gions. There are no annotations, but it is useful.
           Cf. Pearson, 015; Hopwood, 009.

004.   Clements, Frank, compiler. *The Emergence of Arab Na-*
           tionalism from the 19th Century to 1921: A Bibliog-
           raphy. London: Diploma Press, 1976. x + 290 pp.

       An annotated guide on the rise of Arab nationalism
       from its Ottoman origins to the conflicts and confusion
       following World War I. Major sections deal with the
       Ottoman administration and international relations, the
       origins of the Arab nationalist movement, the Arab re-
       volt and Allied policy during World War I, the Peace
       Conference, the Cairo Conference, Arab reactions to
       partition and mandate, and works on Iraq, Syria, Jor-
       dan and Palestine under the mandate. The annotations
       are descriptive and useful.
           Cf. Grimwood-Jones, 005; Pearson, 015; Sauvaget, 016;
       Dawn, 434; Antonius, 430; Haim, 437.

005. Grimwood-Jones, Diana, Derek Hopwood, and J.D. Pearson,
     et al., editors. *Arab Islamic Bibliography: The
     Middle East Library Committee Guide.* London: Har-
     vester Press, 1977. xvii + 292 pp.

     Based on Gueseppe Gabrieli's *Manuele di bibliografia
     musulmana.* Provides a wide-ranging survey of the lit-
     erature on Arab Islamic countries, with 20 sections,
     each compiled by members of the Middle East Library
     Committee. Most entries are not annotated, though each
     section is introduced by a brief essay. Contents in-
     clude surveys of bibliographies, reference works, Ara-
     bic grammars, who's who's, periodicals, atlases, fest-
     schriften, institutions doing research in the United
     Kingdom, the U.S., France and Germany, archives, li-
     braries, and booksellers.
     Cf. Pearson, 015; *American Archivist*, 019.
     Reviews: *ARBA* 9 (1978):150.

006. Halstead, John, and Serafino Procari. *Modern European
     Imperialism: A Bibliography of Books and Articles,
     1815-1972.* 2 volumes. Boston: G.K. Hall, 1974.

     Examines the literature on imperialism both as a
     process and as the subject of political and academic
     debate. Volume 1 surveys the general literature on im-
     perialism and the general and specific literature on
     the British Empire and imperialism. Volume 2 covers
     other empires--France, Italy, Germany, Portugal, etc.
     Russia is not covered. Material is divided into gen-
     eral subject headings and sub-divided into further de-
     scriptive subject headings. Material is arranged al-
     phabetically and is not annotated. There are over
     33,000 books and articles listed. The present work
     builds on the pioneer study, *The Literature of European
     Imperialism: A Bibliography, 1815-1939*, 3rd edition
     (Washington, D.C.: Pearlman, 1947), edited by Lowell
     Ragatz. Provides a brief guide to documents and papers,
     mainly published sources on such collections.
     Cf. Winks, 017.
     Reviews: *CRL* 36 (1975): 67.

007. Hanham, H.J., editor. *Bibliography of British History,
     1851-1914.* Oxford: Clarendon Press, 1976. xxvii +
     1606 pp.

     A comprehensive, topically arranged survey with over
     10,000 entries, with useful annotations, especially on
     the contents of edited works and festschriften. An in-
     valuable guide. The range of publications dealing with

British historical sources is daunting; one of the best
sources of on-going bibliographic information is contained in various journals. In addition to the reviews
and books listed in such journals as the *English Historical Review*, *American Historical Review*, *Journal of
Imperial and Commonwealth History*, *Journal of British
Studies*, *Journal of Modern History*, *Journal of Contemporary History*, *British Institute of Historical Research*,
Middle Eastern Studies, *Middle East Journal*, *International Journal of Middle East Studies*, *Economic History
Review*, and *History*, see the following: *Bibliography of
Historical Works Issued in the United Kingdom*, published
at various times by the Anglo-American Conference of
Historians; the *British National Bibliography*, a weekly
survey of monographic material received for publication
and published by the Council of British National Bibliography since 1950; Geoffrey Elton, *Modern Historians
on British History, 1485-1945: A Critical Bibliography*
(London: Methuen, 1970); the *Annual Bulletin of Historical Literature*, published by the British Historical
Association; the American Historical Association's
Guide to Historical Literature (Cambridge: Harvard University Press, 1961), which is now dated; the *International Bibliography of Historical Sciences* (Paris), a
continuing yearly survey of historical literature in
all European languages; and *Writings on British History*,
published in cumulative volumes by the Institute of
Historical Research (London).
    Reviews: *ARBA* 8 (1977):210; *CRL* 38 (1977):329.

008.   Higham, Robin, editor. *A Guide to the Sources of Brit-
       ish Military History*. Los Angeles: University of
       California Press, 1971. xxi + 630 pp.

    Surveys bibliographic sources and historiographic
trends and suggests topics for further research. Provides information on the location and use of special
collections and archives in Britain, Australia, New
Zealand, and Canada, not necessarily restricted to military history. It is divided into 25 chapters, written
by 27 contributors who survey the literature on the development of the British army and navy from prehistoric
times to the end of World War II. Has sections on science and technology, colonial wars, major European conflicts, medicine, and military law. Each section is
introduced by an essay outlining the major themes and
points of interest in historiography as well as in the
events under discussion, and briefly compares and eval-

uates the most important works mentioned. Useful,
though it does not cover periodical literature.
  Cf. Bayliss, 002; Albion, 001; Marder, 131.
  Review: *CRL* 33 (1972):326.

009. Hopwood, Derek, and Diana Grimwood-Jones, editors. *The
      Middle East and Islam: A Bibliographical Introduction.*
      London: Inter Documentation, 1972. viii + 368 pp.

      Surveys relevant literature on Islamic history from
      the earliest times to the present. Twenty-five con-
      tributors, including George Atiyeh, Peter Avery, C.E.
      Bosworth, J.A. Boyle, Richard Hill, and Albert Hourani,
      were invited to submit an annotated list of the 50 most
      essential works in their specialty. The various sec-
      tions concentrate on reference sources in European and
      Middle Eastern languages--dictionaries, guides, peri-
      odicals, surveys; on general works on Middle Eastern
      geography, history, political science, economics; and
      on more specific studies on individual countries. Each
      section is introduced by a brief bibliographic essay.
      An important reference tool, but uneven in its entries
      and annotations and does not give full publication in-
      formation.
        Cf. Pearson, 015; Littlefield, 011; Grimwood-Jones,
      005; Sauvaget, 016.
        Review: *MEJ* 28 (1974):340-2, George N. Atiyeh.

010. Khalidi, Walid, and Jill Khalidi. *Palestine and the
      Arab-Israeli Conflict: An Annotated Bibliography.*
      Beirut: Institute for Palestine Studies, 1974. xxi
      + 736 pp.

      Detailed survey of published and unpublished material
      on Palestine, the mandate, and the origins and develop-
      ment of the Arab-Israeli conflict. Relevant sections
      cover the background to the Palestine problem, the de-
      velopment of Jewish settlement, Ottoman administration,
      the growth of Arab nationalism and European administra-
      tion. Most of the work concentrates on the post-World
      War II period but provides a useful survey of background
      material.
        Cf. Porath, 530; Wasserstein, 535; Tibawi, 533;
      Caplan, 520.
        Review: *CRL* 36 (1975):314.

011. Littlefield, David. *The Islamic Near East and North
      Africa: An Annotated Guide to Books in English for*

Non-Specialists. Littleton, Colo.: Libraries Unlim-
ited, 1977. 375 pp.

Surveys some 1200 works, divided into sections covering major bibliographies, reference works, general histories, international relations, languages, literature,
the arts, biographies, travel, and a country-by-country
survey of key materials. Annotations are detailed,
though the work tries to do too much in a limited space.
Well-balanced and useful. A handy complement to
Sauvaget, item 016.
    Cf. Grimwood-Jones, 005; Pearson, 015; Clements, 004.
    Reviews: *ARBA* 9 (1978):151; *MEJ* 31 (1977):371-2,
J.E. Peterson.

012. Matthews, William, compiler. *British Diaries: An Anno-
        tated Bibliography of British Diaries Written between
        1442 and 1942*. Berkeley: University of California
        Press, 1950. xxxiv + 339 pp.

Surveys diaries with brief annotations. Complement
with Matthews, *British Autobiographies: An Annotated
Bibliography of British Autobiographies Published or
Written Before 1951* (Berkeley: University of California
Press, 1955). Also see Charles L. Mowat, *Great Britain
Since 1914, The Source of History: Studies in the Uses
of Historical Evidence* (Ithaca, N.Y.: Cornell University Press, 1971), which compares the value of various
biographies and memoirs, as well as examining how to
use them, and state papers and secondary sources. For
brief sketches of key figures, see the *Dictionary of
National Biography*.
    Cf. Cook, 030; Bidwell, 026.

013. Patai, Raphael. *Jordan, Lebanon and Syria: An Annotated
        Bibliography*. Behavior Science Bibliographies. New
        Haven, Conn.: HRAF Press, 1957. vii + 289 pp.

An annotated guide, sponsored by the Human Relations
Area File, that concentrates on the people, culture,
social science and human geography of Syria, Lebanon
and Jordan. Divided into four parts: general, which
covers reference sources, and one section for each of
the three countries. Archival sources on Syria, Jordan
and Palestine are not extensive. Consult Grimwood-
Jones, *Arabic Islamic Bibliographies*, item 005; and
Pearson, item 015. In addition see S. Humphrey's
"Opportunities and Facilities for Research in Syria,"
Middle East Studies Association Bulletin 8 (1974):16-21;

J. Mandaville, "The Ottoman Court Records of Syria and Jordan," *Journal of the American Oriental Society* 86 (1966):311-9; and M.C. Hudson, "Research Facilities in Lebanon," *Middle East Studies Association Bulletin* 6 (1972):17-25.

014.   Pearson, J.D., *et al*.   *Index Islamicus: A Catalogue of Articles on Islamic Subjects in Periodicals and Other Collective Publications*.   Cambridge: Heffer (since 3rd supplement, Scholar Mansell), continuing publication.

The single most comprehensive survey of periodical literature on the Middle East in Western languages, covering the years 1906 to the present, with quarterly reports that include major monographs as well as articles.   Surveys over 500 journals that have material on the Middle East and is a handy guide.   Material is divided topically and by country and subdivided into subjects with author entries arranged alphabetically, with a comprehensive author index.   A similar survey of periodical literature, though not as comprehensive, is contained in issues of the *Middle East Journal* published by the Middle East Institute, Washington, D.C. In addition see Florence Ljunggren and Mohammad Hamdy, *Annotated Guide to Journals Dealing with the Middle East and North Africa* (Cairo: American University of Cairo, 1964) which is a list of some 356 journals in European languages and Arabic dealing with the Islamic Middle East, providing publication information and a brief description of contents and main fields of interest covered by the respective journals.

Also see Peter Rossi and Wayne White, editors, *Articles on the Middle East, 1947-1971: A Cumulation of the Bibliographies from the Middle East Journal*, 4 vols. (Ann Arbor, Michigan: Pierian Press, 1980), which supersedes a number of similar cumulative indexes to the articles contained or mentioned in the *Middle East Journal*.   The most ambitious index of historical periodical literature is *The Combined Retrospective Index to Journals in History, 1838-1974*, Annebel Wile, executive editor, 11 vols. (Washington, D.C.: Carroleton Press, 1977).   This work surveys some 928 journals, largely English language; the material is divided into 342 subject categories with author's name and keywords of the title represented.   Volumes 10 and 11 are the author index and users will need the user's guide by Even Farber in Volume 1.   Volume 4 deals with the Middle

East. There are omissions, but the information retriev-
al is impressive. The single most comprehensive survey
of historiography is, of course, *Historical Abstracts*,
which not only surveys works dealing with the period
1775 to the present in diplomatic, economic, social,
political and cultural history in journals from all
over the world, but also gives a brief synopsis of each
entry.

015. Pearson, J.D. *Oriental and Asian Bibliography: An Introduction with Some Reference to Africa*. London:
Crosby Lockwood, 1966. xvi + 261 pp.

A bibliography of the literature on Asia, including
the Middle East, as well as a brief account of the
nature of Oriental studies, the institutions in Europe
and America that carry on research, and an account of
their facilities. The work is divided into three main
parts: (1) producers of the literature, which discusses
the main institutions in Europe and America dealing with
Oriental studies; (2) the literature and its control,
which discusses manuscript collections, reference works,
and periodicals; and (3) storehouses of the literature,
which is a survey of major orientalist libraries in the
United Kingdom, Europe, America and Asia. Though dated
it is still essential. Supplement with Reeva Simon,
*The Modern Middle East: A Guide to the Research Tools
in the Social Sciences*, item 039.

In addition see Ann Schultz, *International and Regional Politics in the Middle East and North Africa:
A Guide to Information Sources* (Detroit, Michigan:
Gale, 1977), which, though covering more contemporary
events, offers a useful guide to information sources
from Afghanistan to Morocco. Supplement this with
Florence Ljunggren and Charles Geddes, editors, *An International Directory of Institutes and Societies Interested in the Middle East* (Amsterdam: Djambatan,
1962), which lists societies, universities and some
libraries that carry on or promote research in the
Middle East, with addresses, statements of purpose and
mention of any publications by the agency listed. Also
see two brief introductions to research facilities on
or in the Middle East: Nancy Searles, *Study and Research
in the Middle East and North Africa, 1976* (Washington,
D.C.: Africa-Middle East Educational Training Service,
1976); and Thomas Martin, *North American Collections
of Islamic Manuscripts* (Boston: Hall, 1978).

016. Sauvaget, Jean. *Introduction to the History of the*
      Muslim East: A Bibliographical Guide. Based on the
      2nd edition as recast by Claude Cahen. Los Angeles:
      University of California Press, 1965. xiii + 252 pp.

      An enlarged, revised edition by Claude Cahen, of
      Sauvaget's classic study, though it does not manage to
      be as thorough on some subjects as the original French
      edition. Surveys material on Islamic and pre-Islamic
      Middle Eastern history, listing archives and manuscript
      collections, major works in history, literature, social
      life, etc. in European and Middle Eastern languages,
      and various research aids. The handiest general intro-
      duction to Middle Eastern history, though it concentrates
      on the pre-1900's. Pages 16-21 and 193-201 deal with
      archives in the Middle East and Ottoman Enpire and in
      France. Dated but still useful. Bibliographies on the
      Middle East date quickly. See Richard Ettinghausen, *A*
      Selected and Annotated Bibliography of Books and Peri-
      odicals in Western Languages Dealing with the Near and
      Middle East: With Special Emphasis on Medieval and Mod-
      ern Times (Washington, D.C.: Middle East Institute,
      1954) for a general survey. A useful source, though
      covering a more contemporary period, is George Atiyeh,
      compiler, *The Contemporary Middle East, 1948-1973: A*
      Selected and Annotated Bibliography (Boston: Hall, 1975).
      This work has a brief guide to bibliographies and a
      survey of periodicals. Also see Philip Talbot, general
      editor, *A Selected Bibliography: Asia, Africa, Eastern*
      Europe, Latin America (New York: American Universities
      Field Staff, 1960); and the cumulative supplement 1961-
      1971, general editor, Teg Grondahl, which are brief sur-
      veys of the literature for undergraduate use. Other
      works include: Charles Geddes, *Analytical Guide to the*
      Bibliographies on the Arabian Peninsula, Bibliographic
      Series, no. 4 (Denver, Colorado: American Institute of
      Islamic Studies, 1974); and *Analytical Guide to the Bib-*
      liographies on Modern Egypt and the Sudan, Bibliographic
      Series, no. 2 (Denver, Colorado: American Institute of
      Islamic Studies, 1972), short works that survey bibliog-
      raphies on the economy, politics and history of Egypt,
      the Sudan, and Arabia. Also see Richard L. Hill, *A*
      Bibliography of the Anglo-Egyptian Sudan: From the Ear-
      liest Times to 1937 (Oxford: Oxford University Press,
      1939); J.H. Stephens and R. King, *A Bibliography of*
      Saudi Arabia (Durham: Centre for Middle Eastern and
      Islamic Studies, 1973); Frank Clements, *Saudia Arabia,*

World Bibliographical Series, no. 5 (Oxford: Clio Press,
1973); Geoffrey Handley-Taylor, *Bibliography of Iran*,
5th edition (London: n.p., 1969); Hafez Farmayan, *Iran:
A Selected and Annotated Bibliography* (Washington, D.C.:
Library of Congress, 1958).
Cf. Shaw, 038; Sluglett, 357; Pearson, 035.

017. Winks, Robin, editor. *The Historiography of the British
Empire-Commonwealth: Trends, Interpretations, and Resources.* Durham, N.C.: Duke University Press, 1966.
xiv + 596 pp.

Surveys recent trends in the historiography of the
Empire-Commonwealth, largely between 1939-1963. Twenty-
one essays by scholars in the field on various aspects
of imperial history from the American colonies to the
end of empire. Essays attempt to assess the literature,
identify trends, suggest how they developed, and point
out areas for further study. Of particular note are
the following: Robert O. Collins, "Egypt and the Sudan,"
279-95; John Galbraith, "The Empire Since 1783," 46-68;
Wm. Roger Louis, "Great Britain and International Trusteeship: The Mandate System," 296-311; and Joseph Jones,
"Commonwealth Literature: Developments and Prospects,"
493-522. Other essays cover Canada, Australia, New
Zealand, India, Africa, Ireland, etc. The work is now
dated, but provides a general introduction to sources
that is useful for background information and interpretation of the relative importance of the works discussed.
There is also some information on the location and contents of relevant archives in Britain, America and the
Commonwealth.
Cf. Halstead, 006; Mansergh, 129; Langer, 093; Ward,
210; Hall, 119.

Guides and Atlases

018. Alsberg, Paul A., editor. *Guide to the Archives of
Israel.* Jerusalem: Israel Archives Association,
1973. 257 pp.

Original edition published in Hebrew in 1966, inven-
tories archives, and major collections of documents,
papers and monographs dealing with Zionist, Jewish or
Israeli history, sciences, politics, etc. Comprehensive
and informative.

In addition, see Bernard Wasserstein, "Libraries and
Archives 12: Israel," *History* 60 (1975):56-61, which is
a handy guide to and brief history of the collections
in the Jewish National Library, the Hebrew University
Library, the Central Zionist Archives, the Weizmann
Archives, the Yad Vashem Archives, the Histadrut Archives and the Jabotinsky Institute. Also, see W.R.
Brinner, "Research Facilities in Israel," *Middle East
Studies Association Bulletin* 7 (1973):42-8; and the
archival sources on Jewish history and Zionism in *Studies on Palestine*, item 527.
   Cf. Public Records--Middle East, 037; *American Archivist*, 019.

019. *American Archivist.*

   Quarterly journal published by the Society for American Archivists. Contains articles and communications
on archives, and on archival practices, procedures and
theories. Frequently contains articles on special collections or archives in various countries with information on contents and problems associated with using
them. There are a number of similar journals, and
though largely useful only to professional archivists,
they do contain insights into locations and use of archives. In particular see *Archivum: Revue Internation-
ale des Archives*, published under the auspices of the
International Council of Archives (Paris), which from
time to time has information on archival sources in
the Middle East, the state of collections, their availability and the laws governing their use. In addition,
see the *Journal of the Society of Archivists* (Great
Britain); and *Archives: The Journal of the British Records Association*, which deals mainly with archives and
manuscript collections in Britain. Historical and professional journals, such as *History*, the *Journal of
Imperial and Commonwealth History*, the *American Historical Review*, the *English Historical Review*, and the
Bulletin of the Institute of Historical Research either
have regular features or occasional studies on archives
or bibliographies on current monographs and articles,
and reviews of recent theses.
   The state of most Middle East archives, outside Israel
and Turkey, is variable, and information on them is
difficult to find and often unreliable. See Public
Records--Middle East, item 037. Such professional
journals as the *Middle East Journal* and the *International Journal of Middle East Studies* give some archival

and bibliographical information; while the *Middle East
Studies Association Bulletin* and the *British Society
for Middle East Studies Bulletin* provide studies on
archives in Britain, America, and the Middle East as
well as reviews of specialist literature, programs,
and theses in progress or completed. For a study on
how to use archives, see Philip Brooks, *Research in
Archives: The Use of Unpublished Primary Sources* (Chicago: University of Chicago Press, 1969).

 Cf. Sauvaget, 016; Monger, 098; Sluglett, 357;
Greaves, 416; Watt, 189; Public Records--Great Britain,
035.

020. Angel, Herbert E. "Iran Archives." *American Archivist*
  35 (1972):173-82.

 A study not of archives *per se*, but of the problems
of archival development in Iran and the efforts to prepare the government Foreign Office material for use.
All this material is now dated, and for the present archival research in Iran offers more than the normal
difficulties. Major archives in Iran include collections at the National Library, the Majlis Library, and
the Library of the University of Tehran, all in Tehran.
For further information in Iranian archives and sources,
see Roy Mottahedeh, "Sources for the Study of Iran,"
Iranian Studies 1 (1968):4-7; Hafez Farmayan, "Observations on Sources for the Study of Nineteenth- and
Twentieth-Century Iranian History," item 044; Firuz
Kazemzadeh, "Recent Iranian Historiography," *Middle
Eastern Studies* 7 (1956):334-40; and Iraj Afshar, "Basic Information on Collecting Persian Materials for the
development of Iranian and Islamic Studies," *Middle
East Studies Association Bulletin* 10 (1976):11-19. The
journal *Iranian Studies* occasionally has articles on
Iranian historiography.

 Cf. *American Archivist*, 019; Issawi, 417; Bakhash,
502.

021. Ash, Lee. *Subject Collections: A Guide to Special Book
  Collections and Subject Emphases as Reported by Uni-
  versity, College, Public and Special Libraries and
  Museums in the United States and Canada.* 4th edition.
  New York: Bowker, 1974. iv + 908 pp.

 Contains about 70,000 entries arranged alphabetically
by subject. Each entry briefly describes the contents
of major holdings, with relevant addresses. Persists

in calling the "Middle East" the "Near East," and lists
Islam under the inappropriate heading of "Mohammadanism."
Limited by the fact that not all libraries or special
collections responded to the editor's enquiries, but is
fairly comprehensive nonetheless. For example, it gives
a brief account of collections at the Library of Congress, the New York Public Library, and the libraries
of Columbia, Harvard and the University of California
at Los Angeles and the Hoover Institution on War, Revolution and Peace.

Cf. Young, 042; Wilson, 041; Cook, 030; Pearson, 035.

022. *Aslib Index to Theses Accepted for Higher Degrees in
       the Universities of Great Britain and Ireland.* Lon-
       don: Aslib, continuing publication since 1950.

Annual list of British dissertations arranged by subject, listing thesis title, degree, year and awarding
institution. Availability of theses varies from university to university and there is no regular system
for microfilming and making theses available. Applica-
tion must be made on an individual basis and some institutions will not loan theses; more recent theses may
have a bar placed on access by the author.

Cf. Bloomfeld, 027; *American Archivist,* 019.

023. Bacharach, Jere. *A Near East Studies Handbook, 570-
       1974.* Seattle: University of Washington Press, 1974.
       x + 147 pp.

An essential quick reference guide to the study of the
Middle East. Contains a list of various Middle East dynasties; a table of rulers; genealogies of the major
ruling dynasties (including, where applicable, Europeans); a historical atlas with, for example, the Sykes-
Picot division of the Middle East and various Allied
plans for Middle East partition; a comparative calendar
for converting Hijira dates into their equivalent Christian dates [a much easier chart than that contained in
G.S.P. Freeman-Grenville, *The Muslim and Christian Calendar* (London: Oxford University Press, 1963); and definitely more usable than the comprehensive but formidable *Wastenfeld-Mahlersche Vergleichungs-Tabellen der
mohammadischen und Christlichen Zeitrechnung* by E.
Mahler (Weisbaden, 1961)]; and a brief chronology of
major events. In addition there is comment on the puz-
zles of transliterating Middle Eastern languages into
English, and a list of abbreviations of major journals

on the Middle East and of organizations in or dealing
with the Middle East. Also see C.E. Bosworth, *The Islamic Dynasties: A Chronological and Genealogical Handbook*, Islamic Surveys, no. 5 (Edinburgh: Edinburgh University Press, 1967), which is, however, not as useful
on more modern times.
Cf. Bidwell, 043; Cook, 218; Holt, 490.

024. Banks, Arthur, and Allan Palmer. *A Military Atlas of
      the First World War*. London: Heinemann, 1975. xii
      + 338 pp.

Expanded version of Martin Gilbert's *First World War
Atlas* (London: Weidenfeld & Nicolson, 1970), with commentary by Allan Palmer. Contains 20 pages of maps on
Gallipoli and maps on other campaigns in the Middle
East. Also see Martin Gilbert, *Recent History Atlas,
1860-1960* (London: Weidenfeld & Nicolson, 1966), which
has maps of various changes in the Middle East—the
decline of the Ottoman Empire, the Sykes-Picot Agreement, the war against Turkey, and the war between Greece
and Turkey. On aspects of Islamic history represented
by maps, see Roelf Roolvink, *Historical Atlas of the
Muslim People* (Amsterdam: Djambatan, 1957); Harry Hazard,
Atlas of Islamic History (Princeton, N.J.: Princeton
University Press, 1951); and Norman Pounds, *An Atlas of
Middle Eastern Affairs* (New York: Praeger, 1964), which
covers more contemporary material.
For a guide to atlases see Kenneth Winch, editor, *International Maps and Atlases in Print*, 2nd edition (London: Bowker, 1976), which lists atlases published around
the world. Also see S. Padraig Walsh, *General World
Atlases in Print, 1972-1973: A Comparative Analysis*
(London: Bowker, 1973), which surveys atlases available,
comparing their usefulness, and describing the characteristics of atlases and how to evaluate them. For a
survey of maps and atlases on the Middle East, see
Gerry Hale, "Maps and Atlases of the Middle East,"
Middle East Studies Association Bulletin 3 (1969):17-
39, which also discusses the state of mapping in Middle
Eastern countries.
Cf. James, 313; Moberly, 315; Littlefield, 011.

025. Bechtold, Peter K. "Research Facilities in the Sudan."
      Middle East Studies Association Bulletin 7 (1973): 23-
      31.

Examines facilities available, mainly in Khartoum,
describing their use and availability. Gerry and Sandra

Hale update Bechtold in "Research Facilities in the
Sudan: Addendum," *Middle East Studies Association Bul-
letin* 9 (1975):30-5. Also see P.M. Holt, item 379, and
"The Source Material for the Sudanese Mahdia," *Middle
Eastern Affairs*, no. 1, St. Antony's Papers, no. 4
(London: Chatto & Windus, 1958):107-19. Private pa-
pers of some British officials in the Sudan are held
by the Middle East Centre, Sudan Archive, University
of Durham, England. Also available is the now-dated
work by Richard Hill, *A Bibliography of the Anglo-
Egyptian Sudan: From the Earliest Times to 1937* (Oxford:
Oxford University Press, 1939).

026. Bidwell, Robin. *Bidwell's Guide to Government Ministers.*
      3 volumes. London: Frank Cass, 1973-4.

Surveys the major officeholders in various parts of
the world from 1900 to 1972. Volume 1, *The Major Powers
and Western Europe, 1900-1971*, lists heads of state and
officeholders in the major ministries; volume 2, *The
Arab World, 1900-1972*, does the same as well as listing
the chief representatives from foreign powers; volume
3, *The British Empire and Successor States, 1900-1972*,
does the same for Britain and the Commonwealth. Useful, but the arrangement of material and format make
it difficult to extract information or cross-reference
it from year to year or country to country. A similar
but more comprehensive work, easier to use but with
more gaps in the information supplied is Bertold Spuler,
Rulers and Governments of the World, 3 vols. (German
edition, 1953; London: Bowker, 1977). Volume 2 covers
the years 1492 to 1929, surveying heads of state and
chief officeholders in every major and most minor countries.

027. Bloomfield, Barry, compiler. *Theses on Asia: Accepted
      by Universities in the United Kingdom and Ireland,
      1877-1964.* London: Frank Cass, 1967. xi + 127 pp.

Lists by subject Ph.D. and M.A. theses in history and
other fields on Asia, including the Middle East. There
are a number of sources listing theses. These include
P.M. Jacobs, compiler, *History Theses, 1901-1970: Historical Research in the Universities of the United Kingdom* (London: Institute of Historical Research, 1976);
S. Peter Bell, *Dissertations on British History, 1815-
1914: An Index to British and American Theses* (Folke-
stone [Eng.]: Bailey & Swinfen, 1974), which concentrates on domestic history and does not cover foreign

and colonial policies; and Roger Bilboul, compiler, *Retrospective Index to Theses of Great Britain and Ireland, 1716-1950* (Santa Barbara, California: American Bibliographical Center–Clio Press, 1975), which covers material before the *Aslib Index to Theses for Higher Degrees in the Universities of Great Britain and Ireland*, item 022. Lists of North American theses are contained in *Dissertation Abstracts* and in *Index to American Doctoral Dissertations*, and theses are available on microfilm from University Microfilms, Ann Arbor, Michigan. Also see George Selim, *American Doctoral Dissertations on the Arab World, 1883-1974*, 2nd edition (Washington, D.C.: Library of Congress, 1976), which is a quick reference to 1,825 theses on Arab countries and North Africa. In addition to these sources, *Middle East Studies Association Bulletin* and *British Middle Eastern Studies Association Bulletin* and the *Bulletin of the Institute of Historical Research* give information on dissertation research, completed dissertations, and various research programs and special collections for research.

028.   Bond, Maurice, editor. *Guide to the Records of Parliament*. London: HMSO, 1971. x + 352 pp.

Describes the range of records of both Houses of Parliament preserved at Westminster. Provides a general introduction to the records and the major publications and their contents, classification and use.
Cf. Cook, 030.

029.   Butler, David, and Anne Sloman. *British Political Facts 1900-1975*. 4th edition. London: Macmillan, 1975. xix + 432 pp.

A guide to basic facts about British political history, listing who held office, what office, and when. Also gives brief biographical sketches on the chief individuals mentioned. Chapter 1 covers ministers; 2, parties; 3, Parliament; 4, elections; 5, political place names; 6, well-known political quotations; 7, the civil service; 8, royal commissions; 9, the administration of justice; 10, social conditions; 11, employment and trade unions; 12, the economy; 13, nationalization; 14, local government; 15, royalty; 16, the British Isles; 17, the Commonwealth; 18, international relations (listing major treaties and British ambassadors); 19, the armed forces; 20, the press; 21, the broadcasting authorities; 22, religion; 23, interest groups; and 24, a brief bibliographical survey of relevant sources. A mine of useful information that saves time in running down general but elusive information. Cf. Cook, 031; Bidwell, 043; Bond, 028.

030. Cook, Chris, editor. *Sources in British Political History 1900-1951.* 5 volumes. London: Macmillan, 1975-77.

An essential source for locating manuscript collections on all subjects in British social and political history, providing comprehensive coverage of the location of the official papers of government officials, influential individuals, publicists and persons of note. The idea originated at a 1967 conference of historians and archivists at Nuffield College, Oxford to discuss the problem of the lack of any single source on the location, contents and accessibility of the personal papers of public figures. The first fruits of this collaboration was *A Guide to the Papers of British Cabinet Ministers*, edited by Cameron Hazelhurst and Christine Woodward (London: Royal Historical Society, 1974). This work lists principal cabinet ministers for whom information on their papers is available, and gives lengthy descriptions of the type and number of papers contained in the respective collections. *Sources in British Political History* largely supersedes this first effort. Volume 1 in this set is a guide to the archives of various organizations and societies, and constitutes a ready source book on the location and policies of a wide variety of libraries and archives in the United Kingdom. Volume 2 is a guide to the papers of public servants; volumes 3 and 4 cover the papers of members of Parliament; and volume 5 deals with the papers of writers, intellectuals and publicists. Also available is the now-dated work, *The Prime Ministers' Papers, 1801-1907* by John Brooke (London: HMSO, 1968). Cf. Butler, 029; Bidwell, 043; Bond, 028; Public Records--Great Britain, 035.

031. Cook, Chris, and Brendan Keith. *British Historical Facts, 1830-1900.* London: Macmillan, 1975. xi + 279 pp.

Provides information on British leadership, listing the main figures in politics, the military, and administration. It also provides some statistical informa-

tion on voting patterns, population, newspaper circula-
tion, debts and investment, and imperial affairs. A
handy but limited reference tool which complements Robin
Bidwell, *Guide to Government Ministers*, item 043.

Complement with Brian Mitchell, editor, *European Historical Statistics, 1750-1970* (London: Macmillan, 1975);
and Mitchell and Phyllis Deane, *Abstract of British Historical Statistics* (Cambridge: Cambridge University
Press, 1962), which provide charts and graphs on ex-
ports and imports, interest rates, finance, etc. In
conjunction with Butler and Sloman's *British Political
Facts*, item 029, these provide a ready reference guide
to relevant political and economic information.

Cf. Saul, 238; Carrington, 215; Platt, 237; Watt, 189.

032.   Gibb, H.A.R., Bernard Lewis, *et al.*, editors. *Ency-
       clopaedia of Islam*. 2nd edition. Leiden: Brill,
       1960+.

A comprehensive reference source on Islamic history,
culture and linguistics. Entries are arranged alphabetically; each has been written by an expert and generally contains a bibliography for further study. Contains biographical essays; descriptions of theological
terms; essays on taxation, law, religious controversies;
dynasties and local histories; and on key terminology;
art; architecture; and literature. The new edition,
currently four volumes, is still in progress, appearing
in fascicles as new sections are completed.

033.   Mansoor, Menahem, compiler. *Political and Diplomatic
       History of the Arab World, 1900-1967: A Chronological
       Study*. 16 volumes. Washington, D.C.: Microcard Edi-
       tions, 1972-74.

Divided into three major parts, these volumes give a
day-by-day account of events of international significance pertaining to the Arab Middle East and North
Africa with a biographical sketch of the major individuals involved and a collection of documents relating
to the events presented in the chronology. Volumes 1-
7 contain the chronology, often with brief descriptions
of the event listed; volume 8 contains the biographical
material; and volumes 9 through 16 contain the supporting documents along with information on sources and
works about the documents and their background. Volume
1 covers the period 1900-1941, which is a disappointing
compression. An invaluable reference tool.

Cf. Hurewitz, 048.

034. *Parliamentary Debates of the United Kingdom of Great Britain and Ireland.* 5th series. London: HMSO, continuing publication.

An essential source. Though members of Parliament generally left foreign affairs to the Foreign Secretary, some did ask probing or embarrassing questions that forced answers. In addition there were debates on policy or funding, and the record on these should be consulted along with other official papers. For a brief guide to members of Parliament, see Butler, item 029; and Cook, item 030. Also see Michael Stenton and Stephen Less, *Who's Who of British Members of Parliament*, Vol. 2: *1886-1918* (Hassocks, Sussex: Harvester Press, 1978).
Cf. Cook, 031; Bond, 028.

035. Pearson, J.D. *Oriental Manuscripts in Europe and North America: A Survey.* London: Inter Documentation, 1971. lxxviii + 515 pp.

Result of a seminar on national libraries in Asia held in Manila in 1964. Covers manuscript collections in all the main Asian languages, ancient and modern, held in libraries, special collections or research facilities in Europe and North America. Material is grouped by language with an alphabetical, country-by-country survey of holdings. Also includes important bibliographic information on other sources for locating archives. The lengthy introduction is a useful survey of the state of oriental studies.
Cf. Public Records--Middle East, 037; *American Archivist*, 019.

036. Public Records--Great Britain.

The chief repository of public records in Britain, with over 80 miles of shelving, is the Public Record Office, Kew, Richmond, Surrey, TW9. The archives contain surviving materials from all departments of government and some private papers. The nature and organization of the PRO, plus the major classes of documents, is described in the official publication, *Guide to the Contents of the Public Record Office*, 3 volumes (London: HMSO, 1968). In addition, a number of handbooks, all published by Her Majesty's Stationery Office, deal with individual classes of documents, including *The Records of the Colonial and Dominion Offices*; *List of Cabinet Papers, 1880-1914*; *List of Papers of the*

Committee of Imperial Defence, to 1914; *List of Colonial Office Confidential Prints, to 1916*; *The Cabinet Office to 1945*; *List of Cabinet Papers, 1915 and 1916*; *The Records of the Cabinet Office to 1922*; and *The Records of the Foreign Office, 1782-1939*. See John Pemberton, compiler, for a list of *British Official Publications* (Oxford: Pergamon Press, 1971), which contains information on publications relating to records sources.

Other record repositories in London include the Imperial War Museum, Lambeth Rd., SE1, which has a small reading room; the India Office Library, Orbit House, Blackfriars Rd., SE1; the British Museum; and the Houses of Parliament. The Imperial War Museum has an extensive library relating to all aspects of war, plus a diverse collection of private papers and memoirs by military figures. Access is open but prior arrangements must be made to use the facilities. The India Office Library contains an extensive collection of books and manuscripts related to India; in addition the Library also houses the extant records of the India Office and the East India Company (see Sutton, item 040). The British Museum houses one of the largest collections of private papers available, including those of A.J. Balfour, William Robertson, and Arnold Wilson (see Cook, 030; Busch, 352; Monger, 098; Greaves, 416; Sluglett, 357; Cohen, 398; and Watt, 189). The Parliament Library houses the records of Parliament and many private papers (see Bond, item 028). For the location of other archives, consult the Historical Manuscripts Commission and the National Register of Archives, Quality Court, Chancery Lane, WC2, which keeps on-going information on private holdings, the location of records, and their availability. Information on the location of archival material is also available upon request from the Political Archives Investigation Committee of the London School of Economics Library, Houghton St., WC2. Also see Robert Collison, compiler, *Directory of Libraries and Special Collections on Asia and North Africa* (London: Crossby Lockwood, 1970), which gives information on archives and libraries in Britain with relevant collections.

Cf. Albion, 001; Bayliss, 002; *American Archivist*, 019; Cook, 031.

037. Public Records--Middle East

Archives in the Middle East are generally not as well organized or as readily usable as archives in Europe or

America. The best facilities are those in Israel, Egypt, and Turkey, though the Egyptian and Ottoman archives are not completely open and, indeed, are not completely catalogued. For surveys of relevant archives, see Grimwood-Jones, item 005; and Pearson, item 035. On the Ottoman archives, see Shaw, item 038; on Egypt, see Holt, item 490. Also see H.A. Rivlin, *The Dar al-Watha'iq in 'Abden Palace of Cairo as a Source for the Study of the Modernization of Egypt in the Nineteenth Century* (Leiden: Brill, 1970); F.R. Hunter, "The Cairo Archives for the Study of Elites in Modern Egypt," *International Journal of Middle East Studies* 4 (1973): 476-88; and John Williams, "Research Facilities in the U.A.R.," *Middle East Studies Association Bulletin* 4 (1970):47-54. On Iran, see Angel, item 020. On Israel and Palestine, see Ma'oz, item 527; and Alsberg, item 018. On Syria, Jordan and Lebanon, see Patai, item 013. On the Sudan, see Bechtold, item 025. On Iraq, see Sluglett, item 357.

Cf. *American Archivist*, 019; Public Records--Great Britain, 036.

038. Shaw, Stanford J. "Ottoman Archival Materials for the Nineteenth and Early Twentieth Centuries: The Archives of Istanbul." *International Journal of Middle East Studies* 6 (1975):94-114.

A brief, descriptive look at the Ottoman archives in Istanbul, their problems and methods of use, and major classes of documents. The Ottoman archives are difficult to use and not all classes of documents are open for use. For a brief description of the archives as well as published sources on them, see Sauvaget, item 016, 193-201. Also see other articles by Shaw: "Archival Sources for Ottoman History: The Archives of Turkey," *Journal of the American Oriental Society* 80 (1960):1-12 (supplemented with Frank Tachau, "Research Facilities in Turkey," *Middle East Studies Association Bulletin* 9 (1975):20-9; "The Archives of Turkey--An Evolution," *Wiener Zeitschrift für Kunde des Morgenlandes* 69 (1977): 91-8; and "The Ottoman Archives as a Source for Egyptian History," *Journal of the American Oriental Society* 83 (1963):447-52. Also see the following articles by Bernard Lewis: "Studies in Ottoman Archives," *British Society for Oriental and African Studies* 16 (1954):469-501; "The Ottoman Archives as a Source for the History of the Arab Lands," *Journal of the Royal Asian Society* (1951):139-55; and "Sources for the Economic History of the Middle East," *Studies in the Economic History of the Middle East*, item 218, 78-92. Many of these articles deal mainly with pre-19th century material and are reprinted in Lewis' *Studies in Classical and Ottoman Islam* (London: Variorum, 1976).

    Cf. Grimwood-Jones, 005; Public Records--Middle East, 037; *American Archivist*, 019; Shaw, 481.

039.   Simon, Reeva. *The Modern Middle East: A Guide to Research Tools in the Social Sciences*. Westview Special Studies on the Middle East. Boulder, Colorado: Westview Press, 1978. xv + 283 pp.

    A handbook of reference tools and major monographs on social sciences from 1900 on, dealing with the geographic area from Afghanistan to North Africa, Turkey, and the Arab countries. Includes material in Turkish, Persian, Arabic and Hebrew. Deals primarily with resource material such as bibliographies, guides to primary sources, newspapers, data files and reference sources such as dictionaries, handbooks, biographic and geographical studies. Annotations are ruthlessly succinct.

    Cf. Pearson, 035; Grimwood-Jones, 005; Young, 042.

040.   Sutton, Stanley Cecil. *A Guide to the India Office Library: With a Note on the India Office Records*. London: HMSO, 1967. xii + 122 pp.

    Description of the holdings and a guide for the use of the library. Short section on the India Office Records, which contain the records of the East India Company and the India Office. The Library also has an important collection of books and manuscripts in Asian and European languages which, along with the British Museum and the library of the School of Oriental and African Studies of the University of London, form a considerable research pool. Sutton gives an account of the nature of the resources, categories, and the current availability of material. Dated, but more current information is obtainable upon writing the Keeper of Records, Commonwealth Relations Office, India Office Library, Orbit House, Blackfriars Rd., London.

    For a more recent description of the India Office Records, the nature of the holdings and procedures for use, see Joan Lancaster, "The Scope and the Use of the India Office Library and Records with Particular Reference to the Period 1600-1947," *Asian Affairs* [formerly the *Jour-*

nal of the Royal Central Asian Society] 9 (1978):31-43.
Also see Malcolm E. Yapp, "The India Office Records as
a Source for the Economic History of the Middle East,"
Studies in the Economic History of the Middle East,
item 219, 501-13, which gives a brief introduction to
materials available.
Cf. Sluglett, 357; Cohen, 394; Busch, 352.

041. Wilson, Brian J. *Aslib Directory*. 2 volumes. London:
Butler & Tanner, 1968-70.

Concentrates on listing information sources, mainly
well-developed libraries. Volume 2, *Information Sources in Medicine, the Social Sciences and the Humani-
ties*, surveys holdings in the British Isles with the
entries arranged alphabetically by city, with an alphabetical listing of each library or information source.
Provides a brief description of the holdings and gives
the pertinent details on how to contact the various libraries, and lists any publications by the respective
agencies relating to their holdings.
Cf. Public Records--Great Britain, 036; *American Archivist*, 019; Cook, 030.

042. Young, Margaret L., Harold Young, *et al.*, editors.
*Directory of Special Libraries and Information Cen-
ters*. 3rd edition. 3 volumes. Detroit, Michigan:
Gale, 1974.

A guide to libraries, archives, newspaper collections,
and collections of business, history, science and social
science in the U.S. and Canada. List of about 14,000
holdings with information on content and extent of the
libraries and collections and on the services provided,
with names of staff and addresses of the institutions.
Supplementing this is the 5-volume set, *Subject Directory of Special Libraries and Information Centers* (Detroit, Michigan: Gale, 1975), also by Young, *et al.*
Volume 4, in particular, lists social science and hu-
manities libraries. In addition see the *National Union
Catalog of Manuscript Collections*, 9 volumes (Washington, D.C.: Library of Congress, 1959+), which lists
over 25,000 collections in over 800 repositories in
the U.S., giving brief summaries of holdings. Also see
Richard Lewanski, *Subject Collections in European Libraries*, 2nd revised edition (London: Bowker, 1978),
which has information on libraries and special collections in Britain and Europe.
Cf. Wilson, 041; Ash, 021; Cook, 030.

Treaties and Documents

043.   Bidwell, Robin, editor. *The Affairs of Kuwait, 1896-1905:*
       Foreign Office Prints: Correspondence Respecting Af-
       fairs of Kuwait, 1896-1905. New edition. 2 volumes.
       London: Frank Cass, 1971.

       Robin Bidwell, Secretary of the Middle East Centre
       at Cambridge, has compiled the Confidential Prints on
       Kuwait, along with an introductory essay outlining the
       historic background of Anglo-Kuwaiti relations. There
       are also explanatory notes identifying key individuals,
       places and some events mentioned in the text. Confi-
       dential Prints were a selection of letters and tele-
       grams printed for reference purposes and later circu-
       lated to other departments as the need arose to keep
       them informed. Their selected nature makes them of
       limited value, but they are useful keys to the general
       tone of relations. The first in a series of three
       edited by Bidwell; the others deal with *The Affairs of*
       Arabia, 1905-1906 new edition, 2 volumes (London: Frank
       Cass, 1971) and *The Affairs of Asiatic Turkey, 1908-*
       1913 (which has not appeared), each along similar lines
       with useful introductory material. Complements *British*
       Documents, item 045. Confidential Prints may be ob-
       tained on microfilm from the Public Record Office, Kew,
       London.
            Cf. Busch, 404; Kelly, 407; Wilson, 358; Lorimer, 410.

044.   Farmayan, Hafez. "Observations on Sources for the Stu-
       dy of Nineteenth- and Twentieth-Century Iranian His-
       tory." *International Journal of Middle East Studies*
       5 (1974): 32-49.

       A brief introduction to the major Persian historical
       sources, mainly chronicles or memoirs. Unfortunately
       much of the pertinent primary material is secreted away
       in private hands, or worse, lost. Gives a brief de-
       scription of the holdings of the Majlis (Parliament),
       the National, and the University of Tehran Libraries.
       The current situation in Iran does not suggest the best
       climate for research, however.
            Cf. Angel, 020; Public Records--Middle East, 037.

045.   Gooch, George Peabody, and Harold Temperley, editors.
       British Documents on the Origins of the War, 1898-
       1914. Assisted by Lillian M. Penson. 11 volumes.
       London: HMSO, 1926-1938.

The major collection of published documents on British foreign policy leading up to World War I, covering such issues as the end of isolation, the mounting tension with Germany, the rapprochement with France and Russia, relations in the Near and Far East, the Baghdad Railway, etc. Though the selections are good, they remain incomplete and generally lack the vital minutes that help in evaluating the significance of the documents. Should be used as a reference tool and not as a substitute for primary research. Volumes 1-3 deal mainly with Britain's growing awareness of political isolation and the resulting attempts to find friends, if not Allies. Volume 4 deals with the Anglo-Russian Convention of 1907; volume 5 with the Balkans and Turkey; volume 6 with strains in Anglo-German relations and the search for a way to end these tensions; volume 7 concerns the Agadir Crisis; and volumes 9 and 10, each in two parts, deal with the Balkan Crises and tension in the Middle East. For a complementary collection of documents, mostly treaties, speeches or statements of policy, see Joel Wiener, editor, *Great Britain: Foreign Policy and the Span of Empire, 1689-1971: A Documentary History*, 4 volumes (London: Chelsea House, 1972). On pre-war diplomacy, see the section on International Rivalry, 1890-1914: General; especially see Steiner, 307 and 137; Taylor, 308; and Monger, 098.

Cf. Toscano, 052; Grenville, 085; Benians, 196; Albertini, 284; Rolo, 265; Nish, 100; Greaves, 248; Churchill, 243; Hurewitz, 048; Hinsley, 086; Lowe, 095-6.

046.   Grenville, John Ashley Soames, editor. *The Major International Treaties, 1914-1973: A History and Guide with Texts*. London: Methuen, 1974. xxix + 575 pp.

A valuable selection of treaties of major international significance. Grenville's introductory essay on treaties, their construction, method of ratification, frequently used terms, and the nature of alliance systems is a handy reference tool. Contains the relevant treaties concerning the Middle East during and immediately after World War I, with brief essays on the background to the documents themselves. Complements Hurewitz, item 048.

Reviews: *H* 60 (1975):130, C. Howard.

047.   Hurewitz, Jacob Coleman. *Diplomacy in the Near and Middle East: A Documentary Record, 1535-1956*. 2 volumes. 1956. Reprint. New York: Octagon, 1972.

A reference work on the major treaties, agreements,
proclamations, conventions, and an assortment of official papers relating to Middle Eastern affairs and the
relations of the Great Powers with each other and with
local states in the Middle East. The commentary by
Hurewitz is useful. These volumes have been superseded
by his *Middle East and North Africa in World Affairs*,
item 048, but these latter volumes do not reproduce all
the documents of the earlier volumes.
    Cf. Grenville, 046.
    Reviews: *JMH* 29 (1957):118-9, R.C. Mowat; *MEJ* 11
(1957):95-6, Harry Howard.

048.   Hurewitz, Jacob Coleman, editor and compiler. *The*
       Middle East and North Africa in World Politics: A
       Documentary Record. 2nd edition, revised and en-
       larged. 3 volumes. New Haven, Conn.: Yale Univer-
       sity Press, 1975.

A new, enlarged edition of *Diplomacy in the Near and*
Middle East, item 047, these volumes contain the major
treaties, agreements, statements of policy, reports on
economics and politics, from the granting of capitulatory rights to France in 1535 to relevant contemporary
documents. Each item is introduced with an explanatory
essay, varying in length from brief to rather long and
involved, that helps put the documents in perspective
and gives some bibliographic information for further
study. Very useful and more convenient than the length-
ier treaty series. Has a useful bibliography.
    Works with similar collections but with a broader
perspective include the following: Michael Hurst, ed.,
Key Treaties of the Great Powers, 1814-1914, 2 volumes
(Newton Abbot, [Eng.]: David & Charles, 1972); J.A.S.
Grenville, ed., *Major International Treaties*, item 046;
and Fred Israel, ed., *Major Peace Treaties of Modern*
History, 1648-1967, with an introduction by Arnold
Toynbee, commentaries by Emanuel Chill, 4 volumes (New
York: Chelsea House in association with McGraw-Hill,
1967). In addition, see Clive Parry, editor, *The Con-*
solidated Treaty Series, 175 volumes (Dobbs Ferry, N.Y.:
Oceana, 1964+), which is a survey of world treaties
from 1648 to 1918 when the League of Nations treaty
series begins. Also see Charles Aitchison, compiler,
A Collection of Treaties, Engagements and Sanads Re-
lating to India and Neighboring Countries, 5th edition
(Calcutta: Government of India Central Publishing
Branch, 1929).

Cf. Toscano, 052; Prescott, 050; Gooch, 045; Woodward, 053; Ingrams, 049.
Review: *MEJ* 29 (1975):461, Harry Howard; *MEJ* 34 (1980):86-7, Carl Brown; *PSQ* 96 (1976):372-3, William Quandt.

049.   Ingrams, Doreen. *Palestine Papers, 1917-1922: Seeds of Conflict.* London: J. Murray, 1972. xii + 198 pp.

Presents a collection of relevant British Cabinet and State papers on the origins of British policy in Palestine beginning with the Balfour Declaration in 1917 and ending with the first White Paper in 1922. Documents are chronologically presented to show the development of a policy or line of thought. One of its values is that it presents the departmental minutes accompanying memoranda, revealing the thinking of various members within a department and how their ideas, in combination with others, emerged as a policy. Useful, though very selective. Complement with Woodward, 053; Kedourie, 346; Klieman, 298; and Hurewitz, 047.
Cf. Stein, 531; Sykes, 532; Porath, 530; Hurewitz, 048; Tibawi, 533; Caplan, 520; Wasserstein, 535; Friedman, 521.
Review: *MEJ* 27 (1973):384-5, Ann Lesch.

050.   Prescott, John R.V. *Map of Mainland Asia by Treaty.* Melbourne: University of Melbourne, 1975. xx + 518 pp.

A survey of the treaties that established the boundaries of various Asian countries including those between Russia and China from 1869 to 1915, Afghanistan and Russia, Afghanistan and Iran, and India and China. An unhappy omission is the settlement of the Russo-Persian and the Turco-Persian borders, but the documents and accompanying explanatory text with guides to sources are invaluable aids.
Cf. Hurewitz, 048; Grenville, 046.

051.   Temperley, Harold, and Lillian Penson. *A Century of Diplomatic Blue Books, 1814-1914.* 1938. Reprint. London: Frank Cass, 1966. xvi + 600 pp.

Blue books were collections of documents issued by the Foreign Office on specific matters of policy solicited by command, by Parliament or in reply to addresses. These blue books, often extracted under pressure, were undated, and this work dates them and places the vari-

ous Blue Books from Castlereagh to Grey in their context, showing how and why they were issued and tailored,
and what they said about policy formation at the time.
The book is divided into sections that reflect the tenure of successive Foreign Secretaries, each new section
being introduced by an essay describing that particular
Foreign Secretary's policy towards Blue Books. The
work is continued by Robert Vogel in *A Breviate of
British Diplomatic Blue Books, 1919-1939* (Montreal:
McGill University Press, 1963).

052.   Toscano, Mario, compiler. *An Introduction to the History of Treaties and International Politics. The
Documentary and Memoir Sources*, volume 1. *The History
of Treaties and International Politics.* Baltimore,
Md.: Johns Hopkins University Press, 1966. xv +
685 pp.

Surveys the literature and published archival sources
on the origins of World War I and II. There are extensive commentaries on contents and usefulness and the
method of selection and arrangement of collections of
published documents from European archives. There are
also extensive comments on memoirs and an attempt to
assess their veracity or usefulness. This enlarged
edition was first published in Italian in 1963; more
volumes are promised but none have appeared, or are
unknown to me. Useful for students and for scholars
as a guide to sources.
    Cf. Hurewitz, 048; Gooch, 045; Woodward, 053; Alber-
tini, 284.

053.   Woodward, E.L., *et al.*, editors. *Documents on British
Foreign Policy, 1919-1939.* 1st series. 21 volumes.
London: HMSO, 1947.

The major collection of documents, in three series,
dealing with British policy during the interwar years.
The documents, largely command papers, are extensive
and well-annotated but should be used mainly as a reference tool or as a guide to the contents of Foreign
Office papers. Relevant documents on the Middle East
down to 1921 are in volumes 1 and 2, dealing with the
Peace Conference; volume 3, on San Remo and the Turkish
dilemma; volume 4, on Palestine, Syria, Turkey and
Persia in 1919; volume 13, on Turkey down to December
1920, Arabia, Syria and Palestine to January 1921, and
Persia to March 1921; and volume 17, on Turkey to 1922.

As one reviewer noted, this is an incredible record of the clumsiness, folly and bad luck revealed in the diplomatic process.

Cf. Hurewitz, 048; Busch, 285; Klieman, 298; Howard, 322; Kedourie, 333; Nevakivi, 324; Olson, 424; Lewis, 477.

Theory: Economic Imperialism and Free Trade

054. Eldridge, C.C. *England's Mission: The Imperial Idea
      in the Age of Gladstone and Disraeli: 1868-1880.*
      London: Macmillan, 1973. xvii + 288 pp.

      Examines the stresses the British empire went through
      in the 1860's to 1880's and the impact these stresses
      had on subsequent developments and thinking about empire
      and imperial unity. Studies the evolution of the ideas
      of imperialism in Victorian Britain and gives a valuable
      review of the debate on empire and the importance of
      free trade. Strikes a balance in the debate on "infor-
      mal" empire and the question of anti-imperialism, show-
      ing that there was at least some political pressure in
      the 1870's for surrendering imperial possessions. Has
      a useful summary and comparison of Robinson and Galla-
      gher's ideas and views of their major critics, D.C.M.
      Platt and Oliver MacDonagh. Also see Eldridge's less
      successful follow-up study, *Victorian Imperialism*
      (London: Hodder & Stoughton, 1978).
         Cf. Fieldhouse, 055; Robinson and Gallagher, 072;
      Platt, 071; Louis, 066; MacDonagh, 067; Thornton, 078;
      Hyam, 091; Owen, 070.
         Reviews: *AHR* 81 (1976):140-1, A.P. Thornton; *EHR* 90
      (1975):921-2, D.K. Fieldhouse; *H* 60 (1975):317, P.J.
      Cain; *JICH* 2 (1974):361-3, J.H. Davidson; *JMH* 47 (1975):
      519-29, Ralph A. Austen.

055. Fieldhouse, David Kenneth. *Economics and Empire, 1880-
      1914.* Ithaca, N.Y.: Cornell University Press, 1973.
      527 pp.

      Develops Fieldhouse's exocentric arguments for British
      imperial activity. Stresses the inadvertent nature of

empire brought on by responses to threats to security
and the adventurism and careerism of a few individuals
at the periphery of empire. Downplays economic motives,
or a clear link between political and economic motives
of expansion, continuing Fieldhouse's assault on the
Hobson-Lenin ideas of economic imperialism. Complements Robinson and Gallagher's arguments in *Africa and
the Victorians*, item 072. Divided into four main sections: Explanations of Empire; Case Studies in European
Expansion, 1830-80; Case Studies, 1880-1914; and Conclusions. Concentrates on European expansion in Asia
and Africa. Fieldhouse's earlier work, *The Colonial
Empires: A Comparative Survey from the Eighteenth Century* (London: Weidenfeld & Nicolson, 1966), covers the
period before 1830 and makes some of the same points,
though *Economics and Empire* finds more of a place for
economic factors. See the various works cited herein
on imperialism, especially Louis, item 066; and Platt,
item 071. For a review of Fieldhouse and much of the
historiography on imperialism, see Kemp, 060; Hodgart,
item 059; Stokes, item 076; Owen, item 070.

Reviews: *AHR* 80 (1975):941-2, Richard Wolff; *EcHR* 27
(1974):514-5, S.B. Saul; *EHR* 90 (1975):665, Trevor
Reese; *H* 59 (1974):243-9, P.J. Cain; *HJ* 18 (1975):409-
16, Eric Stokes; *JMH* 47 (1975):519-29, Ralph Austen.

056. Fieldhouse, David Kenneth. "'Imperialism,' An Historical Revision." *Economic History Review* 14 (1961):
187-209.

Questions the basic arguments presented by John Hobson in his classic study, *Imperialism: A Study* (1902).
Fieldhouse places Hobson's views in a context of dis-
illusionment in Britain over the Boer War and shows
that this sentiment was an important element in Hobson's
anti-imperialism. Hobson saw events in South Africa
firsthand and his experiences led him to see a narrow
economic motive for British involvement. Fieldhouse
attacks Hobson's contentions by showing that the export
of surplus capital, which Hobson saw as the besetting
sin, far from flowing into underdeveloped areas and
pulling the British Government in with it to safeguard
the interests of bankers and industrialists, in fact
went to developed areas. The race for colonies was
more the result of strategic concerns and diplomacy
than economics. Compare these views with Koebner, item
062; Kemp, item 060; and Lloyd, item 065.

Cf. Owen, 070; Fieldhouse, 056; West, 079; Hodgart,
059; Stokes, 076; Robinson, 073; Platt, 237; Thornton,
078; Cairncross, 214; Saul, 238.

057.   Galbraith, John S. "The 'Turbulent Frontier' as a Fac-
       tor in British Expansion." *Comparative Studies in
       Society and History* 2 (1960):150-68.

       British statesmen did not want to acquire new colonial
       territories or increased responsibilities for government
       and defence in India or Africa. Despite this determi-
       nation the empire of territory and responsibility grew.
       A combination of forces accounts for this, but one of-
       ten decisive ingredient was the "turbulent frontier"--
       the lack of order, the confusion, that lapped around
       the edge of British "islands" of stability and threat-
       ened to spill over into them. The local administrators
       could not ignore this threat and were sucked into ex-
       pansion, sometimes willingly; and sometimes they were
       the source of disorder, disrupting local patterns and
       relationships. Galbraith touches on similar themes
       in his "Myths of the 'Little England' Era," *American
       Historical Review* 67 (1961):34-48. Interesting.
       Cf. Robinson, 072; Fieldhouse, 055; Schreuder, 074;
       Landes, 063; Sanderson, 208.

058.   Hammond, Richard J. "Economic Imperialism: Sidelights
       on a Stereotype." *Journal of Economic History* 21
       (1961):582-98.

       Downplays economic explanations of imperialism, show-
       ing that there is no direct relationship between expan-
       sion and economic interest. In the same vein as William
       Langer, item 064, which is not mentioned in the foot-
       notes. D.K. Fieldhouse, items 055 and 056, pursues the
       same theme.
       Cf. Hodgart, 059; Kemp, 060.

059.   Hodgart, Alan. *The Economics of European Imperialism.*
       Introduction by V.G. Kiernan. Foundations of Modern
       History. London: Edward Arnold, 1977. xi + 88 pp.

       A brief introduction to pre-Marxist and Marxist think-
       ing on economic imperialism. Examines Marx's views and
       the major interpreters and critics of economic imperi-
       alism, e.g., J.S. Mill, Adam Smith and J.A. Hobson.
       Also provides a summary and critique of modern Marxist
       interpretations. Attempts to develop a working theore-
       tical and analytical structure and definition of eco-

nomic imperialism, arguing that many previous theoretical frameworks have been more interested in self-justification and self-fulfillment than in analyzing and interpreting facts. Argues that interest in improving living standards led people to explore economic resources in more and more areas, the result being a reallocation of resources on an international scale to the benefit of one group that was supported by superior technology and power. Does not limit this motivation to capitalism, but includes socialist countries as well. Rather abbreviated. One of the standard neo-Marxist interpretations of economic imperialism is Paul Sweezy's *Theory of Capitalist Development* (New York: Monthly Review Press, 1968).

Cf. Owen, 070; Thornton, 078; Fieldhouse, 055; Kemp, 060; West, 079.

Reviews: *EcHR* 31 (1978):317-8, Forest Capie; *H* 64 (1979):305, P.J. Cain; *JEH* 38 (1978):1004-5, D.K. Fieldhouse; *JICH* 7 (1978):82-3, D.K. Fieldhouse.

060. Kemp, Tom. *Theories of Imperialism*. London: Dennis Dobson, 1967. viii + 202 pp.

Nine studies by Kemp of imperialism as a theory, constructed around a Marxist point of view. Examines the ideas of leading Marxist writers, including Rosa Luxemburg and Lenin, and subsequent interpretations, including the development of a Marxist orthodoxy. Contrasts these views with other interpretations of imperialism that denigrate or de-emphasize an economic interpretation. Gives a critique of the views of Robinson and Gallagher, item 072; Fieldhouse, item 055; Hobson, in item 065; and Koebner, "The Concept of Economic Imperialism," item 062. Aims to develop a comprehensive theory of imperialism that covers all instances and emphasizes the role of capitalism and economic exploitation as the principal characteristics. The chapter "Objections and Re-statements," 151-74, is a thoughtful attack on critics of the idea of economic imperialism, making a strong case for the combination of motivating factors in 19th century imperialism. Helps redress an imbalance but then creates a new one. Reality lies somewhere between the extremes.

For a collection of the major theoretical works on the ideas of capitalist imperialism, pro and con, from Adam Smith to Robinson and Gallagher, see D.K. Fieldhouse, *The Theory of Capitalist Imperialism* (London: Longmans, 1967). For other collections of essays and

documents on imperialism, see Louis Synder, editor, *The
Imperialism Reader: Documents and Readings on Modern
Expansionism* (Princeton, N.J.: Van Nostrand, 1962);
Robin William Winks, editor, *British Imperialism: Gold,
God, Glory* (New York: Holt, Rinehart and Winston, 1963);
and Harrison Wright, editor, *The 'New Imperialism':
Analysis of Late Nineteenth-Century Expansion*, Problems
in European Civilization (Boston: Heath, 1961). In ad-
dition, see Victor Kiernan, *Marxism and Imperialism:
Studies* (London: Edward Arnold, 1974); and Michael Bar-
ratt Brown, *The Economics of Imperialism* (Baltimore,
Md.: Penguin, 1974), for other Marxist views.
       Cf. Owen, 070; Winks, 017; Louis, 066; Stokes, 076;
Fieldhouse, 056.

061.   Kiernan, E. Victor Gordon. *The Lords of Human Kind:
       European Attitudes Towards the Outside World in the
       Imperial Age.* Subtitle in U.S. edition: "Black Man,
       Yellow Man, and White Man in An Age of Empire."
       London: Weidenfeld & Nicolson, 1969. xv + 336 pp.

       Studies European attitudes and behavior towards the
       non-European world, concentrating on the 19th century.
       A Marxist view that concentrates on the dark side of
       European attitudes, detailing a history of prejudice,
       brutality and exploitation. Imperialism presents a
       different picture at the day-to-day level, as opposed
       to the esoteric ideals that are featured in pro-impe-
       rialist literature or in some recent scholarship. Looks
       at the conquest and rule of India, contact and relations
       with the Islamic world, the Far East, the South Seas,
       Africa, and Latin America.
          Cf. Hodgart, 059; Kemp, 060; Fieldhouse, 055; Hyam,
       090; Beloff, 080; Taylor, 209; Carrington, 215; Saul,
       238; Robinson, 072.
          Reviews: *AHR* 75 (1970):1415-6, Graham W. Irwin; *EHR*
       86 (1971):434, R.J. Moore.

062.   Koebner, Richard. "The Concept of Economic Imperialism."
       Economic History Review 2 (1949):1-29.

       Reviews various views of economic imperialism summa-
       rized as Fabian, Marxist and American. Like Langer,
       item 064, Koebner argues that the concept of economic
       imperialism has passed through four stages: the first
       was characterized by J.A. Hobson; the second was an
       adoption of Hobson into a Marxist framework; the third
       stage was an expansion of the view by Marxists and non-

Marxists that economic imperialism fettered humanity; and fourth, this effort coalesced into a political movement. Koebner examines the first of these three stages, demonstrating that the critics of empire have failed to show a sufficient correlation between capital investment and territorial expansion. Read in conjunction with Tom Kemp, item 060, for a comparative view. Also see Koebner and H. Schmidt, *Imperialism: The Story and Significance of a Political Word, 1840-1960* (Cambridge: Cambridge University Press, 1964), which examines the evolution in the meaning of the word "imperialism," showing the various uses to which it has been put.

Cf. Fieldhouse, 056; Robinson, 073; Owen, 070; Platt, 071; Stokes, 076.

063. Landes, David. "Some Thoughts on the Nature of Economic Imperialism." *Journal of Economic History* 21 (1961): 493-512.

Distinguishes between the theory of economic imperialism, as a monistic interpretation, and economic imperialism, as an aspect of imperialism--the domination of one group over another. After surveying the origins of various theories of economic imperialism, showing that a refutation of one particular theory does not invalidate the idea that there were economic motives in imperialism, Landes sets out a new argument that accounts for economic and non-economic motives. In brief, Landes argues that imperialism is "a multifarious response to a common opportunity that consists simply in the disparity of power. Whenever and wherever such disparity has existed, people and groups have been ready to take advantage of it. It is, one notes with regret, in the nature of the human beast to push other people around...." Disparity of power creates opportunity, and then other factors encourage the powerful to take advantage of it.

Cf. Robinson, 072; Louis, 066; Platt, 071; Stokes, 076; Kemp, 060; Owen, 070.

064. Langer, William L. "A Critique of Imperialism." *Foreign Affairs* 15 (1935):102-15.

Attacks economic interpretations of imperialism as both too narrow and too broad: while imperialism is attributed to economic motives the various Marxist views, based on Hobson, fail to show any connection

between investment and territorial expansion. Compare
with the views expressed by Tom Kemp, item 060. Also
see Eric Stokes, item 076, for a discussion of the connection between the views of Hobson and Lenin.
   Cf. Owen, 070; Fieldhouse, 056; Robinson, 073;
Koebner, 062; West, 079.

065. Lloyd, Trevor. "Africa and Hobson's Imperialism."
      Past and Present 55 (1972):130-53.

      Defends Hobson's account of economic imperialism by
      showing where and how the major critics (see in partic-
      ular Langer, item 064; Koebner, item 062; and Field-
      house, item 073) have misinterpreted Hobson's argument.
      John Hobson's *Imperialism* (1902) identifies the need
      to employ excess capital as a primary motive in Euro-
      pean overseas investment and expansion, hence imperial-
      ism. Lloyd argues that Hobson used imperialism to mean
      a variety of different things, and did not declare it
      an inevitable process or one that was always and in
      every circumstance economically motivated. Trevor com-
      pares and contrasts Hobson's views with those of his
      critics, especially R.J. Hammond, item 058; and D.K.
      Fieldhouse, item 056. Using this as a springboard,
      Lloyd then discusses the development of economic in-
      terests in Africa and the effect those interests had
      on European diplomacy and expansion. Also see P.J.
      Cain, "J.A. Hobson, Cobdenism and the Radical Theory of
      Economic Imperialism, 1898-1914," *Economic History Re-
      view* 31 (1978):565-84.
         Cf. Stokes, 076; Robinson, 072; Louis, 066.

066. Louis, William Roger, editor. *Imperialism: The Robinson
      and Gallagher Controversy.* Modern Scholarship on
      European History Series, Henry A. Turner, Jr., general
      editor. New York: New Viewpoints, 1976. xii + 252
      pp.

      The Robinson and Gallagher controversy, begun with
      their article, "The Imperialism of Free Trade," item
      073, and handsomely expanded into their major monograph,
      Africa and the Victorians, item 072, occasioned a his-
      toriographical reconsideration of the nature of late
      19th-century European imperial expansion. Roger Louis
      has collected the various essays by Robinson and Galla-
      gher and joined them together with a series of articles
      published over the years by their major supporters and
      critics, and also included a collection of brief com-

mentaries written for the volume on the nature of the
debate and points made in it. Louis' introductory essay also provides an analysis of the Robinson and Gallagher thesis and contrasts it with the views of their
critics and supporters. An essential book for studying
one of the major historiographical controversies on empire. See the other works mentioned in this section,
particularly those by Platt, item 071; Eldridge, item
054; Fieldhouse, item 055; Hyam, item 091; Owen, item
070; and MacDonagh, item 067.

Reviews: *AHR* 83 (1978):424-5, Robin W. Winks; *HJ* 20
(1977):761-9, Paul Kennedy.

067. MacDonagh, Oliver. "The Anti-Imperialism of Free Trade."
     Economic History Review 14 (1962): 489-501.

Questions any straightforward link between mid-
Victorian free-trade policies and imperial control or
informal manipulation; and argues that Robinson and
Gallagher, item 072, by a certain looseness in terminology, have ignored important distinctions in the nature of trade and empire, and the resistance to informal
and formal control by those who espoused the free-trade
doctrine. MacDonagh argues that Richard Cobden and the
Manchester School, the chief spokesman and representative
body of free-trade doctrine, were influential and anti-
imperial. Contrast with J.S. Galbraith, "Myths of the
'Little England' Era," *American Historical Review* 67
(1961):34-48, who questions the concept of "Little
Englanders" and suggests continuity in imperial expansion if not a continuity in motives for expansion.
B.A. Knox, "Reconsidering Mid-Victorian Imperialism,"
Journal of Imperial and Commonwealth History 1 (1973):
155-72, in turn, supports MacDonagh and Platt, items 067
and 071, and attacks Robinson and Gallagher, showing
that there was anti-imperial sentiment as proved by the
fact that Britain passed up or gave away certain colonial possessions or the opportunity to intervene "informally" before the "new imperialism." See Louis, item
066; Eldridge, item 054; Hyam, item 091; and Owen, item
070, for discussions of the major issues. Also see
R.J. Moore, who notes in "Imperialism and 'Free Trade'
Policy in India, 1853-4," item 069, that there was a
gap between the theories of an anti-imperialist lobby
and what governments had to do in practice.

068. Mathew, W.M. "The Imperialism of Free Trade: Peru,
     1820-70." *Economic History Review* 21 (1968):562-79.

Examines aspects of Britain's economic and political
policies towards Peru in order to show the characteristics of informal control. It is not simply a question of the economic relations between states that de-
termines informal control, but the way the stronger
state employs its power. Shows that in Peru Britain
did not pursue informal empire even though the motive
and opportunity were present. Compare with Feis, item
222; Platt, item 237; Moore, item 069; and of course
Robinson and Gallagher, items 072 and 073, with whom
Mathew takes issue.

For other studies on informal empire and free trade,
see Peter Harnetty, "The Imperialism of Free Trade:
Lancashire and the Indian Cotton Duties, 1859-1862,"
Economic History Review 18 (1965):333-49; Peter Winn,
"British Informal Empire in Uruguay in the Nineteenth
Century," *Past and Present* 73 (1976):100-26; and A.G.
Hopkins, "Economic Imperialism in West Africa, Lagos,
1880-92," *Economic History Review* 21 (1968):580-606.
Also D.C.M. Platt, editor, *Business Imperialims, 1840-
1930: An Inquiry Based on British Experience in Latin
America* (Oxford: Clarendon Press, 1977), which thorough-
ly explores British business investment in Latin America.
Cf. McLean, 421, Kent, 398.

069.   Moore, R.J. "Imperialism and 'Free Trade' Policy in
        India, 1853-4." *Economic History Review* 17 (1964):
        135-45.

Argues that there was a difference between free trade
ideology and practice. Criticizes MacDonagh, item 067,
for his emphasis on the principles espoused by free-
traders as opposed to their practical political actions.
In India in the period covered the free-traders encouraged a policy of economic development that strengthened the imperial connection.

070.   Owen, E.R.J., and R.B. Sutcliff. *Studies in the Theory
        of Imperialism*. London: Longmans, 1972. 392 pp.

A collection of 13 interpretative essays by Marxists
and non-Marxists, arising from a seminar held at Oxford
in 1969-70 that examined aspects of imperialism, mainly
economic aspects, both in theory and practice. The essays are divided into three parts. Part 1 examines and
criticizes theories of imperialism (mainly Marxist-
Leninist and economic and social theories), as well as
non-European ideas of imperialism, cooperation with and

resistance to imperialism, and the Robinson and Gallagher
thesis. Part 2 examines mid-19th to 20th century forms
of imperialism. Part 3 examines imperialism in action
in Egypt, India, Africa and Latin America. The focus
is on economic imperialism; thus such alternatives as
Schumpeter's theory are not considered. Contributors
include: Tom Kemp, Robert Sutcliff, Michael Barratt
Brown, Robert Owen, Ronald Robinson, Jean Stengers, A.S.
Kanya-Forstner, and D.C.M. Platt. Contains a useful
annotated bibliography on imperialism. For an excellent
comparative review of this volume, Fieldhouse's *Economics
and Empire*, item 055, and others, see Ralph Austen's
"Economic Imperialism Revisited: Late-Nineteenth Century
Europe and Africa," *Journal of Modern History* 48 (1975):
519-29.
Cf. Robinson, 072; Hyam, 091; Louis, 066.
Review: *JICH* 2 (1973):101-2, Kenneth Robinson.

071. Platt, D.C.M. "Economic Factors in British Policy During the 'New Imperialism.'" *Past and Present* 39
(1968):120-38.

Platt is the chief critic of Robinson and Gallagher's
arguments for an imperialism of free trade and of their
idea of "official mind." In this article he sets out
to rebut Robinson and Gallagher's, item 072, and Fieldhouse's, item 055, over-emphasis on political motives
for empire development, and shows that J.A. Hobson (see
item 065), while wrong on particulars, pointed out the
importance of trade and the threat of economic competition in imperial expansion. Security of empire and
security of trade went hand-in-hand as motives for expansion, especially as imperial rivalry increased.
Platt develops these themes and continues his attack on
Robinson and Gallagher in "The Imperialism of Free Trade:
Some Reservations," *Economic History Review* 21 (1968):
296-306; and in "The National Economy and British Imperial Expansion before 1914," *Journal of Imperial and
Commonwealth History* 2 (1973):3-14. Many of the main
arguments and articles in the Robinson-Gallagher debate,
including Platt's article "Further Objections to an
'Imperialism of Free Trade, 1830-60,'" are presented in
William Roger Louis' *Imperialism*, item 066. Support for
some of Platt's contentions concerning trade may be
found in Cohen's *British Policy in Mesopotamia*, item
394.
Cf. Fieldhouse, 056; Platt, 237; Feis, 222.

*   Platt, D.C.M. *Finance, Trade and Politics in British
       Foreign Policy, 1815-1914.* Cited as item 237.

072.   Robinson, Ronald, and John Gallagher, with Alice Denny.
       *Africa and the Victorians: The Official Mind of Im-
       perialism.* Published in paperback by Anchor Press,
       1968, subtitled "The Climax of Imperialism." London:
       Macmillan, 1961. xii + 491 pp.

       "Expansion in all its modes seemed not only natural
       and necessary but inevitable; it was pre-ordained and
       irreproachably right." Thus did the mid-Victorians see
       their duty—to expand trade, but also the benefits of
       their achievements, their genius for order and govern-
       ment. Once thrust upon the world stage, with an empire
       to husband as they faced jealous rivals, the British
       found that expansion had a momentum of its own and re-
       sponsibilities that often out-weighed advantages. But
       the alternative of surrendering the colonies and thus
       the responsibilities was not considered. Accepting
       this the British had to defend their position, and in
       the late 19th century this often produced further ex-
       pansion. Robinson and Gallagher examine this "new"
       expansion in Africa, underscoring the concern for the
       strategic defence of India as the rationale. They con-
       centrate on the "official mind" of government leaders
       and diplomats, who knew little geography and shunned
       finance, but who shared similar backgrounds and outlooks
       and were determined to protect the Indian Empire and
       the routes there and back. An essential feature of
       their argument is the concept of "informal empire,"
       which holds that the British preferred to exercise in-
       direct influence in local states to achieve their ends
       and avoid the burdens of direct rule, but that if this
       failed they were prepared to assume direct control. In
       their argument they stress the importance of imperial
       rivalry with France and Germany and local conditions—
       the turbulent frontier—as factors that forced expan-
       sion, concentrating on the occupation of Egypt in 1882
       and the crises with the Boers in South Africa. This
       argument, plus an earlier article, "The Imperialism of
       Free Trade," item 073, reassesses the nature of impe-
       rialism and demotes the importance of economic factors.
       Needless to say, this created a stir, and the Robinson
       and Gallagher thesis has become the subject of heated
       debate, much of which is summarized in William Roger
       Louis' *Imperialism*, item 066. Also see Chapter 22,
       "The Partition of Africa," in the *New Cambridge Modern*

History, vol. 11, item 099, for further developments by
Robinson and Gallagher of their thesis. For a comprehensive review of *Africa and the Victorians*, see Ronald
Hyam, "The Partition of Africa," *Historical Journal* 7
(1964):154-69.

  Cf. Platt, 071; Hyam, 091; West, 079; MacDonagh, 067;
Eldridge, 054; Stokes, 076; Landes, 063 and 232;
Koebner, 062; Sanderson, 208; Owen, 070; Fieldhouse,
055; Galbraith, 057.

  Reviews: *AHR* 67 (1962):1020-1, Margaret Bates; *H* 48
(1963):249-52, W.L. Burn; *JMH* 35 (1963):199-200, Holden
Furber.

073. Robinson, Ronald, and John Gallagher. "The Imperialism
      of Free Trade." *Imperialism*, item 066, 54-72.

  The opening salvo in a reconsideration of mid-Victorian
imperialism. Orthodoxy holds that the guiding principle
of mid-19th century economic thought was "free trade,"
a doctrine of open, non-protectionist commerce, and that
this doctrine opposed the acquisition of colonies.
Reasoning from this, it is held that the new expansion
of empire after the 1870's marked a gradual drift away
from free trade principles and thus there was a clear
division, a new imperialism. Robinson and Gallagher
confront this and argue for continuity, that there was
no such neat division between mid- and late-Victorian
expansion. They argue that free trade anti-imperialism
was a persuasive philosophy but that it counted for
little in practice; and that the Victorians expanded
their trade and the protection of it as necessary.
Furthermore, they argue that the common feature of
British overseas interests was a concern for the security necessary to carry-on trade. This security meant
local security and security from international threats
or competition. The British were willing to leave local
affairs to the locals if satisfied that the locals would
accept trade on British terms; but if local conditions
or foreign rivalry jeopardized trade, then the British
were prepared to assume direct control of an area to
ensure a British peace. This argument holds that the
British Empire expanded both formally *and* informally,
and that one of the significant changes of the late 19th
century was not a sudden passion for empire, but a
change in circumstances that forced a shift from informal to formal control. For expansion on these ideas,
see Robinson, "Imperial Problems in British Policies,
1880-95," *Cambridge History of the British Empire*, item

196, 127-80; Robinson and Gallagher, "The Partition of Africa," *Imperialism*, item 066, 73-127; and Robinson, "Non-European Foundations of European Imperialism: Sketch for a Theory of Collaboration," *Imperialism*, item 066, 128-52.

Cf. Kemp, 060; Fieldhouse, 055; MacDonagh, 067; Eldridge, 054; Hyam, 091; Owen, 070; Kiernan, 061; Hodgart, 059; Shannon, 107.

074.   Schreuder, D.M. "The Cultural Factor in Victorian Im-
         perialism: A Case Study of the British 'Civilising
         Mission.'" *Journal of Imperial and Commonwealth His-
         tory* 4 (1976):283-317.

Examines the impact of the administrative framework in South Africa on imperial expansion as opposed to the "reluctant" imperialism of the officials in London. Shows influence of the Victorian mentality on civiliz- ing the frontier and making a profit at the same time. Compare with Galbraith, item 057.

075.   Semmel, Bernard. *The Rise of Free Trade Imperialism:*
         Classical Political Economy, the Empire of Free Trade
         and Imperialism, 1750-1850. Cambridge: Cambridge Uni-
         versity Press, 1970. x + 250 pp.

A necessary introduction to classical and Marxist economic thought that shaped the intellectual background to the debate on economic imperialism. Explores the economic thought surrounding the ideas of "free trade" and "free trade imperialism," comparing and contrasting the views of the key intellectual figures in the inter- pretation of economics and empire. In addition, see two works by R.L. Schuyler, *The Fall of the Old Colonial System: A Study in British Free Trade, 1770-1870* (Lon- don: Oxford University Press, 1945), and "The Climax of Anti-Imperialism in England," *Political Science Quarter- ly* 36 (1921):537-60.

Cf. Semmel, 106; Kemp, 060; Owen, 070; Fieldhouse, 055; Eldridge, 054; Langer, 064; Louis, 066; Robinson, 072; Platt, 071.

Reviews: *AHR* 77 (1972):513-4, Sar Desai; *ASPR* 67 (1973):1125-6, Kirk R. Emmert; *EHR* 87 (1972):892-3, D.K. Fieldhouse; *H* 57 (1972):289-90, Boyd Hilton; *PHR* 41 (1972):122-4, Daniel B. Valentine.

076.   Stokes, Eric. "Late Nineteenth-Century Colonial Expan-
         sion and the Attack on the Theory of Economic Imperi-

alism: A Case of Mistaken Identity?" *Historical Journal* 12 (1969):285-301.

Examines the attack on Lenin's analysis of the connection between monopoly finance capitalism and imperialism. The arguments of such critics as Robinson and Gallagher, item 072; Fieldhouse, item 056; and Koebner, item 062, have denigrated the relevance of the theory of economic imperialism in accounting for the so-called scramble for Africa between 1870 and 1900. In this attack the arguments of J.A. Hobson and Lenin are inseparably linked, the one rising or falling on the validity of the other. Stokes argues, however, that this linkage is inaccurate. Lenin never argued with Hobson that the scramble was the result of monopoly finance capitalism. Lenin argued that this form of capitalism followed in the wake of the scramble; the period 1870-1900 was a transitional period to monopoly capitalism. Stokes develops a finely balanced attack on the notions of Robinson and Gallagher, Fieldhouse and Koebner, by showing that Lenin's views were not the orthodox interpretations of economic imperialism everyone presumed them to be. A truer picture of imperial activity emerges from combining Robinson and Gallagher's argument for the "official mind," item 073, and Lenin's views on finance and monopoly capitalism and the destabilizing effect of European economic activities on less advanced countries that could create crises for which the solution became annexation.
Cf. Louis, 066.

077.   Taylor, A.J.P. "Economic Imperialism." *Englishmen and Others. Historical Essays.* London: Hamish Hamilton, 1956, 76-80.

Examines the validity of the Hobson-Lenin heritage and the origins of economic interpretations of imperialism. The world is less rational and the motives for action less straightforward than economic interpretations would allow, despite the cleverness of the argument--power, not money, is the besetting sin.
Cf. Landes, 063; Hodgart, 059.

078.   Thornton, Archibald Paton. *Doctrines of Imperialism.* New York: John Wiley, 1965. ix + 246 pp.

Examines the nature of imperialism, its psychological and economic motives, its supporters, analysts and critics. Three main "doctrines" are considered: the doc-

trines of power, profit, and civilization. An interpretative essay that takes a wide-ranging view of imperialism, not limiting it to an economic or political
phenomenon among nations, but seeing it as a question
of dominance that grows out of natural relationships,
whether between the sexes, nations, economic groups, or
leaders and led. The quest for power, security, and
profit, sustained by a belief in the correctness of
one's own arrangements and the right to force others
to act accordingly, is a profound motive in human relations not restricted to time or place. Might be described as a look at the "mind of imperialism" as opposed to a study of empires or monocausal explanations
of empire.

Cf. Fieldhouse, 055; Owen, 070; Hodgart, 059.

Reviews: *AHR* 72 (1966):125-6, Helen Manning; *APSR* 61
(1967):557-8, James W. Roberts; *EHR* 82 (1967):633, D.K.
Fieldhouse; *JAH* 53 (1966):179, A.P. Thornton; *JP* 28
(1966):858-9, William M. Johnston; *S&S* 31 (1967):119-22,
Tom Kemp.

079.   West, Katherine. "Theorising about 'Imperialism': A
       Methodological Note." *Journal of Imperial and Common-
       wealth History* 1 (1973):147-54.

A calm assessment of how historians and social sci-
entists think about imperialism. Underlines the fact
that much of this thinking is freighted with an ideological framework that seeks to condemn a process it
sees as reprehensible without going any further. Sets
out no new theory but compares and contrasts various
existing notions, pointing out their methodological
shortcomings.

Imperial Reorganization: The End of Isolation

080.   Beloff, Max. *Britain's Liberal Empire, 1887-1921. Im-
       perial Sunset*, vol. 1. London: Methuen, 1969. xii
       + 387 pp.

Examines the problems facing Britain that contributed
to imperial decline. The problems of imperial organization and coordination, of defense, of the challenges
presented to Britain by Russia, France and Germany, and
of declining industrial capacity overtaxed the abilities

of British statesmen to find solutions. An excellent
overview and analysis. See the other works cited herein on imperialism, commonwealth and imperial reorganization.
   Cf. Taylor, 209; Hyam, 090; Grenville, 085; Monger,
098.
   Reviews: *AHR* 75 (1970):1729-30, Bernard Semmel; *EHR*
86 (1971):373-5, Nicholas Mansergh; *H* 57 (1972):305-6,
Donald Southgate; *PSQ* 86 (1971):522-3, Stephen Koss.

081.   Bourne, Kenneth. *The Foreign Policy of Victorian Eng-
       land, 1830-1902.* Oxford: Clarendon Press, 1970.
       xii + 531 pp.

   Emphasizes an Eurocentric view. The book is divided
into two main parts: an essay; and a collection of supporting documents. There is an excellent bibliography,
and the essay is a critical integration of research on
the nature of mid-Victorian imperialism and the problems facing British statesmen in the late 19th century.
Contrast with Fieldhouse, item 055; Monger, item 098;
and Howard, item 089.
   Cf. Gooch, 045; Benians, 196; Lowe, 096.
   Reviews: *AHR* 76 (1971):1547-8, Zara Steiner; *EHR* 88
(1973):205-6, C.W. Crawley; *H* 56 (1971):462-3, M.R.D.
Foot; *JMH* 44 (1972):118-9, J.B. Conacher.

082.   D'Ombrain, Nicholas. *War Machinery and High Policy:
       Defence Administration in Peacetime Britain, 1902-
       1914.* Oxford Historical Monographs. London: Oxford
       University Press, 1973. xii + 302 pp.

   Examines the role of the Committee of Imperial Defence
and the growth of the Cabinet Office in Britain's efforts to improve the efficiency of strategic planning
and coordination. The CID before the war had a check-
ered career. Begun as a body to coordinate strategic
planning, reflecting a concern for imperial defence,
the Committee's influence declined after 1906 to become little more than a technical review board with
little power, largely as a result of personal jealous-
ies and attempts to protect existing patterns of power
within the govenment. It was rescued from complete
oblivion by Maurice Hankey. An excellent study, if a
bit narrow, of institutional change and inter-departmental rivalry. For a brief summary of the evolution
of the Committee of Imperial Defence, see John Ehrman,
Cabinet Government and War, 1890-1940 (Cambridge: Cambridge University Press, 1958).

Cf. Bond, 110; Hamer, 121; Searle, 105; Johnson, 123;
Mackintosh, 128; Marder, 131; Hankey, 292; Roskill, 186;
Tunstall, 141; Gooch, 114; Judd, 167.
    Reviews: *AHR* 80 (1975):978-9, Zara Steiner; *H* 60
(1975):146-7, Brian Bond.

083. Edwards, E.W. "The Japanese Alliance and the Anglo-
        French Agreement of 1904." *History* 42 (1957):19-27.

      The Alliance was Britain's first step from "isolation"
      and contributed to the making of the Anglo-French en-
      tente of 1904. Relies heavily on published sources.
      Complement with Monger, item 098; Grenville, item 085;
      and Penson, items 101 and 102.
        Cf. Nish, 100; Steiner, 108; Lowe and Dockrill, 096;
      Rolo, 265; Lowe, 097; Rothwell, 104.

084. Fraser, Thomas G. "India in Anglo-Japanese Relations
        During the First World War." *History* 63 (1978):366-
        82.

      Studies the perennial British anxiety for the security
      of the eastern empire, most particularly India. The
      challenge of Germany and Britain's declining ability
      to protect all its interests simultaneously produced
      the need for agreements to reduce responsibilities and
      establish a set of priorities for imperial defence.
      The Japanese alliance, first concluded in 1902, was one
      such agreement. But Japanese expansion and dynamism
      --plus its appeal to Asian nationalists after 1905 as
      an Asian power that had defeated a major European state,
      Russia--caused increasing concern in British circles
      that Japan would replace Germany as the main threat to
      empire. During the war this British worry undermined
      the former friendship.
        Cf. Nish, 100; Rothwell, 104; Lowe, 097.

085. Grenville, John Ashley Soames. *Lord Salisbury and
        Foreign Policy: The Close of the Nineteenth Century.*
        University of London Historical Studies, no. 14.
        London: Athlone Press, 1964. x + 451 pp.

      Details changes in Britain's foreign policy in the
      period 1895-1902. Does not argue "end of isolation"
      but shows that Salisbury favored non-alignment, a pol-
      icy of association based on temporary needs and not on
      long-term promises. The increase of pressures on im-
      perial defence eroded British confidence, and Salis-
      bury's successors began searching for alliances or ar-

rangements to compensate for the loss of self-reliance
in strategic defence. The crisis was made manifest when
the navy made it clear that they could not maintain
Britain's traditional policy of interceding at Constantinople to protect the Turk from the Russians. Excellent study. Complement with Lillian Margery Penson's
studious *Foreign Affairs under the Third Marquis of
Salisbury*, Creighton Lecture in History (London: Athlone
Press, 1962).

Cf. Monger, 098; Greaves, 415; Taylor, 209; Gillard,
245; Robinson, 072; Shannon, 107.

Reviews: *AHR* 70 (1964):127-8, Henry Winkler; *EHR* 81
(1966):205-6, F.V. Parsons; *H* 49 (1969):396-8, E.W.
Edwards; *HJ* 7 (1964):340-4, Zara Steiner; *PSQ* 80 (1965):
640-2, Bernard Semmel.

086. Hinsley, Francis Harry, editor. *British Foreign Policy
under Sir Edward Grey*. Cambridge: Cambridge University Press, 1977. viii + 702 pp.

A collection of 31 articles divided into four sections
covering aspects of Grey's foreign policy: Introductory;
Before the War: Europe and the Near East; Before the
War: The Far East and the World; The Outbreak of War
and the War Years. There is an attempt to see that the
articles complement one another. Of interest are K.G.
Robbins, "The Foreign Secretary, The Cabinet, Parlia-
ment and the Parties," 3-21; Zara Steiner, "The Foreign
Office," item 388; K.G. Robbins, "Public Opinion, the
Press and the Pressure Groups," 70-88; A.K. Hamilton,
"Great Britain and France," item 263; Beryl Williams,
"Great Britain and Russia," item 258; Marian Kent,
"Constantinople and Asiatic Turkey, 1905-1914," item
372; Jonathan Steinberg, "The German Background to Anglo-
German Relations, 1905-1914," item 277; D.W. Sweet,
"Great Britain and Germany," item 278; D.W. Sweet and
R.T.B. Langhorne, "Great Britain and Russia," item 257;
M.L. Dockrill, "British Policy During the Agadir Crisis
of 1911," 271-87; R.T.B. Langhorne, "Great Britain and
Germany, 1911-1914," item 274; C.J. Lowe, "Grey and the
Tripoli War, 1911-1912," 315-23; K.A. Hamilton, "Great
Britain and France," item 263; I.H. Nish, "Great Brit-
ain, Japan and North-East Asia, 1905-1911," 362-7;
E.W. Edwards, "China and Japan, 1911-1914," 368-81;
M. Ekstein, "Russia, Constantinople and the Straits,
1914-1915," item 318; Marian Kent, "Asiatic Turkey,
1914-1916," 436-51; I.H. Nish, "Japan and China, 1914-
1916," 452-65; Zara Steiner, "The Foreign Office and

the War," 517-31; and K.G. Robbins, "Foreign Policy,
Government Structure and Public Opinion," 532-46.

In combination with Monger, item 098; Grenville, item
085; Lowe, item 095; Mowat, item 099; and Taylor, item
209, these essays give an excellent overview of late
19th- and early 20th-century British policy. One of the
chief complaints about the volume is that there is no
article devoted to Anglo-Persian relations. In addition the articles are basically narrative and not analytical. Useful, with a handy bibliography on secondary
sources.

Cf. Robbins, 184; Steiner, 137; Grey, 160; Warman,
142; Nish, 100.

Reviews: *AHR* 83 (1978):731-2, Lyle A. McGeoch; *H* 64
(1979):135-6, Keith Robbins; *PSQ* 93 (1978):716-7,
Robert L. Jervis.

087.   Howard, Christopher H.D. *Britain and the Casus Belli,
       1822-1902: A Study of Britain's International Posi-
       tion from Canning to Salisbury.* London: Athlone Press,
       1974. xiv + 204 pp.

An interpretative essay on Britain's commitment, or
lack of commitment, to permanent alliances. Argues that
British policy was pragmatic, not isolationist, and that
Britain did commit itself to limited treaties though
never on the scale of the Triple Alliance. In that
sense, the Triple Entente was the epitome of British
diplomacy--informal commitment based on a mutuality of
interests, which is what governs the validity of treaties, formal or otherwise.

Cf. Penson, 102.

Reviews: *AHR* 81 (1976):137, Richard A. Cosgrove;
EHR 90 (1975):921-2, D.K. Fieldhouse; *JMH* 61 (1976):130,
Kenneth Bourne.

088.   Howard, Christopher H.D. *Splendid Isolation: A Study
       of Ideas Concerning Britain's International Position
       and Foreign Policy During the Later Years of the Third
       Marquis of Salisbury.* New York: St. Martin's Press,
       1967. xv + 120 pp.

Was there a policy of isolation? Did Britain con-
sciously seek it or was it the result of circumstances?
Did Salisbury pursue it and his successors scramble to
undo it? Howard argues that though there may have been
no specific policy of isolation, Britain found itself
isolated in the late 19th century, or the British be-

lieved this to be true and sought ways to end it.
Salisbury, credited with pursuing isolation, was not
an isolationist but derived his ideas of limiting commitments to foreign powers from an assessment of the
British style of government--Parliamentary review--that
theoretically limited the extent to which any government could unequivocally commit Britain to a foreign
alliance. Howard is not concerned with whether or not
there was "splendid isolation," but how contemporary
statesmen and public opinion conceived Britain's position and what they did to meet necessities. He explores
similar ideas in "Splendid Isolation," *History* 47 (1962):
32-41, and "The Policy of Isolation," *Historical Journal* 10 (1967):77-88. A related study is Howard's *Casus Belli*, cited above.
Cf. Monger, 098.
Reviews: *AHR* 73 (1968):1534-5, Max Beloff; *H* 53
(1968):159-60, Zara Steiner.

089. Howard, Michael Eliot. *The Continental Commitment: The
Dilemma of British Defense Policy in the Era of the
Two World Wars*. The Ford Lectures in the University
of Oxford, 1971. London: Temple Smith, 1972. 176 pp.

Examines the tension in British imperial thinking between the need to defend an overseas empire and the
need to protect the Home Islands, a concern brought into sharp focus by the Boer War. A perceptive study of
the institutional changes and mental reorientations
that resulted from this tension and the need to set
priorities. The weight of decision favored a reorganization to confront a continental threat, but the British still found themselves unable to pursue clear-cut
policies when overseas interests were threatened; thus
the "sideshows" of World War I.
Cf. Tunstall, 141; Gooch, 114; Johnson, 123; Bond,
110; d'Ombrain, 082.
Reviews: *EHR* 89 (1974):137-40, David Dilks.

090. Hyam, Ronald. *Britain's Imperial Century, 1815-1914:
A Study of Empire and Expansion*. New York: Barnes
& Noble, 1976. 462 pp.

Surveys aspects of the growth of the British empire
and of the factors that motivated it, making a case that
the export of excess emotional energy was a motivating
factor in expansion. Integrates economic and ideological imperatives in interpreting British imperialism.

Of particular note is the discussion on the growing
awareness in Britain of the empire's vulnerability after 1860 as challenges began to multiply. The discussions of the role of sex, pessimism, sports, emotional
energy, and religion as factors in imperialism in the
first part of the book are provocative, while the study
of the decline of British industry, the growth of America, Germany and Japan as imperial rivals along with
Russia and France, the increasing spirit of independence of the self-governing Dominions, plus the crisis
of confidence in British governing circles, is a sound
exploration of British imperial trauma. Argues that
empire existed more as an idea than as a reality, and
Hyam himself does not develop a clear definition of
empire, which is a handicap in coming to terms with
some of the evidence and the conclusions. Nor are all
the assumptions closely supported by evidence; but much
of the work is interpretative.
    Cf. Robinson, 072; Porter, 103; Shannon, 107; Taylor,
209; Fieldhouse, 055; Kiernan, 061.
    Reviews: *AHR* 82 (1977):361-2, Henry R. Winkler; *EHR*
92 (1977):915-6, R.F. Holland; *HJ* 20 (1977):761-9, Paul
Kennedy; *JICH* 5 (1977):234-6, Bernard Porter; *VS* 21
(1978):273-5, William N. Rogers II.

091. Hyam, Ronald, and Ged Martin. *Reappraisals in British*
      Imperial History. Cambridge Commonwealth Series.
      London: Macmillan, 1975. viii + 234 pp.

      Dispels the myth that there was a British Empire, at
      least in the sense that it was a coordinated, integra-
      ted, logical whole, administered wisely and uniformly
      from the center. Ten separate essays on topics as di-
      verse as imperial interests and the Paris Peace of 1763
      to the influence of the Durham Report (on Canada) of
      1839, illustrate the theme of the disparate and indi-
      vidual nature of the empire. Of particular interest
      is Martin's critique of Robinson and Gallagher's *Africa*
      and the Victorians, item 072. The essay, pp. 139-55,
      questions the emphasis Robinson put on the strategic
      response to local crisis as an explanation for expan-
      sion in Africa, or that there was any single triggering
      event, in this case the occupation of Egypt in 1882.
      Martin makes the important point that it was not just
      Africa that was being divided, but the available world,
      and that the partition of Africa was part of this move-
      ment and that this division had no single motive, such
      as the response to local pressures. Other essays of

interest are "'Anti-Imperialism' in the Mid-Nineteenth
Century and the Nature of the British Empire, 1820-70,"
88-120; "The Idea of Imperial Federation," 121-38; and
"Introduction: Personal and Impersonal Forces and the
Continuity of British Imperial History," 1-20.
  Cf. Robinson, 073; Louis, 066; Eldridge, 054; Mac-
Donagh, 067; Platt, 237; Fieldhouse, 055.
  Reviews: *EHR* 92 (1977):442-3, A.F. McC. Madden.

092. James, Robert Rhodes. *The British Revolution: British
      Politics, 1880-1939*. 2 volumes. London: Hamish
      Hamilton, 1976.

  Relates the course of late empire, especially the
  role of British politics and politicians in handling
  the problems that Britain faced. Vol. 1, *From Gladstone to Asquith, 1880-1914*, concerns the Irish Question, the Boer War, and the political climate before
  World War I. Vol. 2, *From Asquith to Chamberlain,
  1914-1939*, has useful information on the British conduct of the war.
    Cf. Taylor, 308; Shannon, 107; Mackintosh, 174.
    Reviews: *AHR* 83 (1978):1013-4, Michael Bentley.

093. Langer, William Leonard. *The Diplomacy of Imperialism:
      1890-1902*. 2nd edition. 2 volumes. Reprint. in
      one volume. New York: Alfred Knopf, 1972.

  One of the classic studies of European diplomacy in
  the age of imperialism, analyzing the whole system of
  European international relations and the worldwide consequences of European maneuverings. Argues that stalemate in Europe between competing power blocs forced
  European attention overseas in new, more aggressive activities, and spurred imperial rivalry which then had
  consequences in Europe. Chapter 3 attempts to define
  aspects of British imperialism as the example *par ex-
  cellence* of empire, incorporating economic motives, but
  downplaying their role in a definition of imperialism
  that stresses the role of political personalities,
  popular-social imperialism and international rivalry.
  The work continues from Langer's *European Alliances and
  Alignments, 1871-1890* (New York: Knopf, 1931). Langer's
  views on economic imperialism are expanded in "A Critique of Imperialism," item 064. In addition, see
  Parker T. Moon, *Imperialism and World Politics* (New
  York: Macmillan, 1947), which covers many of the same
  topics but with a more anti-imperial bias, showing the
  agressiveness of new imperialism.
    Cf. Taylor, 209; Grenville, 085; Fieldhouse, 055.

094.   Low, Donald Anthony. *Lion Rampant: Essays in the Study
        of British Imperialism*. Studies in Commonwealth Pol-
        itics and Society, no. 1. London: Frank Cass, 1973.
        vii + 230 pp.

   A look at some of the "problems" in Empire–Commonwealth history, areas that need further study. Why,
   for instance, did some countries accept or cooperate
   with imperial domination? The first chapter deals with
   this, examining the idea of cooperation, the use of
   force, the coerciveness and attractiveness of efficient administration and what factors could initiate an
   "imperial" situation. Further chapters examine aspects
   of imperial rule--social engineering, economic changes,
   political shifts--the impact of Christianity, the
   struggles for independence, and the aftermath of empire.
   A useful introduction to problems and issues with suggestions for areas of research.
      Cf. Fieldhouse, 055; Thornton, 109; Hodgart, 059;
   Kemp, 060.
      Reviews: *AHR* 81 (1976):140-1, A.P. Thornton; *JICH*
   3 (1978):302-3, John Hargreaves; *PSQ* 90 (1975):183-5,
   John W. Cell.

095.   Lowe, Cedric James, and M.L. Dockrill. *The Mirage of
        Power*. 3 volumes (1: *British Foreign Policy 1902-
        1914*; 2: *British Foreign Policy 1914-1922*; 3: *Docu-
        ments*). Foreign Policy of the Great Powers Series.
        London: Routledge & Kegan Paul, 1972.

   Examines various aspects of Britain's international
   relations between the end of the Boer War and the final
   peace settlements after World War I. Volume 1 covers
   the period 1902-1914, and discusses the Anglo-French
   entente, Anglo-German, Anglo-Russian, and Anglo-American
   relations, plus a chapter on the European diplomatic
   atmosphere before World War I. Volume 2 covers the war
   years--strategies, war aims, and the peace settlements
   --with chapters on the Middle East and the Allied intervention in Russia. Volume 3 is a collection of supporting documents, mostly unpublished. Such a brief
   collection is bound to be spotty and should be used
   more as a sampler of what is available than as a source
   book. Essays have a European bias and concentrate on
   major events. Excellent introductory material. Functional bibliography. Use in conjunction with *British
   Documents on the Origins of the War*, item 045.

Cf. Taylor, 209; Robinson, 072; Beloff, 080; Steiner, 307; Churchill, 243; Busch, 404; Platt, 237; Guinn, 291; Hinsley, 086.
Reviews: *AHR* 78 (1973):445-6, Arthur Marsden.

096. Lowe, Cedric James. *The Reluctant Imperialists: British Foreign Policy 1878-1902*. 2 volumes (1: *British Foreign Policy, 1878-1902*; 2: *Documents*). London: Routledge & Kegan Paul, 1967.

Examines aspects of British foreign policy from the Congress of Berlin of 1878 to the Anglo-Japanese alliance in 1902. Essays cover the European context, British concern for the security of empire, the defence of India, the situation in East Asia, Africa and the Middle East. The initial essay, "The Anatomy," is a thoughtful overview of main elements and motives in British foreign policy, stressing concern for control of the seas, the moral underpinnings of policy, and the basically amateurish character of British policy-making. Eurocentric in viewpoint. Bibliography is more in the line of "Suggested further reading." Documents are merely supportive. Excellent introduction to foreign policy for students.
Cf. Taylor, 209; Beloff, 080; Nish, 100.
Reviews: *AHR* 75 (1970):1117-8, M.A. Fitzsimmons; *EHR* 84 (1969):630-1, A.E. Campbell; *H* 54 (1969):309-10, E.W. Edwards.

097. Lowe, Peter. "The British Empire and the Anglo-Japanese Alliance, 1911-1915." *History* 54 (1969):212-225.

The Anglo-Japanese alliance represented one feature of the movement in Britain to rationalize imperial defence, reducing commitments at the periphery in order to strengthen Britain's position vis-a-vis Germany. This reappraisal, although supported in principle by the Dominions, caused difficulties in intra-imperial relations. Most particularly Australia and New Zealand distrusted Japanese motives and saw the alliance and the subsequent naval reorganization as an abandonment of their interests. Lowe presents a more complete study of Anglo-Japanese relations in his book, *Great Britain and Japan, 1911-1915: A Study of British Far Eastern Policy* (London: Macmillan, 1969). The decline in Anglo-Japanese relations is detailed in Malcolm Kennedy, *The Estrangement of Great Britain and Japan,*

1917-1935 (Berkeley: University of California Press, 1969).

Cf. Nish, 100; Steiner, 137; Gordon, 116.

098.   Monger, George W.   *The End of Isolation: British For-
       eign Policy, 1900-1907.*   London: Thomas Nelson, 1963.
       vi + 343 pp.

The Boer War demonstrated to British statesmen the
dangers of having no friends in Europe and the over-
extended nature of Britain's imperial resources.   This
realization led to a searching re-examination of policy and strategic commitments that produced changes in
the organization of the army, navy, the government and
to some extent the empire.   It also forced British
statesmen to seek friends, which led to the alliance
with Japan and agreements with France and Russia.
Monger is one of the first to explore this change and
the work remains essential.   Focus is generally restricted to diplomacy and politics but the information
is well-handled.   A brief version of this study that
examines the main themes is his "The End of Isolation:
Britain, Germany and Japan, 1900-1902," *Transactions
of the Royal Historical Society*, 5th series, 13 (1963):
103-21.   Good bibliography with a convenient summary
of all the main archival sources used, with their locations.   See the sections following on imperial defence for the impact the "end of isolation" had on
British institutions.

Cf. Anderson, 195; Taylor, 209; Benians, 196;
Robinson, 072; Greaves, 248; Churchill, 243; Williamson,
211; Howard, 088; Nish, 100; Rolo, 265; Koch, 273;
Langhorne, 275; Woodward, 279.

Reviews: *EHR* 80 (1965):638-9, W.N. Medlicott; *HJ* 7
(1964):340-4, Zara Steiner.

099.   Mowat, Charles Loch.   *The Shifting Balance of World
       Forces, 1898-1945.*   New Cambridge Modern History,
       vol. 12.   2nd revised edition.   Cambridge: Cambridge
       University Press, 1968.   xxvii + 845 pp.

The *Cambridge Modern History* has a long history.
First planned by Lord Acton as a beginning of a uni-
versal history, the original edition appeared in 1910,
edited by A.W. Ward.   In 1960 a *New Cambridge Modern
History*, with volume 12, entitled *The Era of Violence,
1898-1945*, edited by David Thomson appeared; and finally in 1968 this larger, revised edition appeared.   One

of the major changes in the two volumes was that the
Middle East, Southeast Asia and India, and Japan and
China received more individual attention in essays by
Elie Kedourie, D.G.E. Hall and Percival Spear, and
J.W. Davidson and Colin Forster, respectively; whereas
in the Thomson edition all had been lumped under one
essay by Bernard Lewis. Many of the essays remain the
same, although some have been enlarged, and some are
new contributions. Thus, in the Mowat edition, Brian
Bond's more incisive essay replaces C.T. Atkinson's on
the First World War. Both volumes survey the chief
diplomatic, economic, social and cultural events from
1898 to the end of World War II. All such collections
have gaps and are open to criticism, but they provide
useful summaries of major issues. For more detailed
studies on areas covered here, see the many other Cambridge Histories: Richard Grey, editor, *Cambridge History of Africa*, 5 vols. (1975), especially, volume 5,
which covers the period 1790-1870; Ernest Benians,
Cambridge History of the British Empire, item 196; A.W.
Ward, editor, *Cambridge History of British Foreign Policy*, item 210; and P.M. Holt, *Cambridge History of Islam*, item 438.

Cf. Taylor, 209; Williamson, 211; Tunstall, 141;
Steiner, 307; Gifford, 201 and 202.

Reviews: *EHR* 85 (1970):18-20, M.N. Medlicott.

100. Nish, Ian Hill. *The Anglo-Japanese Alliance: The Diplomacy of Two Island Empires, 1894-1907*. University
of London Historical Studies, no. 18. London: Athlone
Press, 1966. xii + 420 pp.

The Anglo-Japanese alliance was the first time Britain
committed itself to a manifest alliance involving a
casus foederis since the Crimean War. The alliance,
designed to relieve Britain of certain defence commitments in Asia, so it could re-deploy the fleet, was
initially aimed at the Franco-Russian alliance, though
it was renegotiated on the basis of a rising German
threat. Nish's definitive study of both the British
and Japanese sides of the negotiations, carried to a
conclusion in his *Alliance in Decline: A Study in Anglo-
Japanese Relations, 1908-1923* (London: Athlone Press,
1972), examines the strategic factors that influenced
the alliance negotiations and the cautious attitude in
Britain to committing itself to a definitive alliance,
much less to an alliance with an unproven Asian power.

For a background study to British interest in Japan,
see Grace Fox, *Britain and Japan, 1858-1883* (Oxford:
Clarendon Press, 1969). Complementary studies are
Peter Lowe's *Great Britain and Japan, 1911-1913: A
Study of Britain Far Eastern Policy* (London: Macmillan,
1969); and Malcolm Kennedy's *The Estrangement of Great
Britain and Japan, 1917-1935* (Berkeley: University of
California Press, 1969). For a study of how the treaty
affected internal imperial relations, see Nish, "Australia and the Anglo-Japanese Alliance, 1901-1911," *Aus-
tralian Journal of Politics and History* 9 (1963):201-
12; and Donald Gordon, *The Dominion Partnership in Imperial Defence, 1870-1914*, item 116, and "The Admiralty
and Dominion Navies, 1902-1914," item 115. On other
aspects of the alliance, see E.W. Edwards, "The Japanese
Alliance and the Anglo-French Agreement of 1904," item
083; Peter Lowe, "The British Empire and the Anglo-
Japanese Alliance, 1911-1915," item 097; and V.H. Rothwell, "The British Government and Japanese Military Assistance, 1914-1918," item 104.

Cf. Lowe, 096; Monger, 098; Steiner, 137; Tunstall,
141.

Reviews: *AHR* 72 (1967):530-1, Chitoshi Yanaga; *EHR*
82 (1967):869-70, A. Fraser; *H* 52 (1967):363-4, E.W.
Edwards; *JAS* 27 (1967):151-21, Akira Iriye; *JMH* 41
(1969):394-5, M.G. Fry; *PA* 39 (1966):182-3, Harold M.
Vinacke.

101.   Penson, Lillian Margary. "The New Course in British
        Foreign Policy, 1892-02." *Royal Historical Society
        Transactions*, 4th series, 25 (1943):121-38.

In the late nineteenth century Britain and Germany,
long-term friends, began to gradually drift apart.
Despite numerous efforts to maintain or renew the ties,
Germany's quest for a place in the sun and Britain's
growing anxiety over imperial security erected barriers
between the two powers. In this period Britain began
to give up its old policy of cooperation with other
powers over specific issues as the need arose, for a
policy of formal and informal alliance. It was not so
much that Britain gave up a policy of isolation but
that the European powers were forming long-term alliances
that threatened Britain with isolation if it did not
make commitments to one or the other of the alliance
groups. The difficulties with Germany made a drift toward France easier. Examines political developments,

the opinion of statesmen, and the effects of public opinion on policy.
    Cf. Grenville, 085; Monger, 098; Taylor, 209; Steiner,
137.

102. Penson, Lillian Margary. "Obligations by Treaty: Their
      Place in British Foreign Policy, 1898-1914." *Studies
      in Diplomatic History and Historiography in Honour
      of J.P. Gooch*. Edited by A.O. Sarkissian. London:
      Longmans, 1961, pp. 76-89.

    One of the first works to re-examine the idea of late
19th-century policy as being one of "isolation." If
there was such a policy, Penson argues that it ended
in 1905 with Britain's support of France against Germany over Morocco, which extended the meaning of the
simple settlement of 1904 (although the Anglo-Japanese
treaty of 1902 seems a better date). Reviews various
treaties and the types of commitments, stated or implied,
they entail. For an interpretative study of the meaning of alliances and Britain's commitments without formal treaties, see Christopher Howard, *Britain and the
Casus Belli*, item 087.
    Cf. Steiner, 307; Monger, 098; Grenville, 085; Taylor,
308.

103. Porter, Bernard. *The Lion's Share: A Short History of
      British Imperialism, 1850-1970*. London: Longmans,
      1975. xiii + 408 pp.

    Argues that Britain's turn to "new imperialism" in
the 1870's and the fevered acquisition of new territories was a symptom of British decline and loss of
resilience in economic competition. The scramble for
new territories was undertaken as a remedy but it merely extended Britain's commitments and further strained
resources by forcing defence measures on a grand scale.
Takes a Eurocentric line and makes some rather bold
claims, arguing that if in World War I Britain had lost
in France it would have meant the loss of empire; while
victory in France would have meant that any colonies
lost during the war, while Britain concentrated in
Europe, could have been recovered.
    Cf. Taylor, 209; Shannon, 107; Fieldhouse, 055;
Robinson, 072; Hyam, 090; Eldridge, 054; Low, 074.
    Reviews: *AHR* 82 (1977):361-2, Henry R. Winkler; *HJ*
20 (1977):761-9, Paul Kennedy, *JICH* 5 (1977):344-5,
Andrew Porter.

104.   Rothwell, V.H.   "The British Government and Japanese
       Military Assistance, 1914-1918."   *History* 56 (1971):
       35-45.

   Studies the inconsistent attitude in British official
circles toward the prospect of Japanese participation
in World War I.   The Japanese alliance, negotiated originally in 1902, bound the two together in a defensive
alliance, and its existence had enabled the British to
reorganize the distribution of the navy into home waters
to meet the threat of the growing German navy; but by
World War I and during the war the British began to
suspect their ally of disingenuousness, of seeking to
profit by the war and of designs on British interests.
Although opinion fluctuated during the war, concern
over Japanese intentions prevented any attempt to involve the Japanese directly in the military effort in
the Middle East.
   Cf. Nish, 100; Steiner, 137.

105.   Searle, Geoffrey Russell.   *The Quest for National Effi-*
       ciency: A Study in British Politics and Political
       Thought, 1899-1914.   Oxford: Blackwell, 1971.   x +
       286 pp.

   Examines the efforts of a cross-section of British
public opinion to diagnose and find remedies for Britain's failures in the Boer War, as well as the empire's
seeming weakness and isolation.   A study of the climate
of imperial defensiveness and insecurity that generated
attempts to reorganize the army, the navy, the government, social life, and the relations between the Home
Country and the Empire to make the Empire stronger.
Searle concentrates on the ideology of the movement,
its leading elements, such as the Liberal-Imperialists,
their aims and success, and briefly looks at the opposition to it.   As with Semmel, *Imperialism and Social*
Reform, item 106, Searle does not make entirely clear
how influential "national efficiency" as an ideology
was, or how coherent.   John Gooch's *Plans of War*, item
114, illustrates a more practical side of the reform
effort in this period and shows how political and bureaucratic in-fighting, apart from ideology, could influence the scope and success of reform ideas, no matter how brilliantly conceived or discussed; while Robert
James' work on Rosebery, item 167, illustrates the failure of personal leadership that affected the success of
the movement.   See the other works in the sections on
imperial reorganization and imperialists.

Cf. Matthew, 178; Marder, 131; Shannon, 107.
Reviews: *AHR* 77 (1972):793, Reba Soffer; *EHR* 88
(1973):933-4, P.E. Clarke; *H* 57 (1972):458-9, José
Harris; *HJ* 17 (1974):223-4, Henry Pelling; *JMH* 44
(1972):627-8, Peter Stansky; *PSQ* 88 (1973):138-40,
Richard Lyman.

106. Semmel, Bernard. *Imperialism and Social Reform: English Social-Imperial Thought, 1895-1914.* Studies in
Society, no. 5. London: Allen & Unwin, 1960. 283 pp.

Examines the functional relationship between socialism and imperialism, the attempt to establish a broad,
mass base for imperialism, with the idea of using this
support to strengthen the empire, and using the empire
to see to the welfare of the working classes. Semmel
examines the intellectual origins of this movement and
its supporters, drawn from all spectra of late 19th-
century British society. The search for social imperialism attracted such individuals as Chamberlain,
Milner, the Webbs, the Liberal-Imperialists and significant elements in the Unionist wing of the Conservative party as well as many Conservatives. Compare
with Searle, *National Efficiency*, item 105, which han-
dles similar subjects more effectively.
Cf. Matthew, 178; Gollin, 158; Hyam, 090.
Reviews: *AHR* 66 (1961):715-6, Richard Wilde; *H* 46
(1961):277-81, Christopher Howard; *JMH* 34 (1962):107-8,
Gordon Goodman.

107. Shannon, Richard T. *The Crisis of Imperialism, 1865-
1915.* Paladin History of England. London: Paladin,
1974. x + 512 pp.

Britain's empire was a hodge-podge of states and diverse areas acquired in a variety of fashions, held together by trade and the limited use of power. In the
late 19th century Britain's leaders began to realize
that survival as a Great Power hinged on turning that
loose assortment of holdings into some coherent body
run on recognizable principles with rational use of
available resources. For Britain there was a "new"
imperialism. This did not mean a new scramble for possessions but the repudiation of earlier assumptions
about empire and British power that saw some natural
relationship with the external world that would allow
Britain to keep its empire without a struggle. New
imperialists hoped to forge new methods of rule

and new institutions to carry out imperial defence.
Shannon examines this reorganization, looking at Britain's internal and external affairs, and contrasting
the domestic and foreign policies of the Liberals and
Conservatives as they faced external threats and a
crisis of confidence. Thoughtful study. Compare with
Bernard Porter, item 103.
    Cf. Beloff, 080; Hyam, 090; Taylor, 209; Robinson,
072; Monger, 098; Grenville, 085; Low, 094.

108. Steiner, Zara S. "Great Britain and the Creation of
        the Anglo-Japanese Alliance." *Journal of Modern His-
        tory* 31 (1959):27-36.

      "Isolation," splendid or otherwise, receives yet
another blow as a description of British policy before
1900. After abortive attempts to secure an alliance
with Germany, Britain looked elsewhere and the Japanese
became a possibility. Lacks Steiner's usual quality.
      Cf. Steiner, 137; Nish, 100; Monger, 098; Grenville,
085.

109. Thornton, Archibald Paton. *The Imperial Idea and Its
        Enemies: A Study in British Power*. New York: St.
        Martin's Press, 1959. xiv + 370 pp.

      In the late 19th century, challenges to the empire
forced the British to seriously consider their position, the requirements for holding and defending an
empire, and the morality upon which the empire was
based. From this emerged a conception of British imperial duty to promote peace, commerce and the rule of
law. At the same time antagonists of this idea--do-
mestic critics and foreign powers and local national-
ists--challenged its validity. Thornton examines the
clash between these opponents and the fate of the imperial idea from the late 1800's to the 1940's. In
this struggle the opponents of the imperial idea gained
the upper hand, and the empire and British power collapsed.
      Cf. Porter, 183; Shannon, 107.
      Reviews: *AHR* 65 (1960):596-7, John S. Galbraith; *JMH*
32 (1960):184-5, Paul Knaplund.

Imperial Reorganization:
The Commonwealth and Imperial Defence

110. Bond, Brian James. *The Victorian Army and the Staff
     College, 1854-1914.* London: Eyre Methuen, 1972.
     xvii + 350 pp.

     Examines the rise of professionalism in the British
     army, most particularly the growth of the Staff College
     and the General Staff, from the Crimean War to World
     War I. Concentrates on the attempts to modernize the
     education of army officers and to organize the army on
     an efficient, modern basis, especially in light of the
     deficiencies exposed by the Boer War, in order to bring
     it into line with developments in the continental armies.
     An excellent study of military conservatism and the im-
     portance of personalities and interpersonal rivalries
     in politics. Reform is never a neutral business, even
     if everyone agrees on its necessity. Complement with
     d'Ombrain, item 082; Gooch, item 114; and Hamer, item
     121.
     Cf. Tunstall, 141.
     Reviews: *AHR* 78 (1973):1468-9, Richard Blanco; *H* 58
     (1973):464-5, A.J.A. Morris; *JMH* 45 (1973):509-10, W.S.
     Hamer.

111. Corp, Edward T. "Sir Eyre Crowe and the Administration
     of the Foreign Office, 1906-1914." *Historical Jour-
     nal* 22 (1979):443-54.

     Crowe was an important figure in the direction of re-
     forms in the administrative practices of the Foreign
     Office. Examines Crowe's influence on policy and on
     reform. Compare with R.A. Cosgrove, "The Career of
     Eyre Crowe," *Albion* 4 (1972):193-200.

     Cf. Steiner, 137.

*   D'Ombrain, Nicholas. *War Machinery and High Policy:
     Defence Administration in Peacetime Britain, 1902-
     1914.* Cited as item 082.

112. Dunlop, John Kinninmont. *Development of the British
     Army, 1899-1914: From the Eve of the South African
     War to the Eve of the Great War, with Special Refer-
     ence to the Territorial Force.* London: Methuen,
     1938. xii + 337 pp.

Examines the changes within the structure of the
British Army to accommodate the lessons of the Boer
War and the changing nature of imperial defence.
Though dated it is still a useful study of the Army,
attempted reforms, and the development of the General
Staff. Complement with Bond, item 110; and John Gooch,
item 114.

113. Gooch, John. "Sir George Clarke's Career at the Com-
        mittee of Imperial Defence, 1904-1907." *Historical
        Journal* 18 (1975):555-70.

Examines Clarke's career and his role in the early
development of the Committee of Imperial Defence. The
development of the Committee of Imperial Defence reflected British awareness that modern strategic demands
required more consistent and coordinated means for developing defence plans and imperial priorities. The
years of Clarke's secretariat and the manner of his
departure show the muddle that accompanied attempts to
introduce reforms designed to end muddle. For a detailed study see Franklyn Johnson, item 123.
        Cf. Tunstall, 141; Roskill, 186.

114. Gooch, John. *The Plans of War: The General Staff and
        British Military Strategy c. 1900-1916.* London:
        Routledge & Kegan Paul, 1974. xiv + 348 pp.

Details the important role the General Staff had in
influencing the nature and direction of British foreign
and military policy. The years before World War I were
years of considerable reorganization in British institutions in response to new imperial challenges. Britain in the 1880's and 1890's lacked a General Staff or
any regular system for war-planning, a fact that became
painfully obvious in South Africa. The creation of a
General Staff was an arduous task and required years of
bureaucratic in-fighting; and even after its creation
its usefulness varied according to the attitudes of
leading generals and politicians. Like the Committee
for Imperial Defence, it suffered from jealousy and
neglect. The General Staff, though it lacked sophis-
tication by European standards, initially enjoyed tal-
ented leadership and emerged as an influential body,
especially when contrasted with the navy where a similar centralized body for planning failed to develop.
Gooch examines the development of the General Staff and
its role in strategic planning, as well as the complex

administrative background essential in understanding
the processes of reform, and the problems encountered
during World War I with the cumbersome Cabinet structure and the pervasive weight of Lord Kitchener in military matters. Contrast with Howard, item 089, which
takes a more Eurocentric view than Gooch, who discusses
the importance of the defence of India and Egypt in
British thinking.

Cf. Hamer, 121; Bond, 110; d'Ombrain, 082; Williamson,
211; Cassar, 151.

Reviews: *AHR* 81 (1976):145, Paul Guinn; *EHR* 91 (1976):
230-1, Zara Steiner; *H* 60 (1975):481, P.J.V. Rolo.

115.   Gordon, Donald Craigie. "The Admiralty and Dominion
       Navies, 1902-1914." *Journal of Modern History* 33
       (1961):407-22.

Imperial reorganization was a major theme beginning
in the late 1880's and accelerating after 1900 and the
lessons of the Boer War. Part of the rationalization--
schemes designed by the Home Government to meet challenges, particularly from Germany--was a reorganization
of the navy, which involved concentrating the bulk of
the main battlefleets in and around home waters. This
necessitated stripping the naval frontiers of the empire, an action that disturbed the chief Dominions, most
particularly Australia and New Zealand. Designed to increase coordination of imperial naval resources, the
move induced the Dominions to pursue increasing independence in their defence measures, a trend that gradually increased the political gap between London and
the Dominions, making imperial unity impossible.

Cf. Marder, 131; Woodward, 279.

116.   Gordon, Donald Craigie. *The Dominion Partnership in
       Imperial Defence, 1870-1914.* Baltimore, Maryland:
       Johns Hopkins University Press, 1965. xiv + 315 pp.

Examines the changing relations between Britain and
its English-speaking dependencies, tracing the growth
of the independence of the latter from the former, and
its consequences for imperial unity and strategic defence. At the same time as threats to the Empire began
to develop and the Home Government began to re-allocate
the priorities for defence, the self-governing colonies
began to pursue increasingly independent policies that
reflected local imperatives and perspectives, placing
strains on imperial relations.

Cf. Kendle, 124; Benians, 196; Mansergh, 129.
Reviews: *AHR* 72 (1966):196-7, Theodore Ropp; *H* 54
(1969):315-6, David McIntyre; *JMH* 38 (1966):441-2,
J.B. Conacher; *PSQ* 81 (1966):470-2, Gerald S. Graham.

117. Haggie, Paul. "The Royal Navy and War Planning in the
      Fisher Age." *Journal of Contemporary History* 8
      (1973):113-32.

      Examines the crucial role of Admiral John Fisher in
      reshaping Britain's navy. Fisher appreciated the de-
      mands that technology made on continued naval develop-
      ments, but he failed to grasp completely the importance
      of reorganization in planning for war. Thus he opposed
      a permanent War Staff because he lacked strategic vi-
      sion. On the Fisher era, see Marder, items 131 and 175;
      and MacKay, item 173. Also see P.K. Kemp, editor, *The
      Papers of Sir John Fisher*, 2 volumes (London: Navy Rec-
      ords Society, 1962).
        On aspects of technological change and its effects
      on policy, see Bryan Ranft, editor, *Technical Change
      and British Naval Policy, 1860-1939* (London: Hodder &
      Stoughton, 1977); and Gerald Jordon, editor, *Naval War-
      fare in the Twentieth Century, 1900-1945: Essays in
      Honour of Arthur Marder* (London: Croom Helm, 1977).
        Cf. Woodward, 279.

118. Hall, H. Duncan. "The British Commonwealth and the
      Founding of the League Mandate System." *Studies in
      International Relations: Essays Presented to W. Nor-
      ton Medlicott*, item 197, 345-67.

      Details the growth of the mandate system idea as a
      compromise between British imperial interests, self-de-
      termination, and the attitudes of the major Dominions
      that had acquired and wanted to keep conquered terri-
      tories.
        Cf. Temperley, 309; Monroe, 304; Klieman, 298;
      Sluglett, 357; Wasserstein, 535.

119. Hall, H. Duncan. *Commonwealth: A History of the Brit-
      ish Commonwealth of Nations*. London: Van Nostrand,
      1971. xxxvi + 1015 pp.

      A comprehensive survey of the origins and development
      of the Commonwealth as an idea and as a functioning
      reality. Concentrates on the period after 1887 and
      the first Colonial Conferences. Examines the crisis
      of imperial reorganization that pitted the strategic

interests of Britain against those of the colonies, the tariff question, and vexing problems of coordinating imperial defence. Dry and overlong, but a useful survey and reference source.

Cf. Kendle, 124; Knaplund, 126; McIntyre, 127; Mansergh, 129; Tunstall, 141; Benians, 196.

Reviews: *JMH* 46 (1974):350-1, Milton Israel.

120. Halpern, Paul G. *The Mediterranean Naval Situation, 1908-1914*. Harvard Historical Studies, no. 86. Cambridge: Harvard University Press, 1971. x + 415 pp.

Studies the nature of British naval policy towards the Mediterranean in the light of the rapprochement with France and the threat posed by Germany and Italy. Also surveys the activities of other naval powers-- Russia, Spain, Turkey, and Greece--in the region. Details the effects of changing technology and political rivalry on strategic thinking and the demands of imperial defence as Britain tried to re-distribute its limited resources to the best effect. For a brief documentary account of the naval situation, see E.W.R. Lumby, editor, *Policy and Operations in the Mediterranean, 1912-14* (London: Navy Records Society, 1970).

Cf. Williamson, 211; Marder, 131; Kennedy, 125.

Reviews: *EHR* 88 (1977):217, Christopher Howard; *H* 57 (1972):303-4, Jonathan Steinburg; *IJMES* 4 (1973):370-2, Roderic Davison; *JMH* 44 (1972):286-8, Daniel Horn.

121. Hamer, William Spencer. *The British Army: Civil-Military Relations, 1885-1905*. Oxford: Clarendon Press, 1970. xii + 293 pp.

After the Crimean War the British army underwent a major reorganization to rectify the deficiencies exposed by that war. A similar revolution occurred after the embarrassments of the Boer War, when the army, along with almost every other imperial or government institution, underwent some form of reorganization to make it more efficient. Hamer examines the later period of change, but he also does far more. Some of the best work on imperial reorganization has been done by naval and military historians, and this is one of the better jobs. Analyzes not only the influences making for change but also the debates over the nature of this change and the struggle between conservatives and progressives in the army and in the civilian administra-

tion for control over the change. The forces of change
won out but a spirit of cooperation and united purpose
did not develop and so many of the changes were ren-
dered impotent. Contains a useful bibliography and
guide to archival sources. For a general survey of the
British army and its place in British society, see
Correlli Barnett, *Britain and Her Army, 1509-1970: A
Military, Political and Social Survey* (London: Allen
Lane, 1970).

Cf. d'Ombrain, 082; Bond, 110; Dunlop, 112.

Reviews: *AHR* 77 (1972):520-1, A.V. Tucker; *H* 56
(1971):466-7, John Gooch; *HJ* 14 (1971):859-60, Michael
Howard; *JMH* 44 (1972):121, Theodore Ropp.

122.   Hancock, I.R. "The 1911 Imperial Conference." *His-
       torical Studies of Australia and New Zealand* 12
       (1966):356-72.

       Examines the quest for common grounds for imperial
       unity between Britain and the Dominions. Starting in
       the late 1880's and almost every four years afterwards,
       conferences were held in London between officials of
       the Home Government and the principal Dominions to
       settle on the appropriate framework for promoting mu-
       tual economic and strategic concerns. There was a
       gradual evolution towards imperial federalism, though
       a definitive structure was never worked out, and the
       1911 Conference was an attempt to set up more precise
       guidelines. It failed. The Dominions were too con-
       cerned with local problems and the Home Government too
       distracted by imperial ones for suitable compromise.
       Cf. Kendle, 124; Tunstall, 141.

*   Hankey, Maurice. *The Supreme Command, 1914-1918.*
       Cited as item 292.

123.   Johnson, Franklyn Arthur. *Defence by Committee: The
       British Committee of Imperial Defence, 1885-1959.*
       London: Oxford University Press, 1960. x + 416 pp.

       An exhaustive study of the origins, function and fate
       of the Committee of Imperial Defence. Originally de-
       signed to be an advisory body to the Cabinet (combining
       Cabinet members, the service chiefs and needed experts)
       to devise and coordinate plans for imperial defence,
       the CID began its serious career in the Balfour Govern-
       ment in 1903-4, though it had some earlier stirrings.
       It declined in importance when the Liberals came to

power in 1906, but was resurrected during World War I,
thanks largely to Maurice Hankey. It was an important
innovation in government coordination, though it suffered the bureaucratic fate of becoming ensnarled in
personal, political in-fighting; and it represented an
attempt at institutional change to cope with the necessities of coordinated strategic planning as the British Empire faced more challenges after 1900. An excellent study, with a substantial bibliography, though it
was written before the relevant cabinet documents were
open.
    Cf. Gooch, 114; Tunstall, 141; Brett, 149; Hankey,
292; Roskill, 186.
    Reviews: *AHR* 66 (1961):724-5, W. Ross Livingston;
H 46 (1961):165-6, Brian Tunstall; *JMH* 33 (1961):459-60,
Robin Higham.

124. Kendle, John Edward. *The Colonial and Imperial Confer-
        ences, 1887-1911: A Study in Imperial Organisation.*
        Royal Commonwealth Society Imperial Studies, no. 28.
        London: Longmans, 1967. x + 264 pp.

    Details the evolution of attempts to promote imperial
unity by converting an informal system of conferences
into a semi-federal system composed of British and
Dominion officials to discuss and resolve imperial problems. Concentrates on the period after 1902 and the
debate over the necessities of imperial defence as a
result of the weaknesses exposed by the Boer War and
Britain's diplomatic isolation. Kendle argues that
there were no clear lines drawn between avowed "cen-
trists" and adamant "autonomists" in the efforts at
imperial coordination but, rather, individuals responded to circumstances and interests. The differences
of opinion, however, over defence priorities and economic preference, the distances involved and the incompatibility of some of the personalities, plus lack
of communication between the Home Government and the
Dominions over crucial matters of preference, undermined unity efforts and tended to reinforce regionalism.
The Dominions came to Britain's defence in World War I,
but this was more the result of fellow-feeling than the
operation of a system designed to coordinate an imperial response.
    On relations with the colonies and aspects of the
operation of the Colonial Office, the chief liaison between the colonies and the Home Government, see John
Cell, *British Colonial Administration in the Mid-Nine-*

teenth Century: The Policy-Making Process (New Haven:
Conn.: Yale University Press, 1970); Brian Blakely,
The Colonial Office, 1868-1892 (Durham, N.C.: Duke University Press, 1972); and Ronald Hyam, *Elgin and
Churchill at the Colonial Office, 1905-1908: The Water-
shed of the Empire-Commonwealth* (London: Macmillan,
1968). In particular, see Robert Kubichek, *The Administration of Imperialism: Joseph Chamberlain at the
Colonial Office* (Durham, N.C.: Duke University Press,
1969). Chamberlain, who was very interested in imperial unity, tried while at the Colonial Office to devise a better system of cooperation. Also see Donald
Gordon, *The Dominion Partnership in Imperial Defence,
1870-1914*, item 116, which studies the colonial response.
    Cf. Benians, 196; Mansergh, 129.
    Reviews: *AHR* 74 (1969):999-1000, H. Duncan Hall; *EHR*
84 (1969):879-80, A.F.McC. Madden; *H* 53 (1968):465,
J.A. Cross.

125. Kennedy, Paul M. *The Rise and Fall of British Naval
      Mastery.* London: Allen Lane, 1976. xviii + 405 pp.

      Surveys the role of sea power in British history from
the 17th century to the post-World War II period. Main-
tains that Britain's naval rise and fall was closely
related to its economic fortunes; that sea power exerted
its greatest influence upon world affairs between the
early 16th century and the late 19th century; and that
it was by a combination of sea and land power that
Britain acquired a dominant world position--and then
lost it. Chapters 7, 8, and 9 on the decline of Britain's industrial and military capacity, the rise of naval rivals, and the World War I era are of particular
note, discussing in detail the Fisher Era, the debate
in Britain over army and navy reform, the redistribution
of resources, and the performance of the navy in the war.
    Cf. Marder, 131; MacKay, 173; Graham, 203; Woodward,
279; Tunstall, 141.
    Reviews: *AHR* 82 (1977):356, C.J. Bartlett; *EHR* 92
(1977):912, Paul Hayes; *JMH* 50 (1978):515.

126. Knaplund, Paul. *Britain, Commonwealth and Empire,
      1901-1955.* London: Hamish Hamilton, 1956. xii +
      541 pp.

      Surveys the development of the Commonwealth arguing
that participation in World War I gave the self-governing dependencies a new feeling of self-confidence and

independence that promoted the idea of a commonwealth of nations over an empire with an imperial center. Survey, country by country, of political, economic and social developments, the impact of war and depression, and examines the question of imperial defence and the efforts to effect a coordinated system for imperial defence.

Cf. Mansergh, 129; Tunstall, 141.

Reviews: *AHR* 63 (1958):407-8, H. Duncan Hall; *JMH* 29 (1957):395, A.L. Burt.

127. McIntyre, W. David. *The Commonwealth of Nations: Origins and Impact, 1869-1971*. Europe and the World in the Age of Expansion Series, no. 9. Edited by Boyd Shafer. Minneapolis: University of Minnesota Press, 1977. xvii + 596 pp.

A comprehensive survey of the development of the Commonwealth, with useful information on 19th and 20th century political figures, trade and the question of imperial preference, the development of nationalism, the pull for imperial unity, and the efforts to coordinate imperial defence. Concentrates on political events. Useful, with a generous bibliography.

Cf. Benians, 196.

Reviews: *AHR* 83 (1978):975-6, Richard Preston; *CJH* 13 (1978):315-7, Robert Kubichek; *EHR* 94 (1979):606-8, D.K. Fieldhouse; *H* 64 (1979):133-4, Bernard Porter.

128. Mackintosh, John. "The Role of Committee for Imperial Defence Before 1914." *English Historical Review* 77 (1962):490-503.

A survey of the main features of the Committee for Imperial Defence and an evaluation of the historiography dealing with it. Mackintosh deals particularly with the fate of the CID under the Liberals, showing its decline in importance and the failure to use it effectively as a body to coordinate defence planning. Instead it became little more than a group for discussing technical details with little policy function, though it did on occasion have an important liaison function when matters arose affecting the interests of various departments.

Cf. Johnson, 123; Tunstall, 141.

129. Mansergh, Philip Nicholas Seton. *The Commonwealth Experience*. London: Weidenfeld & Nicolson, 1969. xix + 471 pp.

A comprehensive survey of the growth of the Commonwealth as an idea and as a political reality, concentrating on the self-governing colonies and their relations with the Home Government. Chapters 1 through 6
cover the formative period, the question of imperial
defence, the evolution of imperial conferences, the
attitudes of officials and populations in the Dominions
and in London, the question of economic preference, and
the personalities and conflicts that shaped events down
to the end of World War I.

There is an extensive literature on the empire-commonwealth. Concern for the empire and the need for unity
were epitomized by such contemporary publications as
The Round Table, *United Empire*, *Royal Colonial Institute*; and such works as A.B. Keith, *Imperial Unity and
the Dominions* (Oxford: Clarendon Press, 1916). On the
historiography of the Commonwealth, see Robin Winks,
editor, *The Historiography of the British-Commonwealth*,
item 017. Also see W.K. Hancock, *Survey of British
Commonwealth Affairs, 1918-1936*, 2 vols. (Oxford: Oxford University Press, 1937); James Williamson, *A Short
History of British Expansion: The Modern Empire and
Commonwealth* (London: Macmillan, 1964); Vol. 3, *Cambridge History of the British Empire*, item 196; and
J.D.B. Miller, *The Commonwealth and the World*, 3rd edition (London: Duckworth, 1965).

Cf. Kendle, 124; Beloff, 080.

Reviews: *AHR* 75 (1970):854-5, Robin Winks; *EHR* 86
(1971):435, A.F.McC. Madden.

130.   Marder, Arthur Jacob. *The Anatomy of British Sea Power:
       A History of British Naval Policy in the Pre-Dreadnought
       Era, 1886-1905*. London: Frank Cass, 1964. xix +
       580 pp.

The revolution in ship design in the late 19th century
jeopardized Britain's naval superiority, for it meant
Britain's long-held lead in wooden warships disappeared
virtually overnight. The evolution of the steamship and
the ironclad unleashed a technological arms race for
which there is still no end in sight. Marder studies
the importance of the navy in the British psychology,
its principles of use, the response to naval challenges,
the international and domestic political climate that
influenced thinking about the navy and its use, and
the consequences of reform. More than just a study of
ships and guns, but a sociology of the navy, a study of
its personalities. Complements Marder's *From Dread-*

nought to Scapa Flow, discussed below. For a general, thematic survey of Britain's naval concerns, see Gerald Graham, *The Politics of Naval Supremacy* (Cambridge: Cambridge University Press, 1965). Compare with Kennedy, *British Naval Mastery,* item 125.
Cf. Woodward, 279.

131. Marder, Arthur Jacob. *From the Dreadnought to Scapa Flow: The Royal Navy in the Fisher Era, 1904-1919.* 5 volumes. London: Oxford University Press, 1961-70.

The navy stood between Britain and the world; the British economy depended on ships, and Britain's power was based on control of the seas. For most of the 19th century Britain faced no serious naval rivals; but beginning in the 1880's the British began to worry about potential naval competitors, an anxiety that grew more febrile as anticipation grew into reality. In response to the challenge Britain began to revamp the navy, inaugurating the battleship era and redistributing the fleet. A key figure in promoting these changes was Admiral John Arbuthnot Fisher. Marder examines Fisher's career, the changes in the navy and in British defence thinking, and the navy's performance in World War I. In volume 1, *The Road to War, 1904-14,* Marder especially highlights Fisher's innovative brilliance but his lack of strategic insight that led him to introduce significant changes in ship design and certain institutional changes within the navy, but kept him from seeing the necessity of developing a naval staff for overall strategic planning and coordination with the military. Volume 2, *The War Years to the Eve of Jutland, 1914-1916,* examines not only the navy's activities but also the political background to the Dardanelles disaster, and the crucial roles of Churchill and Fisher, Kitchener and others. Volume 5, *1918-1919: Victory and Aftermath,* has a useful bibliography and useful information on archival sources. An excellent study of the British navy and naval policy.
Cf. MacKay, 173; Kennedy, 125.
Reviews: (vol. 1) *AHR* 67 (1962):393-4, Bernadotte Schmitt; *H* 48 (1963):104-6, F.H. Hinsley; *JMH* 34 (1962): 458-9, Oron Hale; (vol. 2) *H* 52 (1967):238-9, F.H. Hinsley; *JMH* 39 (1967):199-200, Bernadotte Schmitt; (vol. 3) *AHR* 72 (1967):592, Robin Higham; *JMH* 40 (1968): 442-3, Bernadotte Schmitt; (vol. 4) *AHR* 75 (1970):1731-2, Paul Guinn; (vol. 5) *AHR* 77 (1972):794-5, Raymond Callahan; *EHR* 87 (1972):653-4, R.B. McCallum; *H* 56

(1971):299-300, F.H. Hinsley; *JMH* 43 (1971):341-3,
Robert Grant.

132. Morris, A.J. Anthony. "Haldane's Army Reforms 1906-8:
      The Deception of the Radicals." *History* 56 (1971):
      17-34.

      Examines the tensions in the Liberal Party between
      the Radicals, who opposed army development, and Haldane,
      who represented the more imperialist element within the
      Party. The Radicals could never conceptualize the na-
      ture of Haldane's reforms or how to combat them without
      isolating their position. On problems of imperial re-
      organization and tensions within the government, see
      Koss, item 170; Porter, item 183.

133. Murray, John A. "Foreign Policy Debated: Sir Edward
      Grey and His Critics 1911-1912." *Power, Public Opin-
      ion, and Diplomacy*. Edited by L.P. Wallace and Wil-
      liam Askew. Durham, N.C.: Duke University Press, 1959,
      pp. 140-71.

      Studies the storm of opposition that developed in
      mid-1911 over Grey's handling of foreign policy. The
      opposition was a curious alliance of anti-imperialist
      Radicals and arch-imperialists like Lord Curzon, who
      were able to unite in opposition to Grey's secretive-
      ness, the entente he concluded with Russia, and his
      seeming anti-German bias. Grey survived because none
      of his critics was willing to bring down the Liberal
      Government (though Lord Curzon may have not been so
      reluctant).
      Cf. Steiner, 137; Robbins, 184; Hinsley, 086.

134. Platt, D.C.M. *The Cinderella Service: British Consuls
      Since 1825*. London: Longmans, 1971. x + 272 pp.

      Surveys the nature and political and juridical func-
      tion of the British Consular Service from the early
      1800's to 1914. The consular service was the step-
      child of the diplomatic-foreign service establishment,
      though consuls through their reports and observations
      could be instrumental in shaping policy by the views
      they sent back of local conditions. Platt's pioneer
      study, after exploring the training, duties and func-
      tion of the consular service, looks at the consular
      role in East Asia and the Levant. For further studies
      on the consular service in the Middle East, see Gordon
      Iseminger, "The Old Turkish Hands: The British Levan-

tine Consuls, 1856-1876," *Middle East Journal* 22 (1968): 297-316; D.C.M. Platt, "The Role of the British Consular Service in Overseas Trade, 1825-1914," *Economic History Review* 15 (1962):494-512; Alan Cunningham, "'Dragomania': The Dragomans of the British Embassy in Turkey," *Middle Eastern Affairs*, no. 2, St. Antony's Papers, no. 11, edited by Albert Hourani (London: Chatto & Windus, 1961), 81-167; and Peter Bird, "Regional and Functional Specialisation in the British Consular Service," *Journal of Contemporary History* 7 (1972):127-45.

Reviews: *AHR* 77 (1972):789-90, H. Duncan Hall; *EHR* 87 (1972):890-1, P.M.H. Bell; *JICH* 1 (1972):119-20, John Miles; *JMH* 44 (1972):600-2, Robert Bunselmeyer; *PSQ* 88 (1973):299-301, Henry M. Wriston.

135. Satre, Lowell J. "St. John Brodrick and Army Reform, 1901-1903." *Journal of British Studies* 15 (1976): 117-39.

Examines the domestic political consequences stemming from efforts to reform the army after the reverses during the Boer War and in light of the realization that a set of priorities was necessary to handle the new strategic situation after 1900. Brodrick failed to develop a scheme and get it past critics who objected to a large, standing army based on a European model. It remained for Haldane eight years later to achieve the reforms.
Cf. Hamer, 121; Gooch, 114; d'Ombrain, 082; James, 165.

* Searle, Geoffrey. *The Quest for National Efficiency: A Study in British Politics and Political Thought, 1899-1914*. Cited as item 105.

136. Sharp, Alan. "The Foreign Office in Eclipse 1919-22." *History* 61 (1976):198-218.

One of the consequences of World War I was the decline of the Foreign Office's independence in developing foreign policy. Grey's shortcomings in the earlier years of the war; the necessities of more coordination in strategic planning--a feature that had begun before the war; plus the inadequacies of the Asquith government that brought Lloyd George to power, with the consequent streamlining of the cabinet; and Lloyd George's tendency to act without consulting the Foreign Office combined to gradually erode that office's former independence. See the various works by Zara Steiner discussed below.
Cf. Warman, 142.

137.   Steiner, Zara S. *The Foreign Office and Foreign Policy,*
        1898-1914. London: Cambridge University Press, 1969.
        xii + 262 pp.

   A definitive study of the operation of the British
Foreign Office, its personnel and the changes in its
operations in order to handle increasing business.
After surveying the characteristics of the old Foreign
Office, Steiner examines the reforms in procedure begun under Lansdowne (1901-1905), the increasing importance of the permanent officials in influencing policy
formation, and how the reformed Foreign Office dealt
with foreign relations problems, other departments of
government, the Press, and Parliament. Describes the
importance of personalities and political rivalries in
shaping policy, concentrating on Grey's tenure from
1906 to 1914. Steiner has pursued this administrative-
foreign policy study in a number of other essays discussed here. On aspects of the Foreign Office, see
Donald Bishop, *The Administration of British Foreign
Policy* (Syracuse, N.Y.: Syracuse University Press, 1961);
Ray Jones, *The Nineteenth Century Foreign Office: An
Administrative History* (London: Weidenfeld & Nicolson,
1971); John Cornell (pseudonym for John Henry Robinson),
*The "Office": The Story of the British Foreign Office,
1919-1951* (New York: St. Martin's Press, 1958); and
Lord Strang, *The Foreign Office* (London: Allen & Unwin,
1955). Also see Steiner, "The Last Years of the Old
Foreign Office, 1898-1905," *Historical Journal* 6 (1963):
59-90, for a supplementary study.
   Cf. Grenville, 085; Monger, 098; Robbins, 184;
Hinsley, 086; Grey, 160.
   Reviews: *AHR* 75 (1970):2062, Henry Winkler; *EHR* 87
(1972):595-7, F.R. Bridge; *HJ* 16 (1973):857-64, Richard
Langhorne; *JMH* 42 (1970):688-94, Samuel Williamson;
PSQ 86 (1971):325-7, Stephen Koss.

138.   Steiner, Zara S. "The Foreign Office under Sir Edward
        Grey, 1905-1914." *British Foreign Policy under Sir
        Edward Grey*, item 086, 22-69.

   Part of Steiner's thorough study of the British Foreign Office. Concentrates on intra-departmental relations and the role of the permanent officials in shaping policy before World War I. The increasing role of
these officials after Salisbury's departure is one of
the significant changes in the structure of the Foreign
Office to handle increasing demands and need for exper-

tise. But the Foreign Office still tended to function
in a vacuum, with an elitist view of the world and limited understanding of the strategic implications of
the hostility with Germany and the military-naval talks
with France. The compartmentalization of British policy-
making hurt Britain's efforts to conduct a modern war.
See Steiner, "The Foreign Office and the War," *British
Policy under Sir Edward Grey*, item 086, for a discussion of Grey's handling of the war.
Cf. Busch, 352; Kedourie, 346.

139.   Steiner, Zara S. "Grey, Hardinge and the Foreign Office, 1906-1910." *Historical Journal* 10 (1967):415-
39.

One of the important figures in the transitional period 1900-1914 was Sir Charles Hardinge, who was permanent under-secretary at the Foreign Office from 1906
to 1910 and again from 1916 to 1918. Hardinge was a
career diplomat and had considerable experience in
political circles. He, along with other permanent officials (particularly William Tyrell and Eyre Crowe),
helped to transform the working of his department,
streamlining procedures and enhancing the role of permanent officials in directly influencing the development of foreign policy.
Cf. Hinsley, 086; Robbins, 184; Lowe, 095; Grey, 160;
Hardinge, 163; Corp, 111.

140.   Tucker, Albert. "The Issue of Army Reform in the
Unionist Government, 1903-5." *Historical Journal* 9
(1966):90-100.

Examines the difficulties of reforming the army--
overcoming internal opposition to change, deciding on
appropriate priorities and juggling personalities. Reform was not a neutral policy and despite its value
many worked against it to protect their parochial interests. And many of the reform efforts were not well
thought out or efficiently implemented. In addition,
see John McDermott, "The Revolution in British Military
Thinking from the Boer War to the Moroccan Crisis,"
Canadian Journal of History 9 (1974):159-77; T.H.E.
Travers, "Technology, Tactics, and Morale: Jean de
Bloch, the Boer War, and British Military Theory,
1900-1914," *Journal of Modern History* 51 (1979):264-
86; J.K. Dunlop, *The Development of the British Army,
1899-1914*, item 112; Hampden Gordon, *The War Office*

(London: Putnam, 1935); J.E. Tyler, *The British Army and the Continent, 1904-1914* (London: Edward Arnold, 1938); Correlli Barnett, *Britain and Her Army, 1409-1970* (London: Allen Lane, 1970).

Cf. d'Ombrain, 082; Hamer, 121; Shannon, 107; Gooch, 114; Tunstall, 141.

141. Tunstall, W.C.B. "Imperial Defense, 1897-1914." *Cambridge History of the British Empire*, item 196, 563-604.

Surveys efforts to reform the army and navy and to coordinate imperial defence with the self-governing colonies. Reform was not simply a matter of new arms or ships or improvements in training and equipment, but of broad changes in thinking about imperial defence. Tunstall traces the evolutionary stages in this transformation, highlighting the main issues, and problems, and failures. Coordination and cooperation, integrated planning and efficiency were the goals; even though achievement fell short, enough was done to help Britain and the empire survive the first major modern war. Also see Luke Trainor, "The Liberals and the Formation of Imperial Defense Policy, 1892-5," *Bulletin of the Institute of Historical Research* 42 (1969):187-200; and "The British Government and Imperial Economic Unity, 1890-1895," *Historical Journal* 3 (1970):68-84.

Cf. Gooch, 114; Gordon, 116; Kendle, 124; Johnson, 123; Shannon, 107; Williamson, 211.

142. Warman, Roberta. "The Erosion of Foreign Office Influence in the Making of Foreign Policy, 1916-1918." *Historical Journal* 15 (1972):133-59.

Examines the decline in the independence of the Foreign Office as a consequence of the pressure of World War I and the need for greater, overall coordination of strategic planning; and as a result of personality clashes.

Cf. Steiner, 137; Sharp, 136; Hinsley, 086; Mowat, 098.

Proconsuls, Bureaucrats and Administrators

143. Adelson, Roger. *Mark Sykes: Portrait of an Amateur.* London: Jonathan Cape, 1975. 336 pp.

Sykes was the British representative who concluded
the agreement with Picot, the French representative,
setting out Franco-British claims in the Middle East
in 1916. Almost immediately after the settlement the
British began to have second thoughts, and Sykes tried
to undo his original agreement. Adelson examines Sykes'
career, an amateur in politics, and his role in shaping
British Middle East policy. Sykes was an independent
agent, sort of a trouble-shooter (some thought trouble-
maker) whose contacts with Lord Kitchener and the Foreign Office gave him influence. Updates Shane Lesley's
biography, *Mark Sykes, His Life and Letters* (London:
Cassel, 1923). A brief account of Sykes' role in trying to secure Palestine for Britain can be found in
Elie Kedourie, "Sir Mark Sykes and Palestine, 1915-16,"
Arab Political Memoirs, item 444, 236-42. Sykes was
also an acute observer of the East; for his views on
the Ottoman Empire, see *The Caliph's Lost Heritage*
(1915; reprint; New York: Arno Press, 1973).
Cf. Cassar, 151; Kedourie, 346 and 363; Busch, 352;
Nevakivi, 324.
Reviews: *GJ* 143 (1977):461.

144. Aitken, William Maxwell, Lord Beaverbrook. *Politicians
and the War, 1914-1916*. 2 volumes. London: Thornton
Butterworth, 1928.

William Maxwell Aitken, Lord Beaverbrook (1879-1964),
a British politician, and as he would have liked, a
personality, had a long and diverse career, most noted
for his newspaper and political work and his years of
friendship with men in power, among them Lloyd George
and Winston Churchill. His account of the inner workings
of the British cabinets is a masterpiece, though disappointingly vague on the fall of the Asquith Government in 1916. Still it is a must. A further work,
Men and Power, 1917-1918 (London: Hutchinson, 1966) is
also a must, especially for the brief, entertaining
biographical sketches of major political figures that
introduce it. Both works are full of the anecdotes
Beaverbrook loved, but his views need to be balanced
with other accounts. The "history" of Beaverbrook is
A.J.P. Taylor's *Beaverbrook* (New York: Simon and
Schuster, 1972), a comprehensive and loving study.
Cf. Gilbert, 156; Hazelhurst, 295; McEwen, 302; Lloyd
George, 172; Churchill, 153; Asquith, 146.

145. Amery, Julian. *The Life of Joseph Chamberlain.* Volumes
4-6. London: Macmillan, 1951-69.

Continuation of J.L. Garvin's official history of
Chamberlain first begun in 1915. Amery takes up the
study with Chamberlain's career in the early 1900's
and his campaign to strengthen the empire. Chamberlain's
pursuit of imperial unity and social reform through
tariff reform went against Unionist principles and led
to a split within the Conservative Party. Intricate
history.

Cf. Searle, 105; Semmel, 106; Dugdale, 154; Judd,
167 and 168; Young, 193; Shannon, 107.

Reviews: *AHR* 57 (1952):432-4, Richard D. Challener,
AHR 75 (1970):1730-1, Trevor Lloyd.

146.   Asquith, Herbert Henry. *Memories and Reflections, 1852-
       1927*. 2 volumes. Edited by Alexander MacKintosh.
       London: Cassell, 1928.

These memoirs of the Earl of Oxford and Asquith, long-
time politician and Prime Minister from 1908-1916,
covers his political career, and gives valuable character sketches and insights into events. Much of volume 2 is concerned with justifying Asquith's handling
of the war and the "palace coup" that toppled his government in 1916. Compare accounts of the Dardanelles
adventure, the Coalition of 1915 and the fall of the
Liberal Government in December 1916 with Churchill,
item 153. Asquith remains underdone by biographers.

On the Liberal Government, see Peter Rowland, *The
Last Liberal Governments: The Promised Land, 1905-1910*
(London: Cresset Press, 1968); Trevor Wilson, *The Down-
fall of the Liberal Party, 1914-1935* (London: Collins,
1966). On Asquith, see Roy Jenkins, *Asquith* (London:
Collins, 1964); Stephen Koss, *Asquith* (London: Allen
Lane, 1976); and, of course, the official biography by
J.A. Spender and Cyril Asquith, *Life of H.H. Asquith,
Lord Oxford and Asquith*, item 187.

Cf. Blake, 148; Hazelhurst, 295; Beaverbrook, 144;
McEwen, 302; Taylor, 308.

147.   Baring, Evelyn, Lord Cromer. *Modern Egypt*. 2 volumes.
       London: Macmillan, 1908.

Cromer's classic account of how he governed Egypt.
Reviews the background of Britain's involvement in
Egypt and the history of the occupation and subsequent
British presence in Egypt. A superb proconsular study.
For a different view by one of Baring's contemporaries,
see Wilfred Scawen Blunt, *Secret History of the English*

*Occupation of Egypt: Being a Personal Narrative of
Events*, 2nd edition (London: Fisher Unwin, 1907). Also
see Alfred, Lord Milner, *England in Egypt* (London: Arnold, 1892).

Cf. al-Sayyid, 387; Marlow, 382; Owen, 386; Tignor,
390; Holt, 378; Vatikiotis, 391; Safran, 495.

148. Blake, Robert, Baron of Braydeston. *The Unknown Prime
Minister: The Life and Times of Andrew Bonar Law,
1858-1923*. London: Eyre & Spottiswoode, 1955. 556
pp.

A blow-by-blow account of Bonar Law's political career. Bonar Law was Balfour's successor as head of the
Unionist wing of the Conservative Party, and during
World War I was leader of the "loyal opposition" within
the War Cabinet. Bonar Law was an ally of Chamberlain's
over tariff reform, but this did not keep him from con-
testing Chamberlain's control over the Conservative
Party after Balfour's resignation in 1911. During the
early days of World War I Bonar Law guided his party
in close support of the Asquith Government, but his
disenchantment over war management, his dislike of
Churchill and the failures at the Dardanelles led him
to seek a coalition government in 1915, and play a role
in the fall of the Asquith Government in 1916. Blake
provides insights into the internal mechanisms of government and the importance of personalities in politics.

Cf. Taylor, 308; Hazelhurst, 295; McEwen, 302; Gilbert, 156; Beaverbrook, 144; Lloyd George, 172; Churchill, 153; Asquith, 146; Mackintosh, 174.

149. Brett, Reginald, Viscount Esher. *The Captains and
Kings Depart: Journals and Letters of Reginald Vis-
count Esher*. Edited by Oliver, Viscount Esher. New
York: Charles Scribner's Sons, 1938. ix + 307 pp.

Esher (1852-1930) was instrumental in efforts to reform the War Office and the army after the Boer War.
A powerful figure, though personally modest, he was a
key figure in reforming the War Office, in the creation
of a General Staff, and in trying to modernize and
streamline Britain's strategic planning. Along with
Lord Fisher, item 173, and Haldane, item 170, Esher was
one of the chief contributors to improving Britain's
preparedness for a major modern war. This volume, plus
The Journals and Letters of Reginald Viscount Esher,
4 volumes, edited by Maurice Brett (London: Nicolson &

Watson, 1934), contains a substantial collection of
Esher's correspondence, reflecting his political contacts and activities and his thoughts. Volume 3 contains material on his activities as Chairman of the War
Office Reconstruction Committee. For a study of Esher's
political career, see Peter Fraser, *Lord Esher, A Political Biography* (London: Davis, MacGibbon, 1973).
    Cf. Bond, 110; d'Ombrain, 082; Gooch, 114; Johnson,
123; Koss, 170.

150. Buchanan, George William. *My Mission to Russia and
        Other Diplomatic Memories.* 2 volumes. New York:
        Cassell, 1923.

    Buchanan was Britain's Ambassador to Russia in the
crucial years before and during World War I. His account, though limited and somewhat self-serving, is an
important source for inside information on the diplomatic relations of World War I. See the memoirs of
two contemporaries, the French Minister to Russia,
Maurice Paleologue, *An Ambassador's Memoirs*, 3 volumes,
translated by F.A. Holt (London: Hutchinson, 1923); and
the Russian Foreign Minister, Sergei Sazanov, *Fateful
Years, 1906-1916: The Reminiscences of Sergei Sazanov*
(London: Jonathan Cape, 1928). Also see *British Documents on the Origins of the War*, item 045, for a variety of views and points of comparison.
    Cf. Grey, 160.

151. Cassar, George. *Kitchener: Architect of Victory.*
        London: Kimber, 1977. 573 pp.

    The definitive biography of Field-Marshall Herbert
Kitchener and his influence on British strategic policy
during World War I. Relieves Kitchener of the hero-
worship and calumny that surround his name, presenting
a balanced view of his efforts to put the British army
on a par with the continental armies when World War I
broke out. Many of Kitchener's "failures" during the
war were the result of the clumsiness of the cabinet
system (suited to peace, not war), the underdeveloped
state of the General Staff, and the competition within
the government and the army for influence and priorities. Kitchener, however, aggravated matters by his
aloofness, secrecy and lack of grasp of political realities.
    See Philip Magnus, *Kitchener, Portrait of an Imperial-
ist* (London: Murray, 1958), for a slightly different

view with more information on Kitchener's earlier career.
 Cf. Guinn, 291; Taylor, 308; Hazelhurst, 295.

152. Chamberlain, M.E. "Lord Cromer's 'Ancient and Modern
 Imperialism': A Proconsular View of Empire." *Journal
 of British Studies* 12 (1972):61-87.

 Examines Cromer's view of empire and imperial necessity, as discussed in his volume of the same name.
Cromer did not glorify expansion but saw it resulting
from a combination of circumstances, sometimes beyond
control, that forced the issue. An early proponent of
the "turbulent frontier" idea of expansion (see Galbraith, item 057), Cromer also believed in acquiring
areas to keep other powers out if their interests jeopardized the security of an existing British possession.
Cromer had a low opinion of oriental governments.
 Cf. Baring, 147; al-Sayyid, 387; Tignor, 389; Owen,
386; Holt, 378; Vatikiotis, 391.

153. Churchill, Winston L.S. *The World Crisis*. 6 volumes.
 London: Butterworth, 1923-31.

 Churchill's reconstruction of his experiences during
World War I, the nature of the challenges facing Britain and the niceties of political rivalry within the
British government. Interesting account of the decisions to make the attempt on the Dardanelles, the failure of which almost cost Churchill his political career. As with all memoirs-cum-histories, it must be
used judiciously: as A.J. Balfour wryly noted, "Winston
has written an enormous book about himself and called
it *The World Crisis*."
 The material on Churchill is extensive. In addition
to the sources cited in this section, see Stephen
Roskill, *Churchill and the Admirals* (London: Collins,
1977); Peter Stansky, *Churchill: A Profile* (London:
Macmillan, 1973); and Kenneth Young, *Churchill and
Beaverbrook: A Study of Friendship and Politics* (London: Eyre and Spottiswoode, 1966).
 Cf. Hazelhurst, 295; James, 165 and 313; Gilbert,
156; Liddell Hart, 294; Taylor, 308; Beaverbrook, 144;
Klieman, 298; Marder, 131.

154. Dugdale, Blanche E.C. *Arthur James Balfour, First Earl
 of Balfour*. 2 volumes. London: Hutchinson, 1936.

A sensitive, useful study of Balfour by his niece.
Contains insights into the inner workings of British
politics, with important information on the reorganization of the empire after 1900, the formation of the
Committee of Imperial Defence, and the Balfour Declaration.   In addition to the works on and by imperialists
in this section, see Kenneth Young, *Arthur James Balfour*, item 193.
   Cf. Johnson, 123; Mackintosh, 128; Kendle, 124; Judd,
167; Stein, 531.

155.   Gardner, Brian. *Allenby of Arabia: Lawrence's General.*
       London: Cassell, 1965. xxxii + 314 pp.

   Popular account of the life of General (later Field-
Marshall) Edmund Allenby, who commanded the British
campaign against the Turks in Palestine, and after the
war became High Commissioner of Egypt. For more infor-
mation on Allenby, see the semi-official biography by
Field-Marshall Archibald Wavell, *Allenby: Soldier and
Statesman* (1941; reprint; London: White Lion Press,
1974).
   Cf. MacMunn, 314.
   Reviews: *MES* 1 (1965):409–13, Elie Kedourie.

156.   Gilbert, Martin. *Winston S. Churchill*, volumes 3 and
       4. London: Heinemann, 1971.

   Resumes Randolph S. Churchill's biography of his
father, though with a more objective eye. Gilbert's
volumes, each of which has a companion volume of documents, cover Churchill's performance in government during World War I and afterward. Volume 3, *1914–1916*,
examines Churchill's tenure at the Admiralty and his
role in the Dardanelles campaign, his fall from power,
and his return to Parliament to fight an uphill battle
to restore his reputation. Volume 4, *1916–1922*, examines Churchill's return to office, and his accomplish-
ments at the War Office and Colonial Office, posts he
held after the war. Gilbert's analysis of Churchill's
role in the Asquith Government and its fall, in planning the Dardanelles campaign, and his attempts to resolve problems in the Middle East at the Cairo Conference in 1921 are of particular note. The section dealing with the Dardanelles is, perhaps, the single best
account of the political muddle surrounding that event,
though it goes easy on Churchill's role.
   Cf. James, 165; Churchill, 153; Taylor, 308; Marder,
131; Klieman, 298.

Reviews: (vol. 3): *AHR* 78 (1973):641-8, Raymond
Callahen; *H* 58 (1974):133-5, Henry Pelling; (vol. 4):
AHR 81 (1976):865-6, Joseph M. Hernon, Jr.; *EHR* 91
(1976):611-13, Henry Pelling; *PSQ* 91 (1976):550-1,
Walter L. Arnstein.

157. Gilbert, Martin. *Sir Horace Rumbold: Portrait of a
Diplomat, 1869-1941.* London: Heinemann, 1973. xvii
+ 496 pp.

Rumbold was a career diplomat with extensive experience in the Middle East. His superior and condescend-
ing attitudes towards foreigners and especially Middle
Easterners was a typical element in the thinking and
responses of more than one British diplomat. Though
some diplomats had a "feel" for the Middle East, the
importance of views of such men as Rumbold, who was
more than the exception, must not be overlooked in
evaluating the nature of British policy in the area.
Cf. Nicolson, 182; Hardinge, 163; Baring, 147.
Reviews: *EHR* 90 (1975):942-3, P.J.V. Rolo; *JICH* 3
(1978):298-9, Max Beloff; *MEJ* 29 (1975):230-1, Evan W.
Wilson.

158. Gollin, Alfred. *Proconsul in Politics: A Study of Lord
Milner in Opposition and in Power, with an Introductory Section, 1854-1905.* London: Blond, 1964. xiii
+ 627 pp.

A political biography of Alfred, Lord Milner, that
studies his ideas, activities and encounters with the
leading figures of his day. Milner was a controversial
figure, a practical idealist who sought to preserve the
British Empire. He loathed democracy and opposition
and tried to create an imperial race to carry out his
dreams. Gollin concentrates on the period after Milner
left South Africa, with his activities during World War
I receiving greatest attention. Has copious footnotes
but no bibliography. Other aspects of Milner's career
can be found in Vladimir Halperin, *Lord Milner and the
Empire: The Evolution of British Imperialism* (London:
Oldhams Press, 1952); John Kendle, *The Round Table
Movement and Imperial Union* (Toronto: University of
Toronto Press, 1975); John Marlowe, *Milner, Apostle of
Empire*, item 176; Terence O'Brien, *Milner, Viscount of
St. James's and Cape Town* (London: Constable, 1979);
and Walter Nimocks, *Milner's Young Men: The Kindergar-
den in Edwardian Imperial Affairs* (Durham, N.C.: Duke

University Press, 1969). A published collection of
Milner's papers is Cecil Headlam, editor, *The Milner
Papers*, 2 volumes (London: Cassell, 1931, 1933).
   Cf. Amery, 145; Judd, 168; Taylor, 308.
   Reviews: *AHR* 70 (1965):765-6, Joseph Baylen; *EHR* 81
(1966):209-10, A.F.McC. Madden; *H* 50 (1965):100-2,
Michael Hurst; *JMH* 37 (1965):394, A.P. Thornton.

159. Graves, Philip P. *The Life of Sir Percy Cox.* With a
      foreword by Sir Arnold Wilson. London: Hutchinson,
      1941. 350 pp.

      Surveys the diplomatic career of Sir Percy Cox (1864-
      1937), who for many years was Persian Gulf Resident,
      then Chief Political Officer with the British expedi-
      tionary force in Mesopotamia, special representative
      to Persia, and High Commissioner of British-occupied
      Mesopotamia. Cox was an authority on Arabs and was
      respected by local tribal leaders, and his views and
      activities during and after World War I were instrumen-
      tal in influencing the direction of British policy in
      the Middle East. He was the chief local negotiator of
      the ill-fated Anglo-Persian Agreement of 1919; and it
      was Cox who originated the idea of creating an "Arab
      façade" for British rule in Mesopotamia, though he by
      no means "created" the determination of Curzon and
      others to stake out a permanent position in Iraq. This
      is the only biography, and Cox needs a new examination.
         Cf. Nicolson, 182; Winstone, 192; Wilson, 358;
      Sluglett, 357; Busch, 285 and 352; Olson, 424.

160. Grey, Viscount Sir Edward. *Twenty-Five Years, 1892-
      1916.* 2 volumes. New York: Stokes, 1925.

      Explains Grey's views and policies, and his conduct
      of foreign policy as Foreign Secretary from 1906 to
      1916. Gives details on relations with Germany, France,
      Russia and America, and on Grey's attitudes towards
      lesser powers such as Turkey and Persia. Provides in-
      sight into the inner workings of the Foreign Office and
      its handling of World War I. A useful memoir which must
      be used cautiously.
         Cf. Robbins, 184; Steiner, 137 and 307; Hinsley, 086;
      Lowe, 095; Monger, 098; Williamson, 211; Churchill,
      243.

161. Hancock, William Keith. *The Sanguine Years, 1870-1919.*
      Smuts, vol. 1. Cambridge: Cambridge University Press,
      1962. xiii + 619 pp.

The definitive biography of Smuts, his period and
his achievements. Volume 1 covers his early years, his
activities during the Boer War, and his efforts on Britain's behalf during World War I. Provides insight into
Smuts' role in the Easterner vs. Westerner controversy
in British planning during World War I. Though he believed in a knock-out blow in Palestine, he still supported the ill-fated Flanders offensive. Hancock also
discusses Smuts' role at the Paris Peace Conference and
the general atmosphere of the Conference and the ideas
and goals of the respective delegations. Lacks a bibliography but has extensive notes. Also see Sarah G.
Millin, *General Smuts*, 2 vols. (London: Faber & Faber,
1936); and Smuts' *Autobiography: Jan Christian Smuts*
(New York: William Morrow, 1952).
  Cf. Guinn, 291; Taylor, 308; Busch, 285.
  Reviews: *H* 48 (1963):255-6, J.L. McCraken; *JMH* 35
(1963):88-9, P.D. Curtin.

162. Hancock, William Keith, and Jean van der Poel. *Selec-*
    tions from the Smuts Papers. 7 volumes. Cambridge:
    Cambridge University Press, 1966-73.

The first four volumes cover the period 1886-1919,
roughly the years covered in volume one of Hancock's
biography of Smuts discussed above. The volumes contain letters to and from friends and political acquain-
tances that reflect Smuts' life, thought and experiences. Interesting material especially on World War I
and Smuts' support of the Zionist cause after the war.
  Reviews: *AHR* 72 (1967):665-6, H. Duncan Hall; *AHR* 80
(1975):979-80, H. Duncan Hall; *EHR* 90 (1975):232-3,
A.F. Madden; *MES* 4 (1967):113-4, Elie Kedourie; *PSQ* 83
(1968):99-101, David Owen.

* Hankey, Maurice. *The Supreme Command, 1914-1918*.
    Cited as item 292.

163. Hardinge, Charles. *Old Diplomacy: The Reminiscences*
    of Lord Hardinge of Penhurst. London: Murray, 1947.
    xi + 288 pp.

Hardinge was a career diplomat who served in a variety of diplomatic posts overseas, as Viceroy to India,
1910-1916, and as Permanent Under-Secretary of State
for Foreign Affairs. Among his many posts, Hardinge
was Charge d'Affaires at the British Legation in Tehran
in the late 19th century. His account of the affairs

of Persia, the conduct of British and Russian relations in Iran, and his later depictions of the ins-and-outs of diplomacy are illuminating. Complement this study with Sir Henry Drummond-Wolff, *Rambling Recollections*, 2 vols. (London: Macmillan, 1908); and *The Letters and Friendships of Sir Cecil Spring-Rice: A Record*, 2 vols., edited by Stephen Gwynn (Boston: Houghton-Mifflin, 1929), works that cover aspects of British diplomacy in Persia and the Middle East in the late 19th and 20th centuries. Both Wolff and Spring-Rice were British ministers to Persia, in 1889-91 and 1905-7, respectively. In addition see Martin Gilbert, *Horace Rumbold*, item 157; Agatha Ramm, *Sir Robert Morier: Envoy and Ambassador in the Age of Imperialism, 1876-1893* (Oxford: Clarendon Press, 1973); and Arthur Hardinge, *A Diplomatist in the East* (London: Jonathan Cape, 1928), for studies of diplomats and how their opinions can affect policy or relations between nations.
Cf. Steiner, 139; Goold, 354; Grey, 160; Nicolson, 182.

164.   Higgins, Trumbull. *Winston Churchill and the Dardanelles: A Dialogue in Ends and Means*. New York: Macmillan, 1963. xi + 308 pp.

A damning account of Churchill's strategic vision and of the value of the Dardanelles campaign as a measure for ending World War I more quickly. Surveys briefly developments in British strategic and naval thinking and views on the importance of the Straits before World War I, and then examines the political process by which the decision to attack the Dardanelles was reached. Is very much taken up with the Westerners view of the war that saw an attempt outside Europe to get at Germany as so much wasted effort. Rather tendentious, and settles nothing. If the Dardanelles had succeeded...?
Cf. James, 165 and 313; Guinn, 291; Hazelhurst, 295; Hankey, 292; Gilbert, 156.
Reviews: *AHR* 69 (1964):748-9, Henry Winkler.

165.   James, Robert Rhodes. *Churchill: A Study in Failure, 1900-1939*. London: Weidenfeld & Nicolson, 1970. xvi + 372 pp.

Studies Churchill the politician and evaluates his performance in terms of ideals and goals versus achievements and failures. Churchill had a meteoric career, going up rapidly before World War I, declining drama-

tically during the War and after, and then suddenly
catapulted into prominence again on the eve of World
War II. Details the inner-political life of Churchill
and his relations with the political leadership, dwells
on Churchill's activities during World War I--the clash
with Fisher, the Dardanelles fiasco, the fall of Asquith
--but devotes little attention to Churchill's activities
while at the Colonial Office on the Middle East, though
there is no information on the politics of the Chanak
Affair.

Cf. James, 313; Hazelhurst, 295; Churchill, 153;
Beaverbrook, 144; Taylor, 308; Hankey, 292; Walder,
316.

166.   James, Robert Rhodes. *Rosebery: A Biography of Archi-
       bald Philip, Fifth Earl of Rosebery.* London: Weiden-
       feld & Nicolson, 1963. xiv + 534 pp.

Rosebery was the sometime-leader of the Liberal Party
in the late 1800's and early 1900's after the departure
and death of Gladstone. Rosebery was the spiritual
leader of the "Limps," the Liberal-Imperialists, that
element of the Liberal Party interested in strengthen-
ing the empire, but never fulfilled the expectations
of his supporters and abdicated leadership of the party
to Campbell-Bannerman.

For a study of Rosebery and Liberal-Imperialism, see
Peter Jacobson, "Rosebery and Liberal-Imperialism, 1899-
1903," *Journal of British Studies* 13 (1973):83-107, who
argues that Liberal-Imperialism was a device used by
some elements within the Liberal Party to capture control of the party. For a study of Liberal Party in-
fighting, see Peter Stansky, *Ambitions and Strategies:
The Struggles for Leadership of the Liberal Party in
the 1890's* (Oxford: Clarendon Press, 1964).

Cf. Searle, 105; Semmel, 106; Matthew, 178; Wilson,
190; Shannon, 107.

Reviews: *EHR* 80 (1965):197-8, Peter Marshall; *H* 48
(1963):395-6, Christopher Howard.

167.   Judd, Denis. *Balfour and the British Empire: A Study
       in Imperial Evolution, 1874-1932.* New York: St.
       Martin's Press, 1968. 392 pp.

"Balfour was perpetually able to see both sides of a
problem. Unfortunately he was not always ready to make
decisions." (p. 15) Balfour had a long and varied ca-

reer, being Prime Minister halfway through his career,
from 1902–1906, and then holding a number of positions
afterwards, including Foreign Secretary in the Lloyd
George government, 1916–1920. He was a guiding figure
in attempts to promote imperial unity and develop more
coordination in imperial defence. This theme is well-
studied in relation to plans for military reform and
the Committee of Imperial Defence, the South African
War, the collision with Chamberlain over tariff reform,
and the policies and attitudes towards India, the Colonies and the Dominions. Tends to concentrate too much
on personalities, lacks a clear definition of ideas of
empire, and is a bit brisk in handling some subjects,
such as the origins of the Balfour Declaration and
Balfour's role in World War I. See Alfred Gollin,
*Balfour's Burden: Arthur Balfour and Imperial Prefer-
ence* (London: Blond, 1965), for a more detailed look
at the problems of imperial unity and free trade. Two
less satisfactory works on Balfour are Sydney Zebel,
Balfour: A Political Biography (Cambridge: Cambridge
University Press, 1973); and Kenneth Young, *Arthur James
Balfour*, item 193.

   Cf. Johnson, 123; Kendle, 124; Searle, 105; d'Ombrain,
082; Gollin, 158.

   Reviews: *EHR* 85 (1970):870–1, D.K. Fieldhouse; *H* 54
(1969):439–40, Peter Fraser.

168. Judd, Denis. *Radical Joe: A Life of Joseph Chamberlain.*
      London: Hamilton, 1977. xvi + 310 pp.

   Joseph Chamberlain epitomized the crisis in British
imperial thinking and helped shape that crisis. The
decline in Britain's world power and the rise of powerful competitors aroused concern for the survival of the
empire and drove generations of imperialists, from scholars to politicians, to propound on the nature of the
problem and to seek remedies. One of these seekers, a
convert, was Joseph Chamberlain, who sought to combine
ideas of socialism with imperial unity. Judd examines
Chamberlain's career and analyzes his successes and
failures, in particular Chamberlain's role in the Boer
War and the fight for tariff reform. A sympathetic
biography.

   For more detailed studies of Chamberlain's views on
empire, see Peter Fraser, *Joseph Chamberlain: Radicalism and Empire, 1868–1914* (London: Cassell, 1969); and
Richard Rempel, *Unionists Divided: Arthur Balfour and
Joseph Chamberlain and the Unionist Free Traders*

(Newton Abbot [England]: David & Charles, 1972). For
Chamberlain's activities as Colonial Secretary and the
influence of Lord Milner, see Robert Kubichek, *The Administration of Imperialism: Joseph Chamberlain at the
Colonial Office* (Durham, N.C.: Duke University Press,
1969). For details on Chamberlain and tariff reform,
see Sydney Zebel, "Joe Chamberlain and the Genesis of
Tariff Reform," *Journal of British Studies* 7 (1967):
131-157.
   Cf. Amery, 145; Searle, 105; Semmel, 106; Monger,
098; Robinson, 072; Gollin, 158.

169. Koss, Stephen Edward. *John Morley at the India Office,
      1905-1910*. New Haven, Conn.: Yale University Press,
      1969. viii + 231 pp.

   The crisis of empire touched individuals and they influenced their surroundings. The need for greater coordination in imperial defence produced reforms in virtually every area of government, and John Morley (Secretary of State for India, 1905-1910), reacting to this
mood, and a personal interest in seeing the empire based
on Liberal principles, sought to limit the traditional
independence of the Government of India and subordinate
its foreign policy to the imperatives as seen from London. Koss studies Morley's political career, his attitudes towards India and Indians, his efforts at reform
in India, and his determination to subordinate the
Viceroy's policies to Whitehall.
   Two other studies complement the views developed here:
see D.A. Hamer, *John Morley: Liberal Intellectual in
Politics* (Oxford: Clarendon Press, 1968), which deals
more thoroughly with Morley's life, career, and his
writings; and Stanley L. Wolpert, *Morley and India,
1906-1910* (Berkeley: University of California Press,
1967), which is an excellent study of the Morley-Minto
reforms and imperial decline. Also see Edward Alexander, *John Morley* (New York: Twayne, 1972); and M.N.
Das, *India under Morley and Minto* (London: Allen &
Unwin, 1964).
   Cf. Hardinge, 163.
   Reviews: *AHR* 75 (1970):1120-1, Robert Crane; *BSOAS*
34 (1971):174-5, P.D. Reeves; *H* 55 (1970):298-300,
D.A. Hamer; *JAS* 3 (1970):199-200, Milton Israel; *JMH*
42 (1970):687-8, Peter Stansky.

170. Koss, Stephen Edward. *Lord Haldane: Scapegoat for Lib-
      eralism*. New York: Columbia University Press, 1969.
      ix + 263 pp.

Richard Burdon, Viscount Haldane (1856-1928), was a prominent Liberal, a "Roseberyite" Liberal-Imperialist, and one of the leading elements in attempts to reform the army along modern lines after 1900. He was also an admirer of aspects of German culture, and had urged a rapprochement with Germany before World War I. These sympathies may have been the cause of his being dropped by his friend Asquith from the coalition government formed in May 1915. Koss examines Haldane's philosophy, his political activities, his years at the War Office (1906-1915) and his army reforms, the coming of the war and the attacks on Haldane as pro-German, the circumstances of his departure from government and his subsequent return to favor in the 1920's. Underlying this is a study of the collapse of the Liberal Party, the decline of its morale and sense of purpose. The best study of Haldane's army reforms, though unreliable on other points, is Sir Frederick Maurice's *Haldane, 1856-1915: The Life of Viscount Haldane of Cloan, K.I., O.M.* (London: Faber & Faber, 1937); a general study on Haldane's life is Dudley Sommer, *Haldane of Cloan: His Life and Times, 1856-1928* (London: Allen & Unwin, 1960). Also see Haldane's *Autobiography* (London: Hodder & Stoughton, 1931). In addition see Peter Rowland, *The Last Liberal Governments: The Promised Land, 1905-1910* (London· Cresset Press, 1968), which discusses the problems of Liberalism as well as defence planning and army reform.

Cf. Bond, 110; Monger, 098; Johnson, 123; Dunlop, 112; Shannon, 107; Steiner, 307.

Reviews: *AHR* 75 (1970):852-4, Mary Mack; *EHR* 86 (1971):196-7, C.L. Mowat; *H* 55 (1970):150-1, Arthur Marwick; *JMH* 42 (1970):430-5, Robert Rhodes James.

171.   Lawrence, Thomas Edward. *Seven Pillars of Wisdom: A Triumph*. London: Jonathan Cape, 1935.   672 pp.

The controversial figure of Lawrence still attracts and repels, still springs most readily to Western minds that turn to the Middle East and the Arab Revolt. The *Seven Pillars* remains a stunning evocation and a piece of literature, an excellent memoir, though its historical accuracy is questionable. For a collection of Lawrence's articles between 1917 and 1922 on the Arabs and the Middle East that are less romantic and self-serving, see Stanley and Rodelle Wintraub, editors, *Evolution of a Revolt: Early Postwar Writings* (University Park, Penn.: Pennsylvania State University Press,

1968). Also see Lawrence's *Revolt in the Desert* (Garden City, N.Y.: Doubleday, 1927). For a study of the stylistic and intellectual elements that influenced Lawrence in writing *Seven Pillars*, see Jeffrey Meyers, *The Wounded Spirit: A Study of "Seven Pillars"* (London: Brian and O'Keeffe, 1973).

The literature on Lawrence is extensive, some of it lurid, some of it disappointingly simplistic. For a brief overview of Lawrence's Middle Eastern career and the literature on him, see Linda Tarver, "In Wisdom's House: T.E. Lawrence in the Near East," *Journal of Contemporary History* 13 (1978):585-608; and Uriel Dann, "Lawrence of Arabia--One More Appraisal," *Middle Eastern Studies* 15 (1979):154-62. For one of the best overall studies, which is a psychological analysis of Lawrence's character and of his impact, see John Mack, *A Prince of Our Disorder: The Life of T.E. Lawrence* (London: Weidenfeld & Nicolson, 1976). The standard biography of Lawrence's military exploits is Basil Liddell Hart's *T.E. Lawrence: In Arabia and After* (London: Jonathan Cape, 1934), published in America as *Colonel Lawrence: The Man Behind the Legend* (New York: Dodd & Mead, 1934). Other works include Phillip Knightly and Colin Simpson, *The Secret Lives of Lawrence of Arabia* (London: Nelson, 1969), and Knightley's brief *Lawrence of Arabia* (London: Sedqueck & Jackson, 1976); Peter Brent, *T.E. Lawrence* (London: Weidenfeld & Nicolson, 1975), which is a book for young students; Desmond Stewart, *T.E. Lawrence* (London: Hamish Hamilton, 1977), which attacks the Lawrence mystique, and along with Richard Aldington's *Lawrence of Arabia: A Biographical Inquiry* (London: Collins, 1955), is among the most unsympathetic views. Also see the quaint work by Paul J. Marriott, *Oxford's Legendary Son--The Young Lawrence of Arabia, 1888-1910* (Oxford: Blackwell's, n.d.); and Lowell Thomas, *With Lawrence in Arabia* (New York: Century, 1924). An Arab view that debunks Lawrence's image as a friend of the Arabs is Suleiman Mousa, *T.E. Lawrence: An Arab View* (London: Oxford University Press, 1966). For a quick reference guide to the literature by and on Lawrence, see Frank Clements, *T.E. Lawrence: A Reader's Guide* (Plymouth: Latimer Trend, 1973), which surveys the extensive bibliography on Lawrence and on World War I in the Middle East.

Cf. Antonius, 430; Clements, 004; Busch, 352; Kedourie, 345.

172. Lloyd George, David. *War Memoirs of David Lloyd George.*
      6 volumes. Boston: Little, Brown, 1933-37.

      One of the most colorful and controversial of all
      British politicians, around whose name charges of scan-
      dal, ruthlessness, and underhandedness still circulate.
      Lloyd George was a skillful organizer and adept politi-
      cian, whose clear-sightedness during World War I was a
      certain contribution to Britain's war effort. As Prime
      Minister from 1916 to 1922, he restructured the Cabinet
      so that it could cope with the war more efficiently.
      He alienated many military leaders, especially Field-
      Marshalls William Robertson and Henry Wilson, with his
      tactics and his advocacy of "sideshow" campaigns. He
      also undermined the independence of the Foreign Office
      by pursuing policies of his own without consulting his
      Foreign Secretary, A.J. Balfour. His memoirs make in-
      teresting reading, but coming as they did after most
      other war memoirs, especially of those of some of his
      critics, they have an aura of self-righteous justifica-
      tion. Compare his views of the fall of the Asquith
      Government with Beaverbrook, item 144; Asquith, item
      146; and Churchill, 153; and his views of the military
      conduct of the war with Robertson, 185. Also see Lloyd
      George, *Memoirs of the Peace Conference* [English title:
      The Truth About the Peace Treaties], 2 vols. (New
      Haven, Conn.: Yale University Press, 1939).
      Cf. Davis, 286; Hazelhurst, 295; McEwen, 302; Gilbert,
      156.

*   McEwen, J.M. "The Struggle for Mastery in Britain--
      Lloyd George versus Asquith, December, 1916." Cited
      as item 302.

173. MacKay, Ruddock F. *Fisher of Kilverstone.* Oxford:
      Clarendon Press, 1973. xvi + 539 pp.

      John Arbuthnot Fisher (1841-1920) was one of the
      first leaders in Britain to see the crisis of empire as
      one of having to choose where to defend the empire, that
      an all-over defence was beyond the means of imperial re-
      sources in the face of rising challenges. Fisher per-
      ceived this and had a talent for technical evaluation
      that he put to use to reform the British navy, putting
      it on a firm path towards modernization, making the
      fleet a first-class fighting force. MacKay examines
      Fisher's training, the influences that shaped his ideas,
      his career in the navy and as First Sea Lord, his fail-

ure to grasp the necessity of a Naval Staff for war
planning, and his role in the Dardanelles campaign. An
excellent, sensitive study. The official biography of
Fisher is Admiral Sir R.H. Bacon, *The Life of Lord
Fisher of Kilverstone*, 2 vols. (London: Hodder & Stoughton, 1929), though it has been superseded by a more
popularized biography by Richard Hough, *First Sea Lord:
An Authorized Biography of Admiral Lord Fisher*, 2nd edition (London: Severn House, 1977). Some of Fisher's
papers covering his efforts on naval reform are contained in the *Papers of Sir John Fisher*, 2 vols., edited by Peter Kemp (London: Navy Records Society, 1964).
The largest published collection of Fisher's correspondence is edited by A.J. Marder, item 175. See Fisher's
Memoirs (London: Hodder & Stoughton, 1919) for his personal views on politics and reform.
　　Cf. Marder, 131; Kennedy, 125; Woodward, 279; Gilbert,
156; Johnson, 123.
　　Reviews: *AHR* 80 (1975):979, Raymond Callahan; *EHR* 90
(1975):938-9, Paul M. Kennedy.

174.　Mackintosh, John Pitcairn, editor. *Balfour to Chamber-
　　　lain. British Prime Ministers in the Twentieth Cen-
　　　tury*, Vol. 1. London: Weidenfeld & Nicolson, 1977.
　　　288 pp.

　　　A collection of essays on 20th century British Prime
Ministers in two volumes. Volume 1 contains, among
others, essays on Arthur Balfour by Peter Fraser, Henry
Campbell-Bannerman by José F. Harris and Cameron Hazelhurst, H.H. Asquith by Cameron Hazelhurst, and on David
Lloyd George by Kenneth O. Morgan. The essays concentrate on the personalities of the Prime Ministers, their
intra-party relations, their handling of the government
machinery, and their dealings with Parliament. Fraser's
study of Balfour examines aspects of the development of
the Committee for Imperial Defence, and the studies on
Asquith and Lloyd George have useful observations on
political intrigues in the Liberal Government during
World War I (see McEwen, item 302). Handy, brief
sketches and surveys.
　　Cf. James, 092; Watt, 189.
　　Reviews: *AHR* 83 (1978):1017, Henry R. Winkler.

175.　Marder, Arthur Jacob, editor. *Fear God and Dread
　　　Nought: The Correspondence of Admiral of the Fleet,
　　　Lord Fisher of Kilverstone*. 3 volumes. London:
　　　Jonathan Cape, 1952.

Marder has collected a broad range of Fisher's letters
that cover his career and reflect his wit and intelligence, his vision, and his relationships with friends
and enemies. Volume 1, *The Making of an Admiral, 1854-
1904*, is divided into two parts, covering Fisher's ap-
prenticeship and his rise to influence. Volume 2,
Years of Power, 1904-1914, covers Fisher's activities
as First Sea Lord and his efforts to reform the navy.
Volume 3, *Restoration, Abdication, and Last Years,
1914-1920*, deals with Fisher's return to the Admiralty
during the war, his clash with Churchill over the Dardanelles and his resignation. Each section of letters
is introduced by a brief summary of the major events
that were the subjects of Fisher's comments or barks.
Fisher's letters make excellent reading.

Cf. Marder, 131; MacKay, 173.
Reviews: *JMH* 27 (1955):428, and 30 (1958):405, Wayne
Stevens.

*   Marlowe, John. *Cromer in Egypt*. Cited as item 382.

176.   Marlowe, John. *Milner, Apostle of Empire: A Life of
        Alfred George, the Right Honourable Viscount Milner
        of St. James's and Cape Town, K.G., G.C.B., G.C.M.G.,
        1854-1925*. London: Hamilton, 1976. xi + 394 pp.

Studies the shaping of Milner's character and ideas,
his political activities to give effect to his imperial
vision, his activities in South Africa, the "Kinder-
garden," his years out of power after the Boer War, his
role in World War I, and his career in Egypt. A good,
general study. A more academic study is Terence H.
O'Brien, *Milner: Viscount Milner of St. James's and Cape
Town, 1854-1925* (London: Constable, 1979). On various
aspects of Milner's views on empire and his efforts to
foster a "school" of imperially-minded administrators
and propagandists, see Vladimir Halperin, *Lord Milner
and the Empire: The Evolution of British Imperialism*
(London: Oldhams Press, 1952); John Kendle, *The Round
Table Movement and Imperial Union* (Toronto: Toronto
University Press, 1975); and Walter Nimocks, *Milner's
Young Men: The Kindergarten in Edwardian Imperial Affairs* (Durham, N.C.: Duke University Press, 1968). A
useful but limited collection of Milner's papers in two
volumes is Cecil Headlam, editor, *Milner Papers, 1897-
1905* (London: Cassell, 1931-33).

Cf. Gollin, 158; Judd, 168; Shannon, 107; Robinson,
072; Hazelhurst, 295.

177. Marlowe, John. *Late Victorian: The Life of Sir Arnold Talbot Wilson.* London: Cresset, 1967. xii + 418 pp.

Arnold Wilson (1884-1940) spent much of his career in the Indian Political Service in the Persian Gulf, and his book *The Persian Gulf* (London: Allen & Unwin, 1928), is a classic study of the area and of the rise of British interests. After World War I Wilson became Acting Civil Commissioner in British-controlled Mesopotamia, eventually to become the mandate of Iraq. Wilson's tenure was clouded by controversy surrounding Arab revolts in 1920, and Wilson's handling of them led to his replacement. A sympathetic biography that follows Wilson to his death during World War II. See Wilson's account of his experiences in Mesopotamia, item 358.
Cf. Graves, 159; Sluglett, 357; Busch, 352; Monroe, 304; Klieman, 298; Winstone, 192.
Reviews: *GJ* 133 (1967):564.

178. Matthew, Henry Colin Gray. *The Liberal Imperialists: The Ideas and Politics of a Post-Gladstonian Élite.* Oxford Historical Monographs. London: Oxford University Press, 1973. xvi + 331 pp.

Explores the ideology and actions of a diverse group within the Liberal Party, mainly drawn from young Liberals, who sought to reconsider Liberal principles and restore the Party's strength, unity, sense of purpose, and leadership in the late 19th century when the Liberal Party was out of power and racked by internal strife following Gladstone's departure and death. The principal "Lib-Imps" or "Limps" were Richard Burdon Haldane, Herbert Henry Asquith, Edward Grey, and the 5th Earl of Rosebery. They aimed at regenerating the empire as well as a host of other reforms. Matthew examines this group, their ideas and attempts to gain control of the Liberal Party and win control of the government, concentrating on the period 1895-1905. On Lord Rosebery, see Robert Rhodes James, item 166. On the careers of Asquith, Haldane and Grey, see Spender, 187; Koss, item 170; and Robbins, item 184; respectively. Also see T. Boyle, "The Liberal Imperialists, 1892-1906," *Bulletin of the Institute of Historical Research* 52 (1979):48-82, for a detailed breakdown of the imperial elements in the Liberal Party.
Cf. Searle, 105; Semmel, 106; Shannon, 107; Beloff, 080; Porter, 183.

Reviews: *AHR* 79 (1974):152-3, Bernard Semmel; *EHR* 89
(1974):919-20, Trevor Lloyd; *H* 60 (1975):138-9, Paul
Smith; *PSQ* 88 (1973):713-24, Stephen Koss.

179. Mellini, Peter. *Sir Eldon Gorst: The Overshadowed Pro-
      consul*. Hoover Colonial Studies. Edited by Peter
      Duignan, et al. Stanford, California: Hoover Insti-
      tute Press, 1977. xxv + 316 pp.

Eldon Gorst had the misfortune of succeeding Lord
Cromer, whose majesterial presence obscured the fact
that when he left Egypt problems associated with his
policies were beginning to emerge. Gorst, an unpopular
figure in British circles to begin with, was left with
the unwelcome task of coping with economic problems and
growing restiveness in the Egyptian population. In addition, much of Cromer's administrative structure had
been geared to his personality and did not respond to
new leadership. Problems compounded and Gorst was held
responsible. Mellini's study of Gorst's personality
and his abilities is the only monograph on Gorst; it
is useful but not definitive.
     Cf. Tignor, 390; Vatikiotis, 391; Holt, 378; al-
Sayyid, 387; Marlowe, 381; Mansfield, 381.
     Reviews: *AHR* 83 (1978):1012-3, Robert Heussler; *MEJ*
34 (1980):78-9, Arthur Goldschmidt, Jr.

180. Monroe, Elizabeth. *Philby of Arabia*. London: Faber &
      Faber, 1973. 322 pp.

An exploration of H. St. John Philby's character and
career (1885-1960). Philby journeyed to Arabia and the
Levant with the British army in World War I to make war
on the Turks and remained among the Arabs for most of
his life. Philby joined Sir Percy Cox's staff in 1915
and was to use his linguistic talents to work among the
Arabs to win their support for Britain's war effort.
Philby, following Captain Shakespear (see item 191),
was sent to ibn Saud to seek his support. Thus began
the "Arabization" of Philby. Monroe examines Philby's
career among the Arabs, his friendship with ibn Saud,
personal peccadilloes and his influence of lack of influence on British policy among the Arabs. Philby made
less of an impression on the popular mind than Lawrence,
but he was more of a friend to the Arabs, though not
particularly well-liked by his biographer. The bibliography and guide to archival sources is very useful.
     Philby was also a prolific writer. Among his works
see *The Heart of Arabia*, 2 vols. (London: Constable,

1922), which deals with his exploits in Arabia during World War I; and *Arabia and the Wahhabis* (London: Constable, 1928), which completes his account of his exploits with ibn Saud's army during World War I. Also see *Arabian Days: An Autobiography* (London: Robert Hale, 1938), which is a general recounting of his life and adventures.

Cf. Graves, 159; Marlow, 177; Winstone, 192; Wilson, 358; Busch, 352; Monroe, 304; Sluglett, 357; Troeller, 411.

Reviews: *BSOAS* 37 (1974):469-70, C.F. Beckingham; *MEJ* 28 (1974):187-8, William Sands; *MES* 13 (1977):144-5, J.B. Kelly.

181. Nicolson, Harold George. *Curzon: The Last Phase, 1919-1925: A Study in Post-War Diplomacy.* London: Constable, 1934. xvi + 416 pp.

George N. Curzon had a vision of achieving the empire's permanent security. A "pro-consul" of the old school, he had urged a forward policy of imperial defence, mainly for protecting India from Russia; and as Viceroy in the late 19th and early 20th centuries he had endeavored to force the Home Government to undertake a vigorous defence posture. After World War I Curzon became Foreign Secretary and saw an opportunity to capitalize on Britain's post-war victory and the collapse of Russia to achieve his dream and create a chain of buffer states in the east to permanently shield India and British routes east from foreign threats. Unfortunately for Curzon his vision ran counter to the prevailing views of his contemporaries or to the realities of British power. Curzon found it impossible to settle with Turkey or Persia, or convince his colleagues of the necessity of more vigorous military measures to forestall the Bolsheviks and defend the empire in southern Russia. Nicolson examines Curzon's frustration over Turkey and Persia and his relations with his cabinet colleagues. Newly available documents make much of this work outdated, but it is still a perceptive view of Curzon and the nature of policy formation. Curzon's views are made clear in his monumental work on Persia, *Persia and the Persian Question*, item 412.

The standard biography of Curzon is Lord Ronaldshay, *The Life of Lord Curzon*, 3 vols. (London: Benn, 1928). A detailed study of Curzon's years in India and his views on empire is David Dilks, *Curzon in India*, 2 vols. (London: Rupert Hart-Davis, 1969-70), which updates

Lovat Fraser's *India under Curzon and After* (London: Heineman, 1911). A more general biography of Curzon's life and his environment is Kenneth Rose's *Superior Person: A Portrait of Curzon and His Circle in Late Victorian England* (London: Weidenfeld & Nicolson, 1969).

Cf. Busch, 285; Olson, 424; Klieman, 298; Walder, 316; Jeffrey, 296.

182. Nicolson, Harold George. *Sir Arthur Nicolson, Bart., First Lord Carnock: A Study in the Old Diplomacy.* London: Constable, 1930. xvi + 456 pp.

Nicolson's biography of his father. A study of Arthur Nicolson's career as diplomat and as Permanent Under-Secretary at the Foreign Office, 1910-1916. Contains useful information on Nicolson's views and his role in the crucial negotiations with the French and the Russians that formed the basis for the Triple Entente. Nicolson believed adamantly in the necessity of an Anglo-Russian rapprochement, and worked assiduously to promote and maintain it, despite reasons to doubt its utility.

Cf. Steiner, 137 and 138; Grey, 160; Hardinge, 163; Cohen, 394 and 217.

183. Porter, Bernard. *Critics of Empire: British Radical Attitudes to Colonialism in Africa 1895-1914.* New York: Macmillan, 1968. xvi + 369 pp.

J.A. Hobson was the best-known critic of British imperial expansion in the late 19th and early 20th centuries, but there are many others who attacked the motives and methods of empire, some in a continuing free trade heritage, others for socialistic principles. Porter examines this vocal, if rather small group, tracing the origins of their ideas and their influence and impact. Provides an interesting critique of Hobson's arguments, and gives an excellent survey of the Radical critique of empire. On other aspects of Radical critics of empire, see Howard Weinroth, "The British Radicals and the Balance of Power, 1902-1914," *Historical Journal* 13 (1970):653-82; "Left-wing Opposition to Naval Armaments in Britain before 1914," *Journal of Contemporary History* 6 (1971):93-120; and "British Radicals and the Agadir Crisis," *European Studies Review* 3 (1973):39-61. In addition see A.J. Anthony Morris, *Radicalism Against War, 1904-1914: The Advocacy of Peace and Retrenchment* (London: Longmans, 1972). For a general study of the role of critics in influencing policy, see the provocative essays by A.J.P. Taylor in *The Trouble Makers: Dissent Over Foreign Policy, 1792-1939* (London: Hamish Hamilton, 1957).

Cf. Searle, 105; Semmel, 075 and 106; Thornton, 109; Shannon, 107; Robbins, 184; Lloyd, 065; Kemp, 060.

Reviews: *EHR* 84 (1969):873, D.K. Fieldhouse; *H* 54 (1969):317-8, John Hargreaves; *HJ* 13 (1970):809-11, D.W. Harkness; *PSQ* 86 (1971):324-5, Raymond Betts.

184. Robbins, Keith. *Sir Edward Grey: A Biography of Lord Grey of Falloden*. London: Cassell, 1971. xvii + 438 pp.

Grey left no extensive collection of private papers, so a biography is difficult. Robbins overcomes this disadvantage and examines Grey's public and private life, showing him to be an astute, tough-minded politician, and not the myopic, fly-fisherman of legend. As Foreign Secretary (1906-1916), Grey was a force in international affairs, and his fear of Germany (enhanced by a coterie of Germanophobes at the Foreign Office and in key embassies, such figures as Arthur Nicolson, Charles Hardinge, Eyre Crowe, and Francis Bertie) led him to push for Anglo-French, Anglo-Russian ententes that became the basis of British foreign policy before World War I. Compare with Zara Steiner's views of Grey in *Britain and the Origins of World War I*, item 307. For a study of Grey's view of empire, see Robbins' "Sir Edward Grey and the British Empire," *Journal of Imperial and Commonwealth History* 1 (1973):213-21. Also see Grey's own memoirs, *Twenty-Five Years*, item 160.

Cf. Steiner, 137; Hinsley, 086; Lowe, 095; Searle, 105; Greaves, 248; Shannon, 107; Taylor, 209.

Reviews: *EHR* 88 (1973):468-9, Kenneth Morgan; *H* 57 (1972):460-1, Zara Steiner.

185. Robertson, William. *Soldiers and Statesmen, 1914-1918*. 2 volumes. New York: Scribner, 1926.

Field-Marshall Sir William Robertson became Chief of the Imperial General Staff in late 1915. His account of the inner workings of the British war effort—his assessment of Kitchener's one-man-show mentality, his views on the clumsiness of Asquith's cabinet in dealing with war planning, his opinions of the uselessness of sideshow campaigns outside Europe, his views on civilian-military relations, and his observations on the chief

personalities in the government, their relations with
one another and their conduct of war—is an invaluable
"insider's" memoir. As with all memoirs it is self-
serving, but it provides useful observations and gives
insight into how Robertson, himself, viewed events.
Needs to be contrasted with Lloyd George's memoirs,
item 172; Churchill, item 153; Beaverbrook, item 144;
and Hankey, item 292. Also see Robertson's autobiography, *From Private to Field-Marshall* (London: Constable, 1921). For a brief view comparing civilian-
military views of war aims, and Robertson's relations
with Lloyd George, see John Gooch, "Soldiers, Strategy
and War Aims in Britain, 1914-1918," in Barry Hunt and
Adrian Preston, editors, *War Aims and Strategic Policy
in the Great War, 1914-1918* (London: Croom Helms, 1977).
On Robertson's career, see V. Bonham Carter, *The Life
and Times of Field-Marshall Sir William Robertson, 1860-
1933* (London: Muller, 1963).

Cf. Cassar, 151; Guinn, 291; Liddell Hart, 294;
Roskill, 186; Taylor, 308; Howard, 089.

186.   Roskill, Stephen Wentworth. *Hankey, Man of Secrets.*
       3 volumes. London: Collins, 1970-73.

Maurice Hankey (1877-1963) was an influential man-
behind-the-scenes civil servant. His contribution to
the organization of staff work on the Committee of Imperial Defence before World War I and his organization
of the Cabinet secretariat during the War, plus his expert knowledge of military affairs, made him an *eminence
grise* to a succession of governments and politicians
through the post-World War II era. Roskill examines in
detail Hankey's career, and evaluates his contributions.
A thorough, in-depth study, that occasionally loses
track of Hankey the man. Volume 1 covers Hankey's career to the end of World War I. An essential work that
provides insight into behind-the-scenes government and
the importance of personalities and informal politics.
Hankey's own account of his activities during the war,
item 292, is an excellent study in its own right.
Roskill provides information on relevant archival
sources, has copious footnotes but lacks a bibliography.

Cf. Lloyd George, 172; Asquith, 146; Beaverbrook, 144;
Churchill, 153; Hazelhurst, 295; Johnson, 123; Gooch,
114; Guinn, 291.

Reviews: (vol. 1): *EHR* 88 (1973):220-1, Christopher
Andrew; *H* 56 (1971):132-3, John Gooch; *HJ* 13 (1970):
807-9, John Naylor; (vol. 2): *H* 58 (1973):323, John

Gooch; *HJ* 16 (1973):650-2, John Naylor; *JICH* 1 (1972): 127, Ian Nish; (vol. 3): *AHR* 80 (1975):646-8, Paul Guinn; *EHR* 90 (1975):863-6, Christopher Andrew; *H* 60 (1975):492-3, Paul Addison.

*   al-Sayyid, Afaf Lutfi. *Egypt under Cromer: A Study in Anglo-Egyptian Relations.* Cited as item 387.

*   Skrine, Clarmont. *World War in Iran.* Cited as item 326.

187.   Spender, J.A., and Cyril Asquith. *Life of Herbert Henry Asquith, Lord Oxford and Asquith.* 2 volumes. London: Hutchinson, 1932.

The official history of the life and works of H.H. Asquith (1852-1928) and his political career in the Liberal Party. Volume 1 covers his career to 1911; volume 2 covers his performance as Prime Minister during World War I and follows his life to his death in 1928. For a more up-to-date, though not as thorough, biography see Roy Jenkins, *Asquith* (London: Collins, 1964). For an interesting insider's look at the Asquith Cabinet, see *Inside Asquith's Cabinet From the Diaries of Charles Hobhouse*, edited by Edward David (London: John Murray, 1977).
Cf. Asquith, 146; Hazelhurst, 295; McEwen, 302; Grey, 160; Beaverbrook, 144; Churchill, 153; Hankey, 292; James, 092; Gilbert, 156; Matthew, 178.

188.   Storrs, Ronald. *Orientations.* London: Ivor Nicolson & Watson, 1939. xvii + 557 pp.

Storrs worked in Cromer's Egypt, and then for his successors, teaching the Egyptians to appreciate how they should run their own country. During the war Storrs was a member of the Arab Bureau and involved in the negotiations with Husayn, the Sharif of Mecca, to bring the Arabs into the war with Britain. Storrs recounts his Eastern experiences and the alarms and diversions of war. Given the confused nature of British policy towards the Arabs and Kedourie's observations on the state of the Arab Bureau's expertise, item 346, Storrs could have spent less time savoring Arabic at Cambridge (his expression) and more time studying it. An interesting first-hand account that can now be compared with more thorough recent scholarship.
Cf. Busch, 352; Kedourie, 345 and 333; Klieman, 298; Antonius, 430.

189. Watt, D.C. *Personalities and Policies: Studies in the*
      Formulation of British Foreign Policy in the Twen-
      tieth Century. London: Longmans, 1965. xii + 275 pp.

      A collection of essays by Watt, some of which appeared
      in other formats, on the formation of foreign policy in
      Britain. Most of the essays concern the period from
      the 1930's to the 1950's, but there is useful material
      on the era before World War I and on the interwar years.
      Watt does not concentrate on narrating what British pol-
      icies were, but on describing and analyzing the per-
      sonalities, pressure groups and influences that went
      into the formation of policy--an examination of the
      workings of "unspoken assumptions" (see James Joll,
      item 297). The first essay, "The Nature of the Foreign-
      Policy-Making Elite in Britain," 1-18, examines the
      "oligocratic" nature of British foreign policy, a "so-
      ciology" of the policy-making elite. Essay 7, "Impe-
      rial Defence Policy and Imperial Foreign Policy, 1911-
      39: The Substance and the Shadow," 139-58, examines the
      conflict between the necessities of policy as seen in
      Britain and as seen by the self-governing Dominions.
      Essays 12 and 13 are among the most useful, for they
      survey a wide variety of documentary sources, archival
      collections and published accounts in Britain and Amer-
      ica on aspects of foreign policy. There is also a
      brief survey of documentary materials in all European
      countries. The Appendix, 253-62, provides a list of
      the chief members in the policy-making elite. Useful,
      though most of the comments on available archival in-
      formation is now dated with the opening of more records.
        Cf. Butler, 029; Cook, 031; Gooch, 045; Woodward, 053.
        Reviews: *AHR* 71 (1966):916-7, Joachim Remak; *H* 51
      (1966):282-3, C.L. Mowat; *HJ* 6 (1966):154-5, D.W.
      Brogan.

*   Wilson, Arnold. *Loyalties: Mesopotamia, 1914-1920.*
      Cited as item 358.

190. Wilson, John. *C.B.: A Life of Sir Henry Campbell-*
      Bannerman. London: Constable, 1973. 718 pp.

      Explores the life and times of Campbell-Bannerman
      (1868-1908), tracing his political career and his role
      as leader of the Liberal Party after Gladstone's
      death and Rosebery's "abdication" (see item 166). A
      sympathetic biography, concentrating on political af-
      fairs, whose description of Campbell-Bannerman, as

"easy-going" is difficult to contrast with Campbell-Bannerman's maneuvering to control the Liberal Party, or his adroit deflection of the efforts of Haldane, Grey and Asquith, and other Liberal-Imperialists to use him as a front for their notions of government in 1906. See J.A. Spender, *The Life of the Rt. Hon. Sir Henry Campbell-Bannerman* (London: Hodder & Stoughton, 1923) for a more general, if dated, study. On the struggle for leadership within the Liberal Party, see Peter Stansky, *Ambitions and Strategies: The Struggle for the Leadership of the Liberal Party in the 1890's* (Oxford: Clarendon Press, 1961).

Cf. Hazelhurst, 295; Gilbert, 156; Shannon, 107; Porter, 183; Thornton, 109.

Review: *EHR* 89 (1974):923, P. Waller.

191.   Winstone, Harry Victor Frederick. *Captain Shakespear: A Portrait.* London: Jonathan Cape, 1976.   236 pp.

W.H.I. Shakespear was an Indian Political Officer in Kuwait and a friend of ibn Saud. When World War I broke out and it became likely that Turkey would join Germany, the British hoped to secure the support or neutrality of the Arabs. There was, however, no clear policy of what to do and whom to encourage. The Government of India did not want to involve the Arabs because of the inconvenient promises this would involve; while British officials in Egypt wanted to encourage an Arab revolt against the Turks and looked to Husayn, the Sharif of Mecca, as the best choice. India pursued relations with ibn Saud and Cairo with Husayn. Shakespear, who was sent to present British views to ibn Saud, was frustrated by his government's wavering, believing (as did Philby: see item 180) that ibn Saud should receive support. It failed to develop, and in the course of a battle between ibn Saud and a local rival, Shakespear was killed. Useful study, but flawed and rather light. For details on the muddle in British policy, see Briton Busch, *Britain, India and the Arabs*, item 352; and Elie Kedourie, *In the Anglo-Arab Labyrinth*, item 346.

Cf. Busch, 352; Monroe, 180; Wilson, 358; Silverfarb, 349; Troeller, 350; Barker, 351.

Reviews: *IJMES* 11 (1980):265-6, Elizabeth Monroe.

192.   Winstone, H.V.F. *Gertrude Bell.* London: Jonathan Cape, 1978.   xiii + 322 pp.

Gertrude Bell was a particular breed of Victorian who succumbed to the appeal of faraway places. Attracted

to the Middle East in the late 1890's, she acquired a
love of Persia, Arabia and the Levant that held her interest until her death in Iraq in 1926. Apart from being an intrepid explorer she worked for the Arab Bureau
during World War I and as an administrator in the British Mandate in Iraq until her death. Winstone, whose
biography is based on Bell's papers, is the first major
biography and almost alone in the field. It examines
Bell's ideas and attitudes, her relations with Sir Percy
Cox and Arnold Wilson, her views of Arab independence
and her activities in Iraq. Two less satisfactory studies are Josephine Kamm, *Daughter of the Desert: The
Story of Gertrude Bell* (London: Brodley Head, 1956);
and M.R. Ridley, *Gertrude Bell* (London: Blackie, 1941).
There are also two collections of Bell's letters:
Florence Bell, editor, *The Letters of Gertrude Bell*,
2 vols. (London: Benn, 1927); and Elizabeth Burgoyne,
Gertrude Bell: From Her Personal Papers, 2 vols. (London: Benn, 1958-61). Two of Bell's most interesting
and sensitive works are *Persian Pictures* (London:
Jonathan Cape, 1937); and *The Desert and the Sown* (London: Heinemann, 1907).
  Cf. Marlowe, 177; Wilson, 358; Graves, 159; Sluglett,
357; Bidwell, 403; Monroe, 180.

193. Young, Kenneth. *Arthur James Balfour: The Happy Life
      of the Politician, Prime Minister, Statesman and
      Philosopher, 1848-1930.* London: Bell, 1963. xxvi
      + 516 pp.

  Describes Balfour's career as a politician and contrasts this with Balfour's temperament and his intellectual and moral outlook. Balfour was a complex man,
whose intellectual habits and density of personality
made him seem distant and aloof, always half-amused or
bemused. Provides useful information on Balfour's
years as Prime Minister and leader of the Unionist wing
of the Conservative Party, his relations with Joseph
Chamberlain, his efforts at imperial reform and his activities during World War I. Not, however, a definitive biography. The standard biography, and still one
of the most perceptive studies of Balfour and the political element he moved in, is that by his niece, Blanche
Dugdale, *Arthur James Balfour, First Earl of Balfour,
K.G., O.M., P.R.S., Etc.*, item 154. An excellent study
of Balfour's relations with Chamberlain and his handling of the tariff reform issue is by Alfred Gollin,

Balfour's Burden: Arthur Balfour and Imperial Preference (London: Blond, 1965).

Cf. Judd, 167 and 168; Johnson, 123; Kendle, 124; Gooch, 114; Shannon, 107.

Reviews: *H* 48 (1963):395-6, Christopher Howard.

CHAPTER 3
INTERNATIONAL RIVALRY

International Rivalry, 1890-1914:
Britain and Its Rivals
in the Middle East

General

194. Albrecht-Carrié, René. *Diplomatic History of Europe
    Since the Congress of Vienna*. 2nd edition. London:
    Methuen, 1965. xvi + 736 pp.

    Surveys European diplomacy from 1815 to the 1950's.
    A thoughtful, general study with a Eurocentric bias but
    with useful information on European rivalry in the
    Middle East. Provides an international context for un-
    derstanding European diplomatic relations.
    Cf. Taylor, 209; Fisher, 359; Grenville, 085; Monger,
    098; Steiner, 307; Albertini, 284.

195. Anderson, Matthew Smith. *The Eastern Question, 1774-
    1923: A Study in International Relations*. London:
    Macmillan, 1966. xxi + 436 pp.

    The question of what to do with the Ottoman Empire
    was a nettle in European diplomacy for most of the 19th
    century. Ottoman weakness invited stronger powers to
    take advantage, but the various European powers kept an
    eye on one another lest anyone benefit too much from
    dismembering the Ottoman Empire. Anderson surveys the
    "Eastern Question," updating J.A.R. Marriott's *The
    Eastern Question: An Historical Study in European Di-
    plomacy* (Oxford: Clarendon, 1924); and adds an inter-
    national perspective to R.W. Seton-Watson's *Disraeli,
    Gladstone and the Eastern Question* (London: Macmillan,
    1935). Useful.
    Cf. Lewis, 477; Blaisdale, 273; Millman, 207; Jelavich,
    206; Shaw, 481; Taylor, 209; Kedourie, 333; Howard, 332.

Reviews: *AHR* 72 (1967):1345, L.S. Stavrianos; *MEJ* 21 (1967):409-10, Sydney N. Fisher; *PSQ* 83 (1968):151-2, Roderic H. Davison.

196. Benians, Ernest Alfred, et al., editors. *The Empire-Commonwealth, 1870-1919. Cambridge History of the British Empire*, vol. 3. Bibliography edited by A. Taylor Milne. Cambridge: Cambridge University Press, 1959. xxi + 948 pp.

Reviews the evolution of the commonwealth and the problems of imperial defence, reorganization and coordination that influenced its development. Good bibliography, though now dated.
Cf. Hall, 119; Mansergh, 129; Knaplund, 126; McIntyre, 127; Kendle, 124; Searle, 105; Semmel, 106.
Reviews: *EcHR* 12 (1959):465-6, D.K. Fieldhouse; *HJ* 3 (1960):96-8, D.G. Creighton; *JMH* 31 (1959):137-8, A.L. Burt.

197. Bourne, Kenneth, and D.C. Watt, editors. *Studies in International History: Essays Presented to W. Norton Medlicott*. London: Longmans, 1967. xiii + 446 pp.

Twenty-one essays on aspects of international relations in the late 19th and 20th centuries. Of interest are the articles by Gillard, "Salisbury and the Indian Defence Problem, 1885-1902," item 246; Kurat, "How Turkey Drifted Into World War I," item 335; Nevakivi, "Lord Kitchener and the Partition of the Ottoman Empire, 1915-1916," item 339; and Hall, "The British Commonwealth and the Founding of the League Mandate System," item 118.
Reviews: *AHR* 74 (1968):546-7, William Franklin; *H* 54 (1969):322-3, P.A. Reynolds; *JMH* 41 (1969):522-4, Raymond J. Sontag.

198. Clayton, G.D. *Britain and the Eastern Question: Missolonghi to Gallipoli*. London History Studies, no. 8. London: University of London Press, 1971. 256 pp.

An introductory text for students, outlining the major features of the Eastern Question and Britain's policy in the area.
Cf. Anderson, 195; Millman, 207.
Reviews: *MEJ* 26 (1972):215-6, Harry N. Howard.

199. Daniel, Norman. *Islam, Europe and Empire*. Edinburgh: Edinburgh University Press, 1966. xvii + 619 pp.

A survey of Middle Eastern-European relations in the
age of imperialism to 1900. Interesting review of the
background, the impressions the West had of Islam and
the East had of the West, the impact of the French revolution, Western economic expansion and superior power
in the Middle East, and the response of the Middle East
to Western encroachment. Somewhat biased account in
favor of Islam.
Cf. Rosenthal, 456; Hourani, 439; Sharabi, 457; Lewis,
449; Cottam, 506.
Reviews: *AAPSS-A* 373 (1967):263-4, S.D. Goitein; *AHR*
73 (1967):94-5, John B. Christopher; *H* 54 (1969):162-4,
M.E. Yapp; *JEH* 29 (1969):556-8, Kemal H. Karpat.

200. Farnie, Douglas Anthony. *East and West of Suez, The*
      Suez in History, 1854-1956. Oxford: Clarendon Press,
      1969. ix + 860 pp.

      A comprehensive, if densely written, study of British
      policy in the eastern Mediterranean and the strategic
      importance of the Suez Canal. Most of the research ma-
      terial cited, however, is not contemporary scholarship
      or newly-available archival material. Skirts a variety
      of issues, but still a useful summation. For a brief
      study of the financial aspects of the Suez Canal, see
      Bent Hanssen and Khairy Tourk, "The Profitability of
      the Suez Canal as a Private Enterprise, 1859-1956,"
      Journal of Economic History 38 (1978):938-58.
      Cf. Robinson, 072; Holt, 378; Richmond, 494; Vati-
      kiotis, 391; Marlowe, 383.
      Reviews: *AHR* 75 (1970):1418-9, Charles Issawi; *EHR* 87
      (1972):138-9, F.V. Parsons; *H* 55 (1970):319, M.E. Yapp;
      JEH 30 (1970):882-3, Max Fletcher.

201. Gifford, Prosser, and William Roger Louis, editors.
      Britain and France in Africa: Imperial Rivalry and
      Colonial Rule. New Haven, Conn.: Yale University
      Press, 1971. xix + 989 pp.

      Contains 23 essays, including a bibliographic survey,
      on Anglo-French rivalry and aspects of their colonial
      experience in Africa in the period of "new" imperialism,
      c. 1870-1939. Of note are the following articles:
      Henri Brunschwig, "Anglophobia and French African Poli-
      cy," 3-34; Agatha Ramm, "Great Britain and France in
      Egypt, 1876-1882," 73-120; G.N. Sanderson, "The Origins
      and Significance of the Anglo-French Confrontation at
      Fashoda, 1898," 285-332; and Pierre Guillen, "The En-
      tente of 1904 as a Colonial Settlement," 333-68. The

focus of the essays is on European diplomacy and methods
of government and ignores the local peoples, but the
essays were intended to examine European attitudes and
methods.

Cf. Louis, 301; Taylor, 209; Sanderson, 208; Robinson
and Gallagher, 072.

Reviews: *EHR* 88 (1973):864-6, Roger Bullen; *VS* 16
(1973):352-4, John Galbraith.

202. Gifford, Prosser, and William Roger Louis, editors.
*Britain and Germany in Africa: Imperial Rivalry and
Colonial Rule.* With the Assistance of Alison Smith.
New Haven, Conn.: Yale University Press, 1967. xvii
+ 825 pp.

A collection of 24 essays, including a historiographical review, on Anglo-German rivalry in Africa and
the nature of their respective colonial experiences;
in three sections. The essays in Part 1, "Imperial Rivalry," are important for bringing together articles on
the nature of imperial rivalry. Of particular note are
the studies by William Roger Louis, "Great Britain and
German Expansion in Africa, 1884-1919," 3-46; S.L.
Mayer, "Anglo-German Rivalry at the Algeciras Conference," 215-44; Gaddis Smith, "The British Government
and the Disposition of the German Colonies in Africa,
1914-1918," 275-300; and Jean Stengers, "Britain and
German Imperial Rivalry: A Conclusion," 337-47. Has an
excellent bibliography. See the companion volume discussed above for views on Anglo-French rivalry. Also
see L.H. Gann and Peter Duingan, *Colonialism in Africa,
1870-1960*, 4 volumes (Cambridge: Cambridge University
Press, 1964).

Cf. Louis, 301; Robinson and Gallagher, 072; Sanderson, 208; Taylor, 209.

Reviews: *AHR* 74 (1969):948-9, Margaret L. Bates;
BSOAS 33 (1970):235-6, G.N. Sanderson; *EHR* 84 (1969):
816-7, A.J.P. Taylor; *H* 54 (1969):148-9, R.C. Bridges.

203. Graham, Gerald. *Great Britain in the Indian Ocean: A
Study of Maritime Enterprise, 1810-1850.* Oxford:
Clarendon Press, 1967. xii + 479 pp.

With the defeat of Napoleon and the consolidation of
the position in India, Britain gradually acquired a
paramount position in the Indian Ocean. Graham studies
this evolution, the increasing British interest in Egypt
and the Persian Gulf--routes connecting east and west--
and the development of trade and strategic thinking.

For an examination of the major themes in British naval strategy, the problems facing Britain with increasing competition, see Graham's *The Politics of Naval Supremacy* (Cambridge: Cambridge University Press, 1965); and, of course, for a study of the influence and importance of sea power, see Alfred Thayer Mahon, *The Influence of Sea Power upon History, 1660-1783*, (1890; reprint. New York: Hill & Wang, 1957). On the development of British interests in the Red Sea area, see Thomas Marston, *Britain's Imperial Role in the Red Sea Area, 1800-1878* (Hamden, Conn.: Shoe String Press, 1961).
Cf. Hoskins, 362; Kelly, 407; Busch, 404; Kumar, 409; Farnie, 200; Fieldhouse, 055.
Reviews: *AHR* 74 (1969):989-90, Bruce T. McCully; *EHR* 84 (1969):362-4, A.N.Ryan; *GJ* 134 (1968):134, A. Preston; *H* 54 (1969):297-8, Freda Harcourt; *PA* 41 (1968): 467-8, John Curtis.

204.   Hale, Oron James. *The Great Illusion, 1900-1914.* The Rise of Modern Europe, no. 17. New York: Harper & Row, 1971. xv + 361 pp.

Surveys the climate of European diplomatic, political and social life before World War I, trying not to see the era looking backward from the war. Captures the complexity of the situation and underscores the hopes and confusions that characterized the period. Wide-ranging and perceptive.
Cf. Albrecht-Carrié, 194; Lafore, 299; Taylor, 209; Rolo, 265; Albertini, 284; Joll, 297.
Reviews: *AHR* 77 (1972):780-1, Joachim Remak.

205.   Hayes, Carlton Joseph Huntley. *A Generation of Materialism, 1871-1900.* The Rise of Modern Europe Series. New York: Harper & Brothers, 1941. xii + 390 pp.

An evocative survey of European political, social and economic life in the late 19th century. It covers the period before that covered by Oron Hale, item 204, and examines nationalism, liberalism, imperialism, the arts, industry and aspects of politics to capture the climate of an age. Hayes' work, which is scholarly, in conjunction with Barbara Tuchman's *The Proud Tower: Portrait of the World Before the War, 1890-1914* (London: Hamilton, 1966), which is not a scholarly work, helps towards understanding how the age saw its world, rather than our view looking backward. In the same vein, James Morris' *Pax Britannica: The Climax of an Empire* (London:

Faber, 1968), though filled with glittering generalizations, captures some of the social and political context
and the mood of the world of the British empire.
   Cf. Hyam, 090; Shannon, 107; Langer, 093.

206.   Jelavich, Barbara. *The Ottoman Empire, the Great Powers,*
       and the Straits Question, 1870-1887. Bloomington:
       Indiana University Press, 1973. xi + 209 pp.

   The question of what to do with the Ottoman Empire
and who was to get control of the Straits connecting
the Mediterranean and Black Sea was a long-term consideration in European diplomacy, affecting the interests
of Britain, Germany, Austria, Russia and, of course,
the Ottomans, who were caught by their own weaknesses
in European rivalries.
   Examines the effects of shifting European alliances
on Ottoman integrity, concentrating particularly on
Anglo-Russian rivalry and the changing British attitude
towards the Ottoman Empire and the Straits.   The opening of the Suez Canal, Ottoman weakness and their handling of the Armenian question inclined the British to
begin to reconsider their policy of defending Ottoman
territorial integrity, though keeping Russia in check
remained a goal.   For a different view, one that argues
that Britain did not really change its mind about defending Turkey, as opposed to the Straits, until the
Admiralty vetoed ideas that the fleet could be used,
see Margaret Jefferson, "Lord Salisbury and the Eastern
Question, 1890-1898," *Slavonic and East European Review*
38 (1960):44-60.   Also see W.N. Medlicott, "Lord Salisbury and Turkey," *History* 12 (1927):244-7, for a similar argument.   Also see Cedric Lowe, *Salisbury and the*
Mediterranean, 1886-1896 (London: Routledge & Kegan
Paul, 1965); and Lillian Penson, "The Foreign Policy
of Lord Salisbury, 1878-1880: The Problem of the Ottoman Empire," in Alfred Coville and Harold Temperley,
editors, *Studies in Anglo-French History during the*
Eighteenth, Nineteenth, and Twentieth Centuries (1935;
reprint. Freeport, N.Y.: Books for Libraries Press,
1969), 125-42.   A more detailed, though dated, study of
aspects of the period is W.N. Medlicott, *The Congress*
of Berlin and After: A Diplomatic History of the Near
Eastern Settlement, 1878-1880 (1938; reprint. London:
Cass, 1963).
   Cf. Anderson, 195; Millman, 207; Monger, 098; Grenville, 085.
   Reviews: *AHR* 79 (1974):556-7, C. Ernest Dawn; *MEJ* 28
(1974):210-1, Harry N. Howard.

*   Kelly, J.B. *Britain and the Persian Gulf*. Cited as
        item 407.

207.   Millman, Richard. *Britain and the Eastern Question,*
        1875-1878. Oxford: Clarendon Press, 1979. xv +
        613 pp.

        In the 1830's and in 1854 Britain took steps to pro-
        tect the integrity of the Ottoman Empire. British an-
        xiety over the spread of the Russian Empire was an im-
        portant element in their efforts; and the fate of the
        Ottoman Empire, the "Eastern Question," was a principal
        element in this anxiety. In the 1870's the Turks faced
        revolts from within and had to wage a losing war with
        Russia that threatened to bring an abrupt end to the
        Empire in Europe. Britain, determined to defend Otto-
        man integrity and thereby contain Russia, interceded
        diplomatically in the peace that followed the war and
        obliged the Russians to modify their terms. Examines
        in particular the role of Disraeli and Salisbury in
        shaping British policy towards the Eastern Question,
        though it does not concern itself exclusively with the
        diplomatic background, instead concentrating on the
        British domestic influences and interpersonal relations
        that were important in determining policy. Sheds im-
        portant light on the shift in British policy away from
        upholding Ottoman integrity as disillusionment set in.
        An exhaustive, essential study capitalizing on recent
        scholarship and documentary material. A useful bibli-
        ography. Also see Ann Saab, *The Origins of the Crimean*
        Alliance (Charlottesville: University of Virginia Press,
        1977), for a detailed study of British and French in-
        terest in the Ottoman Empire as seen from Constantinople.
        One of the few works to do this. Compare with Jelavich,
        item 206.
           Cf. Anderson, 195; Monger, 098; Grenville, 085;
        Taylor, 209; Blaisdell, 213; Langer, 093.
           Reviews: *AHR* 85 (1980):618-9, Barbara Jelavich; *MEJ*
        34 (1980):236-7, A.P. Saab.

*   Mowat, Charles. *The Shifting Balance of World Forces,*
        1898-1945. Cited as item 099.

*   Robinson, Ronald, and John Gallagher, with Alice Denny.
        Africa and the Victorians. Cited as item 072.

208.   Sanderson, George Neville. *England, Europe and the*
        Upper Nile, 1882-1899: A Study in the Partition of

Africa. Edinburgh: Edinburgh University Press, 1965. xiv + 465 pp.

Control of the Nile at its source, Anglo-French rivalry, and the unpredictable qualities of the politics of local states (such as the Mahdists in the Sudan, and Ethiopia) produced a climate of tension, diplomatic uncertainty and war. The British became increasingly concerned that an unfriendly power controlling the sources of the Nile could deny Egypt water and thereby undermine Britain's position. The main candidate for this maneuver was the French, who smarted over the fact that Britain had acquired a predominant influence in Egypt. Sanderson examines the development of British and French interests in the Upper Nile and the subsequent rush to control it. He does not attempt a new interpretation of imperial history but examines the diplomatic and military strategies and maneuvers of the parties involved. An excellent study of the diplomatic atmosphere with a useful bibliography on Egypt and the Sudan. Also see Robert Collins, *King Leopold, England and the Upper Nile, 1899-1909* (New Haven, Conn.: Yale University Press, 1968), which complements Sanderson. In addition see the separate articles by Sanderson which cover much of the same ground: "The Anglo-German Agreement of 1890 and the Upper Nile," *English Historical Review* 78 (1963):49-72; and "England, Italy, the Nile Valley and the European Balance, 1890-91," *Historical Journal* 7 (1964):94-119.

Cf. Taylor, 209; Langer, 093; Robinson, 072; Holt, 378; Grenville, 085; Monger, 098; Rolo, 265; Benians, 196; Mowat, 099.

Reviews: *AAPSS-A* 369 (1967):193-4, K.D.D. Henderson; *AHR* 71 (1966):1031-3, William L. Langer; *EHR* 82 (1967): 194-5, D.R. Gillard; *GJ* 132 (1966):292, Roy C. Bridges; *H* 52 (1967):123-4, E.W. Edwards; *MEJ* 20 (1966):233, Roderic Davison; *PSQ* 81 (1966):675, Bernard Semmel.

209. Taylor, A.J.P. *The Struggle for Mastery in Europe, 1848-1918*. Oxford History of Modern Europe. Allan Bullock and F.W.D. Drakin, general editors. Oxford: Clarendon Press, 1954. xxxvi + 638 pp.

A masterful survey of European power politics and the balance of power ranging over every major diplomatic confrontation or exchange from the abortive 1848 revolutions to the end of World War I. Argues a Eurocentric line, that events and relations in Europe were what set

the tempo for the relations among European empires overseas. Chapters 17, "The Era of 'World Policy,' 1897-
1902," 372-401; 18, "The Last Years of British Isolation:
The Making of the Anglo-French Entente, 1902-5," 403-
26; 19, "The Formation of the Triple Entente, 1905-9,"
427-56; 20, "The Years of Anglo-German Hostility, 1909-
12," 457-83; and chapter 23, "The Diplomacy of War,
1914-1918," 532-68, provide some of the best summaries
of European diplomacy available, though one may argue
with the interpretations. For European rivalry in
Africa, see Robinson, item 072; Gifford, items 201 and
202; and Louis, item 301; on the Eastern Question, see
Anderson, item 195; Jelavich, item 206; and Millman,
item 207. On changes in British policy, see Grenville,
item 085; and Monger, 098; on the origins of World War
I, see Steiner, item 307.
   Cf. Woodward, 279; Benians, 196; Langer, 093; Williamson, 211; Rothwell, 306.
   Reviews: *AHR* 60 (1955):880-2, Bernadotte Schmitt;
JMH 28 (1956):304-5, E.C. Helmreich.

210. Ward, A.W., and G.P. Gooch, editors. *1866-1919. Cam-*
      bridge History of British Foreign Policy, 1783-1919,
      vol. 3. 1922. Reprint. Cambridge: Cambridge Uni-
      versity Press, 1970.

      Examines the formation and execution of British for-
      eign policy in response to the major issues and inter-
      ests that affected Britain's international position.
      Essays tend to be narrative and are now outdated by the
      availability of generous quantities of documentary ma-
      terial. Chapter 8, "The Foreign Office," 539-630, by
      Algernon Cecil, is a useful summary of the workings and
      transformations of the Foreign Office and its chief
      personnel; but most of the work in this volume has been
      superseded.
         Cf. Grenville, 085; Monger, 098; Shannon, 107; Lowe,
      095 and 096; Steiner, 137 and 307; Hinsley, 086; Gooch,
      045; Benians, 196.

211. Williamson, Samuel Ruthven, Jr. *The Politics of Grand*
      Strategy: Britain and France Prepare for War, 1904-
      1914. Cambridge: Harvard University Press, 1969.
      xvii + 409 pp.

      The Entente Cordiale of 1904 resolved Anglo-French
      colonial differences. This settlement formed the basis
      of a more general Anglo-French rapprochement that took
      on a special meaning for the two nations as German power

grew to threaten the interests of both. Williamson explores that evolution and its consequences for European diplomacy before World War I. Valuable because it places Anglo-French relations in a regional and global context, showing how the growing coordination of defence policies between the two nations limited or enhanced their European and world positions. The quasialliance with France, the re-alignment of Britain's strategic forces plus the reorganization of military and government institutions were indications of the major shifts in Britain's world position after 1900. An essential study, to be read in conjunction with Rothwell, item 306; Woodward, item 279; Rolo, item 265; and the works mentioned under "imperial reorganization."

Cf. Steiner, 307; Shannon, 107; Robinson, 072; Gooch, 114.

Reviews: *AAPSS-A* 394 (1971):153-4, Howard M. Sachar; *AHR* 75 (1970):2039-40, Richard Ullman; *EHR* 87 (1972): 449, Michael Howard; *H* 56 (1971):131, Jonathan Steinburg; *JMH* 43 (1971):167-9, Theodore Ropp.

Economic Rivalry

212. Anderson, Olive. "Great Britain and the Beginnings of the Ottoman Public Debt, 1854-55." *Historical Journal* 7 (1964):47-63.

Furnishes an account of the background and circumstances of the crucial loans of 1854 and 1855 and what role they played in bringing about European financial control of Turkey's debt. Updates Blaisdell, discussed below, on the basis of new documentary evidence. However, much remains to be done on the economic aspects of Ottoman-European contacts.

Cf. Feis, 222; Platt, 237; Lewis, 477; Shaw, 481; Karpat, 475; Issawi, 227.

213. Blaisdell, Donald Christy. *European Financial Control in the Ottoman Empire: A Study of the Establishment, Activities, and Significance of the Administration of the Ottoman Public Debt.* New York: Columbia University Press, 1929. x + 243 pp.

The Ottoman Government, heavily in debt to European financial interests--mainly French and British--defaulted in 1875. The Sublime Porte was forced to accept a measure of foreign financial control over imperial revenues as a means of resuming payments to its creditors.

This system of financial control impaired Ottoman integrity and allowed various European powers to insinu-
ate their imperial interests into the management of the
Empire. Blaisdell traces the background of Ottoman bor-
rowing, the formation of the Ottoman Public Debt and
the functioning of the Debt as an expression of European imperialism. Dated but still useful.
    Cf. Feis, 222; Anderson, 195; Platt, 237; Berkes,
465; Davison, 466; Devereaux, 468.

214. Cairncross, Alexander Kirkland. *Home and Foreign In-
      vestment, 1870-1913: Studies in Capital Accumulation.*
      1953. Reprint. Clifton, N.J.: Kelly, 1975. xvi +
      251 pp.

      A collection of essays by Cairncross dealing with
capital accumulation and market fluctuation, concentrating on British foreign and home investment, the dynamics of internal and international trade and the migra-
tion of capital and labor, with a view to the effects
these had on economic development. The concluding chapter examines Victorian economic theories and notes that
two defects of Victorian economic thinking that retarded
the development of a comprehensive theory of investment
derived from a failure to account adequately for interest rates, depression, and monetary fluctuation; and
their neglect of the influence of monetary policy, concentrating on ideal models of a real-exchange economy.
Chapter 9 considers the question of whether or not foreign investment paid. Concludes with a qualified "yes,"
but 1870-1914 was a peculiar period and subsequent years
may have made the prospects less rewarding, especially
as local nationalism raised the spectre of expropriation.
      Cf. Fieldhouse, 055; Platt, 237; Feis, 222; Saul, 238.

215. Carrington, Charles Edmund. *The British Overseas: Ex-
      ploits of a Nation of Shopkeepers.* Cambridge: Cam-
      bridge University Press, 1950. xxi + 1092 pp.

      Surveys the exploits of various British imperialists
overseas. Of limited value, but contains priceless
anecdotes and biographical information; it lacks a bibliography and footnotes. Compare with Holder Furber,
Rival Empires of Trade in the Orient, 1600-1800 (Minneapolis: University of Minnesota Press, 1976), which,
even though covering an earlier period, gives insights
into the nature of overseas encounters and imperial rivalries.

Cf. Fieldhouse, 055; Beloff, 080; Eldridge, 054; Hyam, 090; Porter, 103; Kiernan, 061; Saul, 238.

Reviews: *AHR* 56 (1951):555-6, Howard Robinson; *JMH* 24 (1952):427-8, Holden Furber; *MEJ* 5 (1951):247-8, William Aiken.

216.   Chapman, Maybelle Kennedy. *Great Britain and the Bagh-
       dad Railway, 1888-1914.* Smith College Studies in
       History, no. 31. Northhampton, Mass.: Smith College,
       1948. x + 248 pp.

Details Anglo-German friction over the construction of the Baghdad Railway, exploring aspects of railway development in the Ottoman Empire and British interest in that development in the decade before the Germans received the Baghdad concession. The history of the railway says a great deal about the nature of imperial rivalry and Great Power relations with lesser powers. Relies on *British Documents*, item 045, for its primary material, and is more solidly based than Earle, item 209, but recent access to the major archives, both German and British, date the work. A new, detailed study of the Baghdad railway capitalizing on Ottoman and Western sources remains to be done. For one of the best recent accounts, see Cohen, item 394.

Cf. Karkar, 230; Platt, 237; Feis, 222; McLean, 234; Kent, 398; Schoenberg, 374; Benians, 196.

*   Cohen, Stuart. *British Policy in Mesopotamia, 1903-
         1914.* Cited as item 394.

217.   Cohen, Stuart. "Sir Arthur Nicholson and Russia: The
       Case of the Baghdad Railway." *Historical Journal* 18
       (1975):863-72.

Nicolson was a firm adherent of the Anglo-Russian entente, so much so that he turned a blind eye to Russian violations of both the letter and spirit of the 1907 Convention (see Churchill, item 243), believing Britain needed Russia's friendship in the Middle East. In the case of the Baghdad Railway, Nicolson was able to carry his point that Britain had to accommodate Russia's determination to participate in the Baghdad Railway. Revealing of inter-departmental maneuvering and policy-making, or unmaking. On the Baghdad Railway, see Earle, 219; Chapman, 216; Karkar, 230; Corrigan, 329; Cohen, 394; Feis, 222; Platt, 237; and Francis, 223. On inter-departmental rivalry, see Kedourie, 346; Busch, 352;

and Steiner, 137 and 307. On Nicolson, see the biography by his son, Harold Nicolson, item 182.

218. Cook, Michael Allan, editor. *Studies in the Economic
      History of the Middle East: From the Rise of Islam to
      the Present Day.* London: Oxford University Press,
      1970. ix + 526 pp.

      A collection of 27 essays divided into three parts on
      various aspects of Middle Eastern economic history and
      source materials. Part 3 concerns the 19th and 20th
      centuries. The most relevant articles are: Ahmad Ashraf,
      "Historical Obstacles to the Development of a Bourgeoisie
      in Iran," 308-332; Mohammad Salman Hasan, "The Role of
      Foreign Trade in the Economic Development of Iraq, 1864-
      1964: A Study in the Growth of a Dependent Economy,"
      346-72; Charles Issawi, "Middle East Economic Develop-
      ment, 1815-1914: The General and the Specific," 395-
      411; E.R.J. Owen, item 385. The papers are the result
      of a conference at the School of Oriental and African
      Studies of the University of London in 1967.
        Cf. Issawi, 227; Baer, 487; Holt, 490; Kedourie, 231;
      Polk, 453.
        Reviews: *MEJ* 26 (1972):91-2, Oded Remba.

219. Earle, Edward Mead. *Turkey, the Great Powers and the
      Baghdad Railway: A Study in Imperialism.* London:
      Macmillan, 1923. ix + 364 pp.

      The classic, if dated, study of imperialism, the clash
      of Great Powers and the Baghdad railway. Discusses the
      origins and development of the German project and the
      reaction of Britain, France and Russia to it. For a
      further study that corrects and expands Earle's obser-
      vations, see J.B. Wolff, "The Diplomatic History of the
      Baghdad Railroad," *University of Missouri Studies* 11
      (1936). Both these works, however, were written before
      the opening of the major archives or the publication of
      British Documents, item 045. For a contemporary study
      that capitalizes on newly-available primary material,
      see Stuart Cohen, item 394.
        Cf. McLean, 234 and 373; Kent, 398; Francis, 223;
      Busch, 404; Benians, 196.

220. Entner, Marvin Lee. *Russo-Persian Commerical Relations,
      1828-1914.* University of Florida Monographs. Social
      Sciences, no. 28. Gainesville: University of Florida
      Press, 1965. 80 pp.

Describes Russian commercial activity in Iran.
Through the course of the 19th century, Russia used its
political power to expand its influence and indirect
control over Iran, and used economic activities to further this control. The process of Russian expansion
alarmed the British, just as British economic power and
expansion disturbed the Russians. Iran was caught between these rival anxieties and paid the cost. One of
the few detailed studies of Persia's economic relations.

Cf. Issawi, 417; Curzon, 412; Kazemzadeh, 251; Ramazani, 425.

Reviews: *AHR* 71 (1966):1292, C.M. Foust; *JAS* 25
(1966):540-1, Ronald R. Rader; *JEH* 26 (1966):248-9,
Walther Kirchner; *MEJ* 20 (1966):415, Geré Lecompte.

221. Fatemi, Nasrollah Saifpour. *Oil Diplomacy: Powderkeg
     in Iran.* New York: Whittier Books, 1954. 405 pp.

Covers the development of Iran's oil industry from
the D'Arcy concession to the difficulties in Anglo-
Iranian relations in the 1930's and 1950's when Iran
nationalized the oil industry. Tendentious and biased,
but useful and expressive of local sentiments.

Cf. Ferrier, 413; Longrigg, 233; Kent, 398; Jones,
229; Ramazani, 425.

Reviews: *JMH* 28 (1956):74-5, T.H. Vail Motter; *MEJ* 9
(1955):90-1, George Lenczowski.

222. Feis, Herbert. *Europe, the World's Banker, 1870-1914:
     An Account of European Foreign Investment and the
     Connection of World Finance with Diplomacy Before the
     War.* New Haven, Conn.: Yale University Press, 1930.
     xiii + 469 pp.

The classic study of European--mainly British, French
and German--investment in Asia, most particularly the
Ottoman Empire, Persia, China, and Japan. Divided into
three parts, examining the nature and chief characteristics of the investment patterns of the major European
powers, the relations between lenders and borrowers and
government involvement in favor of finance and trade,
and case studies of the consequences of European investment and rivalry on the affairs of regional states.
Though dated, it remains a pertinent source.

Cf. Platt, 237; Cairncross, 214; Saul, 238; Hoffman,
226.

223. Francis, Richard M. "The British Withdrawal from the
      Baghdad Railway Project in April 1903." *Historical
      Journal* 16 (1973):168-78.

      The standard interpretation maintains that Britain
      withdrew from the Baghdad Railway project because of
      the pressure of public opinion and a vigorous press
      campaign. This is only part of the answer. The oppo-
      sition of Joseph Chamberlain and a general realization
      within the cabinet that the negotiations with the Ger-
      mans were not going to produce an agreement giving due
      respect to British commercial or strategic interests,
      together with public opposition, combined to abort the
      agreement. On the impact of public opinion, see the
      dated, but still useful, *Publicity and Diplomacy: With
      Special Reference to England and Germany, 1890-1914*
      (New York: Appleton-Century for the Institute of Research
      in the Social Sciences of the University of Virginia,
      1940), by Oron J. Hale; also K.G. Robbins, "Foreign
      Policy, Government Structure and Public Opinion," *Brit-
      ish Foreign Policy*, item 086, 532-45.
      Cf. Earle, 219; Chapman, 216; Platt, 237; Feis, 222;
      Kent, 398; Cohen, 394.

224. Henderson, W.O. "German Economic Penetration in the
      Middle East." *Studies in German Colonial History*.
      London: Frank Cass, 1962, pp. 74-86.

      The Baghdad railway attracts most attention when con-
      sidering German economic activities in the Middle East,
      but there were other important ventures. Henderson
      studies German economic penetration of the Ottoman Em-
      pire, as well as increasing German political efforts;
      though, like the British, the Germans saw technical and
      military advisors as a means to bolster the Turks and
      assure their recovery. This was viewed by other Powers
      as a sign of an aggressive German intent. Based on
      limited research but adequate as a general introduction.
      Other parts of the book review aspects of German colo-
      nial expansion and policy. Germany started in the co-
      lonial field late and made mistakes, not only in colo-
      nial administration but in its relations with other
      colonial powers. In addition see M.L. Flannigam, "Ger-
      man Eastward Expansion, Fact and Fiction: A Study in
      German-Ottoman Trade Relations, 1890-1914," *Journal of
      Central European Affairs* 14 (1955):319-33. See Immanuel
      Geiss, *German Foreign Policy, 1871-1914* (London: Rout-
      ledge and Kegan Paul, 1976), for a general introduction
      to major themes in German foreign policy.

Cf. Hoffman, 226; Jack, 370; Earle, 219; Karkar, 230; Martin, 276; Staley, 240.

225. Hershlag, Z.Y. *Introduction to the Modern Economic History of the Middle East.* 2nd revised edition. Leiden: Brill, 1980.

Explores the political, social and economic features of Middle Eastern life, concentrating on three primary areas--Persia, Egypt, and the Ottoman Empire--that help account for the failure of the Middle East to adjust to the Western challenge. Examines not only the impact of the West but internal structural weaknesses that inhibited a successful response. Divided into two main parts, the first examining Middle Eastern economic patterns from 1800 to the end of World War I, and the second exploring the economic and social changes in the interwar period. Interesting and informative, but most of the material is based on secondary or European sources. Complement with Issawi, items 227 and 228; Cook, item 218; Polk, item 453; and Holt, item 490.
   Cf. Anderson, 195.
   Reviews: (1st edition) *MEJ* 19 (1965):93-4, Charles Issawi.

226. Hoffman, Ross John Swartz. *Great Britain and the German Trade Rivalry, 1875-1914.* 1933. Reprint. New York: Russel & Russel, 1964. xii + 363 pp.

Describes the decline of British industrial-trade supremacy and the challenges presented by Germany to Britain's worldwide economic position. Hoffman examines the growth and nature of the rivalry, the influence it had on British business and government, and the British response to German competition. Has an interesting section on the Baghdad Railway and Anglo-German trade rivalry in the Middle East, including Persia, Mesopotamia and Turkey. Economic rivalry between the two states preceded naval rivalry, but may have influenced it--both because navies were needed to protect growing overseas trade; and as a source for creating a climate of hostility between the two powers that aggravated relations before naval rivalry began. The British believed German economic rivalry was politically motivated and supported--a belief supportable to a degree because economic benefits had political advantages--and suspected and resented German penetration of British markets. Dated but useful. On the influence of anti-German public opinion on British policy, see Oron Hale's

*Publicity and Diplomacy: With Special Reference to Eng-
land and Germany, 1890-1914* (New York: Appleton-Century
for the Institute of Research in the Social Sciences of
the University of Virginia, 1940). Also see Derek
Aldcroft, editor, *The Development of British Industry
and Foreign Competition, 1875-1914: Studies in Industrial Enterprise*, University of Glasgow Social and Economic Studies, no. 12 (London: Allen & Unwin, 1968);
and W.O. Henderson, *The Rise of German Industrial Power,
1834-1914* (London: Temple Smith, 1975).
   Cf. Feis, 222; Platt, 237; Hoskins, 362; Earle, 219;
Kent, 398; Cohen, 394; Busch, 404; Steiner, 307;
Martin, 276.

227. Issawi, Charles, editor. *The Economic History of the
      Middle East, 1800-1914: A Book of Readings*. Chicago:
      University of Chicago Press, 1966. xv + 543 pp.

      Details the major features of Middle Eastern economic
      development, or stagnation, in the years of increasing
      contact with the West. Provides a brief introduction
      to Middle Eastern economic realities and then, by pre-
      senting articles or original studies, examines in de-
      tail aspects of the economic life of the Ottoman Empire
      and its chief geographical units--Egypt, the Sudan,
      Arabia, Syria, Palestine, and Iraq. The material in-
      cludes studies on industrial policy, transport, decline
      in trade, population statistics, exports and imports,
      migration, agriculture, local industries and finance.
      Though the piecemeal collection of material gives a
      fragmented view of a complex topic, this is one of the
      few general surveys of Middle Eastern economies and is
      essential.
         Cf. Issawi, 417; Baer, 487; Holt, 490; Hershlag, 225.
         Reviews: *JEH* 27 (1967):258-9, Nikki Keddie; *MEJ* 21
      (1967):410-1, Helen Rivlin; *PSQ* 82 (1967):665-6, Kemal
      H. Karpat.

228. Issawi, Charles. "Middle East Economic Development,
      1815-1914: The General and the Specific." *Studies in
      the Economic History of the Middle East*, item 218,
      395-411.

      Using population growth, foreign capital investment,
      mechanical transport and foreign trade, Issawi examines
      changes in Middle Eastern economic patterns to conform
      to the demands of the international economic system
      that developed in the century between Napoleon and

World War I. Shows the effect of this process of integration, which, in combination with European political
dominance, stimulated certain areas of the economy but
in an unbalanced fashion that had deleterious effects
on Middle East political independence, social order,
and prosperity.
    Cf. Issawi, 417; Landes, 232; Blaisdell, 213; Entner,
220.

229. Jones, G. Gareth. "The British Government and the Oil
    Companies, 1912-1924: The Search for an Oil Policy."
    Historical Journal 20 (1977):647-72.

    Argues that most studies of the relationship between
government and industry have been studies of government
policy towards industry, largely ignoring the reverse--
industry's efforts to involve government. In particular
Jones looks at oil company efforts, mainly the Anglo-
Persian Oil Company, to attract official British support,
to involve the government directly in promoting and sus-
taining the company. The company was successful, not
because the government realized the strategic value of
petroleum, but because the Foreign Office and other departments were anxious to preserve or promote all-British
companies in sensitive areas like Persia and Mesopotamia.
Even the Admiralty, pointed to by some as the bastion of
oil-thinking, lacked a coherent, well-thought out oil
policy before World War I. One of the best and most in-
telligently considered studies of the development of
British oil policy.
    Cf. Kent, 398; Cohen, 394; Mejcher, 235; Sluglett,
357; Longrigg, 233; Shwadran, 239; Fatemi, 221; Monroe,
304; Ferrier, 413.

230. Karkar, Yakub. *Railway Development in the Ottoman Em-
    pire, 1856-1916.* New York: Vantage, 1972. 181 pp.

    Surveys the development of the various railway pro-
jects in the Ottoman Empire, discussing the motives behind the different lines (which were often the result
of European interests and not Ottoman needs), their economic value, and their strategic impact. Unfortunately
not much new information is added to the history of the
Baghdad Railway, but this is a useful survey.
    Cf. Earle, 219; Haddad, 472; Lewis, 477; Schoenberg,
374; McLean, 373.
    Reviews: *IJMES* 4 (1974):503-6, Donald Quataert.

231. Kedourie, Elie, editor. *The Middle East Economy: Studies in Economics and Economic History.* London: Frank Cass, 1977. 185 pp.

A collection of seven essays on aspects of Middle Eastern economic development, reprinted from a special issue of *Middle Eastern Studies* 12 (1972). The articles deal with Egypt, Iran, Central Asia, and Turkey and have no common theme or period. Three of the articles are of use: Justin McCarthy, "Nineteenth Century Egyptian Population," 1-40, which is an excellent survey; Robert Tignor, "The Egyptian Revolution of 1919: New Directions in the Egyptian Economy," 41-68; and Marius Deeb, "Bank Misr and the Emergence of the Local Bourgeoisie in Egypt," 69-86. The Deeb article covers the interwar period, but has useful observations on capital formation in Egypt. The most valuable article is by Tignor, which traces the impact of the 1919 revolution on British control of Egypt and how the economy developed as Egypt moved towards independence.
Cf. Holt, 490; Cook, 218; Issawi, 227; Tignor, 390; Deeb, 488.
Reviews: *JEH* 38 (1978):569-71, Charles Issawi.

*   Kent, Marian. *Oil and Empire: British Policy and Mesopotamia, 1900-1920.* Cited as item 398.

232. Landes, David Saul. *Bankers and Pashas: International Finance and Economic Imperialism in Egypt.* London: Heinemann, 1958. xvi + 354 pp.

A classic study of international finance, the penetration of regional economies by European interests, the role of personalities in business, and the economic and political consequences of the integration of two dissimilar economic systems when one is far stronger and more dynamic than the other. Based on correspondence between two French businessmen, Alfred André and Edouard Derieu, the former in Paris and the latter the private banker of the Khedive of Egypt in the 1860's, it is an intimate study of imperialism and important as background information.
Cf. Blaisdell, 213; Anderson, 195; Platt, 237; Feis, 222.
Reviews: *MEJ* 13 (1959):205-6, Roderic Davison.

233. Longrigg, Stephen H. *Oil in the Middle East: Its Discovery and Development.* 3rd edition. Royal Institute

for International Affairs. London: Oxford University Press, 1968. xii + 519 pp.

The update of Longrigg's comprehensive survey of the development of the Middle East oil industry contains much new material on the period between 1954 and the late 1960's. Chapters 1-7 survey the granting of concessions, political rivalry, economic factors, the growth of the industry, and technical information on oil, its extraction and uses in each major oil producing area—the Ottoman Empire, Iraq, Persia and Arabia. An excellent survey. Another survey that gives more historical background on some of the concessions is George Stocking, *Middle East Oil: A Study in Political and Economic Controversy* (Nashville, Tenn.: Vanderbilt University Press, 1970). Also see George Lenczowski, *Oil and State in the Middle East* (Ithaca: Cornell University Press, 1960), though it has little on the early oil industry.

Cf. Fatemi, 221; Shwadran, 239; Kent, 398; Jones, 229; Cohen, 394; Mejcher, 235; Sluglett, 357; Ferrier, 413.

Reviews: (1st ed.): *MEJ* 8 (1954):461-2, John DeNovo; (2nd ed.): *JMH* 28 (1956):74-5, T.H. Vail Motter; (3rd ed.): *MEJ* 22 (1968):359-60, David Finnie.

*   McLean, David. "British Finance and Foreign Policy in Turkey: The Smyrna-Aidin Railway Settlement, 1913-1914." Cited as item 373.

234. McLean, David. "Finance and 'Informal' Empire Before the First World War." *Economic History Review* 29 (1976):291-305.

Did trade and finance follow the flag, or act as instruments for the extension of power? Argues that there was an irrefutable informal empire, not one concerned with trade but with security. Studies examples in Turkey, Persia and China of British use of informal measures to protect security interests. Sides with Robinson and Gallagher, items 072 and 073, downplaying economic motives by putting them in a context of political and strategic concerns. Contrast with Platt, item 237; Mejcher, item 235; Kent, 398; and Cohen, 394. Informal political influence is not the same thing as "informal empire"; and despite McLean's assertion, his examples do not irrefutably establish the existence of an informal empire. See the section on imperialism for

works dealing with empire and the Robinson and Gallagher debate.
Cf. McLean, 421.

*   Martin, Bradford. *German-Persian Diplomatic Relations, 1873-1912*. Cited as item 276.

235.   Mejcher, Helmut. *Imperial Quest for Oil: Iraq, 1910-1928*. With Foreword by Elizabeth Monroe. Middle East Monograph, no. 6. London: Ithaca Press for the Middle East Centre, St. Antony's College, Oxford, 1976.

Explores the development of Britain's interest in Middle Eastern oil, the acquisition of oil concessions, and the subsequent British monopoly on Iranian and Iraqi oil. Tends to mistake the lobbying of a group of individuals for an oil policy for the mind of the British government, which leads to over-emphasis on the importance of oil in British thinking before 1918. Makes numerous mistakes in points of detail. Compare with Kent, *Oil and Empire*, item 398, which also tends to see oil in everything, but is a much better study.
Cf. Cohen, 394; Sluglett, 357; Shwadran, 239; Longrigg, 233; Jones, 229; Ferrier, 413; Fatemi, 221.
Reviews: *AHR* 83 (1978):1308, Marian Kent; *IJMES* 11 (1980):270-3, Briton Busch.

236.   Olson, William J. "The Mazanderan Development Project and Hajji Muhammad Hasan: A Study in Nineteenth Century Persian Entrepreneurship, 1884-1898." *Towards a Modern Iran: Studies in Thought, Politics and Society*. Edited by Elie Kedourie and Sylvia Haim. London: Frank Cass, 1980.

Studies the efforts by one of Iran's principal merchants, in cooperation with the Shah and his chief minister, to develop a railway and mining complex in northern Iran, one of many Persian industrial schemes that collapsed because of internal difficulties. There were many railway schemes in Persia, but this was the only all-Persian effort and only one of two schemes that actually managed to lay track. Shows the internal and external political difficulties that affected modernizing programs in Iran.
Cf. Farmayan, 507; Avery, 501; Issawi, 417; Curzon, 412.

237. Platt, Desmond Christopher St. Martin. *Finance, Trade and Politics in British Foreign Policy, 1815-1914*. Oxford: Clarendon Press, 1968. xi + 454 pp.

   Strategic concerns governed much of British thinking about empire, but integral to all thinking and policy was a concern for and interest in promoting trade. Platt makes the point, however, that this realization did not necessarily lead the Government to intervene on behalf of economic interests or push trade, either because preference for one trade interest could harm others, or out of a disdain for such matters. Furthermore, the Government recognized, as did many in business, principles of *laissez faire* government and free trade, facts which influenced officials not to push trade, or to limit the protection of it. Platt strikes a balance between the "official-mind" approach to imperialism, and economic motivations, examining patterns of British trade in and policy toward China, Persia, Turkey, Egypt, Africa and Latin America. Argues against Robinson and Gallagher on a canvas as vast, with generalizations as copious, that are as susceptible to revision. Good selected bibliography. See Zara Steiner's review article, "Finance, Trade and Politics in British Foreign Policy, 1815-1914," *Historical Journal* 13 (1970):545-68, for an excellent critique of Platt's view and its relation to the field of imperial studies. Steiner adds an important note of caution to the over-emphasis on trade and its influence on the Foreign Office.
   Cf. McLean, 234; Feis, 222; Robinson and Gallagher, 072; Eldridge, 054; Fieldhouse, 055; Louis, 066.
   Reviews: *AHR* 74 (1969):990-1, A. Imlah; *EcHR* 22 (1969):142-3, W. Ashworth; *EHR* 85 (1970):588-91, F.V. Parsons; *H* 54 (1969):309, S.B. Paul; *JEH* 29 (1969): 382-3, M. Fletcher.

238. Saul, Samuel Berrick. *Studies in British Overseas Trade, 1870-1914*. Liverpool: Liverpool Press, 1960. ix + 246 pp.

   Explores the growth of Britain's overseas trade, the challenge to Britain's trade predominance, and several key problems facing Britain before World War I. Divided into two parts, with a general introduction and a chapter on the problems associated with an international economy, while the remaining chapters of Part 1 deal with the export of capital, economic policy and tariffs and competition. Part 2 covers trade with the

Empire, concentrating on Canada and India. Compare with
Cairncross, item 214. In addition see James Imlah,
"Economic Elements in the 'Pax Britannica,'" *Studies in
British Foreign Trade in the Nineteenth Century* (Cambridge: Harvard University Press, 1959); and the articles in Alan Ross Hall, editor, *The Export of Capital
from Britain, 1870-1914, Debates in Economic History*
(London: Methuen, 1968). Also see Saul's "Britain and
World Trade, 1870-1914," *Economic History Review* 7
(1950):49-66; and "The Economic Significance of 'Con-
structive Imperialism,'" *Journal of Economic History*
17 (1957):173-92.

  Cf. Hyam, 090; Kiernan, 061; Fieldhouse, 055.
  Reviews: *EcHR* 14 (1961-2):158, J.R.T. Hughes; *H* 45
(1960):286-7, W. Ashworth; *JEH* 21 (1961):127-8, Max
Fletcher; *JMH* 33 (1961):457-8, Albert Imlah.

239. Shwadran, Benjamin. *The Middle East, Oil and the Great
      Powers.* 3rd edition, enlarged and revised. Mono-
      graph Series, the Shiloah Center for Middle East
      and African Studies, Tel Aviv University. New York:
      Wiley, 1973. xviii + 630 pp.

      Surveys the growth of the oil industry in the Middle
      East and the geo-political features of the emergence of
      oil as a strategic commodity. Divided into seven sec-
      tions covering the major areas of oil production. Sec-
      tion 1 is a general introduction examining the impact
      of the West on the Middle East, the history and nature
      of Great Power rivalry in the area and the importance
      of oil. Section 2 looks at the Iranian oil industry
      from the first concessions to the 1970's. Section 3
      examines Iraq; Section 4, Saudia Arabia; Section 5, the
      Persian Gulf; Section 6, Israel, Jordan, Lebanon, Syria,
      Egypt and Turkey; and Section 7 provides a general con-
      clusion, examining modern oil policies of both produc-
      ers and consumers. An excellent survey, though it
      strays on a number of minor factual details.
        Cf. Longrigg, 233; Kent, 398; Mejcher, 235; Jones,
      229; Fatemi, 221.
        Reviews: (1st ed.): *MEJ* 10 (1956):200, George Len-
      czowski; (2nd ed.): *AHR* 63 (1968):683-4, John DeNovo.

240. Staley, Eugene. "Business and Politics in the Persian
      Gulf: The Story of the Wönckhaus Firm." *Political
      Science Quarterly* 48 (1933):367-85.

Examines British concern for maintaining the Persian
Gulf as an exclusive political enclave. Although the
British were not opposed to foreign economic activity
in the Gulf, they had difficulty in distinguishing, in
their own minds, between foreign economic activity and
political meddling. The presence of a thriving German
mining business, the Wönckhaus Firm, is a case in point.
The British were convinced it was a front for the German Government (though Staley shows otherwise), and
seized it during the war, as they did other German assets in the Middle East.
   Cf. Martin, 276; Kent, 398; Cohen, 394.

Russia

241. Alder, Garry John. *British India's Northern Frontier,
      1865-95: A Study in Imperial Policy.* Imperial Stu-
      dies, no. 25. Published for the Royal Commonwealth
      Society. London: Longmans, 1963. xiii + 392 pp.

   Examines the "Great Game" in Central Asia, the role
   that Russian imperial expansion had on Indian defence.
   Alder concentrates on British activities to secure the
   eastern approaches to India; but concern for Indian defence was very much tied to imperial defence as a whole
   and formed an element in British activities elsewhere
   in the Middle East.
   There is a growing body of literature on the Great
   Game; some of the principal works are: Alder's "Britain
   and the Defence of India: The Origins of the Problem,
   1798-1815," *Journal of Asian History* 6 (1972):14-44;
   "India and the Crimean War," *Journal of Imperial and
   Commonwealth History* 2 (1973):15-37; and "The Key to
   India?: Britain and the Herat Problem, 1830-1863,"
   Middle Eastern Studies 10 (1974):186-209, 287-311;
   Edward Ingram's "The Rules of the Game: A Commentary
   on the Defence of British India, 1798-1829," *Journal of
   Imperial and Commonwealth History* 3 (1975):257-79;
   H.W.C. Davis' "The Great Game in Asia, 1800-1844," *Pro-
   ceedings of the British Academy* 12 (1926):227-57; J.L.
   Morison's "From Alexander Burnes to Frederick Roberts:
   A Survey of Imperial Frontier Policy," *Proceedings of
   the British Academy* 22 (1936):117-206; A.P. Thornton's
   "The Reopening of the 'Central Asian Question,' 1864-
   9," *History* 41 (1956):122-36; Adrian Preston's "Sir
   Charles MacGregor and the Defence of India, 1857-1877,"

Historical Journal 12 (1969):58-77; and D.R. Gillard's
"Salisbury and the Indian Defence Problem, 1883-1902,"
item 246.

In addition to these studies there was a whole "the
Russians-are-coming" school in the 19th century that
warned Britain of the dangers of Russian expansion. The
best among these studies are those by Sir Henry Rawlin-
son, *England and Russia in the East: A Series of Papers
on the Political and Geographical Conditions of Central
Asia* (London: John Murray, 1875), and Lord George Curzon,
Persia and the Persian Question, item 412.

Cf. Edwardes, 244; Ingram, 250; Gillard, 245; Millman,
207; Taylor, 209; Greaves, 416; Gleason, 247; Sumner,
256; Lederer, 254.

242. Allworth, Edward, editor. *Central Asia: A Century of
      Russian Rule*. New York: Columbia University Press,
      1967. xiv + 552 pp.

A collection of 16 essays on Russian expansion and
rule in Central Asia. The articles by Hélène Carrière
d'Encausse, covering the Russian conquest, the development of Russian rule, the role of local nationalities
and the collapse of Czarist government, are of particular note. For a study of the development of local nationalism, see Serge Zenkovsky, *Pan-Turkism and Islam
in Russia* (Cambridge: Harvard University Press, 1960).
An excellent study of the development of the Russian
presence is Geoffrey Wheeler, *The Modern History of
Soviet Central Asia* (London: Weidenfeld & Nicolson,
1964); for a critical review of Western and Soviet
scholarship, see David MacKenzie, "Russian Expansion in
Central Asia (1864-1885): Brutal Conquest or Voluntary
Incorporation? A Review Article," *Canadian Slavic Studies* 4 (1970):721-35. For more information on Russian
control of Central Asia, see Seymour Becker, *Russia's
Protectorates in Central Asia: Bukhara and Khiva, 1865-
1924* (Cambridge: Harvard University Press, 1968); Peter
Morris, "The Russians in Central Asia, 1870-1887," *Slavonic Review* 53 (1975):521-38; David MacKenzie, "Expansion in Central Asia: St. Petersburg vs. the Turkestan
Generals (1863-1866)," *Canadian Slavic Studies* 3 (1969):
286-311; and Richard Pierce, *Russian Central Asia, 1867-
1917: A Study in Colonial Rule* (Berkeley: University of
California Press, 1960), and *Soviet Central Asia: A
Bibliography* (Berkeley: University of California Press,
1966). On the Russian impact on Central Asia, see
Wayne Vucinich, editor, *Russia and Asia: Essays on the*

Influence of Russia on the Asian People (Stanford, California: Hoover Institution Press, 1973). For the impact of Russian expansion on British policy, see Ingram, item 250; Edwardes, item 244; Gillard, item 245; and Millman, item 207.
Cf. Lederer, 254; Sumner, 256.
Reviews: *AA* 70 (1968):385-6, Fred Adelman; *GJ* 133 (1967):528, Owen Lattimore; *JAS* 27 (1967):154-5, Marvin L. Entner; *MEJ* 22 (1968):221-2, Charles Hostler; *PA* 40 (1967):156-8, John W. Strong; *PSQ* 83 (1968):444-6, Richard Pipes.

243. Churchill, Rogers Platt. *The Anglo-Russian Convention of 1907.* Cedar Rapids, Iowa: Torch Press, 1939. 365 pp.

The standard study of the 1907 Convention that ostensibly resolved outstanding Anglo-Russian differences in Persia, Afghanistan and Tibet. The work is dated, but has yet to be superseded, though the works by Monger, item 098; Grenville, item 085; and Greaves, item 248, give much more detail on the international and British background. Churchill traces the background to the rapprochement and then recounts the course of the negotiations--much of which can be followed in *British Documents on the Origins of the War*, item 045.
Cf. Klein, 252; Lowe, 095; Sweet, 257; Williams, 258-9.

244. Edwardes, Michael. *Playing the Great Game: A Victorian Cold War.* London: Hamish Hamilton, 1975. viii + 167 pp.

A readable though often garbled account of Anglo-Russian rivalry in Asia from the late 18th century to the early 19th century. Examines the tensions this rivalry caused and the various British attempts to cope with the political and military consequences of Russian expansion. The "Russians-are-coming" school of thought, later to be replaced by the "Germans-are-everywhere" school, was an important element in British strategic thinking. A forthcoming book, *Strategies of British India: Britain, Iran and Afghanistan, 1798-1850* (Oxford: Clarendon Press), by Malcolm Yapp promises to be the definitive study of British defence policy in India.
Cf. Alder, 241; Gillard, 245; Ingram, 250; Greaves, 416.

* Entner, Marvin. *Russo-Persian Commercial Relations, 1828-1914.* Cited as item 220.

245. Gillard, David. *The Struggle for Asia, 1828-1914: A
      Study in British and Russian Imperialism*. London:
      Methuen, 1977. 214 pp.

      The conflict of Anglo-Russian interests in Asia was
      a major element of late 19th- and early 20th-century
      international relations. British concern for the secu-
      rity of India and fear of Russian advance was a sig-
      nificant component in British strategic thinking.
      Gillard studies the "Great Game" and argues that it
      derived from the desire of politicians to control their
      environment and to anticipate and organize effective
      response to threats. Compare Gillard, who covers all
      of Asia, with Alastair Lamb, *Asian Frontiers: Studies
      in a Continuing Problem* (London: Pall Mall Press, 1968);
      and *The McMahon Line: A Study in the Relations Between
      India, China and Tibet, 1904 to 1914*, 2 volumes (London:
      Pall Mall Press, 1966), studies that concentrate on
      east Asia.
        Cf. Alder, 241; Ingram, 250; Greaves, 416.
        Reviews: *EHR* 63 (1978):260, M.S. Anderson; *GJ* 144
      (1978):346; *PA* 51 (1978):269-70, John A. White.

246. Gillard, David. "Salisbury and the Indian Defence Prob-
      lem, 1885-1902." *Studies in International History:
      Essays Presented to W. Norton Medlicott*, item 197,
      236-48.

      Examines the British strategic nightmare of Russian
      pressure on India while presenting Britain with chal-
      lenges elsewhere. Russia was immune to Britain's navy
      and Britain could not afford a military reverse in Asia
      for the adverse effect this might have had on British
      prestige. One of Britain's problems after 1900 was
      trying to decide where and how to defend the empire
      against a growing number of threats that outstripped
      imperial resources. Salisbury was the last Foreign
      Secretary to act with the confidence that Britain could
      confront the challenges alone.
        Cf. Greaves, 415 and 416; Monger, 098; Grenville, 085.

247. Gleason, John Howes. *The Genesis of Russophobia in
      Great Britain: A Study of the Interaction of Policy
      and Opinion*. Harvard Historical Studies, no. 57.
      1936. Reprint. Cambridge: Harvard University Press,
      1950. ix + 314 pp.

      Studies Anglo-Russian relations from the defeat of
      Napoleon to 1841 when the two powers recognized common

goals in preserving the Ottoman Empire. During this period the British had become increasingly alarmed at the prospect of Russian expansion, and relations between the two declined. Studying public opinion, Gleason shows how British misconceptions of Russian motives helped to produce this tension. By ending in 1841, however, he fails to show that there was more justification for suspicion of Russia, whether it expended intentionally or not, than he allows. Perception in politics and scholarship is a significant point of departure. Also see G.H. Bolsover, "David Urquhart and the Eastern Question: A Study in Publicity and Diplomacy, 1833-57," *Journal of Modern History* 8 (1936):444-67.

Cf. Anderson, 195; Millman, 207; Jelavich, 206; Greaves, 416.

Reviews: *EcHR* 5 (1952):1640, M. Vyuyon; *JMH* 25 (1953): 76-7, Vernon Puryear.

248.   Greaves, Rose L. "Some Aspects of the Anglo-Russian Convention and its Working in Persia, 1907-14." In two parts. *Bulletin of the School of Oriental and African Studies* 31 (1968):69-91 and 290-308.

The 1907 Convention was not just a settlement of Anglo-Russian differences in Asia, for it also represented a major change in Britain's European policy. (Or rather, it was another milestone on the way to those changes.) Greaves outlines these changes and then details what they meant for British policy in Persia, where for years policy had been directed towards limiting Russian encroachment. Examines the Persian Revolution of 1906; the appointment and dismissal of Morgan Shuster, an American economics expert hired by the Persian Government; the Russian ultimatum and invasion of 1911 to force the Persians to dismiss Shuster; and the continual violation by Russia of the spirit and letter of the 1907 Convention and why Britain tolerated it. Excellent study of what happens to small powers caught between the conflicting interests of Great Powers.

Cf. Churchill, 243; Williams, 258 and 259; McDaniels, 517; Monger, 098; Langer, 093; Lowe, 095.

249.   Hopwood, Derek. *The Russian Presence in Syria and Palestine, 1843-1914: Church and Politics in the Near East.* Oxford: Clarendon Press, 1969. viii + 232 pp.

Various European Great Powers took it upon themselves to look after the welfare of Christian minorities with-

in the Ottoman Empire. Their motives were a complex
blend of concern for the well-being of Christians in an
Islamic state and the national, imperial interests of
the respective Great Power. It was often difficult to
distinguish between the two, except when the respective
Power had to make the choice, in which case imperial interests came first. Hopwood examines the background and
growth of Russian interest in the Levant, and the consequences of that interest. Concentrates on the Orthodox Palestine Society, the main agency of Russian religious activity, and its relations with local Christians
and Ottoman authorities. A similar study is Theofanis
G. Stavrou, *Russian Interests in Palestine, 1882-1914:
A Study of Religious and Educational Influence* (Thes-
saloniki: Institute for Balkan Studies, 1963); and
"Russian Interest in the Levant, 1843-1848," *Middle
East Journal* 17 (1963):91-103. Also see Abdul Latif
Tibawi, "Russian Cultural Penetration of Syria-Palestine
in the Nineteenth Century," in two parts, *Journal of
the Royal Central Asian Society* 53 (1966):166-82, 309-
323.

Reviews: *AHR* 76 (1971):1521-2, Theofanis G. Stavrou;
BSOAS 33 (1970):393-4, Malcolm E. Yapp; *H* 55 (1970):
144, M.S. Anderson; *MEJ* 24 (1970):387-8, A.L. Tibawi.

250.   Ingram, Edward. *The Beginning of the Great Game in
Asia, 1828-1834.* Oxford: Clarendon Press, 1978.
xi + 361 pp.

The Great Game evolved from Britain's efforts to defend India from Russia--Britain succeeded but lost India
nonetheless. Ingram examines the origins of the Great
Game, connecting it to the Eastern Question. He traces
the peculiarities of the British position in India and
relations with the surrounding areas, showing how local
circumstances plus the threat of Russian expansion
pulled the British into a Persian and Central Asian policy. An important study but given to rhetorical flights
and obscurities. Needs to be read in conjunction with
Rose Greaves, item 416; G.J. Alder, item 471; and David
Gillard, item 245. Also see Ingram's other works: "From
Trade to Empire in the Near East," in three parts, *Middle
Eastern Studies* 14 (1978):3-21, 182-204, 278-306, which
deals with the period 1775-1801 in the Levant; "A Pre-
view of the Great Game in Asia, 1798-1801," in four
parts, *Middle Eastern Studies* 9 (1973):3-18, 157-74,
296-314, and 10 (1974):15-35; "The Defence of British
India," in three parts, *Journal of Indian History* 48

(1970):565-83, and 49 (1971):57-78, and Golden Jubilee
Volume (1973):595-622.
Cf. Edwardes, 244; Anderson, 195.
Reviews: *EHR* 95 (1980):377-8, C.J. Bartlett.

*   Jelavich, Barbara. *The Ottoman Empire, the Great Powers,
    and the Straits Question, 1870-1887.* Cited as item
    206.

251. Kazemzadeh, Firuz. *Russia and Britain in Persia, 1864-
     1914: A Study in Imperialism.* Yale Russian and East
     European Studies, no. 6. New Haven, Conn.: Yale Uni-
     versity Press, 1968. xii + 711 pp.

Persia had the misfortune of being between two empires, one expanding and the other nervous about security. Not an impartial study, but stiff with information, though it has not made the best use of British
archival sources. Needs to be balanced with Greaves,
item 416. There is no other study that deals as exten-
sively with Russian activities in Iran in this period.
Has an excellent bibliography. On other aspects of
Russian activities in Iran, see Kazemzadeh's "Russian
Imperialism and Persian Railways," *Harvard Slavic Studies* 4 (1957):355-73; and "The Origins and Early Development of the Persian Cossack Brigade," *American Slavic
and East European Review* 15 (1956):351-63.
   Cf. Entner, 220; Churchill, 243; Gillard, 245; Curzon,
412; Sykes, 426.
   Reviews: *AHR* 74 (1969):449-50, A.P. Thornton; *BSOAS*
33 (1970):402-3, A.K.S. Lambton; *H* 54 (1969):310-1,
G.J. Alder; *JMH* 42 (1970):264-71, J.B. Kelly; *MEJ* 23
(1969):83-4, T. Cuyler Young.

252. Klein, Ira. "The Anglo-Russian Convention and the Prob-
     lems of Central Asia, 1907-1914." *Journal of Brit-
     ish Studies* 11 (1971):126-47.

Examines Anglo-Russian tensions in Central Asia despite the 1907 Convention. Britain was weak in Asia,
Russia benefited from a strong strategic position, and
the British (perhaps numbed by the threat of Germany)
never made the Convention into a strong instrument to
check Russian expansion. Concentrates on Tibet and
areas east of Persia and thus is a complement to Greaves,
item 248, which Klein curiously overlooks.
   Cf. Gillard, 245.

253. Langer, William Leonard. "Russia, the Straits Question
      and the European Powers, 1904-1908." *English Histori-
      cal Review* 44 (1929):59-85.

      Looks at the background of Russian interest in the
      Straits and Russian diplomatic maneuvering to secure
      them. Useful but dated. For an overview of Russian
      policy and objectives, see the essays in Ivo Lederer,
      editor, *Russian Foreign Policy: Essays in Historical
      Perspective*, discussed below, especially the essays by
      Cyril Black, "The Pattern of Russian Objectives"; and
      Firuz Kazemzadeh, "Russia and the Middle East." A
      general review of Russian foreign policy is G.H. Bol-
      sover's "Aspects of Russian Foreign Policy, 1815-1914,"
      Essays Presented to Sir Lewis Namier, edited by Richard
      Pares and A.J.P. Taylor (London: Macmillan, 1956), 320-
      56.
           Cf. Zotiades, 260; Taylor, 209; Lowe, 095.

254. Lederer, Ivo John, editor. *Russian Foreign Policy: Es-
      says in Historical Perspective*. New Haven, Conn.:
      Yale University Press, 1962. xxiii + 620 pp.

      A collection of 18 essays on various aspects of Rus-
      sia's foreign relations, from internal features to re-
      lations with countries in Europe and Asia. Attempts to
      place Russian views of foreign relations in an interna-
      tional perspective. Of particular interest are Cyril
      Black, "The Pattern of Russian Objectives," 3-38; Robert
      Brynes, "Attitudes Towards the West," 109-41; Raymond
      Garthoff, "Military Influences and Instruments," 243-
      78; Gordon Craig, "Techniques of Negotiation," 351-76;
      Hajo Holborn, "Russia and the European Political Sys-
      tem," 377-416; and Firuz Kazemzadeh, "Russia and the
      Middle East," 489-530.
           Cf. Sumner, 256; Allworth, 242; Kazemzadeh, 251;
      Lenczowski, 322.

*   Lowe, Cedric James, and M.L. Dockrill. *The Mirage of
      Power*. Cited as item 095.

255. Spring, D.W. "The Trans-Persian Railway Project and
      Anglo-Russian Relations, 1909-14." *Slavonic and East
      European Review* 54 (1976):60-82.

      Examines Anglo-Russian cooperation in Persia, in par-
      ticular the negotiations for a trans-Persian railway.
      Railway construction in Persia, a nation without a rail-
      way network until the 1930's, was retarded by imperial

rivalry--British fears of facilitating an invasion of India and Russian fears of facilitating economic competition in areas under its influence and control. German pressure caused the two Powers to reconcile their differences in 1907, and before the war they negotiated for a railway to balance the Baghdad project and to increase their political and economic influence in Persia. Sheds light on the workings of the entente and its effects on Persia.

Cf. Kazemzadeh, 251; Olson, 236; Issawi, 417; Curzon, 412.

256. Sumner, B.H. *Tsardom and Imperialism in the Far East and Middle East, 1880-1914.* Raleigh Lecture on History, 1940. Reprint. Hamden, Conn.: Archon Books, 1968. 43 pp.

A brief survey of the main features and motives in Russian foreign policy. Particularly useful as a look from the Russian point of view at the rivalry with Britain in Asia, especially in Persia and the Ottoman Empire, and at the impact German ambitions and the humiliating defeat by Japan had on Russian policy. In addition see Barbara Jelavich, *A Century of Russian Foreign Policy, 1814-1914* (Philadelphia, Penn.: Lippincott, 1964); and Hugh Seton-Watson, *The Decline of Imperial Russia, 1855-1914* (London: Methuen, 1952).

Cf. Lederer, 254; Allworth, 242; Gillard, 245; Entner, 220.

257. Sweet, D.W., and R.T.B. Langhorne. "Great Britain and Russia, 1907-1914." *British Foreign Policy under Sir Edward Grey*, item 086, 236-55.

Studies the workings of the 1907 Convention in Asia and its impact on European diplomacy. The situation in Persia, Russia's continued pressure on that decaying Oriental monarchy and therefore on Britain's position in the Persian Gulf, put the greatest strain on the Anglo-Russian entente.

Cf. Churchill, 243; Greaves, 248; Monger, 098; Grenville, 085; Beloff, 080; Ward, 210.

258. Williams, Beryl J. "Great Britain and Russia, 1905 to the 1907 Convention." *British Foreign Policy under Sir Edward Grey*, item 086, 133-47.

The challenge of Germany in Europe plus the threat of Russia in Asia forced the British, unable to confront

both powers, to come to some negotiated settlement.
Grey opened negotiations with Russia in June 1906, soon
after taking office, both because of Foreign Office hostility towards Germany and the difficulty of reaching
any substantive agreement with the Wilhelmstrasse.
Nicolson, the Permanent Under-Secretary, wanted an
agreement with Russia at almost any price; Grey, however, was more cautious. Russia was inclined to come
to an agreement with Britain because of internal revolution and the defeat in a war with Japan, plus the
German threat at a time when Russia was thus weakened.
Williams discusses the impact of the Russian revolution
of 1905 in "The Revolution in 1905 and Russian Foreign
Policy," *Essays in Honour of E.H. Carr*, Chimen Abramsky
and Beryl J. Williams, editors (London: Macmillan,
1974). The eventual agreement eased tensions in Asia
but Britain received no reassurances on the Straits or
on respect for their paramount position in the Persian
Gulf.
    Cf. Churchill, 243; Greaves, 248; Monger, 098; Lowe,
095; Beloff, 080; McLean, 421.

259. Williams, Beryl J. "The Strategic Background to the
      Anglo-Russian Entente of August 1907." *Historical
      Journal* 9 (1966):360-73.

      Britain feared for the safety of India's land frontier
and saw Russia as the threat. The Russians, whether
interested or not, were prepared to play on this fear
to paralyze or inconvenience British diplomacy elsewhere. This left a lingering bad odor in Anglo-Russian
relations which was eventually dispelled by the rise of
a threat to both Powers--Germany. This encouragement
led Britain and Russia to compose their outstanding differences in Asia, at least temporarily.
      Cf. Churchill, 243; Monger, 098; Greaves, 248.

260. Zotiades, George B. "Russia and the Question of Con-
      stantinople and the Turkish Straits during the Balkan
      Wars." *Journal of Balkan Studies* 11 (1970):281-98.

      The threat that Bulgaria, or any nation other than
Russia, might gain control over Constantinople and the
Straits was a Russian nightmare, made acute by Ottoman
weakness as demonstrated during the Balkan Wars. At
the same time the Russians were sponsors of Slavic nationalism in the very Balkan nations threatening to
take the Straits and deprive Russia of its long-sought

goal, and were also protectors of Orthodox Christians
in the Ottoman Empire. Russian statesmen found it difficult to juggle their conflicting ambitions. Their
main concern, though, was in delaying any but a Russian
solution to the fate of Constantinople.
    Cf. Anderson, 195; Sumner, 256; Langer, 093; Taylor,
209; Lowe, 095; Ekstein, 318.

France

*   Gifford, Prosser, and William Roger Louis, editors.
       *Britain and France in Africa: Imperial Rivalry and
       Colonial Rule.* Cited as item 201.

261.   Hamilton, Keith A. "An Attempt to Form an Anglo-French
       'Industrial Entente.'" *Middle Eastern Studies* 11
       (1975):47-73.

       The Anglo-French political entente of 1904 did not
       guarantee harmony in Anglo-French relations. In the
       Ottoman Empire commercial rivalry continued, and in
       many instances French and German financial interests
       cooperated to the detriment of British interests. Hop-
       ing to improve the entente with France, the British
       worked to secure more Anglo-French economic cooperation
       in Turkey. These efforts failed, but this fact, while
       tedious, did not upset the political entente; nor did
       continued Franco-German economic cooperation form the
       basis of a rapprochement.
           Cf. Platt, 237; Feis, 222; Kent, 371; Shorrock, 266;
       Spagnolo, 268; Blaisdell, 213; Earle, 219.

262.   Hamilton, Keith A. "Great Britain and France, 1905-
       1911." *British Foreign Policy under Sir Edward Grey*,
       item 086, 113-32.

       Examines Grey's determination to remain committed to
       the entente with France in response to the growing
       power and assertiveness of Germany. Fear of diplomatic
       isolation canalized Grey's foreign policy between 1905-
       1911, when Anglo-French informal military discussions
       began cementing the relationship. Grey was not insen-
       sitive to the idea of a rapprochement with Germany, but
       he found it difficult to overcome the suspicion that
       Germany was Britain's real enemy, an idea reinforced
       by Germany's intransigence over the naval issue. This
       led, by unintended steps, to the military discussions
       with France and the growth of a presumptive alliance.

Cf. Williamson, 211; Steiner, 307; Rolo, 265; Monger, 098; Taylor, 209.

263. Hamilton, Keith A. "Great Britain and France, 1911-1914." *British Foreign Policy under Sir Edward Grey*, item 086, 324-44.

Examines the strains on the Anglo-French entente, such as Britain's attempts to negotiate with Germany. The French were eager to cement more formal ties and promoted naval-military coordination to achieve this. The British were interested in the entente not just because of Germany, but also for the trouble France could cause if it became hostile.
Cf. Rolo, 265; Lowe, 095; Marder, 131.

264. Hargreaves, John D. "The Origin of the Anglo-French Military Conversations in 1905." *History* 36 (1951): 244-48.

Brief look at the timing of the Anglo-French military conversations that eventually converted the entente into an informal alliance. His assumption is that they began before Grey assumed office, but the record is unclear. Dated.
Cf. Williamson, 211; Taylor, 209; Howard, 089; Monger, 098; Grenville, 085; Rolo, 265.

*   Landes, David. *Bankers and Pashas: International Finance and Economic Imperialism in Egypt*. Cited as item 232.

*   Lowe, Cedric James, and M.L. Dockrill. *The Mirage of Power*. Cited as item 095.

*   Lowe, Cedric James, and M.L. Dockrill. *The Reluctant Imperialists: British Foreign Policy, 1878-1902*. Cited as item 096.

265. Rolo, P.J.V. *Entente Cordiale: The Origins and Negotiations of the Anglo-French Agreements of 8 April 1904*. London: Macmillan, 1969. 300 pp.

Summarizes the negotiations for an Anglo-French settlement of outstanding differences, mainly over Egypt, that formed the basis for a close relationship between the two countries, reinforced by the aggressive foreign policy of Germany. Examines the origins of Anglo-French hostility--the occupation of Egypt--and

the factors that eventually led the two powers to
reconcile their differences. The work is based almost
solely on published documents and secondary sources,
but it is a useful survey and summary. A detailed study of both French and British diplomacy on the entente
remains to be done, though the British side has received
considerable attention. On the background to the Anglo-
French Agreement, see Christopher Andrew's *Theophile
Delcassé and the Making of the Entente Cordiale: A Reappraisal of French Policy, 1898-1905* (London: Macmillan, 1968) and its useful bibliography; and his "The
Entente Cordiale from its Origins to 1914," *Troubled
Neighbors: Franco-British Relations in the Twentieth
Century* (London: Weidenfeld & Nicolson, 1971), edited
by Neville Waites, 11-39; as well as his very similar
study, "France and the Making of the Entente Cordiale,"
Historical Journal 10 (1967):89-105. Also see Joseph
Mathews, *Egypt and the Formation of the Anglo-French
Entente of 1904* (Philadelphia: University of Pennsyl-
vania Press, 1939). On aspects of Anglo-French hos-
tility and cooperation, see Arthur Marsden, *British
Diplomacy and Tunis, 1875-1902: A Case Study in Medi-
terranean Policy* (London: Chatto & Windus, 1972); E.W.
Edwards, "The Franco-German Agreement on Morocco,
1909," *English Historical Review* 78 (1963):483-513;
and F.V. Parsons, "The Proposed Madrid Conference on
Morocco, 1887-88," *Historical Journal* 8 (1965):72-94.
   Cf. Monger, 098; Grenville, 085; Taylor, 209; Williamson, 211.
   Reviews: *AHR* 75 (1970):2039, Oron J. Hale; *EHR* 86
(1971):877-8, P.M.H. Bell; *H* 56 (1971):128, Christopher
Howard; *JMH* 42 (1970):688-94, Samuel Williamson.

266. Shorrock, William I. *French Imperialism in the Middle
      East: The Failure of Policy in Syria and Lebanon,
      1900-1914.* Madison: University of Wisconsin Press,
      1976. x + 214 pp.

      Studies the development of French interest in Syria
      prior to World War I, concentrating on French economic
      involvement and the relations with the Christian mi-
      norities, whom France patronized. The sense of commit-
      ment and responsibility France developed for Syria was
      not reciprocated by Muslim Arabs and difficulties arose
      because the two failed to understand one another, a
      fact that was aggravated after World War I when the
      French occupied the area. Also see Shorrock, "French
      Presence in Syria and Lebanon before the First World

War, 1900–1914," *Historian* 34 (1972):293–303.   Compare
with Spagnolo, item 268.
  Cf. Nevakivi, 324; Busch, 352.
  Reviews: *AAPSS-A* 434 (1977):217, Gary L. Fowler; *AHR*
82 (1977):653–4, William W. Haddad; *MEJ* 31 (1977):488–
9, Roderic Davison.

267.   Shorrock, William I.   "The Origins of the French Mandate
       in Syria and the Lebanon: The Railway Question 1901–
       1914."   *International Journal of Middle East Studies*
       1 (1970):133–53.

France had a long-term cultural and economic interest
in the Ottoman Empire, most particularly in Syria.   The
idea of acquiring a mandate for the area did not ori-
ginate with the secret agreements during World War I
but derived from these older concerns.   France, like
other European Powers, recognized Ottoman weakness and
wanted to be assured of a share in any divisions of that
feeble state.   Railways became a means of developing
the economies of local areas as well as instruments of
influence.
  Cf. Earle, 219; Andrew, 317; Hamilton, 261.

268.   Spagnolo, John P.   *France and Ottoman Lebanon, 1861–
       1914.*   Foreword by Albert Hourani.   London: Ithaca
       Press for the Middle East Centre, St. Antony's Col-
       lege, Oxford, 1977.   335 pp.

Argues that French interest in Lebanon grew primarily
from French protection of the Marionite Christians and
from a determination to see that France got its fair
share of any of the spoils in the rivalry among the
European states over the Sick Man of Europe's possessions.   The effect of this rivalry and French interests
disrupted political and economic development in Lebanon,
fostering or aggravating communal and sectarian divisions that created an unstable social environment that
persists today.   Makes extensive use of French archival
material as well as Arab and Turkish source material.
Spagnolo examines the nature and development of aspects
of French imperialism in his article, "The Definition
of a Style of Imperialism: The Internal Politics of the
French Educational Investment in Ottoman Beirut," *French
Historical Studies* 8 (1974):563–84.   Good bibliography.
  Cf. Nevakivi, 324.
  Reviews: *AHR* 83 (1978):1064–5, William Shorrock; *MEJ*
32 (1978):214–5, Malcolm Russell.

269. Spagnolo, John P. "French Influence on Syria Prior to World War I: The Functional Weakness of Imperialism." *Middle East Journal* 23 (1969):45-62.

France had a "traditional" interest in Syria, had economic, emotional and cultural ties, was involved with Christian groups, wanted not to be left out of any partition of the Ottoman Empire and saw it as a matter of national honor to be accorded colonies as the due of an imperial power. These complex motives plus the convolutions of the Eastern Question sucked the French and other Europeans willy-nilly into regional politics--themes that are more ably put in Spagnolo's *France and Ottoman Lebanon*, item 268.

Germany

270. Ekstein, Michael G. "Sir Edward Grey and Imperial Germany in 1914." *Journal of Contemporary History* 6 (1971):121-31.

Grey believed that there was a war party and a peace party in Germany on the eve of World War I, and this assumption determined the nature of his policy. Russia was worried about Germany and wanted to secure a closer relationship with Britain in late 1913, while the Germans, worried about encirclement, wanted to prevent this. To do so the Germans created, for Grey's benefit, the impression that there was a split between German civil and military authorities, and Grey could strengthen the civilian element by holding substantive talks which might resolve the vexing naval question. Grey continued to act on this idea during the Sarajevo Crisis and helped form the impression that the Prussian element in Germany, the military, was responsible for the war. Ekstein does not, however, make sufficiently clear just why this impression was important or what effect it had on British policy. Supports the Fisher argument of a cynical German foreign policy (see item 288).
Cf. Steiner, 307.

271. Friedman, Isaiah. *Germany, Turkey and Zionism, 1897-1918*. Oxford: Clarendon Press, 1977. xiv + 461 pp.

Primarily a study of the growth and development of the German Zionist movement and its role in securing German support for settlement in Palestine. During

World War I the Zionist effort in Germany was as important as Weizmann's activities in Britain in securing
vital European support to protect the tenuous position
in Palestine. One of the few works to study this aspect
of Zionist activity. See Saadia Weltmann, "Germany,
Turkey, and the Zionist Movement, 1914-1918," *Review
of Politics* 23 (1951):246-69, for more information.
Complements Stein, item 531.

Cf. Caplan, 520; Mandel, 525.

Reviews: *AAPSS-A* 438 (1978):143-4, Harry N. Howard;
AHR 83 (1978):1230, Raphael Patai; *EHR* 94 (1979):229-
31, B.M.J. Wasserstein; *H* 64 (1979):146-7, Lionel
Kochan; *MEJ* 33 (1979):223-4, Israel Naamani.

* Gifford, Prosser, and William R. Louis, editors. *Brit-
    ain and Germany in Africa: Imperial Rivalry and Colo-
    nial Rule.* Cited as item 202.

* Henderson, W.O. "German Economic Penetration in the
    Middle East." Cited as item 224.

* Hoffman, Ross. *Great Britain and the German Trade Ri-
    valry, 1875-1914.* Cited as item 226.

272. Kennedy, Paul M. "German World Policy and the Alliance
    Negotiations with England, 1897-1900." *Journal of
    Modern History* 45 (1973):605-25.

    Disputes the view that there ever were any real chances
    for an Anglo-German naval holiday. Argues that Admiral
    Tirpitz's maneuverings in domestic politics to secure
    ever-increasing naval expenditures and German colonial
    ambitions helped to negate any real chances of an Anglo-
    German detente or alliance. This, plus the need of the
    German leadership to use foreign successes and naval
    development to advantage in internal affairs, meant the
    Germans never seriously considered concessions to Brit-
    ain that would have obviated their outstanding differ-
    ences. A Fischer-esque argument.

    Cf. Steiner, 307; Lowe, 096; Grenville, 085; Monger,
    098; Langer, 093; Taylor, 209; Fischer, 288.

273. Koch, H.W. "The Anglo-German Alliance Negotiations:
    Missed Opportunity or Myth?" *History* 54 (1969):378-
    392.

    Did an opportunity for an Anglo-German alliance exist?
    No, argues Koch, because the fundamental priorities of

the two countries were mutually exclusive. An alliance
is based on mutual advantage and on give-and-take, and
the differences between the two states were too great
(though one cannot help but feel that the failure to
secure an agreement followed by World War I has led
some historians to believe in inevitability). Gives a
useful survey of the literature on the subject, though
somewhat dated now. Compare with Kennedy, item 125.
Cf. Monger, 098; Grenville, 085; Taylor, 209; Langer,
093; Steiner, 307.

274. Langhorne, Richard T.B. "Great Britain and Germany,
     1911-1914." *British Foreign Policy under Sir Edward
     Grey*, item 086, 288-314.

Examines Anglo-German attempts to settle their differences. The German naval program, however, dogged
all such efforts, despite some progress in other areas
of difference, i.e., over the Portuguese colonies and
the Baghdad Railway.
Cf. Kennedy, 125; Monger, 098; Grenville, 085; Lowe,
095; Steiner, 307; Taylor, 209; Marder, 131.

275. Langhorne, Richard T.B. "The Naval Question in Anglo-
     German Relations, 1912-1914." *Historical Journal* 14
     (1971):359-70.

Studies the attempts to effect a "naval holiday," a
respite in the naval arms race, between Britain and
Germany. Expands on Woodward, item 279; and complements
Kennedy, item 272. Germany needed the navy as visible
proof of its world-power status, but the drive to
achieve this was the one course bound to alienate Britain.
Cf. Marder, 131; Taylor, 209; Steiner, 307; Langhorne,
274.

276. Martin, Bradford G. *German-Persian Diplomatic Rela-
     tions, 1873-1912.* 's-Gravenhage: Mouton, 1959.
     237 pp.

In 1898 Germany departed from its former foreign policy and sought to enhance its international standing
as a great power. Penetration of the Middle East suited
this new policy. The Persians, eager to involve a third
power in Iran to check the British and Russians and as
a means to sustain their national integrity, looked to
the Germans. The effort failed, as the Germans were
more interested in Turkey, and Iran fell into even more

difficulty. Martin examines German interest in Iran.
Though based on limited research, the work remains vir-
tually the only monograph on German-Persian relations.
For a brief account of German economic activity in the
Middle East, see W.O. Henderson, *Studies in German Co-
lonial History*, item 224.
  Cf. Ramazani, 425; Hoffman, 226; Kazemzadeh, 251.
  Reviews: *MEJ* 15 (1961):226-7, J.C. Hurewitz.

*   Staley, Eugene. "Business and Politics in the Persian
    Gulf: The Story of the Wönckhaus Firm." Cited as
    item 240.

277. Steinberg, Jonathan. "The German Background to Anglo-
      German Relations, 1905-1914." *British Foreign Policy
      under Sir Edward Grey*, item 086, 193-215.

      British diplomacy had to come to grips with Germany's
      dynamism, especially its economic expansion. Looks at
      the internal motivations for German foreign adventures
      and the development of the navy and the arms race with
      Britain. Could Britain have done more to prevent war?
      Or was war inevitable? Also see Steinberg's "The No-
      velle of 1908: Necessities and Choice in the Anglo-
      German Naval Arms Race," *Transactions of the Royal His-
      torical Society*, 5th series, 21 (1971):25-43.
        Cf. Fischer, 288.

278. Sweet, D.W. "Great Britain and Germany, 1905-1911."
      British Foreign Policy under Sir Edward Grey, item
      086, 216-35.

      Grey was not opposed to a rapprochement with Germany,
      although he was not prepared to abandon the entente
      with France to achieve it or to relinquish essential
      British interests. The incompatibility of the respec-
      tive Anglo-German goals precluded a settlement.
        Cf. Steiner, 137; Marder, 131; Woodward, 279; Hoffman,
      226.

279. Woodward, Ernest Llewellyn. *Great Britain and the Ger-
      man Navy*. 1935. Reprint. London: Frank Cass, 1964.
      viii + 524 pp.

      British security needs in the early 20th century re-
      quired that Germany voluntarily accept a position of
      inferiority, at least in naval terms. This clashed
      with a seeming German need for a "conspicuous consump-
      tion" in ships, an urge that menaced the British in the

one area they felt most vulnerable. Resolution of this difference evaded every effort, though by 1913 there were signs of change. The rivalry, however, contributed to the diplomatic revolution before World War I that saw Britain come to terms with Russia and solidify its ties with France.

Cf. Marder, 131; Grenville, 085; Monger, 098; Steiner, 307; Hoffman, 226.

United States

280.   Bryson, Thomas. *American Diplomatic Relations with the Middle East, 1784-1975: A Survey.* Metuchen, N.J.: Scarecrow Press, 1977. viii + 431 pp.

Surveys the American presence in the Middle East from the Barbary Pirates to the Kissinger era. Chapter 5, "Pre-war Middle East: A Time of Transition," 45-57; chapter 6, "World War I and the American Response to Upheaval in the Middle East, 1914-1920," 58-74; chapter 7, "The Inter-War Years and the American Response to Nationalism in the Middle East, 1920-1939," 75-93; and chapter 8, "The Open Door and the American Quest for Middle East Oil, 1919-1939," 96-109, are of note. The book covers a broad topic, concentrating on the post-World War II period, giving only a sketchy account of earlier American activities in the Middle East. For more details on some of the topics discussed by Bryson, see John DeNovo, "The Movement for an Aggressive American Oil Policy, 1918-20," *American Historical Review* 61 (1956):854-76; "Petroleum and the U.S. Navy before World War I," *Mississippi Valley Historical Review* 41 (1955):641-56; and "A Railroad for Turkey: The Chester Project, 1908-13," *Business History Review* 33 (1959): 300-29. Also see James Field, *America and the Mediterranean World, 1776-1882* (Princeton, N.J.: Princeton University Press, 1969); and Michael Hogan, "Informal Entente: Public Policy and Private Management in Anglo-American Petroleum Affairs, 1918-1924," *Business History Review* 48 (1974):187-205. E.M. Earle's "The Turkish Petroleum Company: A Study in Oleaginous Diplomacy," *Political Studies Quarterly* 39 (1924):265-79, is an early study of the clash of American and British interests over oil after World War I. In addition see Bryson's *United States/Middle East Diplomatic Relations, 1784-1978: An Annotated Bibliography* (Metuchen, N.J.: Scarecrow Press, 1979), for a listing of articles and

monographs on American diplomacy, oil interests, phil-
anthropists, and missionary activity.
    Cf. Evans, 330; Howard, 332 and 538.
    Reviews: *AHR* 82 (1977):1355-6, Anthony R. DeLuca;
JAH 64 (1978):1085-6, Justus D. Doenecke.

281. DeNovo, John August. *American Interests and Politics*
      in the Middle East, 1900-1939. Minneapolis: Univer-
      sity of Minnesota Press, 1963. xii + 497 pp.

      Reviews the American presence in the Middle East,
      which initially was largely a missionary one, and tries
      to assess the effects of American activities. American
      cultural interest in the area preceded any political or
      official interest; in fact the activities of mission-
      aries and businessmen occasionally embarrassed the Amer-
      ican Government. Important for tracing the evolution
      of American involvement and how this fit into the local
      scene, as well as its impact on international relations.
      Has a valuable bibliography.
          For an expansion on aspects of the American presence,
      see Phillip Baram, *The Department of State in the Middle*
      East, 1919-1945 (Philadelphia: University of Pennsyl-
      vania Press, 1978). Also see James Field, *America and*
      the Mediterranean World, 1776-1882 (Princeton, N.J.:
      Princeton University Press, 1969). A comprehensive
      study with an excellent bibliography on America and the
      Straits Question from 1830 to the 1960's is Harry Howard,
      Turkey, the Straits and U.S. Policy (Baltimore, Maryland:
      Johns Hopkins Press, 1974); while William Polk's *The*
      United States and the Arab World, revised edition (Cam-
      bridge: Harvard University Press, 1969), gives a general
      survey of American interests in the Middle East from
      the 19th century, though it concentrates on the post-
      World War I period. For a more detailed study on Egypt,
      see L.C. Wright, *United States Policy Towards Egypt,*
      1830-1914 (New York: Exposition Press, 1969). An ac-
      count of some of the Americans, mainly missionaries,
      in the area in the 19th century can be found in David
      Finnie, *Pioneers East: The Early American Experience in*
      the Middle East (Cambridge: Harvard University Press,
      1967). A brief overview of American policy in the
      Middle East from 1800 to the late 1950's is George
      Lenczowski, editor, *United States Interests in the*
      Middle East (Washington, D.C.: American Enterprise In-
      stitute for Policy Research, 1960).
          Cf. Evans, 330; Howard, 538.

Reviews: *AHR* 70 (1964):164-5, Willard Beling: *JMH* 36 (1964):471-2, Robert Daniel; *MEJ* 18 (1964):240-2, Bayard Dodge.

* Evans, Laurence. *U.S. Policy and the Partition of Turkey, 1914-1924.* Cited as item 330.

282. Grabill, Joseph L. *Protestant Diplomacy and the Near East: Missionary Influence on American Policy, 1810-1927.* Minneapolis: University of Minnesota Press, 1971. x + 395 pp.

An excellent account of American Protestant missionary activity in the Middle East, and the attempts of the missionaries to convert Middle Eastern Christians-- local laws prohibited proselytizing among Muslims--and to get the American Government to take a more active role in local matters. One of the few reliable works on Christian groups and World War I. See Robin Waterfield, *Christians in Persia: Assyrians, Armenians, Roman Catholics and Protestants* (London: Allen & Unwin, 1973); and John Joseph, *The Nestorians and Their Non-Muslim Neighbors: A Study of Western Influence on Their Relations* (Princeton, N.J.: Princeton University Press, 1961), for two other valuable studies. For American missionary and philanthropic activity in Syria and Palestine, see Abdul Latif Tibawi, *American Interests in Syria, 1800-1901: A Study of Educational, Literary and Religious Work* (Oxford: Clarendon Press, 1966). Also see Grabill's "Missionary Influence on American Relations with the Near East, 1914-1923," *Muslim World* 58 (1968):43-56, 141-56; and Robert Daniel, *American Philanthrophy in the Near East, 1820-1960* (Athens, Ohio: Ohio University Press, 1970).

Cf. Arberry, 546; Hopwood, 249; Tibawi, 400; Atiyah, 547.

Reviews: *AHR* 77 (1972):831-3, James B. Gidney; *IJMES* 4 (1973):369-70, Richard Hovannissian; *JAH* 59 (1972): 204-5, James A. Field, Jr.; *MEJ* 26 (1972):80-2, Bayard Dodge.

* Howard, Harry. *The King-Crane Commission.* Cited as item 538.

283. Manuel, Frank. *The Realities of American-Palestine Relations.* Washington, D.C.: Public Affairs Press, 1949. viii + 378 pp.

Studies American interests in Palestine from the
1830's to the creation of the state of Israel. Deals
in particular with American policy towards Zionism and
the influence of Zionists and Jews on American policy.
Good review, though pro-Zionist and now rather dated.
Cf. Stein, 531.
Reviews: *AHR* 56 (1950):75-6, Carl Freidrich; *JMH* 23
(1951):179, Sydney N. Fisher.

International Rivalry, 1914-1921:
War and Peace

Origins and Conduct of the War and Peace

284. Albertini, Luigi. *The Origins of the War of 1914*. 3
      volumes. Translated and edited by Isabella M.
      Massey. London: Oxford University Press, 1952-1957.

The most exhaustive study of the origins of World
War I, starting with a review of the European diplomatic environment from the Congress of Vienna (Vol. 1:
*European Relations from the Congress of Vienna to the
Eve of the Sarajevo Murders*). Any work of this size
and scope has strengths and weaknesses. The work is
strongest on European relations and weakest in dealing
with the Eastern Question and Turkish neutrality (see
Vol. 3: *The Epilogue of the Crisis of July 1914*).
Albertini is especially good on German policy and the
impact of railway timetables and technological innova-
tions in determining aspects of policy and planning;
and examines the impact of nationalism, militarism,
economic competition and political incompetence in
helping to create the climate for war. Compare with
Sidney Fay, *The Origins of the World War*, 2 volumes,
2nd edition (New York: Free Press, 1966). Also see
Bernadotte Schmitt, *The Origins of World War I* (London:
Hutchinson, 1958); and Zbynek A.B. Zeman, *A Diplomatic
History of the First World War* (London: Weidenfeld &
Nicolson, 1971), published in the United States as *The
Gentlemen Negotiators* (New York: Macmillan, 1971).
Cf. Lafore, 299; Steiner, 307; Taylor, 308; Rolo,
265; Churchill, 243; Trumpener, 340; Sachar, 480;
Monger, 098; Grenville, 085; Howard, 088; Fischer, 288.
Reviews: *H* 41 (1956), 146-7, M.N. Medlicott; *JMH* 24
(1952):69-74, Bernadotte Schmitt.

*   Busch, Briton. *Britain, India and the Arabs, 1914-*
        1921. Cited as item 352.

285.   Busch, Briton Cooper. *Mudros to Lausanne: Britain's*
        Frontier in West Asia, 1918-1923. Albany: State Uni-
        versity of New York Press, 1976. 430 pp.

        Details British policy, or lack of policy, in the
        Middle East after World War I, showing its pragmatic
        nature and the struggle within the government over
        policy-making. Highlights the difference in views be-
        tween policy-makers in India and those in London. A
        broader-ranging work than others by Busch, items 352
        and 404, and the best, but concentrates far too much
        on the inter-departmental details of British policy.
        Good bibliography. In addition, see Paul Helmreich,
        "Oil and the Negotiations of the Treaty of Sèvres, Decem-
        ber 1918-April 1920," *Middle East Forum* 42 (1966):67-75;
        Joseph Grew, "The Peace Conference of Lausanne, 1922-
        1923," *Proceedings of the American Philosophical So-*
        ciety 98 (1959):1-10; and Roderic Davison, "Turkish
        Diplomacy from Mudros to Lausanne," item 467.
            Cf. Helmreich, 331; Klieman, 298; Kedourie, 333;
        Fitzsimmons, 289; Sachar, 480; Lewis, 477.
            Reviews: *AHR* 82 (1977):641-2, Roger Adelson; *BSOAS*
        40 (1977):397-8, M.S. Anderson; *IJMES* 11 (1980):276-7,
        Harry Psomiades; *MEJ* 31 (1977):213-4, Laurence Evans.

286.   Davis, Rodney. "Lloyd George: Leader or Led in British
        War Aims, 1916-1918." *Power, Public Opinion and Di-*
        plomacy: Essays in Honor of Eber Malcolm Carroll by
        His Former Students. Edited by Lillian Parker; L.P.
        Wallace; and William C. Askew. Durham, N.C.: Duke
        University Press, 1959, pp. 222-43.

        Examines Lloyd George's role in shaping British war
        aims, a study of political maneuvering and adjusting
        to circumstances. Lloyd George was a dynamic individ-
        ual but he was also a political one who adapted his ap-
        proach to suit the times more than a leader who shaped
        them. The bibliography on Lloyd George is extensive,
        some recent accounts including: R.J.Q. Adams, *Arms and*
        the Wizard: Lloyd George and the Ministry of Munitions,
        1915-1916 (London: Cassell, 1978); Michael Fry, *The*
        Education of a Statesman, 1890-1915, vol. 1 of *Lloyd*
        George and Foreign Policy (Montreal: McGill-Queen's
        University Press, 1977); William George, *The Making of*
        Lloyd-George (London: Faber, 1976); Martin Gilbert,

editor, *Lloyd George* (Englewood Cliffs, N.J.: Prentice-
Hall, 1968); Peter Rowland, *Lloyd-George* (London: Barrie
& Jenkins, 1975); and Robert Scally, *The Origins of the
Lloyd-George Coalition: The Politics of Social-Imperial-
ism, 1900-1918* (Princeton, N.J.: Princeton University
Press, 1975).

Cf. Hazelhurst, 295; McEwen, 302; Guinn, 291; Rothwell, 306; Taylor, 308.

287.   Egerton, George W. *Great Britain and the Creation of
       the League of Nations: Strategy, Politics and Inter-
       national Organization, 1914-1919.* London: Scholar
       Press, 1979. xiii + 273 pp.

Examines Britain's commitment to the idea of collective security as embodied in the League of Nations.
Looks at the difficulties facing British statesmen in
reconciling the principles of the League with British
security requirements. What the British wanted--es-
pecially such figures as Jan Smuts, Robert Cecil, and
Lloyd George--was a limited international organization
to prevent war but not interfere with British Imperial
policies. Egerton studies the evolution of British
commitment to the League during the war, to the idea
of Anglo-American cooperation, and Lloyd George's tac-
tical maneuvering to use the League. Also see Michael
Fry, *Illusion of Security: North Atlantic Diplomacy,
1918-22* (Toronto: University of Toronto Press, 1972).

Cf. Temperley, 309; Taylor, 308; Beloff, 080; Rothwell, 306; Fitzsimmons, 289; Lloyd George, 172; Hancock,
161; Hankey, 292; Nicolson, 305.

Reviews: *AHR* 84 (1979):1384-5, Keith Robbins.

288.   Fischer, Fritz. *Germany's Aims in the First World War.*
       Introduction by Hajo Holborn. German edition, 1961.
       New York: Norton, 1967. xx + 652 pp.

This controversial study argues convincingly that
German statesmen after 1890 were bent on a course of
world domination that made a clash on the scale of
World War I likely. The arguments are cogent, but concentrate on Germany. Germany, however, was part of an
international system and as such was not immune to the
climate and pressures of that association. French hostility and efforts to surround Germany with hostile
states; Austria-Hungary's weakness; British paranoia
and measures to contain Germany; and Russian anxiety
about the German army--all of which were factors

the Germans aggravated but did not create--worked to
limit or direct German activities or to give them a
particular cast. The combination of these elements
produced a climate of suspicion and anxiety that influenced decisions and created a frame of reference
that made war seem a reasonable solution for Germany.
See Fischer's *War of Illusion: German Policies from
1911 to 1914*, translated by Marian Jackson (London:
Chatto & Windus, 1975) for a study of the domestic and
international background to the arguments presented in
Germany's Aims. Also see Michael Balfour, *The Kaiser
and His Times* (New York: Norton, 1964); and Volker R.
Berghahn, *Germany and the Approach of War in 1914*
(London: Macmillan, 1973). Some of the controversy is
covered in H.W. Koch, editor, *The Origins of the First
World War: Great Power Rivalry and German War Aims*
(London: Macmillan, 1972); and Fischer's response to
his critics is covered in his *World Power or Decline:
The Controversy over Germany's Aims in the First World
War*, translated by Lancelot Farrar *et al.* (New York:
Norton, 1974).
   Cf. Steiner, 307; Albertini, 284; Benians, 196;
Taylor, 209.
   Reviews: *JMH* 41 (1969):260-7, Gerald D. Feldman.

289.   Fitzsimmons, Matthew Anthony. *Empire by Treaty: Brit-
       ain and the Middle East in the Twentieth Century.*
       Notre Dame, Ind.: University of Notre Dame Press,
       1964. xi + 235 pp.

   The British position in the Middle East was based on
the area's strategic and economic importance, but Britain never incorporated into its empire any of the nations of the Middle East, though it played an important
part in shaping them. Examines British policy in the
interwar years, the nature of Britain's interests, the
mandate and treaty systems that grew up reflecting
those interests, and the impact of nationalism in al-
tering and eventually extinguishing those interests.
The first three chapters are useful in understanding
the nature of Britain's position in the Middle East
after World War I.
   Cf. Monroe, 304; Klieman, 298; Kedourie, 333.
   Reviews: *AAPSS-A* 358 (1965):190-1, Don Peretz; *APSR*
59 (1965):216-7, Steven Muller; *MEJ* 18 (1964):499-500,
John Marlowe.

290.   Gottlieb, Wolfram Wilhelm. *Studies in Secret Diplomacy*
       during the First World War. London: Allen & Unwin,
       1957.   430 pp.

       Delves into the relations among the Allies, their ri-
       valries and maneuvering for position during World War I.
       Examines Turkey's entrance into the war; the negotia-
       tions among the Allies over possession of the Straits
       and other interests in the Middle East; and the role of
       Italy in Allied considerations and the attempt to get
       Italy to join the war.   Tries to look at some of the
       "unspoken assumptions" (see Joll, item 297), and the
       domestic and strategic factors that influenced the re-
       spective policies of Russia, France, Britain and the
       smaller states.   Over-emphasizes hidden motives and ob-
       scures the fact that the Allies wanted victory first
       and that other maneuverings were secondary.   Dated.
       For a more up-to-date general account, see Zbynek A.B.
       Zeman, *A Diplomatic History of the First World War*
       (London: Weidenfeld & Nicolson, 1971).
          Cf. Sachar, 480; Trumpener, 340; Albertini, 284;
       Busch, 352; Rothwell, 306; Steiner, 307.
          Reviews: *H* 43 (1958):262-3, J.E. Tyler; *JMH* 31 (1959):
       263-4, William C. Askew.

291.   Guinn, Paul. *British Strategy and Politics, 1914-1918*.
       Oxford: Clarendon Press, 1965.   xiv + 359 pp.

       It is usually argued, with justice, that Britain en-
       tered World War I without a clear definition of objec-
       tives, other than to beat Germany, and that only during
       the course of the war did the British hammer out a set
       of definite goals and principles.   Britain certainly
       went to war unprepared to fight a continental war.   The
       shock of the Western Front, the necessities of war-
       planning, difficult relations with Allies, and a cum-
       bersome peacetime cabinet system caused confusion in
       the early war effort and aggravated internal rivalries
       as the British groped for a policy to guide the war ef-
       fort and break the stalemate in Europe.   Guinn examines
       the intricacies of British internal politics, the ri-
       valries among politicians and between the generals and
       politicians, and the search for a "grand strategy."
       The Easterner vs. Westerner controversy (between those
       who favored a diversion outside Europe and those who
       believed all effort should be made in Europe) is well-
       presented here.
          Cf. Rothwell, 306; Steiner, 307; Hazelhurst, 295;
       Williamson, 211; Hankey, 292.

Reviews: *AAPSS-A* 367 (1966):164-5, Klaus Epstein;
AHR 71 (1966):961-3, Stephen R. Graubard; *JMH* 39 (1967):
331-2, James G. Godfrey.

292. Hankey, Maurice Pascal Alers. *The Supreme Command,*
      1914-1918. 2 volumes. London: Allen & Unwin, 1961.

      Compiled from Hankey's private diaries, these volumes
      are his account of the inner workings of the War Cabi-
      net during World War I. Examines the changes in Cabinet
      government under the pressure of war, and the importance
      of personalities in politics. Hankey was a key figure
      in the Committee of Imperial Defence and was Secretary
      to the Cabinet. Covers the problems within the Asquith
      Cabinet, the Easterners vs. Westerners controversy, the
      coming to power of Lloyd George and the nature of cab-
      inet government. An essential "insider's" work. Also
      see John Mackintosh, *The British Cabinet*, 2nd edition
      (London: Methuen, 1968), for a study of the general na-
      ture of cabinet government and how it evolved before,
      during and after World War I.
           Cf. Roskill, 186; Guinn, 291; Taylor, 308; Asquith,
      146; Churchill, 153; McEwen, 302; Hazelhurst, 295.

293. Hardach, Gerd H. *The First World War, 1914-1918.*
      Translated by Peter Ross and Betty Ross. Economy in
      the Twentieth Century, no. 2. Edited by Wolfram
      Fischer. Berkeley: University of California Press,
      1977. xvi + 328 pp.

      Examines the effect the war had on European capital-
      ism, the progress of industrialization, structural
      changes in the economies of the belligerents brought
      about by the war, and the development of an interna-
      tional labor movement. A Marxist interpretation that
      tends to miss some of the forest for all the trees, but
      some useful observations and information. A good bib-
      liography.
           Reviews: *AHR* 83 (1978):1247-8, William Harrison; *EHR*
      98 (1978):855-6, Malcolm Falkus; *JEH* 38 (1978):547-9,
      Paul Hohenberg.

294. Hart, B.H. Liddell. *History of the First World War*
      [originally titled *The Real War, 1914-1918*]. 1930.
      Reprint. London: Cassell, 1970. 635 pp.

      Surveys the origins, political objectives and major
      campaigns of the war, concentrating on European land
      battles, though there is a vivid description of the

hand-to-mouth attempts to force the Dardanelles and
knock Turkey out of the war.
Cf. Albertini, 284; Rothwell, 306; Guinn, 291.

295.   Hazelhurst, Cameron. *Politicians at War, July 1914 to
       May 1915, a Prologue to the Triumph of Lloyd George.*
       London: Jonathan Cape, 1971. 346 pp.

       Peers into the fog surrounding Britain's decision to
       commit itself to World War I. The first of three pro-
       jected volumes on Lloyd George's rise to pre-eminence,
       this work covers the first nine months of the war, end-
       ing with the first coalition in May, 1915, with Lloyd
       George's role in the events forming the central theme.
       A patient examination of the inner workings of the Brit-
       ish cabinet, dispelling old myths and adding useful in-
       sight into the activities of the politicians. A mine
       of information. See the bibliography for a guide to
       the relevant archival sources and the footnotes for the
       secondary sources. Reading it, one sometimes loses
       track of the great events that moved beyond the world
       of personal correspondence, but this is the pre-eminent
       atmosphere of politicians that influences and shapes
       their response to the world. Complement with McEwen,
       item 302; and Davis, item 286, and the works mentioned
       in them.
       Cf. Taylor, 308; Beaverbrook, 144; Asquith, 146;
       Hankey, 292; Churchill, 153.
       Reviews: *AHR* 77 (1972):521-2, Michael Kinnear; *EHR*
       88 (1972):597-9, P.F. Clarke; *H* 57 (1972):461-2, Keith
       Robbins.

296.   Jeffrey, Keith. "Sir Henry Wilson and the Defence of
       the British Empire, 1918-22." *Journal of Imperial
       and Commonwealth History* 3 (1977):270-93.

       Britain's victory in World War I, the defeat of Ger-
       many, and the collapse of Russia might have been ex-
       pected to ease British anxiety over imperial defence.
       Far from it. The victory left Britain with even more
       territory to defend after an exhausting war and, neces-
       sarily, the debate over priorities—the best place to
       protect the empire—continued unabated. One of the
       main proponents of limiting imperial expansion and hus-
       banding imperial resources was Field Marshall Sir Henry
       Wilson, Chief of the Imperial General Staff. Concerned
       that Britain's over-taxed military resources threatened
       imperial survival, he waged a struggle within the gov-

ernment, most particularly with Lord Curzon, over new acquisitions, especially in the Middle East. An excellent study of personalities and politics.

For studies of Wilson, see J.B. Collier, *Brasshat: A Biography of Field Marshall Sir Henry Wilson* (London: Secker & Warburg, 1961); Bernard Ash, *The Last Dictator: A Biography of Field Marshall Sir Henry Wilson* (London: Cassell, 1968); and the official study by Sir Charles Callwell, *Field-Marshall Sir Henry Wilson: His Life and Diaries*, 2 volumes (London: Cassell, 1927).

Cf. Taylor, 308; Guinn, 291; Nicolson, 181; Klieman, 298; Busch, 285.

297. Joll, James. "1914: The Unspoken Assumptions." *The Origins of the First World War: Great Power Rivalry and German War Aims*. H.W. Koch, editor. London: Macmillan, 1972, pp. 307-28.

The origins of World War I are well-documented, with mountains of official papers and endless memoirs. Yet there are still debates on the how and why of the war. Joll argues that documents alone do not help penetrate the atmosphere of decision-making. Politicians, in moments of crisis, in situations where they cannot foresee the outcome, fall back on unspoken assumptions, not represented in their despatches, that guide their actions. These assumptions and the contexts that give them legitimacy need to be uncovered to complete the picture of why and how statesmen act the way they do.

Cf. Kedourie, 346; Nicolson, 181; Watt, 189.

298. Klieman, Aaron S. *Foundations of British Policy in the Arab World: The Cairo Conference of 1921*. Baltimore, Maryland: Johns Hopkins Press, 1970. xiv + 322 pp.

World War I brought about the long-awaited disintegration of the Ottoman Empire, the collapse of Russian and German interests in the Middle East, and the considerable enlargement of British political, economic and strategic commitments. The war created new problems-- intensified Anglo-French rivalry, increasing American economic penetration, and the explosion of local nationalism--that forced the British to deal in new ways with their newly-won position. The Cairo Conference of 1921 was the bureaucratic response for finding solutions to the problems of administering British policy in Egypt and the mandated territories. A valuable study, especially on the mixed motives in British policy, but contains nothing particularly new.

Cf. Monroe, 304; Kedourie, 346 and 333; Sluglett, 357; Stein, 531; Rothwell, 306 and 356; Cohen, 353; Nevakivi, 324; Fitzsimmons, 289.

Reviews: *AAPSS-A* 394 (1971):156-7, J. Kenneth McDonald; *AHR* 77 (1972):523, James Jankowski; *JMH* 43 (1971):344-6, William Polk; *MEJ* 26 (1972):446-8, J.B. Kelly.

299. Lafore, Lawrence Davis. *The Long Fuse: An Interpretation of the Origins of World War I.* Critical Periods of History Series. New York: Lippincott, 1965. 282 pp.

Examines the origins of the war in its diplomatic context, concentrating particularly on Austria-Hungary and the Balkans. Provides useful insight into the role of the clash of European interests outside Europe as a contributor to the war; also emphasizes the mistakes of politicians and the importance of the ideas in the minds of diplomats in shaping policy. Excellent short introduction. Complements Albertini, item 284.

Cf. Williamson, 211; Shannon, 107; Steiner, 307; Taylor, 308; Rothwell, 306.

Reviews: *AAPSS-A* 363 (1966):163-4, Dwight E. Lee; *AHR* 71 (1966):514-5, Joachim Remak; *H* 52 (1967):239, W.N. Medlicott; *JMH* 38 (1966):319-20, Marion Siney.

300. Lenczowski, George. *The Middle East in World Affairs.* 3rd edition. Ithaca, N.Y.: Cornell University Press, 1962. xxvi + 723 pp.

Surveys the history and role of the West in the Middle East and the importance of the Middle East in international relations. Though most of the work concentrates on the inter-war years, there is important background material of a general nature on the evolution of local nationalism and the changing nature of international rivalry in the Middle East. The work covers Afghanistan, Turkey, Iran, Israel, and the central Arab states-- Egypt, Yemen, Iraq, Syria, Lebanon.

Cf. Lenczowski, 322; Monroe, 304; Sachar, 480; Klieman, 298.

Reviews: (1st ed.) *MEJ* 6 (1952):473-4, George Kirk; (2nd ed.) *MEJ* 11 (1957):203-4, George Kirk.

301. Louis, William Roger. *Great Britain and Germany's Lost Colonies, 1914-1919.* Oxford: Clarendon Press, 1967. xi + 165 pp.

At the end of World War I the problem of what to do
with and about Germany confronted the Allies. For the
British this included the additional problem of what
to do about the German colonies, most of which had been
occupied by Britain or one of the Dominions. The British did not want to return these areas lest the Germans
use them in the future as forward bases for a renewed
expansion. But world opinion did not favor direct annexation. In this climate the concept of a "mandate"
developed. Relying on extensive primary research, Louis
documents the evolution of Britain's determination to
gain control of Germany's overseas possessions both for
strategic and humanitarian reasons. He shows that while
Britain may not have had well-defined war aims, there
was from the beginning of the war a well-defined intention to seize and retain control of German colonies.
An important study in showing the motivations that result from having a world strategic position--Britain's
view was not and could not be confined to Europe alone.
  Cf. Rothwell, 306; Taylor, 308; Temperley, 309.
  Reviews: *AHR* 73 (1968):1157-8, John Galbraith; *EcHR*
21 (1968):181, D.K. Fieldhouse; *JMH* 40 (1968):597-8,
B.D. Bargar.

302. McEwen, J.M. "The Struggle for Mastery in Britain:
      Lloyd George versus Asquith, December, 1916." *Jour-
      nal of British Studies* 18 (1978):131-56.

Why did Asquith resign as Prime Minister in 1916 and
Lloyd George take over? Doubt still persists, though
rumors of power struggles and unsavory maneuvering
abound. McEwen reviews the various accounts, showing
that Lord Beaverbrook's long-respected story (item 144)
leaves something to be desired; and attempts to recon-
struct the event from published and documentary sources.
Lloyd George was impatient with Asquith for mismanaging
the war and forced a collision. Curiously, McEwen does
not use the Balfour Papers at the British Museum, especially BM 49692. For further details, see Cameron
Hazelhurst's "Asquith as Prime Minister, 1908-1916,"
English Historical Review 85 (1970):502-31; and *Politicians at War: July 1914 to May 1915: A Prologue to the
Triumph of Lloyd George*, item 295, which attacks views
expressed by Stephen Koss in "The Destruction of Britain's Last Liberal Government," *Journal of Modern History* 39 (1967):283-303. Also see P.A. Lockwood,
"Milner's Entry into the War Cabinet, December, 1916,"

Historical Journal 7 (1964):120-34; Trevor Wilson, *The Downfall of the Liberal Party, 1914-1935* (London: Collins, 1966); and the important critique of Wilson's interpretation by Cameron Hazelhurst in "The Conspiracy Myth," *Lloyd George*, edited by Martin Gilbert (Englewood Cliffs, N.J.: Prentice-Hall, 1968), 148-57. Also see Martin Pugh's "Asquith, Bonar Law and the First Coalition," *Historical Journal* 17 (1974):813-36; and for a thorough study of the Lloyd George coalition, Kenneth O. Morgan's *Concensus and Disunity: The Lloyd George Coalition, 1918-1922* (Oxford: Clarendon Press, 1979).

Cf. Lloyd George, 172; Asquith, 146; Churchill, 153; Taylor, 308; Gollin, 158; Dugdale, 154; Gilbert, 156; Hankey, 292; Roskill, 186; Blake, 148; Davis, 286.

303.   Mejcher, Helmut. "British Middle East Policy, 1917-21: The Inter-departmental Level." *Journal of Contemporary History* 8 (1973):81-101.

A study of the making of British foreign policy and the interdepartmental struggle for control of Mesopotamia during the war, in particular, the development of the Middle East Department of the Colonial Office.

Cf. Busch, 352; Klieman, 298; Kedourie, 346; Monroe, 304; Warman, 142; Steiner, 137-9 and 307.

304.   Monroe, Elizabeth. *Britain's Moment in the Middle East, 1914-1956*. London: Chatto & Windus, 1963. 254 pp.

The standard survey of British policy in the Middle East from World War I to the Suez crisis, concentrating on the bifurcation of British policy formation between London and the Government of India, the strategic necessities that motivated British policy, relations with local minorities, local nationalism, and the overextension of British power that sapped imperial resources.

Cf. Busch, 352 and 285; Sachar, 480; Klieman, 298; Kedourie, 333; Howard, 332; Wasserstein, 535; Mandel, 525; Sluglett, 357; Vatikiotis, 391; Troeller, 411.

305.   Nicolson, Harold. *Peacemaking 1919*. 2nd edition, 1945. Reprint. New York: Grosset & Dunlap, 1965. xxii + 311 pp.

Nicolson's personal account of the frustrations of putting the world back together at the end of World War I in the climate of fear, ambition and selfishness at the Paris Peace Conference. A useful, short summary.

In addition, see Howard Elcock, *Portrait of a Decision: The Council of Four and the Treaty of Versailles* (London: Methuen, 1972).

Cf. Temperley, 309; Lloyd George, 172; Egerton, 287; Fitzsimmons, 289.

*   Olson, William J. "The Genesis of the Anglo-Persian Agreement of 1919." Cited as item 424.

306. Rothwell, V.H. *British War Aims and Peace Diplomacy, 1914-1918*. Oxford: Clarendon Press, 1971. ix + 315 pp.

Apart from a determination to defeat Germany and end permanently Germany's threat to the British Empire, Britain had no consistent set of war aims. That policy, like most, fluctuated according to circumstances and was pragmatic to a degree. Rothwell examines the internal government processes of policy formation in response to external events and the exigencies of war-- the need to accommodate the goals of Allies or would-be Allies, the appeal of self-determination insofar as it would draw support away from Germany, and the pressure exerted by various lobbying groups. Through this also floated genuine sentiments of altruism and hopes for a better world, but such noble notions must descend to the level of political in-fighting if they are to emerge in any concrete form.

Cf. Taylor, 308; Guinn, 291; Louis, 301; Hankey, 292; Steiner, 307; Williamson, 211; Stein, 531; Klieman, 298.

Reviews: *EHR* 88 (1973):938-9, M.L. Dockrill; *H* 58 (1973):132, Keith Robbins; *JMH* 45 (1973):164-6, Marvin Swartz.

307. Steiner, Zara Shakom. *Britain and the Origins of the First World War*. The Making of the 20th Century Series. London: Macmillan, 1977. vi + 305 pp.

Assesses Britain's diplomacy and responsibilities for World War I. A thoughtful, perceptive examination which argues that British policy was defensive and reflexive in nature and was the consequence of over-extended responsibilities and declining power in the face of growing challenges. The rise of Germany, plus other challenges, forced the British to reassess their world posture and to align themselves with France and Russia. Steiner shows that Britain's foreign policy was the product of a small group of men who responded to public

opinion but who were largely left to conduct affairs
as they saw fit. Shows clearly that diplomacy is a
mixture of what one intends to do and what circumstances
require. An essential survey of British policy. Read
as a concluding essay to the works mentioned in the sections on imperial reorganization. Also see B. Mitchell
Simpson III, editor, *War, Strategy and Maritime Power*
(Rutgers, N.J.: Rutgers University Press, 1977), for
studies on the shift in European diplomatic relations
and war planning.

Cf. Rothwell, 306; Grenville, 085; Monger, 098; Woodward, 310; Hinsley, 086; Robbins, 184; Steiner, 137;
Taylor, 308.

Reviews: *AAPSS-A* 441 (1979):200; *AHR* 84 (1979):1057-
8, Michael G. Fry; *EHR* 94 (1979):234-5, Agatha Ramm;
H 64 (1979):135-6, C.H.D. Howard.

308. Taylor, A.J.P. *English History, 1914-1945.* Oxford
      History of England, volume 15. Oxford: Clarendon
      Press, 1965. xxvii + 708 pp.

One of the best surveys of British history, foreign
or domestic, available. Examines the role of personalities and pressure groups in politics, the effects of
World War I on Britain and how Britain fought the war,
and studies the post-war changes. An excellent survey
with an annotated bibliography and a list of cabinets.
The footnotes are not to be missed. Also see Donald
Read, *England, 1868-1914: The Age of Urban Democracy*
(London: Longmans, 1979); F.S. Northedge, *The Troubled
Giant: Great Britain Among the Powers, 1916-1939* (London: Bell, 1966); and two works by L.C.B. Seaman, *Victorian England: Aspects of English and Imperial History,
1837-1901* (London: Methuen, 1973), and *Post-Victorian
England, 1902-1951* (London: Methuen, 1966).

Cf. Taylor, 209; Hazelhurst, 295; McEwen, 302; Lloyd
George, 172; Churchill, 153; Beaverbrook, 144.

Reviews: *AAPSS-A* 365 (1966):181, H.R. Winkler; *AHR* 71
(1966):1352-4, David Owen; *JMH* 39 (1967):329-30, Peter
Stansky; *PSQ* 81 (1966):469-70, Richard W. Lyman.

309. Temperley, Harold W.V., editor. *A History of the Peace
      Conference.* 6 volumes. London: Frownde, and Hodder
      & Stoughton, 1920-24.

When the American and British diplomats and their
staffs assembled at Paris they brought along a wide
range of experts in geography, history, military affairs,

and economics to advise them on the instrumentalities of peace and the complex questions associated with trying to put the world back together again. These experts (the American team gathered under the title the "Inquiry") met informally and exchanged views. From these meetings this *History* emerged, written by members of the British and American staffs. The articles cover the range of affairs dealt with at the conference, summarizing the issues and how the Peace Conference attempted to deal with them. Volume 6, Part 1, deals with the Middle East, offering a sketch of the major issues and of the final settlements. There is information on relations with Turkey down to the Lausanne Conference on Syria, Palestine, Egypt, Iraq and Persia, with a number of maps reflecting the decisions made. While useful, many relevant facts were not available or were overlooked; the volumes are dated, but the tone of writing about the non-European settlements and self-determination is itself interesting.

The materials available on the Peace Conference, both archival and published, now constitute a subject for separate treatment. On Anglo-American relations at the Conference, see Seth Tillman, *Anglo-American Relations at the Paris Peace Conference of 1919* (Princeton, N.J.: Princeton University Press, 1961). On official aspects of the conference, see *British and Foreign State Papers, 1919* (London: HMSO, 1923); *Papers Relating to the Foreign Affairs of the United States, 1919: The Paris Peace Conference*, 13 volumes (Washington, D.C.: USGPO, 1942–47); and *Documents on British Foreign Policy*, item 053. Among the numerous memoirs, see David Lloyd George, *The Truth About the Peace Treaties*, 2 volumes (London: Gollancz, 1938), and *War Memoirs*, item 172; Arthur J. Balfour, *Retrospect* (New York: Houghton & Mifflin, 1930); Robert Lansing, *The Big Four and Others of the Peace Conference* (New York: Houghton & Mifflin, 1921), and *Papers Relating to the Foreign Relations of the United States, The Lansing Papers, 1914-1920*, 2 volumes (Washington, D.C.: State Department, USGPO, 1939–40); Maurice Hankey, *Diplomacy by Conference* (London: Benn, 1946); Jan Christian Smuts, *Jan Christian Smuts* (New York: William Morrow, 1952); Georges Clemenceau, *Grandeur and Misery and Victory* (New York: Harcourt, Brace, 1930); and Volume 4 of Churchill's *World Crisis*, item 153. Also see Colonel Stephen Bonsal's memoirs, *Suitors and Supplicants: The Little Nations at Versailles* (New York: Prentice-Hall, 1946). For a brief overview of the conference, see Rohan Butler, "The Peace Settlement of Versailles, 1919-1933," *New Cambridge Modern History*, item 099, 209-41; and Harold Nicolson, *Peacemaking 1919*, item 305.

The whole question of mandates, their purpose and constitution vexed deliberations at the Peace Conference and after. The motives for establishing mandates were, in part, to disguise in acceptable form the annexation of former German colonies or Ottoman provinces. On the mandate system, see Paul Birdsall, *Versailles Twenty Years After* (1941; reprint. Hamden, Conn.: Archon Books, 1962); Parker T. Moon, *Imperialism and World Politics* (New York: Macmillan, 1926); Norman Bentwich, *The Mandate System* (London: Longmans, Green, 1930); Philip Quincy Wright, *Mandates Under the League of Nations* (Chicago: University of Chicago Press, 1930); H. Duncan Hall, *Mandates, Dependencies and Trusteeship* (London: Stevens, 1948); Albert Hyamson, *Palestine under the Mandate, 1920-1948* (London: Methuen, 1935); Stephen Longrigg, *Syria and Lebanon under French Mandate* (London: Oxford University Press under the auspices of the Royal Institute of International Affairs, 1958), which is still the best work on the mandate.

Cf. Gottlieb, 290; Kedourie, 333; Sachar, 480; Busch, 285; Klieman, 298; Nevakivi, 324; Howard, 332; Kinross, 464; Zeine, 545; Hovannisian, 553; Egerton, 287; Ullman, 328; Sluglett, 357; Ireland, 397; Olson, 424.

*   Wasserstein, Bernard. *The British in Palestine: The Mandatory Government and the Arab Jewish Conflict, 1917-1929.* Cited as item 535.

*   Williamson, Samuel. *The Politics of Grand Strategy: Great Britain and France Prepare for War, 1904-1914.* Cited as item 211.

310.   Woodward, Ernest Llewellyn. *Great Britain and the War of 1914-1918.* London: Methuen, 1967. xxxiii + 610 pp.

A general, narrative history of British policy during the war, dealing with the campaigns but concentrating on the domestic and international political climate that influenced the formation of policy. Chapters 5 through 8 examine the Gallipoli campaign and the war in the Middle East. A useful survey that needed a bibliography.

Cf. Albertini, 284; Steiner, 307; Gottlieb, 290; Rothwell, 306; Guinn, 291; Busch, 352; Monroe, 304.

Reviews: *AAPSS-A* 379 (1968):175-6, Bernard Semmel;
AHR 74 (1969):179, Bernadotte E. Schmitt; *H* 54 (1969):
121-2, Arthur Marwick; *JMH* 42 (1970):146-51, Stephen
Graubard.

Military Campaigns

311. Allen, W.E.D., and Paul Muratoff. *Caucasian Battle-*
     fields: A History of the Wars on the Turco-Caucasian
     Border, 1828-1921. Cambridge: Cambridge University
     Press, 1953. xxi + 614 pp.

   Studies the various military campaigns between Turkey
   and Russia for dominance in western Asia. Although it
   concentrates on military aspects, it contains a vast
   array of social and political information on the confrontation between the two empires. One of the few
   studies on the Caucasus.
     Cf. Kazemzadeh, 320; Hovanissian, 552-3.
     Reviews: *H* 40 (1955):371-2, Bernard Lewis; *JMH* 28
   (1956):280-1, Gunther Rothenberg; *MEJ* 8 (1954):224-5,
   Firuz Kazemzadeh.

*   Barker, Arthur James. *The Bastard War: Mesopotamia,*
     1914-1918. Cited as item 351.

312. Cassar, George H. *The French and the Dardanelles: A*
     Study of Failure in the Conduct of War. London:
     Allen & Unwin, 1971. xvii + 276 pp.

   The French, like the British, entered World War I
   without a clear idea of what they aimed to achieve,
   short of beating Germany. But after it became obvious
   that the Western front was a stalemate and the search
   began for other ways to defeat Germany and its allies,
   the French began to worry lest Britain capitalize on
   the situation to partition the Ottoman Empire and German colonies without regard for French interests. This
   worry led the French to participate in the Dardanelles
   fiasco. Cassar, in the only study of its kind, examines
   the French political background to the expedition, the
   military effort, and the relations with Britain. A
   solid study but not inspired.
     Cf. Gottlieb, 290; Nevakivi, 324; Andrews, 317;
   Ekstein, 318.
     Reviews: *AHR* 78 (1973):641-48, Raymond Callahen; *H*
   58 (1975):132, John Gooch.

*   Higgins, Trumbull. *Winston Churchill and the Darda-
      nelles*. Cited as item 164.

313. James, Robert Rhodes. *Gallipoli: The History of a
      Noble Blunder*. London: Pan Books, 1965. xiii +
      384 pp.

      A detailed history of the Dardanelles campaign, con-
      centrating on British military aspects of this effort
      to knock the Ottoman Empire out of the war. The at-
      tempt failed and unleashed a series of post-mortems
      that continue today, the question still being, "was it
      worth it?" It might have succeeded and, if it had, it
      may have meant the Allies could have kept Russia sup-
      plied and thus in the war. Failure almost ruined the
      career of Winston Churchill and contributed to the fall
      of Asquith's government. A less satisfactory study of
      the campaign is Alan Morehead's *Gallipoli* (London:
      Hamish Hamilton, 1956). The memoirs of Sir Ian Hamil-
      ton, British Commander at Gallipoli, *Gallipoli Diary*,
      2 volumes (London: Arnold, 1920), are also useful as
      are those of Ellis Ashmead-Bartlett, *The Uncensored
      Dardanelles* (London: Hutchinson, 1928); and the official
      histories by C.F. Aspinall-Oglander, *Military Opera-
      tions: Gallipoli*, 2 volumes (London: Heinemann, 1932);
      Sir Julian Corbett, *History of the Great War: Naval
      Operations*, volumes 1-3 (London: Longmans, Green, 1923);
      and C.E.W. Bean, *Official History of Australia in the
      War: The Story of Anzac*, 12th edition, 2 volumes
      (Sydney: Angus & Robertson, 1941).
          Cf. Sachar, 480; Trumpener, 340; Higgins, 164; Cassar,
      312; Churchill, 153; Marder, 131; Mackay, 173.
          Reviews: *JMH* 38 (1966):320-1, Louis Martan; *MEJ* 20
      (1966):246-7, Joseph Stallings.

314. MacMunn, George, and Cyril Falls, compilers. *Military
      Operations: Egypt and Palestine*. 2 volumes. London:
      HMSO, 1928.

      The official history of the campaign in the Levant to
      defeat the Turks during World War I. See Frederick
      James Moberly, *The Campaigns in Mesopotamia*, discussed
      below, as well as Sir Alec Seath Kirkbride, *An Awaken-
      ing: The Arab Campaign, 1917-1918* (Tavistock, Eng.:
      University Press of Arabia, 1971); and Archibald P.
      Wavell, *The Palestine Campaigns* (London: Constable,
      1938). In addition, see the colorful memoirs of Richard

Meinertzhagen, a British intelligence officer, *Middle East Diary, 1917-1956* (London: Cresset Press, 1959). Cf. Lawrence, 171.

315. Moberly, Frederick James. *The Campaign in Mesopotamia, 1914-1918: History of the Great War Based on Official Documents.* 4 volumes. London: HMSO, 1927.

The official history of the British war effort in Mesopotamia. Moberly also wrote the official history of Britain's activities in Persia during World War I, which was never published, partly because it was considered too sensitive a topic. See *Operations in Persia*, Public Record Office, CAB 44/37/8871.
Cf. Barker, 351; Cohen, 353; Sluglett, 357; Rothwell, 356; Wilson, 358.

316. Walder, Alan David. *The Chanak Affair.* London: Hutchinson, 1969. xv + 380 pp.

The British defeated the Ottomans in World War I and expected, along with the other Allies, to partition the Empire, leaving only a rump Turkish state in part of Anatolia. Getting the Turks to accept this dispensation, however, proved difficult, the issue hanging fire until 1923 when the Allies accepted Turkish nationalism as a reality and conceded to the Kemalists all of Anatolia, plus Constantinople. Arriving at this state, however, had involved a Greco-Turkish war, and the advance of Turkish nationalist forces on Constantinople almost provoked a war with the British, who were in control of Constantinople and the Straits and were loath to surrender them. Walder describes the near-clash at Chanak, which defended the entrance to the Dardanelles, and examines British and Turkish political maneuvering to settle their differences. A popularized account.
For an account of the Greek attempt to partition the Ottoman Empire, see Michael Llewellyn Smith, *Ionian Vision: Greece in Asia Minor, 1919-1922* (London: Allen Lane, 1973). Also see R.K. Jensen, "The Greco-Turkish War, 1920-1922," *International Journal of Middle East Studies* 11 (1978):553-65. For an examination of Italian interests in the Ottoman Empire, see Richard Bosworth's excellent study, *Italy, the Least of the Great Powers, Italian Foreign Policy Before the First World War* (Cambridge: Cambridge University Press, 1980).

Also see Henry H. Cumming, *Franco-British Rivalry in the Post-War Near East: The Decline of French Influence* (London: Oxford University Press, 1938).
   Cf. Busch, 285; Helmreich, 331; Howard, 332; Evans, 330; Kinross, 463-4; Lewis, 477; Sachar, 480; Monroe, 304; Nicolson, 181.
   Reviews: *AAPSS-A* 391 (1970):225-6, Donald E. Webster; *AHR* 75 (1970):1420-1, Michael Kinnear.

Relations with the Allies

317.   Andrew, Christopher M., and A.S. Kanya Forstner. "The French Colonial Policy and French Colonial War Aims, 1914-1918." *Historical Journal* 17 (1974):79-106.

Like the British, the French did not rush into delineating their war aims. What war aims emerged before 1918, when there was more of an attempt to develop aims in anticipation of the peace conference, were the result of the various agreements with other Powers during the war, e.g., the Straits Agreement and the Sykes-Picot Agreement. The goals that emerged were strongly influenced by the *parti colonial*, a lobbying group that had support within the French foreign ministry. This group sought to make sure that in the post-war settlements Britain would not capitalize on the fact that it had defeated the Turks and the Germans in the Middle East and Africa alone to claim sole possession of former Ottoman provinces and German colonies. The pressure of the colonial party ensured a sustained French interest in Lebanon and Syria and thus contributed to the deterioration in Anglo-French relations following World War I. This excellent study examines the activities of this group and traces how French policy reflected the group's pressure. For further studies of this group, its composition and influence, see C.W. Newbury and A.S. Kanya Forstner, "French Policy and the Origins of the Scramble for Africa," *Journal of History* 10 (1969):253-76; and C.M. Andrew and A.S. Kanya Forstner, "The French 'Colonial Party': Its Composition, Aims and Influence, 1885-1914," *Historical Journal* 16 (1971):99-128.
   Cf. Spagnolo, 268; Shorrock, 266; Nevakivi, 324; Busch, 352; Zeine, 545; Gifford, 201; Cassar, 312.

*   Cassar, George. *The French and the Dardanelles*. Cited as item 312.

318. Ekstein, Michael G. "Russia, Constantinople and the
    Straits, 1914-1915." *British Foreign Policy under
    Sir Edward Grey*, item 086, 423-35.

    The agreement of March 1915 giving Allied recognition
    to Russian claims for control of the Straits and Con-
    stantinople was not the result of a major change in
    British policy concerning the Straits or of Russian
    pressure. Sir Edward Grey used the agreement to keep
    Russian cooperation during the war and to limit the pos-
    sible extent of post-war Russian claims. Ekstein fails
    to note that Grey also used the agreement as leverage
    to secure a settlement of Anglo-Russian differences in
    Persia.
    Cf. Churchill, 243; Greaves, 248; Monger, 098;
    Williams, 258-9; Klein, 252; Beloff, 080; Guinn, 291;
    Jelavich, 206; Renzi, 325; Kerner, 321; Smith, 327;
    Zotiades, 260; Grey, 160; Langer, 253 and 093.

319. Ellis, Charles Howard. *The British 'Intervention' in
    Transcaspia, 1918-1919* [published in Britain as *The
    Transcaspian Episode, 1918-1919*; London: Hutchinson,
    1963.] Berkeley: University of California Press,
    1963. 175 pp.

    An account of British efforts to keep Russia in the
    war against the Germans, an intervention that only gra-
    dually became an anti-Bolshevik crusade.
    Cf. Ullman, 328; Allworth, 242; Kazemzadeh, 320;
    Busch, 285.
    Reviews: *JMH* 36 (1964):105-6, Richard Ullman.

320. Kazemzadeh, Firuz. *The Struggle for Transcaucasia,
    1917-1921*. New York: Philosophical Library, 1951.
    xiii + 356 pp.

    World War I destroyed two empires in the Middle East,
    the Russian and the Ottoman. From their remains various
    minorities tried to set up independent states. In the
    Caucasus, a border area between the two empires, the
    Armenians, Azerbaijani Turks, and Georgians sought to
    organize themselves and secure recognition for indepen-
    dent states from the Allies. Various revolutionary
    parties that had flourished before the war tried to es-
    tablish their programs after the war; the Dashnaktsutiun
    was one such Armenian revolutionary group. Kazemzadeh
    studies this group as well as the efforts by Georgians,
    Armenians and Azerbaijani Turks to establish independent
    states. All the attempts foundered and the Red Army and

the Turks reconquered the areas. For a footnote to
this story, see Richard Hovannisian, "Armenia and the
Caucasus in the Genesis of the Soviet-Turkish Entente,"
International Journal of Middle East Studies 4 (1973):
129–47. For more detailed background on the military
campaigns, see W.D. Allen, item 311.
    Cf. Hovannisian, 522–3; Sarkissian, 557; Busch, 285;
Allworth, 242; Lederer, 254.

321.   Kerner, Robert J. "Russia, the Straits and Constanti-
       nople, 1914-1915." *Journal of Modern History* 1
       (1929):400-15.

       Dated study of the negotiations leading to the agree-
       ment during World War I giving Russia control of the
       Straits.
           Cf. Ekstein, 318; Renzi, 325; Guinn, 291.

322.   Lenczowski, George. *Russia and the West in Iran, 1918-
       1948: A Study in Big-Power Rivalry.* Ithaca, N.Y.:
       Cornell University Press, 1949. xv + 383 pp. *Supple-
       ment to "Russia and the West in Iran."* Ithaca, N.Y.:
       Cornell University Press, 1954. 44 pp.

       Explores aspects of Great Power rivalry in Iran, con-
       centrating on Russian activities and the response of
       Britain and America to them, but with some background
       on German activities in Iran as well. An overview,
       somewhat dated. Lenczowski's *The Middle East in World
       Affairs*, item 300, covers the whole Middle East and
       East-West tension on a similar basis. On the communists
       in Iran, see Sepehr Zabih, *The Communist Movement in
       Iran* (Berkeley: University of California Press, 1966).
           Cf. Monroe, 304; Busch, 285 and 352; Ramazani, 425.
           Reviews: *H* 38 (1953):265-6, B.H. Sumner; *MEJ* 3 (1949):
       478-9, Edwin Wright.

323.   Morris, L.P. "British Secret Missions in Turkestan,
       1918-19." *Journal of Contemporary History* 12 (1977):
       363-79.

       Studies the activities of British agents and the Al-
       lied intervention in southern Russia. The Home Govern-
       ment was often embarrassed by the independent actions
       of its representatives, while the agents were often
       despatched to distant areas with the vaguest of instruc-
       tions for ill-considered or insufficiently thought-out
       purposes. Many first-hand accounts of these missions
       are in various issues of both the *Journal of the Royal*

Asian Society and the *Journal of the Royal Central Asian Society* in the years following the war. Also see the memoirs of Major-General L.C. Dunsterville, *The Adventures of Dunsterforce* (London: Edward Arnold, 1920); Major-General W.E.R. Dickson, *East Persia: A Backwater to the Great War* (London: Edward Arnold, 1924); and L.V.S. Blacker, *On Secret Patrol in High Asia* (London: John Murray, 1922).

Cf. Ullman, 328; Ellis, 319; Kazemzadeh, 320.

324. Nevakivi, Jukka. *Britain, France and the Middle East, 1914-1920.* University of London Historical Studies, no. 23. London: Athlone Press, 1969. xiii + 284 pp.

Examines Anglo-French efforts to coordinate their interests in the Middle East in light of the 1904 settlement of differences. Gives a brief account of Anglo-French relations and interests in the Arab Middle East and Turkey immediately prior to the war and the conflicting set of agreements they negotiated to secure those interests during the war; and then concentrates on the years immediately after the war--from the Paris Peace Conference to San Remo--and the attempts to reconcile Anglo-French interests with all the conflicting claims. For a study of French-Arab relations, see Jan Karl Tannenbaum, *France and the Arab Middle East, 1914-1920*, Transactions of the American Philosophical Society, no. 68, part 7 (Philadelphia, Penn.: American Philosophical Society, 1978); and Rasheeduddin Khan, "The Peace Settlement, Arab Diplomacy and Anglo-French Power Politics, 1919-1920," *Islamic Culture* 42 (1968): 57-73 and 43 (1968):133-49. Also see Henry H. Cumming, *Franco-British Rivalry in the Post-War Near East: The Decline of French Influence* (London: Oxford University Press, 1938).

Cf. Shorrock, 266; Andrew, 317; Cassar, 312; Busch, 352; Zeine, 545; Guinn, 291; Rothwell, 306; Kedourie, 346; Klieman, 298; Monroe, 304; Helmreich, 331.

Reviews: *AAPSS-A* 387 (1970):209-10, Don Peretz; *EHR* 85 (1970):203, Ann Williams; *H* 54 (1969):442, Malcolm E. Yapp; *MEJ* 24 (1970):94-5, Laurence Evans.

325. Renzi, William. "Great Britain, Russia and the Straits, 1914-1915." *Journal of Modern History* 42 (1970):1-20.

Explains why Britain gave up the Straits after defending it against Russia for so long. The Russians

were concerned that control of Constantinople and the
Straits, a long-held dream, would escape them. They
were suspicious of any Allied motions in that direction
during the war, interpreting them as signs of invidious
intent, despite the common war against Germany. To reassure the Russians and forestall any inclination on
their part to conclude a separate peace with Germany,
the British accepted the necessity of surrendering
their aging policy of keeping Russia from the Straits.
   Cf. Ekstein, 318; Guinn, 291; Gottlieb, 290; Grey,
160.

326.   Skrine, Clarmont Percival. *World War in Iran*. London:
       Constable, 1962. xxiv + 267 pp.

       Skrine was a consular official in the Indian Civil
       Service stationed in Persia. Though most of his memoir
       covers the interwar years and World War II, there is
       much useful information on British activities in Iran
       during World War I and immediately after.
          Cf. Wilson, 358; Edmonds, 550; Graves, 159; Marlowe,
       177; Ullman, 328; Lenczowski, 322.

327.   Smith, C. Jay, Jr. "Great Britain and the 1914-1915
       Straits Agreement with Russia: The British Promise of
       November 1914." *American Historical Review* 70 (1965):
       1015-34.

       Using largely the Asquith papers, Smith examines the
       negotiations between Britain, France and Russia over
       the fate of Constantinople and the Straits. Useful
       survey of the bibliographic information (now dated) and
       a look at the British cabinet-political background to
       the negotiations. Argues that Russia had little to do
       with the agreement, which resulted largely from British
       efforts to dislodge the Germans from their position at
       Constantinople. A bit difficult to accept.
          Cf. Ekstein, 318; Renzi, 325; Guinn, 291; Gottlieb,
       290; Grey, 160; Taylor, 308.

328.   Ullman, Richard. *Anglo-Soviet Relations, 1917-1921:
       Intervention and the War*. 3 volumes. Princeton,
       N.J.: Princeton University Press, 1961-72.

       The definitive study of the British response to the
       Russian Revolution, the Allied intervention and the be-
       ginnings of Anglo-Soviet relations. Volume 1 covers
       the initiation of the intervention to keep Russia in
       the war as part of efforts to protect India and defeat

Germany. Volume 2 deals with the growing anti-Bolshevik spirit that began to dominate the intervention from 1918 to 1920. Volume 3 traces the collapse of the White campaigns and the emergence of the Anglo-Soviet accord that ended British intervention in Russia in 1921. This last volume examines the clash of Anglo-Soviet interests in the East, most particularly in Persia, and the confusion and disagreement in official circles over priorities that left British policy in the area at a standstill. An essential study with a generous bibliography and review of archival sources.

On aspects of the intervention in Russia, also see George Brinkley, *The Volunteer Army and Allied Intervention in South Russia, 1917-1921: A Study in the Politics and Diplomacy of the Russian Civil War* (Notre Dame, Indiana: University of Notre Dame Press, 1966); Richard Luckett, *The White Generals: An Account of the White Movement and the Russian Civil War* (New York: Viking Press, 1971); John Wheeler-Bennett, *Brest-Litovsk: The Forgotten Peace, March 1918* (1938; reprint. New York: Norton, 1971); Alexander Park, *Bolshevism in Turkestan, 1917-1927* (New York: Columbia University Press, 1957); Edward H. Carr, *A History of Soviet Russia: The Bolshevik Revolution, 1917-1923*, 3 volumes (London: Macmillan, 1950-53); and John Silverlight, *The Victor's Dilemma: Allied Intervention in the Russian Civil War* (London: Barrie & Jenkins, 1970).

On the effects of the Allied fear of Bolshevism, though an exaggerated account, see Arno J. Mayer, *Politics and Diplomacy of Peacemaking: Containment and Counterrevolution at Versailles, 1918-1919* (New York: Vintage, 1969). In addition there are numerous memoirs or personal accounts by British officers who operated in southern Russia and Persia. Among the most interesting are: Major-General L.C. Dunsterville, *The Adventures of Dunsterforce* (London: Edward Arnold, 1920); Major-General W.E.R. Dickson, *East Persia: A Backwater to the Great War* (London: Edward Arnold, 1924); L.V.S. Blacker, *On Secret Patrol in High Asia* (London: John Murray, 1922); Major-General Sir Edmund Ironside, *High Road to Command: The Diaries of Maj.-Gen. Sir Edmund Ironside, 1920-1922*, edited by Lord Ironside (London: Leo Cooper, 1972); Bruce Lockhart, *Memoirs of a British Agent: Being an Account of the Author's Early Life in Many Lands and of His Official Mission to Moscow, 1918* (London: Putnam, 1932); Charles Howard Ellis, *The British "Intervention" in Transcaspia, 1918-1919*, item 319,

and "Operative in Transcaspia, 1918-1919 and the 26
Commisars Case," *Soviet Affairs*, no. 2, St. Antony's
Papers, no. 6, edited by David Footman (New York:
Praeger, 1959), 129-53; Captain David Norris, "Caspian
Naval Expedition, 1918-1919," *Journal of the Central
Asian Society* 10 (1923):216-40; Sir Percy Sykes, "The
British Flag on the Caspian: A Sideshow of the Great
War," *Foreign Affairs* 2 (1923):282-40; and Major General
Sir Wilfred Malleson, "The British Mission to Turkestan,
1918-1920," *Journal of the Central Asian Society* 9
(1922):96-110. Also see L.P. Morris, "British Secret
Missions in Turkestan, 1918-19," item 323, which gives
a brief account of the major British personalities in
the intervention and their activities.

Cf. Busch, 285; Hovannissian, 552-3; Kazemzadeh, 320;
Allworth, 242.

Reviews: (volume 1): *JMH* 34 (1962):219-20, Arthur
Adams; (volume 2): *AHR* 74 (1968):585-6, Stephen Graubard; *H* 54 (1969):326-7, P.M.H. Bell; (volume 3): *AHR*
79 (1974):115-7, Harry Hanak; *EHR* 89 (1974):646-8,
C.J. Bartlett; *H* 59 (1975):151-2, P.M.H. Bell.

Destruction of the Ottoman Empire

*   Busch, Briton Cooper. *Britain, India and the Arabs,
        1914-1921.* Cited as item 352.

*   Busch, Briton Cooper. *Mudros to Lausanne: Britain's
        Frontier in Asia, 1918-1923.* Cited as item 285.

329.   Corrigan, H.S.W. "German-Turkish Relations and the
        Outbreak of War in 1914: A Re-Assessment." *Past and
        Present* 36 (1967):144-52.

        Questions the view that Germany had a predominant
        position in the Ottoman Empire before the war. Ten-
        sions between Turkey and Germany were on the rise be-
        fore the war and the Germans, like other European pow-
        ers, were looking for ways to pick up some of the
        spoils when the Ottoman Empire finally collapsed. Com-
        pare with Trumpener, item 340; and Weber, item 343.
        Also see Fischer, item 288, on the debate on German
        war aims.

*   Davison, Roderic. "Turkish Diplomacy from Mudros to
        Lausanne." Cited as item 467.

*   Dyer, Gwynne. "The Turkish Armistice." Cited as item
    469.

330. Evans, Laurence. *U.S. Policy and the Partition of
     Turkey, 1914-1924.* Studies in Historical and Polit-
     ical Science, series 82, no. 2. Baltimore, Maryland:
     Johns Hopkins Press, 1965. 437 pp.

     Examines America's involvement in the last phase of
     the Eastern Question, concentrating on official policy
     and its evolution from non-involvement, to participa-
     tion, back to non-involvement. Looks at America's at-
     titude during the war, at the Peace Conference, to the
     Mandate system, and the ultimate resolution of hosti-
     lities with Turkey with the Treaty of Sèvres. Rather
     narrow study that could have benefited from the use of
     more unpublished primary material, but useful for giv-
     ing a perspective on American policy. For a similar
     study, see Roger Trask, *The United States Response to
     Turkish Nationalism and Reform, 1914-1939* (Minneapolis:
     University of Minnesota Press, 1971).
     Cf. Howard, 332; Helmreich, 331; Bryson, 280; DeNovo,
     281; Busch, 285.
     Reviews: *AHR* 71 (1966):1294, H.L. Hoskins; *EHR* 82
     (1967):638, A.J.P. Taylor; *MEJ* 20 (1966):247-8, John
     A. DeNovo.

331. Helmreich, Paul C. *From Paris to Sèvres: The Partition
     of the Ottoman Empire at the Peace Conference of
     1919-1920.* Columbus: Ohio State University Press,
     1974. xiii + 376 pp.

     As with Germany, the Allies were at cross purposes in
     deciding how to dispose of the Ottoman Empire in a way
     that would satisfy conflicting claims. The Ottoman Em-
     pire covered a large area and incorporated numerous
     minorities whom the Allies had encouraged with ideals
     of self-determination in order to secure their support
     in defeating the Central Powers, with which the Otto-
     mans were allied. In addition, the European Allies--
     Greece, Italy, France, and Britain--all had interests
     to promote or protect and wanted a share in the spoils,
     which meant territory and privileges. To complicate
     matters, the Armenians, Arabs and other minorities
     wanted independent states, and the Turks refused to co-
     operate with Allied dispensations. The result was an
     impasse that kept the area in turmoil for years.
     Helmreich surveys this confusion from the Armistice at

Mudros, which ended the war in the Middle East, to the
Treaty of Sèvres, which unsuccessfully tried to resolve
the issue of what to do with Turkey to the Allies'
satisfaction. It is a study of *realpolitik*, of imperial
ambition, nationalism, and personalities; of negotia-
tions in a 19th-century manner to resolve a 20th-century
problem.
   Cf. Busch, 285; Howard, 332; Walder, 316; Kedourie,
333; Klieman, 298; Hovannissian, 552-3; Kinross, 463-4;
Nevakivi, 324; Monroe, 304; Sachar, 480.
   Reviews: *AAPSS-A* 416 (1974):224-6, William Langer;
AHR 80 (1975):634-5, Walter Weiker; *EHR* 91 (1976):686,
Ann Williams; *IJMES* 5 (1974):513-5, Laurence Evans;
MEJ 29 (1975):368-9, John DeNovo.

332.   Howard, Harry Nicholas. *The Partition of Turkey: A
       Diplomatic History, 1913-1923*. 1931. Reprint. New
       York: Howard Fertig, 1966. 486 pp.

       Though dated, this remains a useful study of the po-
       litical background to the break-up of the Ottoman Em-
       pire, carrying the Eastern Question into its final
       phase. Howard examines European diplomatic rivalry,
       the increase of German influence with the Young Turks,
       the war and its consequences for Turkey, concluding
       with the Lausanne Conference. The emphasis he places
       on German influence at the Porte has since been chal-
       lenged (see Trumpener, item 340; and Weber, 343), but
       there is still much of value; and if the Germans were
       not as influential as was believed, the British and
       others were not aware of it at the time and acted as
       if the Germans were in control. Howard studies the
       Straits question and U.S. policy thoroughly in *Turkey,
       the Straits and U.S. Policy* (Baltimore, Maryland: Johns
       Hopkins Press, 1974).
          Cf. Busch, 352 and 285; Kedourie, 333; Cunningham,
       367; Heller, 369; Sachar, 480; Gottlieb, 290; Rothwell,
       306; Nevakivi, 324; Klieman, 298.

333.   Kedourie, Elie. *England and the Middle East: The De-
       struction of the Ottoman Empire, 1914-1921*. 1956.
       Reprint. New York: Harvester Press, 1978. x + 236 pp.

       Examines the background of British interest in the
       Ottoman Empire, the breakdown in relations between the
       two, and how and why the British came to the decision
       to partition the Ottoman Empire. A thoughtful look at
       British policy in the Middle East, paying particular

attention to the role of personalities, especially Mark Sykes and T.E. Lawrence. Discusses the making of the Sykes-Picot Agreement, British attempts to renegotiate the Sykes-Picot Agreement, and British policy in Meso-potamia and Syria. Useful, though Kedourie's *Anglo-Arab Labyrinthe*, item 346, covers much the same ground and is based on new, more thorough research. Compare Kedourie's views of Arab nationalism and British in-terests with George Antonius, *The Arab Awakening*, item 340.

Cf. Busch, 352 and 285; Cohen, 394; Sluglett, 357; Sachar, 480; Adelson, 143; Klieman, 298; Porath, 530; Friedman, 521.

Reviews: *MEJ* 10 (1956):438-9, William Yale.

334. Klieman, Aaron S. "Britain's War Aims in the Middle East in 1915." *Journal of Contemporary History* 3 (1968):237-53.

Britain's failure to keep Turkey neutral in World War I forced a re-orientation in British military and po-litical thinking. The spread of war not only threatened Britain's empire beyond Europe, but it also reopened the question of the partition of the Ottoman Empire, the preservation of which had been a cardinal feature in British policy, even though it declined in the 1870's and afterwards. To consider the implications of Tur-key's entrance into the war, the Cabinet appointed an inter-departmental committee under the chairmanship of Maurice de Bunsen, former ambassador to Vienna, to con-sider British war aims regarding Asiatic Turkey. The committee wanted to preserve parts of the Ottoman Empire, but events swept these saner visions away. The end re-sult was a muddled policy and a muddle of agreements that maximized post-war grievances for minimum wartime gains. Good example of accident vs. intent in the di-rection of government policy.

Cf. Busch, 352; Grey, 160; Robbins, 184; Mejcher, 235; Monroe, 304; Sluglett, 357; Kedourie, 333 and 346; Cohen, 353; Kent, 398; Gottlieb, 290; Guinn, 291; Roth-well, 306.

* Klieman, Aaron. *Foundations of British Policy in the Arab World: The Cairo Conference of 1921.* Cited as item 298.

335. Kurat, Y.T. "How Turkey Drifted into World War I." *Studies in International History*, item 197, 291-315.

Argues that Turkish policy before World War I went
through a change that drew the Turks away from Britain
and France and closer to the Germans, a trend resulting
from Turkish realization that British and French protection of Ottoman integrity against Russia was declining.   The Turks were also annoyed over Anglo-French
policies that supported Turkish minorities against the
state, and the habit of the two Powers of helping themselves to pieces of the empire. When the Germans presented themselves as a foil to British, French and Russian pressures, the Ottomans inclined more toward them.
When war broke out, these existing Allied-Ottoman tensions, combined with the fact that there were pro-
Germans in influential positions in the Ottoman cabinet
(including Cemal Paşa and Enver Paşa), pushed the Ottomans into the arms of the Central Powers.
   Cf. Trumpener, 340 and 342; Sachar, 480; Weber, 343;
Corrigan, 329; Cunningham, 367; Heller, 369; Gottlieb,
290.

*   Lewis, Bernard. *The Emergence of Modern Turkey.*   Cited
         as item 477.

336.   Macfie, A.L. "The British Decision Regarding the Fu-
         ture of Constantinople, November 1918-January 1920."
         Historical Journal 18 (1975):391-400.

The successful conclusion of the war in the Middle
East left Britain with a variety of difficult problems.
Among these was the question of what to do with Con-
stantinople, whether to turn the Turks out or not.
Curzon favored expelling them and received the support
of Lloyd George, but other members of the cabinet and
the French proved less willing to alter the status of
Constantinople. Atatürk's victory made the question
redundant. Also see Abe Attrep, "'A State of Wretched-
ness and Impotence': A British View of Istanbul and
Turkey, 1919," *International Journal of Middle East
Studies* 9 (1978):1-9.
   Cf. Howard, 332; Busch, 285; Helmreich, 331; Montgomery, 338; Walder, 316; Monroe, 304.

337.   Mansfield, Peter. *The Ottoman Empire and its Succes-
         sors.* London: Macmillan, 1973. xi + 210 pp.

A brief survey of the fall and partition of the Ottoman Empire and the subsequent social, economic and political history of the various states that emerged from

the rubble of the Ottoman Empire. Mansfield examines the effects of World War I, the rise of Turkish and Arab nationalism, the intrusion of Great Power interests into the area, and the struggle for independence. Useful.

Cf. Lewis, 477; Shaw, 481; Kinross, 464; Howard, 332; Busch, 285; Monroe, 304.

338. Montgomery, A.E. "The Making of the Treaty of Sèvres of 10 August 1920." *Historical Journal* 15 (1972): 775-87.

Examines Anglo-French attempts to resolve the question of what to do with the Ottoman Empire. The British, who had lost considerable treasure and blood in fighting the Turks in World War I, wanted to see the Ottomans reduced to insignificance. The French--who had suffered less and who had major economic interests in Turkey, and who also began to see value in a restored Turkey as a support for French aims in the East --resisted the British. The resulting negotiations dragged on, aggravating relations between the Allies and giving Atatürk the opportunity to organize Turkish nationalism to resist an imposed partition.

Cf. Howard, 332; Busch, 285; Kinross, 464; Woodward, 053; Sachar, 480.

* Nevakivi, Jukka. *Britain, France and the Middle East, 1914-1920.* Cited as item 324.

339. Nevakivi, Jukka. "Lord Kitchener and the Partition of the Ottoman Empire, 1915-1916." *Studies in International History*, item 197, 316-29.

Looks at Lord Kitchener's role in the decision to partition the Ottoman Empire. Kitchener was among the first to pursue the idea of inciting the Arabs against the Turks, and he hoped to partition the Ottoman Empire so that, though the Russians, Greeks, Italians and French would all get a share, British interests would be insured and insulated from outside pressure.

Cf. Cassar, 151; Kedourie, 333; Busch, 352; Vereté, 534; Monroe, 304; Klieman, 298; Rothwell, 306; Nevakivi, 324.

* Sachar, Howard. *The Emergence of the Middle East, 1914-1924.* Cited as item 480.

340.   Trumpener, Ulrich. *Germany and the Ottoman Empire,*
        1914-1918. Princeton, N.J.: Princeton University
        Press, 1968. x + 433 pp.

        Trumpener's major revisionist work challenging the
        notion that the Ottomans were mere tools in German *Ost-*
        politik. Using a variety of archival sources, though
        no Ottoman sources, Trumpener thoroughly documents the
        tensions in Turko-German relations and demonstrates that
        the Ottomans were anything but cyphers. He examines
        the background to Germany's influence in Turkey, the
        question of the Straits, German economic penetration,
        military missions, and the Baghdad Railway. For two
        Turkish accounts of the war, see Djemal Pasha, *Memoirs*
        of a Turkish Statesman, 1913-1919 (London: Hutchinson,
        1922); and Ahmad Emin [Yalman], *Turkey in the World*
        War, Economic and Social History of the World War: Turk-
        ish Series (New Haven, Conn.: Yale University Press,
        1930).
            Cf. Weber, 343; Corrigan, 329; Kurat, 335; Sachar,
        480; Albertini, 284.
            Reviews: *AAPSS-A* 379 (1968):178, Vernon J. Puryear;
        AHR 75 (1970):821-2, J.C. Hurewitz; *JMH* 41 (1969):628-
        30, Victor R. Swenson; *MEJ* 22 (1968):515-7, Norman
        Itzkowitz.

341.   Trumpener, Ulrich. "Lyman von Sanders and the German-
        Ottoman Alliance." *Journal of Contemporary History*
        1 (1966):179-192.

        Studies the early years of the German military mis-
        sion to Turkey and documents the limits placed on that
        mission by Ottoman resistance to foreign meddling, and
        by the interference of other German agencies, e.g., the
        ambassador. Trumpener develops the theme, expanded
        elsewhere (see item 340), that German influence at the
        Porte was not as extensive before and during World War
        I as was believed at the time, or has been argued by
        some scholars. Compare with Heller, item 369; and
        Kurat, item 335, especially the latter who takes the
        opposite position on German influence. Also see Robert
        J. Kerner, "The Mission of Lyman von Sanders," *Slavonic*
        Review [later titled *Slavonic and East European Review*]
        6 (1927):12-27, 543-60, and 7 (1928-9):90-112; and
        Lyman von Sanders's memoirs, *Five Years in Turkey,*
        translated by C. Reichmann (Annapolis: U.S. Naval In-
        stitute, 1927).
            Cf. Weber, 343; Cunningham, 367; Sachar, 480; Ahmad,
        365.

342. Trumpener, Ulrich. "Turkey's Entry into World War I:
     An Assessment of Responsibilities." *Journal of Mo-
     dern History* 34 (1962):369-80.

     Examines the idea which Trumpener later developed
     fully in *Germany and the Ottoman Empire*, item 340, that
     the Ottomans were not helpless tools in German hands,
     and that Turkey's entrance into World War I was not the
     result of German pressure.
     Cf. Sachar, 480; Howard, 332; Gottlieb, 290; Taylor,
     308; Weber, 343; Cunningham, 367; Heller, 369.

343. Weber, Frank G. *Eagles on the Crescent: Germany,
     Austria and the Diplomacy of the Turkish Alliance,
     1914-1918*. Ithaca, N.Y.: Cornell University Press,
     1970. x + 284 pp.

     Explores the nature of Austro-German relations during
     World War I, showing that the alliance was one of ex-
     pedience, and that in many instances the two countries
     were working at cross-purposes. In particular, the
     Austrians suspected German intentions at the Porte and
     encouraged Turco-German clashes or interfered in German
     efforts to support the Turks. Weber's contention that
     Germany might have abandoned its concern for Turkey had
     not the war broken out seems strained. Useful, though
     somewhat turgid and wrapped up in dispatches and memo-
     randa.
     Cf. Trumpener, 340; Heller, 369; Cunningham, 367;
     Sachar, 480.
     Reviews: *AHR* 77 (1972):131-2, Oron Hale; *H* 57 (1972):
     462-4, F.R. Bridge; *IJMES* 3 (1972):93-4, Roderic
     Davison; *JMH* 44 (1972):288-9, Gerald E. Silberstein;
     MEJ 25 (1971):108-9, Laurence Evans.

The Arab Revolt

*   Busch, Briton Cooper. *Britain, India and the Arabs,
     1914-1921*. Cited as item 352.

344. Friedman, Isaiah. "The McMahon-Hussein Correspondence
     and the Question of Palestine." *Journal of Contem-
     porary History* 5 (1970):83-122.

     The negotiations with and promises made to the Arabs
     leading to the Arab revolt against Turkey in World War
     I remain the subjects of debate. What was meant by
     what was said, or not said? What were the perceptions

and motives of the participants? Did the British re-
nege on their promises after the war, or did the Arabs
exaggerate, intentionally or not, what had been promised? These issues bedevilled the original participants, and avoid definitive explanation now. Husayn
had his goals and the British had their own, and both
were willing to negotiate to see how much they could
get while giving up as little as possible. The results, of course, satisfied no one and recriminations
followed. Useful study, but one wonders if the Arabs
really appreciated all the diplomatic niceties and linguistic distinctions that Friedman shows characterized
the British interpretation of their own statements.
For a commentary on the article, see Arnold Toynbee's
comments and Friedman's response in "The McMahon-Hussein
Correspondence: Comments and a Reply," *Journal of Contemporary History* 5 (1970):185-201. The best monograph
on the whole muddled question is Kedourie, item 346.
    Cf. Antonius, 430; Busch, 352; Storrs, 188.

345. Kedourie, Elie. "Cairo and Khartoum on the Arab Ques-
      tion, 1915-1918." *Historical Journal* 7 (1964):280-97.

    Studies inter- and intra-departmental in-fighting over
the direction of policy and illustrates how these
struggles are key determinants in the formation of policy. A view expanded most admirably in *The Anglo-Arab
Labyrinthe*, item 346. Kedourie builds a convincing case
for the impact of the "official mind" on policy, showing
how a befuddled outlook or confusion in conception,
which is made to appear whole and consistent by a process of rationalization after the fact, can occupy a central place. Britain's Middle Eastern policy seemed particularly susceptible to confusion. This essay is also
contained in Kedourie's *Chatham House Version*, item 363.
    Cf. Busch, 352; Sluglett, 357; Monroe, 304.

346. Kedourie, Elie. *In the Anglo-Arab Labyrinthe: The
      McMahon-Husayn Correspondence and its Interpretations,
      1914-1939*. Cambridge Studies in the History and The-
      ory of Politics. Cambridge: Cambridge University
      Press, 1976. xii + 330 pp.

    Details the inner workings of Anglo-Arab relations
leading to the Arab Revolt against the Ottoman Empire
during World War I and the subsequent debate over what
was or was not promised. An excellent study of departmental rivalry, and the influence of personality, dis-

ingenuousness, and incompetence on policy formation.
Divided into two parts. The first part deals with the
Husayn-McMahon correspondence. The second part inter-
prets the meaning of the correspondence in the development of British policy in the Middle East. Gives an
excellent analysis of the Arab position, a critique of
George Antonius, *The Arab Awakening*, item 430, and the
extent to which the British reneged on promises. Compare with Tibawi, item 533, on this latter point.

Cf. Kedourie, 333; Friedman, 344; Dawn, 433; Zeine,
544; Klieman, 298; Lesch, 524; Porath, 530; Mossek, 529;
Caplan, 520; Wasserstein, 535; Mandel, 525.

Reviews: *AHR* 82 (1977):109-10, Paul Jabber; *BSOAS* 40
(1977):396-7, R.M. Burrell; *MEJ* 31 (1977):366, Briton
Busch.

347. Morris, James Humphry. *The Hashemite Kings*. London:
Faber & Faber, 1959. 231 pp.

Surveys the history of Jordan by concentrating on the
biographies of its rulers. Written by a journalist, it
is general and lacks a bibliography, though Jordan is
not an over-studied subject. For a more serious study,
though itself light, see Ann Dearden, *Jordan* (London:
Hale, 1958). Also see John Bagot Glubb, *The Story of
the Arab Legion* (London: Hodder & Stoughton, 1948),
which is a soldier's account of the history of Jordan,
most particularly of its armed forces; and Frederick
Peake, *History and Tribes of Jordan* (Coral Gables: University of Florida Press, 1958), which also has information on the war in the Jordan area. For an intimate
history of Jordan, see the memoirs of King Abdullah,
Jordan's first monarch, *Memoirs of King Abdullah of
Transjordan*, edited by Philip Graves (London: Jonathan
Cape, 1950), and *King of Jordan: My Memoirs Completed*
(London: Longmans, 1978).

Cf. Klieman, 298; Busch, 352; Troeller, 350 and 411;
Zeine, 544-5.

348. Mousa, Suleiman. "A Matter of Principle: King Hussein
of the Hejaz and the Arabs of Palestine." *International Journal of Middle East Studies* 9 (1978):183-94.

Argues that Husayn was kept ignorant of Britain's
policies regarding the proposed disposition of former
Ottoman territories and shows British efforts to placate Husayn with offers of money when he objected to
the process. Concentrates on the disagreements between

Husayn and the British over the extent of the areas to
be included in an independent state, most particularly
over the fate of Palestine. Husayn refused to sign any
treaty giving up Arab claims and he insisted that Britain honor the pledges made by McMahon and abrogate the
Balfour Declaration. The British had a different interpretation of the pledges made, and kept to the
Balfour Declaration. Attempts to negotiate a settlement failed, the issue only resolving itself when Husayn
fled the Hejaz in the face of an invasion by ibn Saud.
Compare with Elie Kedourie, item 346, on promises and
interpretations made by the various parties.

Cf. Troeller, 350; Friedman, 344; Antonius, 430;
Busch, 352.

349.   Silverfarb, Daniel. "The Philby Mission to ibn Sa'ud,
       1917-18." *Journal of Contemporary History* 14 (1979):
       269-86.

Details British policy towards ibn Saud during World
War I and St. John Philby's personal diplomacy that
went beyond what his superiors intended. Relations
with ibn Saud were complicated by inter-departmental
struggles over the vexed question of whether to promote
an Arab revolt against the Ottomans and, if so, how,
and by whom. The Sharif of Mecca emerged as the main
contender, but ibn Saud remained a matter of concern
because of the threat he posed to Husayn, a fact made
no easier by Philby's independent actions.

Cf. Busch, 352; Monroe, 180; Troeller, 350; Edens,
537; Winstone, 191.

350.   Troeller, Gary. "Ibn Sa'ud and Sharif Husain: A Com-
       parison in Importance in the Early Years of the First
       World War." *Historical Journal* 14 (1971):627-33.

Demonstrates why the British backed Husayn of Mecca
over the ibn Saud of Najd as the candidate most likely
to lead a successful Arab revolt. Husayn was the Sharif
of Mecca and a member of the tribe of Muhammad. This
religious standing made him a logical choice as a symbol of the Arab revolt and sapped the credibility of
Turkey's call for an Islamic *jihad*--fear of which was
more real in British imagination than in fact. Troeller
neglects the fact that British policy was sharply divided over encouraging an Arab revolt and that India,
responsible for contacts with ibn Saud, opposed the
idea; while Cairo and Khartoum, in touch with Husayn,

supported it. The latter two won the day, a not incon-
siderable reason for plumping for the Sharif. Compare
with Busch, item 352; and Kedourie, item 346.
   Cf. Winstone, 191; Troeller, 411; Antonius, 195;
Edens, 537.

Britain and Mesopotamia

351. Barker, Arthur James. *The Bastard War: Mesopotamia,*
      1914-1918 [published in Britain as *The Neglected War:*
      Mesopotamia, 1914-1918, London: Faber & Faber, 1967].
      New York: Dial Press, 1967. 534 pp.

      Details the successes and abysmal failures of the
      British Mesopotamian campaign; an apologist history of
      British rule but a critic of the badly bungled campaign.
      For a detailed study of the major disaster in the cam-
      paign, the capture of General Townshend's force at Kut
      al-Amara, see Barker's *Townshend of Kut: A Biography of*
      Maj.-Gen. Sir Charles Townshend, KCB, DSO (London:
      Cassell, 1967); and Townshend's own memoirs, *My Cam-*
      paign in Mesopotamia (London: Thornton Butterworth,
      1920). A history of the military campaigns in the
      Middle East can be found in Edmund Dane's study, *Brit-*
      ish Campaigns in the Nearer East, 1914-1918: From the
      Outbreak of War with Turkey to the Armistice, 2 volumes
      (London: Hodder & Stoughton, 1919). For a study of the
      Indian Army, which fought the campaign in Mesopotamia,
      see Philip Mason, *A Matter of Honour: An Account of the*
      Indian Army, Its Officers and Men (London: Penguin,
      1977).
         Cf. Wilson, 358; Moberly, 315; Busch, 352; Sluglett,
      357; Cohen, 353; Goold, 354.
         Reviews: *AHR* 73 (1968):865-6, Trumbull Higgins.

352. Busch, Briton Cooper. *Britain, India and the Arabs,*
      1914-1921. Berkeley: University of California Press,
      1971. xii + 522 pp.

      Studies the development of Britain's war effort in
      Mesopotamia. Busch examines the confusion in policy-
      making, the divided nature of the decision-making
      structure, and the competition between the various
      British agencies with interests in the Middle East.
      Confines itself almost exclusively to British internal,
      inter-departmental relations. See the other works by
      Busch, items 285 and 404.

Cf. Kedourie, 346; Klieman, 298; Cohen, 394; Mejcher,
234; Kent, 398; Wilson, 358; Troeller, 411.
    Reviews: *AAPSS-A* 401 (1972):166-7, Don Peretz; *AHR* 77
(1972):1093-4, Linda Rose; *BSOAS* 35 (1972):371-2, E.R.J.
Owen; *JAS* 31 (1972):437-9, John Waterbury; *JMH* 44 (1972):
437-8, Robert McDaniel; *MEJ* 26 (1972):79-80, Joseph
Malone.

353. Cohen, Stuart. "The Genesis of the British Campaign in
      Mesopotamia, 1914." *Middle Eastern Studies* 12 (1976):
      119-32.

      What were the motives for the British campaign in
      Mesopotamia? Cohen suggests three reasons: (1) impe-
      rialist, i.e., it was a drive to participate in the
      dismemberment of the Ottoman Empire; (2) propagandist,
      to keep the Arabs from joining the Turks; (3) to pro-
      tect the oil fields. Cohen argues that oil played less
      of a role than the interest in winning over the Arabs.
      Contrast with Mejcher, item 234; and Kent, item 398.
      For background on the campaign, see Moberly, item 315;
      Barker, item 351; Wilson, item 358; Busch, item 352;
      and Cohen, item 394.

354. Goold, J. Douglas. "Lord Hardinge and the Mesopotamia
      Expedition and Inquiry, 1914-1917." *Historical Jour-
      nal* 19 (1976):919-45.

      The Mesopotamian expedition--the British invasion of
      Iraq--during World War I began as a half-hearted adven-
      ture that gathered momentum as it enjoyed success. With
      the stalemate on the Western front, success in the Middle
      East encouraged dreams that outstripped planning--the
      result was disaster when a British army of 10,000 had
      to surrender to the Turks. Hardinge, as Viceroy of
      India, had encouraged the expansion of the British ef-
      fort in Mesopotamia and received much of the blame for
      the failure.
          Cf. Busch, 352; Barker, 351; Moberly, 315; Sluglett,
      357; Guinn, 291.

*   Kent, Marian. *Oil and Empire: British Policy and Meso-
      potamia, 1900-1920.* Cited as item 398.

*   Mejcher, Helmut. *Imperial Quest for Oil: Iraq, 1910-
      1928.* Cited as item 235.

355. Mejcher, Helmut. "Oil and British Policy towards Meso-
      potamia, 1914-1918." *Middle Eastern Studies* 8 (1972):
      377-91.

Using newly opened records in the Public Records Office, Mejcher studies the influence of oil in shaping British policy in Mesopotamia during the war, most particularly the lobbying role of the Admiralty which had a keen interest in securing safe, British-controlled sources of oil. In light of the recent concentration on all things dealing with oil, Mejcher exaggerates the importance of oil in policy decisions before 1918. More balanced accounts are by Cohen, item 394; and Jones, item 229.

Cf. Kent, 398; Sluglett, 357; Mejcher, 235; Monroe, 304; Shwadran, 239; Longrigg, 233; Kleiman, 298.

356. Rothwell, V.H. "Mesopotamia in British War Aims, 1914-1918." *Historical Journal* 13 (1970):273-94.

The British invasion of Mesopotamia, part of the Ottoman Empire, in November 1914 presented British statesmen with the problem of what to do with the conquered area: keep it; establish an autonomous Arab state (under British tutelage); or leave it under some form of reconstructed Ottoman state. Views changed with successes; with the disappearance of the Russians, who would have had an opinion; with the determination to exclude the Germans or other unwelcome interests from an area of British predominance; with the need to make visible concessions to world opinion hostile to imperial aggrandizement and to local self-determination in order to secure support; and, finally, with the growing awareness that oil and its control was a vital British concern. The result was a hodgepodge of conflicting promises and goals that resulted in a mandate, a political hybrid designed to give minimum independence to the Arabs and maximum control to the British in a form to placate international sentiment.

Cf. Busch, 352; Kedourie, 333 and 346; Cohen, 353; Kent, 398; Mejcher, 235; Sluglett, 357; Guinn, 291; Moberly, 315; Wilson, 358; Adelson, 143; Monroe, 304; Klieman, 298.

357. Sluglett, Peter. *Britain in Iraq, 1914-1932.* St. Antony's Middle East Monographs, no. 4. London: Ithaca Press, 1976. vii + 360 pp.

Assesses the main features of British policy in Mesopotamia from the occupation during World War I, through the development of a local British administration and the mandate, down to Iraq's independence. Well-grounded in primary sources, though mainly British, and both describes and analyzes British policy in Iraq. The main British purpose was to indirectly control Iraq as a means of securing Britain's local interests. Studies the intricacies of British administration and the maneuvering to secure a mandate for Iraq. An essential study.

Cf. Busch, 285; Cohen, 394; Klieman, 298; Kedourie, 333; Monroe, 304; Longrigg, 233; Kent, 398.

Reviews: *AHR* 84 (1979):167-8, Peter Mellini; *IJMES* 11 (1980):270-3, Briton Busch; *MEJ* 31 (1977):213, Neal Lendeman.

358. Wilson, Arnold Talbot. *Loyalties: Mesopotamia, 1914-1920*. 2nd edition. 2 volumes. London: Oxford University Press, 1930.

Sir Arnold Wilson was one of the many competent officials who represented British interests in the Middle East. He was a political officer in the Indian Army and served for many years before World War I in Persia and the Persian Gulf. During the war he was attached to Sir Percy Cox's (see item 159) staff in Mesopotamia, and after the war temporarily replaced Cox as head of the Civil Administration. Wilson recounts his role in the war and in Iraq after the war, when he was held responsible for nationalist uprisings against Britain. These volumes, though self-justificatory, contain a mine of information on British policy both during and after the war, as well as much information of local events, customs and relations. Wilson was a prolific writer, and among his most enduring contributions is a survey of the history of the Persian Gulf and of British interests, *The Persian Gulf: An Historical Sketch from the Earliest Times to the Beginning of the Twentieth Century* (Oxford: Clarendon Press, 1928).

Cf. Marlowe, 177; Busch, 352; Winstone, 192; Sluglett, 357; Longrigg, 540.

General

359. Fisher, Sydney Nettleton. *The Middle East: A History.*
London: Routledge & Kegan Paul, 1960. xv + 606 +
xxxi.

A survey history of the Middle East from the rise of
Islam to the Suez Crisis. Discusses the formation of
the Islamic state, the rise of the Ottoman Empire, the
coming of the West and the emergence of the modern
Middle East. A useful introduction, of which there are
few. Also see Yahya Armajani, *Middle East Past and
Present* (Englewood Cliffs, N.J.: Prentice-Hall, 1970)
for a general textbook concentrating on the last two
hundred years.
Cf. Shaw, 481; Lewis, 477; Avery, 501; Holt, 378;
Hitti, 396; Longrigg, 540; Anderson, 195; Monroe, 304.

360. Fisher, W.B. *The Middle East: A Physical, Social and
Regional Geography.* 1950. Reprint. London: Methuen,
1957. xiii + 522 pp.

Surveys the major geographical features of the Middle
East from Iran to Egypt, Turkey to the Arabian Peninsula.
Discusses aspects of the climate, demography, the soil
and features of the physical environment and their im-
pact on regional agriculture and social organization.
A useful survey.
Cf. Mansfield, 364.

361. Glubb, John Bagot. *Britain and the Arabs: A Study of
Fifty Years, 1908-1958.* London: Hodder & Stoughton,
1959. 496 pp.

Glubb Pasha's history of the rise of Arab nationalism
and Anglo-Arab relations. Contains information on the

Arab Revolt, Lawrence's activities and the military campaigns in Arabia and Palestine. The majority of the
book deals with the period 1919-1958. Also see the
sections on Arab Nationalism, Palestine, Syria, Mesopotamia, and Arabia.
   Cf. Klieman, 298; Monroe, 304.

362. Hoskins, Halford Lancaster. *British Routes to India.*
      1928. Reprint. London: Frank Cass, 1966. xiii +
      494 pp.

The classic study of the evolution of British presence
in the Middle East and the commensurate rise in British
concern for the security of those interests. Concentrates on the lines of communication and trade between
Britain and the Indian empire that developed in Egypt
and Mesopotamia as a result of a search for shorter,
securer routes east. Also studies the internationalization of interests in the Middle East, the opening of
the Suez Canal, the beginnings of the Baghdad Railway,
and the consequences this had for British interests and
on British thinking.
   Cf. Robinson and Gallagher, 072; Cohen, 394; Graham,
203; Busch, 404; Farnie, 200.

363. Kedourie, Elie. *The Chatham House Version, and Other
      Middle Eastern Studies.* London: Weidenfeld & Nicol-
      son, 1970. 488 pp.

A collection of 12 essays written previously by
Kedourie and gathered together here. Although the essays were written at different times, they share a loose
theme--the rise of Arab nationalism and the development
of British policy in the Middle East. The book takes
its title from the last chapter, "The Chatham House Version," 351-94, which is a review of the attitudes towards the Middle East and British policy as developed
in the works emanating from the Royal Institute of International Affairs. Essays of note include "The Middle
East and the Powers," 1-12; "Cairo and Khartoum," item
345; "The Capture of Damascus, 1 October, 1918," 33-47;
"Sir Herbert Samuel and the Government of Palestine,"
52-81; "Sa'd Zaghlul," item 491; "The Genesis of the
Egyptian Constitution of 1923," 160-76; "Egypt and the
Caliphate, 1915-52," 177-207; "Pan-Arabism and British
Policy," 213-35; "Minorities," 286-316; "Religion and
Politics," 317-42. Together with *Arab Political Memoirs*,
item 444, the collection reproduces most of Kedourie's

articles, and brings together useful information. See
the section on Arab nationalism for related studies.
   Cf. Kedourie, 333 and 346; Busch, 352; Klieman, 298;
Deeb, 488; Monroe, 304; Mossek, 529.
   Reviews: *IJMES* 2 (1971):91-2, George Kirk.

364. Mansfield, Peter, editor. *The Middle East: A Political
      and Economic Survey.* 4th edition. London: Oxford
      University Press, 1973. xi + 591 pp.

The fourth edition of the Royal Institute of International Affairs' survey of politics, geography, history and social life of the countries of the Middle
East and North Africa. The first three editions were
edited by Reader Bullard and all remain useful. Much
of the material covers areas and periods not relevant
here, but the surveys, by country, contain valuable historical background. A useful reference on political,
social and economic life. Among the studies is Mansfield's "Arab Political Movements," 66-90, which studies
the major elements in the development of Arab nationalism with useful observations on the period from Napoleon to the collapse of the Ottoman Empire. Also see
the essay by Elizabeth Monroe, "The Origins of the Palestine Problem," 47-65.
   Cf. Fisher, 349; Issawi, 227; Polk, 453; Dawn, 433;
Kedourie, 333; Antonius, 430; Monroe, 304.
   Reviews: *JICH* 3 (1975):419-20, G.N. Sanderson; *MEJ*
25 (1971):108, A.L. Tibawi.

                  Britain and the Ottoman Empire

365. Ahmad, Feroz. "Great Britain's Relations with the
      Young Turks, 1908-1914." *Middle Eastern Studies* 2
      (1966):302-29.

Examines Anglo-Turkish relations from the fall of
Abdül Hamid to the start of World War I. The Young
Turk revolution of 1908 brought an end to the increasingly anti-British sentiment at Constantinople, but
this rapprochement was shortlived. The Turks believed
the British had a hand in a counter-revolutionary movement, and difficulties in resolving differences in
Mesopotamia over oil and the Baghdad Railway alienated
the Young Turks. Nor was British diplomacy very ima-

ginative before the war, locked as it was into the belief that neutrality was in Turkey's best interests.
Ahmad tends to over-emphasize Britain's changing attitude towards maintaining Ottoman integrity after 1908;
the change had been underway for some time.
    Cf. Ahmad, 461; Ramsour, 479; Kushner, 476; Lewis,
477; Shaw, 481; Cunningham, 367; Heller, 369; Hinsley,
086; Sachar, 480; Trumpener, 340.

366.   Bailey, Frank. *British Policy and the Turkish Reform
        Movement: A Study in Anglo-Turkish Relations, 1826-
        1853.* Harvard Historical Studies, no. 51. 1942.
        Reprint. New York: Howard Fertig, 1976. xiv + 312 pp.

    Studies Britain's interest in the Turkish reform move-
ment as a means of maintaining the territorial integrity
of the Ottoman Empire. In 1833 the Russians secured
considerable influence at Constantinople with the Treaty
of Hunkar Iskalesi, which reduced the Turkish state to
a virtual protectorate. The potential for admitting
the Russians to the Mediterranean awakened the British
to the task of shoring-up the ramshackle empire to contain the Russians. Dated and uses only European sources,
but useful. For a background study on British policy
at Constantinople in the 1890's, see Colin Smith, *The
Embassy of Sir William White at Constantinople* (London:
Oxford University Press, 1957).
    Cf. Lewis, 477; Devereaux, 468; Berkes, 465; Davison,
466; Anderson, 195; Findley, 470.

367.   Cunningham, Allan. "The Wrong Horse?--A Study of Anglo-
        Turkish Relations before the First World War." *Middle
        East Affairs*, no. 4, St. Antony's Papers, no. 17.
        London: Oxford University Press, 1965, pp. 56-76.

    Britain gradually lost interest in supporting the
Ottoman Empire, which meant a decline in British influence with the Sublime Porte, a gap soon filled by Germany. When World War I began, the British were unprepared to make concessions to what they considered an
enfeebled Turkey that would have to remain neutral by
force of circumstances, and so they took no vigorous
measures to see that Turkey remained neutral. Useful
interpretive introduction, but dated.
    Cf. Ahmad, 461; Trumpener, 340; Howard, 332; Heller,
369; Jelavich, 106; Millman, 207; Robinson, 072; Taylor,
209; Monger, 098.

368. Heller, Joseph. "Britain and the Armenian Question, 1912-1914: A Study in 'Realpolitik.'" *Middle Eastern Studies* 16 (1980):3-26.

Preservation of the Ottoman Empire remained a British concern, but Ottoman military collapse during the Balkan wars showed that the Empire was on the verge of disintegrating. Amidst these concerns the Armenians worked to establish an autonomous region under European protection, a subversion that threatened to ignite another massacre. Heller examines the British attempt to find a means of preserving the Ottoman state and preventing a massacre in a manner consonant with British interests and that would assure those interests if there were a collapse anyway. Heller examines the intricacies of Anglo-Russian diplomacy and provides insights into the inner workings of British foreign policy.

On aspects of the Armenian problem, see Gwyn Dyer, "Turkish 'Falsifiers' and Armenian 'Deceivers': Historiography and the Armenian Massacre," *Middle Eastern Studies* 12 (1976):99-107; and Roderic Davison, "The Armenian Crisis, 1912-1914," *American Historical Review* 53 (1948):481-505.

Cf. Hovanissian, 552; Shaw, 481; Sarkissian, 557.

369. Heller, Joseph. "Sir Louis Mallet and the Ottoman Empire: The Road to War." *Middle Eastern Studies* 12 (1976):3-44.

Louis Mallet went to Constantinople in 1913 to try to restore a degree of cordiality to Anglo-Ottoman relations lost in petty bickering, and over the massacres of Ottoman subject peoples. But Mallet, who had a certain sympathy for Turkish sentiments, was unable to overcome German maneuvering, Turkish disingenuousness and the unsympathetic or mixed signals he received from the Foreign Office, nor to prevent the Ottomans from joining the Central Powers. Compare with Cunningham, item 367, and Trumpener, item 342. Presumes a certain familiarity with British Foreign Office personnel.

Cf. Trumpener, 340; Kurat, 335; Steiner, 307; Sachar, 480; Ahmad, 461; Howard, 332; Grey, 160.

370. Jack, Marian [later Marian Kent]. "The Purchase of the British Government Shares in the British Petroleum Co., 1912-1914." *Past and Present* 39 (1968): 139-68.

The British Government purchased controlling interest
in the Anglo-Persian Oil Company (later British Petroleum) in 1912. Was this an act of imperialism, motivated by strategic or economic concerns? Was it necessary? Argues that strategic concerns came after the
fact, and that the Admiralty, the chief government
agency intent on buying the shares, bought them because
it recognized a good bargain. The decision to purchase
the shares was not an imperial decision--one aimed at
extending British influence--though the Foreign Office
argued an imperialist line. It is clear that the Admiralty and the Government of India did not contemplate
intervention in a foreign country to protect the oil, a
view supported by Stuart Cohen, item 365, but was interested in securing a cheap, steady supply of oil.
Compare with Jones, item 229.
  Cf. Kent, 399; Sluglett, 357; Cohen, 394; Mejcher,
235; Shwadran, 239; Longrigg, 233; Fatemi, 221; Ferrier,
413; Monroe, 304.

*   Jelavich, Barbara. *The Ottoman Empire, the Great Pow-*
        ers, and the Straits Question, 1870-1887. Cited as
        item 206.

371.   Kent, Marian. "Agent of Empire? The National Bank of
        Turkey and British Foreign Policy." *Historical Jour-*
        nal 18 (1975):367-90.

        The National Bank was not an agent of empire, though
        it tried to be. Founded in 1909, the bank went to an
        unmourned grave in 1931. Bank officials before World
        War I tried to involve the Foreign Office in its rela-
        tions with the Turkish government to help sustain it,
        but Grey would not be drawn. The bank complicated re-
        lations with the French, who regarded financial compe-
        tition askance, and the entente was a major goal for
        Britain. In addition, Britain did not have major in-
        terests at Constantinople to uphold that justified sig-
        nificant support for the bank. Kent reviews the bank's
        background and comments on much of the existing liter-
        ature on Turkey's finances and foreign involvement.
          Cf. Kent, 398; Feis, 222; Platt, 237; McLean, 234;
        Francis, 223; Hamilton, 261.

372.   Kent, Marian. "Constantinople and Asiatic Turkey,
        1905-1914." *Foreign Policy under Sir Edward Grey*,
        item 086, 148-64.

Britain had three aims in its relations with the Ottoman Empire: to maintain paramountcy of influence in the Persian Gulf; protect Britain's commercial interests; and preserve Ottoman territorial integrity. These policies ran into trouble because of poor Anglo-Turkish relations. Kent examines Grey's handling of Anglo-Turkish relations, showing his determination to maintain the status quo at the Straits and to counter German activities at the Porte. Kent carries these views further in "Asiatic Turkey, 1914-1916," in the same volume, 436-51, briefly examining the change in Britain's determination to partition the Ottoman Empire, the efforts to incite an Arab revolt, the negotiations with Russia over the Straits, and the Sykes-Picot agreement. Kent argues that Grey did not distinguish himself in these affairs and must be blamed for the confusion of British promises to the Arabs.
Cf. Lewis, 477; Shaw, 481; Heller, 369; Cunningham, 367; Howard, 332.

373. McLean, David. "British Finance and Foreign Policy in Turkey: The Smyrna-Aidin Railway Settlement, 1913-1914." *Historical Journal* 19 (1976):521-30.

In weak nations where conflicting foreign interests and investments flourish, it is often difficult to separate commercial enterprise from political or strategic concerns. Railways, with their obvious strategic and commerical uses, are a case in point. When the Italians, demanding their share of the European scramble for a piece of the Ottoman economic pie, sought a railway concession that would have competed directly with a British railway company operating in Turkey, a political crisis loomed. The British Government could not afford to abandon the company because of the correlations between economic activity and political influence. An interesting example of how governments could become enmeshed in economic concerns even if they were not particularly keen to do so.
Cf. Platt, 237; Feis, 222; Francis, 223; Karkar, 230.

* Millman, Richard. *Britain and the Eastern Question, 1875-1878.* Cited as item 207.

374. Schoenberg, Philip. "The Evolution of Transport in Turkey (Eastern Thrace and Asia Minor) under Ottoman Rule, 1856-1908." *Middle Eastern Studies* 13 (1977): 359-72.

Studies traditional transport in the Ottoman Empire,
the efforts to introduce railways to improve transport,
and evaluates Ottoman performance in the light of economic, political and geographical obstacles.   Much remains to be done on examining economic activities in
the Middle East as opposed to considering such activity
in the 19th century as merely an adjunct to the European presence. Unfortunately Schoenberg uses no Ottoman sources, nor does he utilize Issawi, item 227.
Complement this study with Donald Quataert, "Limited
Revolution: The Impact of the Anatolian Railway on Turkish Transportation and the Provisioning of Istanbul,
1890-1908," *Business History Review* 51 (1977):139-60.
    Cf. Haddad, 472; Hamilton, 261; Earle, 219; Feis,
222; Karkar, 230; Platt, 237; Cohen, 394; McLean, 234.

Britain, Egypt and the Sudan

*   Abd al-Rahim, Muddathir. *Imperialism and Nationalism
         in the Sudan: A Study in Constitutional and Political
         Development, 1899-1956.* Cited as item 484.

375.   Atkins, Richard. "The Conservatives and Egypt, 1875-
         1880." *Journal of Imperial and Commonwealth History*
         2 (1974):190-205.

         Examines the slow change in British thinking that
         began to see Egypt, not Turkey, as the *point d'appui*
         of imperial defence of the routes to the eastern empire.
         At the same time, Anglo-French cooperation in Egypt be-
         gan to deteriorate as Egyptian finances entered a pe-
         riod of crisis and nationalism threatened the security
         of European interests.
            Cf. Robinson and Gallagher, 072; Marlowe, 383; Cromer,
         147; Jelavich, 206; Millman, 207.

*   Baring, Evelyn, Lord Cromer. *Modern Egypt.* Cited as
         item 147.

376.   Fabunmi, Lawrence Apalara. *The Sudan in Anglo-Egyptian
         Relations: A Case Study in Power Politics, 1800-1956.*
         London: Longmans, 1960. xx + 466 pp.

         Examines the clash of interests between Britain and
         Egypt over the status of the Sudan. Traces how Brit-

ain's interests in the Sudan, backed up by British power, came to take precedence over Egyptian claims in the Sudan. The book is deceptively subtitled and only the first sixty pages concern the pre-1930's, though the topical arrangement of the book means information is scattered throughout. Limited value.

Cf. Holt, 379; Warburg, 392; Robinson and Gallagher, 072; Sanderson, 208; Cromer, 147.

377. Hirszowicz, L. "The Sultan and the Khedive, 1892-1908." *Middle Eastern Studies* 8 (1972):287-311.

Studies the relationship between the Sultan of Turkey and his erstwhile vassal, the Khedive of Egypt. The reign of Muhammad Ali (1769-1849) weakened that connection, and the increasing influence of the European powers, particularly Britain and France, reduced both Ottoman control and Khedival authority over Egypt. In the late 19th century the Khedive Abbas Hilmi (1874-1944) tried to escape this situation by exploring means of getting the Europeans out and at the same time increasing his own influence within the Muslim world, which aroused the apprehension of the Sultan, Abdül Hamid, producing a three-cornered game of political maneuvering between the Khedive, the Sultan and the Europeans.

Cf. Kedourie, 363; Hourani, 439; al-Sayyid, 387; Cromer, 147; Marlowe, 383; Richmond, 494; Vatikiotis, 391; Holt, 378.

378. Holt, Peter Malcolm. *Egypt and the Fertile Crescent, 1516-1922: A Political History.* London: Longmans, 1966. xii + 337 pp.

An important source for the political development of Egypt and Mesopotamia from the Ottoman conquest through the years of increasing Western contact and domination, concentrating on internal developments. Examines the nature of the Ottoman system and its problems, the rise of Muhammad Ali in Egypt, the development of Arab nationalism and the break-up of the Ottoman Empire after World War I. A general introduction. Contains a useful annotated bibliography and brief chronological and genealogical tables.

Cf. Richmond, 494; Vatikiotis, 391; Marlowe, 383; Lewis, 477; Hitti, 396; Longrigg, 540; Haddad, 472; Ma'oz, 527; Busch, 404; Kelly, 407.

Reviews: *AHR* 73 (1967):553-4, R.L. Tignor; *EHR* 83 (1968):393-4, Albert Hourani.

379. Holt, Peter Malcolm. *A Modern History of the Sudan: From the Funj Sultanate to the Present Day.* Revised edition. Asia-Africa Series. London: Weidenfeld & Nicolson, 1961. xii + 242 pp.

A scholarly study of the Mahdist state, the Anglo-Egyptian Sudan, and the development of Sudanese nationalism. Gives a brief historical background on the Sudan and its people and then concentrates on political and administrative matters. For background on Egyptian rule in the Sudan, see Richard Hill, *Egypt in the Sudan, 1820-1881* (London: Oxford University Press, 1959); for the best study of the Mahdist state, see Holt's *The Mahdist State in the Sudan, 1881-1898: A Study in its Origins, Development and Overthrow* (Oxford: Clarendon University Press, 1970); also see Richard Hill, *A Biographical Dictionary of the Sudan*, 2nd edition (London: Frank Cass, 1967). For an administrative history, see Percy Marten, *The Sudan in Evolution: A Study of the Economic, Financial and Administrative Conditions of the Anglo-Egyptian Sudan* (London: Constable, 1921).
Cf. Fabunmi, 376; Abd al-Rahim, 484; Sanderson, 208; Robinson, 072.
Reviews: *JMH* 35 (1963):419, Garland Parker.

380. Issawi, Charles. *Egypt at Mid-Century: An Economic Survey.* London: Oxford University Press, 1954. xiv + 289 pp.

Updates Issawi's *Egypt: An Economic and Social Analysis* (London: Oxford University Press, 1947). Surveys Egypt's geo-political setting, the economic environment, and the major changes and trends in Egypt's economic development from the 18th century to the 1950's. Chapter 3 discusses aspects of the British occupation of 1882 and subsequent economic policies. Other chapters deal with human resources, standard of living, agriculture, industry, transport, finance and foreign trade, economic problems and social and political trends. Although dated, it remains a useful survey, especially in conjunction with Issawi's *Economic History of the Middle East*, item 227. Also see Edward Owen, *Cotton and the Egyptian Economy, 1820-1914: A Study in Trade and Development* (Oxford: Clarendon Press, 1969); and Helen Rivlin, *The Agricultural Policy of Muhammad 'Ali in Egypt*, Harvard Middle Eastern Studies, no. 4 (Cambridge: Harvard University Press, 1961).
Cf. Holt, 490; Baer, 487; Herschlag, 225; Landes, 232; Cook, 218.

381. Mansfield, Peter. *The British in Egypt*. London: Weiden-
        feld & Nicolson, 1971. xiv + 351 pp.

        Surveys the history of British Egypt, of Cromer, the
        civil administration, and the efforts to reconcile
        Egyptian nationalism, from the occupation to indepen-
        dence. Assumes too much too early about Britain's de-
        termination to remain in control of Egypt, but useful
        as a general introduction.
          Cf. Tignor, 390; Holt, 378; Vatikiotis, 391; Marlowe,
        383; Baer, 487; Baring, 147; al-Sayyid, 387.

382. Marlowe, John. *Cromer in Egypt*. London: Elek Books,
        1970. x + 332 pp.

        A survey of British rule in Egypt concentrating on
        the career of Evelyn Baring. Marlowe examines Cromer's
        ideas, his economic and political policies, his diplo-
        macy, his relations with the Khedive and the Egyptian
        administration, and the impact of Cromer's policies.
        The study does not do much with Egyptian attitudes to
        Cromer or the British. A useful summary that should be
        used in conjunction with al-Sayyid, *Egypt and Cromer*,
        item 387.
          Cf. Vatikiotis, 391; Holt, 378; Mansfield, 381; Cromer,
        147; Marlowe, 382; Tignor, 389.
          Reviews: *AHR* 77 (1972):186-7, Helen Rivlin; *IJMES* 4
        (1973):250-2, Roger Allen; *JMH* 44 (1972):119-20, William
        Ochsenwald; *MEJ* 25 (1971):409-10, Arthur Goldschmidt,
        Jr.

383. Marlowe, John. *A History of Modern Egypt and Anglo-
        Egyptian Relations, 1800-1956*. 2nd edition [1st edi-
        tion: *Anglo-Egyptian Relations, 1800-1953*, 1954].
        London: Frank Cass, 1965. 468 pp.

        A useful, readable overview of the relationship of
        Anglo-Egyptian relations from Napoleon to Nasser.
        Marlowe offers a more detailed account of the rise of
        Arab nationalism and British policy in *Arab Nationalism
        and British Imperialism: A Study in Power Politics*
        (London: Cresset Press, 1961), though it concentrates
        on the 1930's and after. He also studies the background
        to Anglo-French relations, exploring the basis for hos-
        tility between the two, in *Perfidious Albion: The Ori-
        gins of Anglo-French Rivalry in the Levant* (London:
        Elek Books, 1971).
          Cf. Holt, 378; Richmond, 494; Mansfield, 381; Owen,
        385; Tignor, 390; Ahmad, 485; Vatikiotis, 491; Safran,
        495.
          Reviews: (1st edition): *H* 41 (1956):317, Douglas Dekin.

*   Mellini, Peter. *Sir Eldon Gorst: The Overshadowed Pro-
        consul.* Cited as item 179.

384.   Mowat, R.C. "From Liberalism to Imperialism: The Case
        of Egypt, 1875–1887." *Historical Journal* 16 (1973):
        109–24.

        Examines the crisis in free trade anti-imperialism
        represented by the case of Egypt and how the British
        gradually conceived the necessity of intervening in
        Egypt to protect their economic interests and the Suez
        Canal.
            Cf. Owen, 385; Tignor, 390; Cromer, 147; Marlowe, 382;
        al-Sayyid, 387; Robinson and Gallagher, 072.

385.   Owen, Edward Roger John. "The Attitudes of British Of-
        ficials to the Development of the Egyptian Economy,
        1882–1922." *Studies in the Economic History of the
        Middle East,* item 218, 485–500.

        Surveys the attitude of certain leading British offi-
        cials in Egypt to economic development. Divides the
        period into three parts: 1882–1906, a period dominated
        by Lord Cromer and his ideas; 1907–1913, a period of
        economic difficulty that forced the British to re-
        examine their economic policies; and 1914–1922, the war
        years and their aftermath that put an end to substantive
        reflection on economics. The officials, generally bu-
        reaucrats and not economists, took their philosophies
        from accepted wisdom and wanted above all orderly de-
        velopment, stressing irrigation and agriculture and a
        limited role for government in economic matters.
            Cf. Issawi, 227; Polk and Chambers, 453; Baer, 487;
        Cromer, 147; Marlowe, 382; Mellini, 179; Holt, 490;
        Owen, 386; Tignor, 390; Robinson and Gallagher, 072;
        al-Sayyid, 387.

386.   Owen, Edward Roger John. "The Influence of Lord
        Cromer's India Experience on British Policy in Egypt,
        1883–1907." *Middle East Affairs,* no. 4, St. Antony's
        Papers, no. 17. London: Oxford University Press,
        1965, pp. 109–39.

        Examines Cromer's policies in Egypt as tutored by the
        British experience of governing non-European races in
        India. Cromer borrowed heavily from his Indian expe-
        rience, which meant he applied Indian solutions to
        Egyptian problems. This worked in the short run but
        proved increasingly ineffective, yet Cromer inflexibly

held to his methods. For a study of Cromer's economic policies in Egypt, see Owen's "Lord Cromer and the Development of Egyptian Industry, 1883-1907," *Middle Eastern Studies* 2 (1966):282-301.
   Cf. al-Sayyid, 387; Marlowe, 382; Baring, 147; Vatikiotis, 391; Holt, 378; Tignor, 390.

* Richmond, John. *Egypt, 1798-1952: Her Advance Towards a Modern Identity.* Cited as item 494.

* Sanderson, George. *England, Europe and the Upper Nile, 1882-1899.* Cited as item 208.

387. al-Sayyid, Afaf Lutfi [later Afaf Lutfi al-Sayyid-Marsot]. *Egypt Under Cromer: A Study in Anglo-Egyptian Relations.* New York: Praeger, 1968. xiii + 236 pp.

   Studies Cromer's role in governing Egypt, the imprint of his personality and the reaction to it. Covers the period 1883-1907, concentrating on Cromer, and the Egyptian elite, stressing the role of personalities in politics. Important for its use of Egyptian sources and the background it gives on Egyptian nationalism. On aspects on Cromer's tenure in Egypt, also R.C. Mowat, "From Liberalism to Imperialism: The Case of Egypt, 1875-1887," item 384. Also see al-Sayyid's study of post-World War I Egypt and the growth of Egyptian nationalism, *Egypt's Liberal Experiment, 1922-1936* (Berkeley: University of California Press, 1977).
   Cf. Marlowe, 382; Tignor, 390; Owen, 386; Vatikiotis, 391; Wendell, 496; Mansfield, 381.
   Reviews: *AHR* 75 (1969):124-6, Stephen E. Koss; *MEJ* 23 (1969):393, Robert Tignor; *PSQ* 86 (1971):673-5, Helen A.B. Rivlin.

388. Taylor, A.J.P. "Prelude to Fashoda: The Question of the Upper Nile, 1894-5." *English Historical Review* 65 (1950):52-80.

   Examines the growing importance of Africa and Egypt in British thinking. Acquisition of the Suez Canal and the re-evaluation of where best to defend the routes east (at Constantinople or in Egypt) alerted the British to the seeming threats posed to their position in Egypt by foreign control of the sources of the Nile.
   Cf. Sanderson, 208; Langer, 093; Monger, 098.

389. Tignor, Robert Lee. "Lord Cromer: Practitioner and
      Philosopher of Imperialism." *Journal of British Stu-*
      dies 2 (1963):142–59.

      Evelyn Baring, Lord Cromer, did not begin his career
      as an imperialist, and despite his role as the virtual
      ruler of Egypt he worked to improve the country as a
      means of putting an end to the British occupation. In
      his last years in Egypt, however, he lost sight of this
      goal, became contemptuous of the Egyptians' efforts to
      reform themselves, and succumbed to the lure of power.
      One of the features of British rule was the gradual em-
      ployment of more former Indian civil servants to work
      in Egypt, reducing or limiting the number of Egyptians
      in important positions in the bureaucracy. The increase
      in British personnel and the "Indianization" of the
      Egyptian civil service, which made bureaucratic prac-
      tice alien to the few trained Egyptians, helped to re-
      inforce the view that Egyptians could not govern them-
      selves. Tignor explores this process in "The 'Indian-
      ization' of the Egyptian Administration under British
      Rule," *American Historical Review* 69 (1963):636–61.
        Cf. Chamberlain, 152; Baring, 147; al-Sayyid, 387;
      Marlowe, 382; Mansfield, 381; Owen, 386.

390. Tignor, Robert Lee. *Modernization and British Colonial*
      Rule, 1882-1914. Princeton Studies on the Near East.
      Princeton, N.J.: Princeton University Press, 1966.
      xi + 417 pp.

      Details the nature and activities of the British ad-
      ministration in Egypt and its impact on Egyptian so-
      ciety. Tignor argues that British administration had
      a modernizing effect on certain areas of society but
      retarded others; and that not everything the British
      planned worked as they intended. For most of the pe-
      riod studied Cromer was Consul-General (1883-1907) and
      virtual ruler of Egypt, and after an introduction to
      the nature of Egyptian society, Tignor concentrates on
      Cromer's policies, the bureaucracy he established, and
      the success or failure of Cromer's efforts. Tignor
      then devotes attention to the policies of Eldon Gorst
      and Lord Kitchener, Cromer's immediate successors. The
      underlying principle in British policy in Egypt was to
      insure local tranquility and stability. The British
      occupied the country with that idea in mind and it re-
      mained the primary concern. An excellent survey and
      examination of the impact of colonial rule.

In addition see *Middle Eastern Studies* 16 (1980) for
a special issue on modern Egypt, in particular the following articles: Gordon Martel, "The Near East in the
Balance of Power: The Repercussions of the Kaulla In-
cident in 1893," 23-41; William Shepard, "The Dilemma
of a Liberal: Some Political Implications in the Writing of the Egyptian Scholar, Ahmad Amin (1886-1954),"
84-97; and Steven Rosenthal, "Urban Elites and the
Foundations of Municipalities in Alexandria and Istanbul, 125-33.

Cf. Tignor, 389; al-Sayyid, 387; Mellini, 179;
Vatikiotis, 391; Richmond, 494; Baer, 487; Holt, 490;
Baring, 147; Marlowe, 382; Owen, 385-6.

Reviews: *AHR* 73 (1968):1213-4, William R. Louis; *EHR*
83 (1968):869, P.M. Holt; *H* 53 (1968):301-2, M.E. Yapp;
MEJ 22 (1968):95-6, Elizabeth Monroe; *PSQ* 83 (1968):
152-4, Charles Issawi.

391. Vatikiotis, Panayiotis J. *The Modern History of Egypt.*
Asia-Africa Series of Modern Histories. Bernard
Lewis, editor. London: Weidenfeld & Nicolson, 1969.
xv + 512 pp.

Surveys the development of the modern Egyptian state
from Napoleon to Nasser, with a brief section on the
establishment of Islam in Egypt, the land and people,
and early contacts with Europe. Deals with the impact
of the West and the Egyptian political and intellectual
response. Pursues three major themes: the continuity
of Egyptian society from ancient times to the present;
how Islam and Arabic influenced and modified this continuity and affected the Egyptian world-view; and the
impact of the West and how Egyptians adjusted to the
dislocation occasioned by foreign domination. Concentrates on internal politics, social development and the
rise of modern Egyptian nationalism. Deals most effectively with the period from the late 19th century
to the present, and is an excellent review of Egyptian
views of British domination missing in many other surveys. For a useful, but general, survey see *Great
Britain and Egypt, 1914-1951* (London: Royal Institute
of International Affairs, 1951).

Cf. Marlowe, 383; Mansfield, 381; Holt, 378; Baring,
147; al-Sayyid, 387; Mellini, 179; Kedourie, 363 and
444; Baer, 487.

Reviews: *AHR* 75 (1970):1164-5, Richard P. Mitchell;
BSOAS 33 (1970):627-30, Gabriel Baer; *MEJ* 25 (1971):
100-1, Thomas Naff.

392.   Warburg, Gabriel. *The Sudan under Wingate: Administra-*
        tion in the Anglo-Egyptian Sudan, 1899-1916. London:
        Frank Cass, 1971. xi + 245 pp.

        In 1898 Kitchener expunged the Mahdist state and
        brought the Sudan under British control, though theore-
        tically under the joint control of Britain and Egypt.
        The first British administrator was Sir Reginald Wingate,
        whose ideas and methods determined much of the char-
        acter of the development of civil administration in the
        Sudan. Warburg examines Wingate's policies, their ef-
        fect and how local conditions or interests, in turn,
        influenced the nature and effectiveness of those po-
        licies. He also examines Wingate's relations with suc-
        cessive authorities in Egypt—i.e., Cromer, Kitchener
        and MacMahon—and with his inspector-general Rudolf C.
        Slatin (known as Slatin Pasha), a German by birth who
        spent most of his life in Egypt and the Sudan. Unfor-
        tunately Warburg never adequately introduces Slatin,
        though he figures prominently throughout. A useful
        study, but much remains to be done.
        On Slatin Pasha, see Richard Hill, *Slatin Pasha*
        (London: Cambridge University Press, 1965); and Slatin's
        own account of his experiences in *Fire and Sword in the*
        Sudan: A Personal Account of Fighting and Serving the
        Dervishes, 1879-1895, translated by F.R. Wingate (Lon-
        don: Edward Arnold, 1896). On aspects of Egyptian rule
        and the Mahdist state in the Sudan, see Richard Hill,
        Egypt in the Sudan, 1820-1881 (London: Oxford Univer-
        sity Press, 1959); and P.M. Holt, *The Mahdist State,*
        (see item 387). On Wingate see the biography by his
        son Ronald Wingate, item 393. On aspects of Sudanese
        nationalism, though mostly devoted to contemporary as-
        pects, see Warburg's *Islam, Nationalism and Communism*
        in a Traditional Society (London: Frank Cass, 1978),
        and his "Religious Policy in the Northern Sudan: Ulama
        and Sufism, 1899-1918," *Asian and African Studies* 7
        (1971):89-119.
        Cf. Holt, 379; Abd al-Rahim, 484; Kedourie, 363.
        Reviews: *MES* 13 (1977):148-50, G.N. Sanderson.

393.   Wingate, Ronald. *Wingate of the Sudan: The Life and*
        Times of General Sir Reginald Wingate, Maker of the
        Anglo-Egyptian Sudan. London: John Murray, 1955.
        xi + 274 pp.

        Britain enjoyed the services of a number of pro-
        consular administrators who gave much of the world a

British sense of order, or at least kept the natives
quiet. One such figure was Reginald Wingate, who was
Governor-General of Sudan from 1899, after the suppression of the Mahdist state by Lord Kitchener, until 1916
when he became High Commissioner in Egypt, though retaining general control over the Sudan. After the war
Wingate was held responsible for the nationalist turmoil in Egypt and returned home under a cloud. The
biography by his son is interesting but rather biased
in favor of Wingate and tends to ignore the local people
except as objects. A more thorough, scholarly study is
Gabriel Warburg's *The Sudan under Wingate*, discussed
above.

Cf. Sanderson, 208; Holt, 379.

Reviews: *MEJ* 10 (1956):445-6, Muhammad Sabry.

Britain and Syria, Mesopotamia and Palestine

394. Cohen, Stuart A. *British Policy in Mesopotamia, 1903-
1914*. St. Antony's College, Oxford, Middle East Monographs, no. 5. London: Ithaca Press for the Middle
East Centre, St. Antony's College, Oxford, 1976. vii
+ 361 pp.

Evaluates the evolution of Iraq's importance in British imperial thinking from a formless strategic concern
to a consistent evaluation of the area's commerical
value and strategic importance. One of the chief causes
for this was the internationalization of interests in
the area, epitomized by the Baghdad Railway and oil interests. Good study of how policy is influenced by interest groups. Places too much stress on commerce over
strategic concerns.

Cf. Kelly, 407; Busch, 404, 352 and 285; Cohen, 353;
Mejcher, 235; Kent, 398; Earle, 219; Chapman, 216;
Robbins, 184.

Reviews: *AHR* 84 (1979):167-8, Peter Mellini; *IJMES*
11 (1980):270-3, Briton Busch.

395. Cohen, Stuart A. "Mesopotamia in British Strategy,
1903-14." *International Journal of Middle East Studies* 9 (1978):171-181.

Examines British interests in Mesopotamia, showing
not only concern for trade and local security but also

a determination not to become militarily involved in
the event of war. Despite this determination the Ottoman drift towards war forced the British to reconsider
their position and embark on a local campaign that involved them ever deeper in an expanding military effort.
   Cf. Hoskins, 362; Klieman, 298; Busch, 404 and 352;
Mejcher, 235; Kent, 398; Kelly, 407; Sluglett, 357.

396. Hitti, Philip Khuri. *Lebanon in History: From the Ear-
         liest Times to the Present.* 2nd edition. New York:
         St. Martin's, 1962. xx + 548 pp.

      A survey of Lebanese history. Chapters 28-33 deal
   with the social, political, economic climate in the
   19th century, the coming of the West, the rise of nationalism, and World War I and the mandate. Has an
   Arab bias but useful for background information. Also
   see Hitti's *History of Syria* (London: Macmillan, 1951),
   which also covers Lebanon and Palestine. For a more
   analytical study of Lebanon and Syria in the late 19th
   and early 20th centuries, see Albert Hourani, *Syria and
   Lebanon: A Political Essay* (London: Oxford University
   Press, 1946).
      Cf. Shaw, 481; Tibawi, 401; Salibi, 542; Spagnolo,
   268; Shorrock, 266.
      Reviews: (1st edition): *JMH* 30 (1958):142-3, Carl
   Anthon.

397. Ireland, Philip W. *Iraq: A Study in Political Develop-
         ment.* London: Jonathan Cape, 1937. 510 pp.

      Surveys the British presence in Mesopotamia from an
   early interest in protecting the routes east, to the
   invasion during World War I, to the establishment of
   the mandate after the war. Though more modern scholarship has access to a wealth of recently-opened documents, this work remains one of the best studies of
   the evolution of the mandate system in Iraq. An excellent bibliography surveys the sources available at the
   time of writing.
      Cf. Cohen, 394; Sluglett, 357; Wilson, 358; Hoskins,
   362; Vinogradov, 543; Penrose, 541.

398. Kent, Marian. *Oil and Empire: British Policy and Meso-
         potamia Oil, 1900-1920.* New York: Barnes & Noble,
         1976. xiii + 273 pp.

      Explores the growing importance of oil in British
   economic and strategic thinking that led to involvement

in Persian and Mesopotamian oil fields. Before World
War I Britain gained control of the Anglo-Persian Oil
Company, which had a monopoly over the Persian oil
fields, and negotiated for a substantial role in the
Turkish Petroleum Company (see J.C. Hurewitz, item 047,
for the text of these agreements). Kent concentrates
on the Mesopotamian fields, and argues that the approaches and policies developed between 1900-1920
shaped subsequent British policy in the area, though
the Government did not always do everything in its power to assist British companies to secure local monopolies. Divided into three parts: background; the conclusion of the Mesopotamian oil concessions, 1900-14;
and the exigencies of war and post-war policies. A
useful, detailed study, but it over-emphasizes the importance of oil in British policy before 1918, mistak-
ing the views of some for an overall policy. This tendency to read backwards is shared by several works, including those by Cohen, item 394; Sluglett, item 357;
and Mejcher, item 235. Compare with Gareth Jones, 229.
  Cf. Longrigg, 233; Shwadran, 239; Lenczowski, 300;
Fatemi, 221; Kent, 370; Klieman, 298; Rothwell, 306;
Moberly, 315.
  Reviews: *BHR* 52 (1977):577-8, Ronald Ferrier; *EHR* 92
(1977):928-9, D.C.M. Platt; *HJ* 20 (1977):516-8, G.
Gareth Jones; *JEH* 37 (1977):823-4, Mira Wilkins; *MEJ*
31 (1977):88-9, Harry N. Howard.

399. Khan, Rasheeduddin. "Mandate and Monarchy in Iraq: A
      Study in the Origin of the British Mandate and the
      Creation of the Hashemite Monarchy in Iraq, 1919-
      1921." *Islamic Culture* 43 (1969):189-213, 255-76.

      Studies the difficulties facing Britain at the end
      of the war when it tried to assume control of Iraq with-
      out appearing to do so. Examines the evolution of the
      mandate idea and how Britain used it to form an Arab
      façade for British control, highlighting Britain's use
      of Feisal and the Arab nationalists' reaction to Brit-
      ish maneuvers. Useful. Compare with Briton Busch,
      items 352 and 285; Stuart Cohen, item 394; Peter
      Sluglett, item 357; and Stephen Longrigg, item 540.
        Cf. Vinogradov, 543; Wilson, 358; Graves, 159;
      Marlowe, 177; Temperley, 309; Monroe, 304; Klieman,
      298; Ireland, 397.

*   Longrigg, Stephen. *Iraq, 1900 to 1959: A Political,
      Social and Economic History.* Cited as item 540.

*   Penrose, Edith, and E.F. Penrose. *Iraq: International
         Relations and National Development.* Cited as item
         541.

*   Sluglett, Peter. *Britain in Iraq, 1914-1932.* Cited
         as item 357.

400.   Tibawi, Abdul Latif. *British Interests in Palestine,
         1800-1906: A Study of Religious and Educational En-
         terprise.* London: Oxford University Press, 1961.
         280 pp.

         Examines early British interests in Palestine, which
         were largely confined to a limited trade and religious
         enterprises. British officials became involved in dis-
         putes between local Christians, competing Protestant
         missionary groups, and Ottoman officials.
             Cf. Hopwood, 249; Shorrock, 266; Grabill, 282.

401.   Tibawi, Abdul Latif. *A Modern History of Syria Includ-
         ing Lebanon and Palestine.* London: Macmillan, 1969.
         441 pp.

         A detailed study of the history of "Greater Syria"
         from Napoleon to the 1960's. Relevant chapters trace
         the origins of Arab nationalism, the main features of
         Ottoman administration, the growth of foreign interests
         and international rivalry in the area, the role of Amer-
         ican, French and British missionaries, the attitudes
         and activities of the various minorities, the coming
         of World War I and the collapse of Ottoman authority,
         and the "betrayal" of the Arabs by the Allies in the
         post-war settlements. Somewhat tendentious but useful.
             Cf. Shaw, 481; Salibi, 542; Haddad, 472; Ma'oz, 527;
         Hitti, 396; Zeine, 544; Dawn, 433; DeNovo, 281; Tibawi,
         533.
             Reviews: *AHR* 75 (1970):2098, C. Ernest Dawn; *EHR* 86
         (1971):888, Ann Williams; *MEJ* 25 (1971):531-2, John P.
         Spagnolo.

                    Britain and the Persian Gulf and Arabia

402.   Abdullah, Muhammad Morsy. *The United Arab Emirates: A
         Modern History.* London: Croom Helm, 1978. 365 pp.

A general introduction to the history of the Trucial
States, now the United Arab Emirates. The work is divided into six major sections, examining the development of British interest in the area from 1892 to the
1960's; the internal developments within the Trucial
states; relations with neighboring states, such as
Saudi Arabia and Iran; the establishment of local boundaries; and a conclusion. Abdullah shows that British
policy, initially concerned with suppressing piracy and
the slave trade, changed after 1890 to concern for protecting Britain's position from foreign encroachment by
other Great Powers or local states, and that this was
achieved by closer relations, not to mention meddling,
with the Trucial States. A similar study that concentrates on the interwar years is Rosemarie Said Zahlan's
*The Origins of the United Arab Emirates: A Political
Social History of the Trucial States* (London: Macmillan,
1978). Also see Donald Hawley, *The Trucial States*
(London: Allen & Unwin, 1970).

Cf. Lorimer, 410; Kelly, 407-8; Busch, 404; Kumar,
409; Hopwood, 406.

Reviews: *AHR* 84 (1979):818-9, Briton C. Busch; *MEJ*
33 (1979):216.

403. Bidwell, Robin. *Travellers in Arabia*. London: Hamlyn,
1976. 224 pp.

A look at various explorers who studied or adventured
in Arabia, concentrating on the 18th through the 20th
centuries. Looks at the world the explorers found and
how they viewed what they found. The main individuals
discussed are Johann Burkhardt (1784-1817); Richard
Burton, who visited Arabia in the mid-1800's; Charles
Doughty, whose *Travels in Arabia Deserta* (1888; reprint.
London: Jonathan Cape, 1927), is still a classic; and
St. John Philby, who became enamored of Arabia in the
early decades of this century. An excellent, light
study, handsomely illustrated, that captures some of
the feeling that moved and motivated the individuals
who were haunted by far places. Earlier studies of
travellers in Arabia include R.H. Keinan, *The Unveiling
of Arabia: The Story of Arabian Travel and Discovery*
(London: Harrap, 1940); and D.G. Hogarth, *The Penetration of Arabia* (London: A. Rivers, 1904). For a general study of adventurers and soldiers of fortune in
Arabia, see Peter Brent, *Far Arabia: Explorers of the
Myth* (London: Weidenfeld & Nicolson, 1977). For a view

that takes some of the romantic edge off travellers in
the East, see Sari Nasir, *The Arabs and the English*
(London: Longmans, 1976). Also see Zahra Freeth, and
H.V.F. Winstone, *Explorers of Arabia: From the Renais-
sance to the End of the Victorian Era* (London: Allen &
Unwin, 1978); and Sarah Searight, *The British in the
Middle East* (New York: Atheneum, 1970). Also see Leslie
Blanch, *The Wilder Shores of Love* (London: Harmondsworth,
1959), a work that takes a rather romantic look at wo-
men adventurers in the Middle East.

Cf. Lawrence, 171; Monroe, 180; Winstone, 191-2;
Lorimer, 410.

Reviews: *GJ* 143 (1977):322.

404.   Busch, Briton Cooper. *Britain and the Persian Gulf,
       1894-1914.* Berkeley: University of California Press,
       1967. xv + 432 pp.

Examines the special status that the Persian Gulf
had for Britain, the nature of the British position in
the Gulf, and their response to foreign encroachment--
namely French, German, Russian, and Ottoman--in the
Gulf. Catalogues the diverse nature of British decision-
making machinery in the area and gives a detailed account of Britain's relations with the littoral states
as the British sought to protect Britain's privileged
position. Taken together with two further volumes
(items 285 and 352), this gives a well-documented if
narrowly diplomatic view of Britain's role in the Gulf
down to the beginning of World War I. See J.B. Kelly's
article, "TLS in the Desert," *Journal of Imperial and
Commonwealth History* 1 (1973):357-79, for some sharp
criticism of Busch's work. For a look at the 18th-
century development of British contacts in the area,
see Abdul Amir Amin, *British Interests in the Persian
Gulf* (Leiden: Brill, 1967). On the 20th century, see
John Marlowe, *The Persian Gulf in the Twentieth Century* (London: Cresset, 1962).

Cf. Kelly, 407; Kumar, 409; Staley, 240; Greaves,
416; Hoskins, 362; Kent, 398; Cohen, 394-5; Hurewitz,
047.

Reviews: *AHR* 74 (1968):236-7, H.D. Jordan; *JAS* 28
(1968):151-2, Robert A. Huttenback; *JMH* 42 (1970):264-
71, J.B. Kelly; *MEJ* 23 (1969):233-4, Christina Harris.

405.   Gavin, R.J. *Aden Under British Rule, 1839-1967.*
       London: Hurst, 1975. x + 472 pp.

Studies the establishment of British rule in Aden
from the foundations of the British colony to independence. Concentrates on British policy and the strategic and economic importance of Aden. See Gordon Waterfield, *The Sultans of Aden* (London: Murray, 1961), for
a more detailed background study that traces the evolution of British interest in Aden from its beginnings
to 1860.

Cf. Kelly, 407; Graham, 203.

Reviews: *AHR* 81 (1976):917-8, Kathleen E. Dunlop;
GJ 143 (1977):114.

406. Hopwood, Derek, editor. *The Arabian Peninsula: Society
and Politics.* London: Allen & Unwin, 1972. 320 pp.

A collection of fifteen articles on the origins of
the contemporary Arabian states. Divided into four
parts on history, politics and international relations,
sociology and economics. The material is lopsidedly
on Oman, and many of the essays concern modern Arabia,
but the following are of use: Ahmad Mustafa Abu-Hakima,
"The Development of the Gulf States," 31-53; George
Rentz, "Wahhabism and Saudi Arabia," 54-66; J.C.
Wilkinson, "The Origins of the Omani State," 67-88;
J.B. Kelly, "A Prevalence of Furies: Tribes, Politics,
and Religion in Oman and Trucial Oman," 107-41; and
R.M. Burrell, "Britain, Iran and the Persian Gulf: Some
Aspects of the Situation in the 1920's and 1930's,"
160-89. Of particular value is the introduction by
Hopwood, which is a bibliographic essay on some of the
best works on Arabia in English.

Cf. Kelly, 407; Busch, 404; Lorimer, 410.

Reviews: *AHR* 78 (1973):1104, Robert G. Landen; *APSR*
68 (1974):1359-60, John G. Merriam.

407. Kelly, John Barrett. *Britain and the Persian Gulf,
1795-1880.* Oxford: Clarendon Press, 1968. xiv +
911 pp.

An exhaustive, if not exhausting, account of the development of British influence in the Persian Gulf.
While it provides details as seen by British officials
--from the records they have left--it does not use
French or Ottoman sources and thus has a one-sided
view. Also does not give much insight into the actual
formation of policy. It does illustrate the tensions
in British policy, how in the area of the Persian Gulf
imperial interests caused Britain to bully the Ottomans
while giving them support at Constantinople against
other powers. A reference source.

For a briefer analysis of aspects of the British position, see Kelly's "The Legal and Historical Basis of the British Position in the Persian Gulf," *Middle Eastern Affairs*, no. 1, St. Antony's Papers, no. 4 (London: Chatto & Windus, 1958), 119-40. For earlier British contacts in the area, see A.A. Amin, *British Interests in the Persian Gulf* (Leiden: Brill, 1967); also see C.J. Lorimer, item 410, for information on the localities and groups mentioned. On other aspects of local history, see Donald Hawley, *The Trucial States* (London: Allen & Unwin, 1970), which, though it deals mainly with the modern period, has useful background information. In addition, see J.F. Standish, "British Maritime Policy in the Persian Gulf," *Middle Eastern Studies* 3 (1967):327-54, and "The Persian War of 1856-1857," *Middle Eastern Studies* 2 (1966):18-45. Also see Muhammad Abdullah, *The United Arab Emirates: A Modern History*, item 402; and Rosemarie Zahlan, *The Origins of the United Arab Emirates: A Political and Social History of the Trucial States* (London: Macmillan, 1978).
Cf. Troeller, 411; Graham, 203.
Reviews: *AHR* 74 (1969):989, Roderic Davison; *EHR* 85 (1970):374-5, C.S. Nicholls; *H* 54 (1969):310-11, G.J. Alder; *HJ* 13 (1969):374-5, Albert Hourani; *MEJ* 23 (1969):392-3, Robert Landen; *MES* 5 (1969), A.K.S. Lambton.

408. Kelly, John Barrett. *Eastern Arabian Frontiers*. London: Faber & Faber, 1964. 319 pp.

Focuses on the boundary dispute over the Buraimi Oasis between Saudi Arabia and her neighbors, Qatar, the Trucial States and Oman. A historical perspective of the nature of the conflicting claims and how Britain became involved in them. Much of the material concerns the post-World War II period, but the book is useful for the background on regional politics from the early 1900's and on the growth of British influence and involvement. Relies exclusively on British archival material.
Cf. Busch, 404; Troeller, 411.

409. Kumar, Ravinder. *India and the Persian Gulf Region, 1858-1907: A Study in British Imperial Policy*. London: Asia Publishing House, 1965. 259 pp.

Explores the strategic importance to Britain of the Persian Gulf area as a route between India and Britain.

Most particularly, Kumar looks at how officials in
India viewed the situation and what they did or encouraged the Home Government to do to protect British
interests. Kumar examines the gradual development of
British economic and political activity in the area,
the efforts to preclude foreign powers from the area,
the rivalry with France and later the Germans, and relations with local states. On aspects on Anglo-Persian
conflicting claims to influence in the Persian Gulf,
see Fereydoun Adamiyat, *Bahrein Islands: A Legal and
Diplomatic Study of the British-Iranian Controversy*
(New York: Praeger, 1955).

Cf. Busch, 404; Graham, 203; Hoskins, 362; Cohen,
394; Monroe, 304; Earle, 219; Sluglett, 357; Lorimer,
410.

Reviews: *AHR* 72 (1967):1351, J.C. Hurewitz; *EHR* 83
(1968):425-6, C.C. Davies; *HJ* 11 (1968):203-5, Beryl
Williams; *JAS* 26 (1967):734-5, A.T. Embree; *PA* 39
(1966):238, R.L. Greaves.

410. Lorimer, J.G. *Gazetteer of the Persian Gulf, 'Oman,
and Central Asia*. 2 volumes in 4. Calcutta: Super-
intendent Government Printing (India), 1908-1915.

One of the most impressive studies of its type. Indian officials informed themselves in great detail about
the geography, culture, and economic, political and social environment of the countries surrounding India.
Indeed, the British had more detailed information on
transport, routes of march, agriculture, tribal history
and local politics on Afghanistan, Persia and the Persian Gulf area than on some areas within the empire.
Among the most complete and authoritative of these is
Lorimer's *Gazetteer*, a comprehensive study, and essential as a reference tool. Similar information may be
gathered from the published reports of official wanders
in Asia in the *Geographical Journal* (London); and to a
lesser extent in the *Journal of the Royal Central Asian
Society*, and the *Journal of the Royal Asian Society*.
Also see S.B. Miles, *The Countries and Tribes of the
Persian Gulf* (1919; reprint. London: Frank Cass, 1966),
which deals largely with Oman.

Cf. Curzon, 412; Sykes, 426.

411. Troeller, Gary. *The Birth of Saudi Arabia: Britain and
the Rise of the House of Sa'ud*. London: Frank Cass,
1975. xxii + 287 pp.

Studies the rise of 'Abd al-Aziz ibn Sa'ud, the founder of modern Saudi Arabia, and his diplomatic relations
with the British. The book concentrates on the period
1910-1926, but Troeller gives a brief account of the
socio-political background of ibn Sa'ud's Arabia. An
important sub-theme is the diversity of opinion in British policy-making, a fact that fragmented British thinking and action in the Middle East. In addition, see
John S. Habib, *Ibn Sa'ud's Warriors of Islam: The Ikhwan
of Najd and Their Role in the Creation of the Sa'udi
Kingdom, 1910-1930* (Leiden: Brill, 1978), for a more
detailed study of internal Saudi affairs.

Cf. Troeller, 350; Kumar, 409; Silverfarb, 349; Busch,
352; Kelly, 407-8; Monroe, 180; Edens, 537; Winstone,
191.

Reviews: *MEJ* 31 (1977):95, George Rentz.

Britain and Persia

412.   Curzon, George N. *Persia and the Persian Question.* 2
       volumes. 1892. Reprint. New York: Barnes and Noble,
       1966.

Curzon's masterful study of Persia and its role in
British imperial politics as he saw it. Curzon was concerned with the defence of India and looked upon Russia
as the main threat to Britain's position. He hoped to
convince his countrymen of the necessity of defending
India as far from the Indian frontier as possible. In
his scheme the erection of buffer states was the answer.
Curzon travelled in Persia gathering information for
his study. He collected a wide range of material on
Persia's political state, social conditions and the
economy to use as arguments for his great goal--to convince British politicians and financeers to take a hand
in bolstering Persia against Russia. The work contains
a wealth of information on economic aspects of Persian
life. An essential reference tool, though more modern
scholarship may show much of Curzon's information to
be inaccurate or incomplete.

Cf. Sykes, 426; Avery, 501; McLean, 421; Issawi, 417.

413.   Ferrier, Ronald W. "The Early Management Organisation
       of British Petroleum and Sir John Cadman." *Manage-
       ment Strategy and Business Development: An Historical*

and Comparative Study. Edited by Leslie Hannah.
London: Macmillan, 1976, pp. 130-47.

Surveys the origins of British Petroleum from the
William Knox D'Arcy concession of 1901 to the birth of
the Anglo-Persian Oil Company in 1909. Ferrier, the
historian of British Petroleum, then gives interesting
information on the company's operations, its relations
with the British Government and the Company's efforts
to get official support.
Cf. Kent, 398; Jones, 229; Fatemi, 221; Amirsadeghi,
500.

414. Garthwaite, Gene R. "The Bakhtiyari Khans, the Government of Iran, and the British, 1846-1915." *International Journal of Middle East Studies* 3 (1972):24-44.

Studies the relations between the British and one of
southwestern Iran's largest and most powerful tribal
confederations. In many respects the British treated
the Bakhtiyari as a state-within-a-state, which to some
extent they were. By doing so they enhanced the prestige of the tribe in local affairs and undermined the
authority of the central government. Despite efforts
to secure Bakhtiyari loyalty the British were never
able to rely on them, a point that became painfully
clear during World War I. Garthwaite expands on
Bakhtiyari internal relations in his article, "The
Bakhtiyari Ilkhani: An Illusion of Unity," *International Journal of Middle East Studies* 8 (1977):145-60.
Cf. Oberling, 423; Wilson, 358; Sykes, 426; Browne,
505; Cottam, 506.

415. Greaves, Rose Louise. "British Policy in Persia, 1892-
1903." *Bulletin of the School of Oriental and African
Studies* 28 (1965):Part I, 34-60; Part II, 284-307.

An examination of Lord Salisbury's policies towards
Persia and the gradual change in those policies as his
influence declined and a new generation of diplomats
took over. This "new course" involved a drift away
from the Triple Alliance and the ultimate entente with
France (1904) and later Russia (1907). Part of the
shift in policy towards Persia, where the British had
tried to bolster a deteriorating oriental monarchy with
financial advice and support against the encroachment
of Russia, also resulted from growing determination to
reach some accommodation with Russia in the face of increasing doubts about German intentions; and because of

a British fear of becoming isolated politically. This
set of articles, plus Greaves' book, *Persia and the
Defence of India*, item 416, and her article on the 1907
Convention with Russia, item 248, are the most thorough
and thoughtful examinations of late 19th- and early
20th-century British policy in Persia to date.
   Cf. McLean, 421; Monger, 098; Grenville, 085; Penson,
101-2; Thornton, 427.

416.   Greaves, Rose Louise. *Persia and the Defence of India,
       1884-1892: A Study in the Foreign Policy of the Third
       Marquis of Salisbury.* University of London Historical
       Studies, no. 7. London: University of London, Ath-
       lone Press, 1959. xii + 301 pp.

       The possession of India made Britain a continental
       power and forced the British to think in terms of a
       land-based defence, since the navy could not protect
       the northwest frontier or bring pressure to bear on
       Russia, the chief threat to India. Concern for the
       defence of India became a key element in the foreign
       policy of Lord Salisbury, who tried to create a buffer
       state system as one means of shoring up India's defences.
       Persia figured prominently in this scheme. An excel-
       lent study with a generous bibliography and information
       on British archival sources, which, together with
       Monger, item 098, and Cohen, item 394, gives a handy
       guide to private papers.
          Cf. McLean, 421; Grenville, 085; Penson, 101; Howard,
       088; Benians, 196; Alder, 241; Gillard, 245; Taylor,
       209.
          Reviews: *AHR* 65 (1960):957-8, James G. Allen; *H* 45
       (1960):70-1, C. Collin Davis; *HJ* 3 (1960):201-3, V.G.
       Kiernan; *JMH* 32 (1960):183-4, Gilbert Hill; *MEJ* 14
       (1960):102-3, Bradford Martin.

417.   Issawi, Charles, editor. *The Economic History of Iran,
       1800-1914.* Publications of the Center for Middle
       Eastern Studies, no. 8. Chicago: University of Chi-
       cago Press, 1971. xv + 405 pp.

       Collected documents on aspects of the economic de-
       velopment of Iran. Discusses the general political,
       social, economic and historical background, and then
       presents articles and original documents by European
       observers or Iranian officials on foreign trade, trans-
       port, agriculture, industry, petroleum and finance.
       Useful not only as a ready reference source but as a

guide to other sources and for pointing out lacunae in
present knowledge on Iran's economic development. Supplements Issawi, *Economic History of the Middle East*,
item 227, and is an essential reference tool.

The Persian economy is still a neglected area. For
two valuable studies, see Gad Gilbar, "Persian Agriculture in the Late Qajar Period, 1860-1906: Some Economic
and Social Aspects," *Asian and African Studies* 12 (1977):
1-54; and "Demographic Developments in Late Qajar Persia, 1870-1906," *Asian and African Studies* 11 (1976):
125-56. Also see W.M. Floor's three articles, "The
Bankers (*sarraf*) in Qajar Iran," *Zeitschrift der
deutschen morgenländischen Gesellschaft* 129 (1979):263-
81; "The Merchants (*tujjar*) in Qajar Iran," *Zeitschrift
der deutschen morgenländischen Gesellschaft* 126 (1976):
101-35; and "The Guilds in Iran--An Overview from the
Earliest Beginnings till 1972," *Zeitschrift der deutschen
morgenländischen Gesellschaft* 125 (1975):99-116. For
the best study of land ownership see Ann K.S. Lambton,
*Landlord and Peasant in Persia: A Study in Land Tenure
and Land Revenue Administration* (London: Oxford University Press, 1953). Also see Lambton's "The Case of
Hajji 'Abd al-Karim: A Study on the Role of the Merchant
in Mid-Nineteenth-Century Persia," *Iran and Islam: In
Memory of Vladimir Minorsky*, edited by C.E. Bosworth
(Edinburgh: Edinburgh University Press, 1971); and "The
Case of Hajji Nur ad-Din, 1823-47: A Study in Land Ten-
ure," *Bulletin of the School of Oriental and African
Studies* 30 (1967):54-72.

Cf. Hershlag, 225; McDaniel, 517; Entner, 220; Olson,
236; McLean, 234; Curzon, 412; Avery, 501.

Reviews: *AHR* 78 (1973):719, Firuz Kazemzadeh; *APSR*
66 (1972):1383-4, Sepehr Zabih; *EcHR* 26 (1973):546-7,
F.J. Fisher; *IJMES* 11 (1980):266-7, Ronald Ferrier;
MEJ 26 (1972):207-8, M. Ali Fekrat; *MES* 10 (1974):251-
2, Julian Bharier.

418. Keddie, Nikki. "The Economic History of Iran, 1800-
       1914: An Overview." *Iranian Studies* 5 (1972):58-78.

Examines the principal features of the 19th-century
Iranian economy, including the sources of government
revenue, foreign investment, demography, trade, agriculture and the effects of international political and
economic activities. Much work on late 19th- and early
20th-century Iranian economics--on the whole Middle
East, for that matter--remains to be done.

For more detailed studies on Iranian economics, see
Robert McDaniel, "Economic Change and Economic Resili-
ency in 19th Century Persia," *Iranian Studies* 4 (1971):
36-49; P.W. Avery and J.B. Simmons, "Persia on a Cross
of Silver, 1880-1890," *Middle Eastern Studies* 10 (1974):
259-86; Julian Bharier, *The Economic Development of
Iran, 1900-1970* (London: Oxford University Press, 1971),
which provides statistical information, but most of it
dealing with the last twenty years; Ahmad Ashraf, "Historical Obstacles to the Development of a Bourgeoisie
in Iran," Cook, item 218, 308-32; Gad Gilbar, "Demographic Developments in Late Qajar Persia, 1870-1906,"
Asian and African Studies 11 (1976):125-56, and "Persian Agriculture in the Late Qajar Period, 1860-1906:
Some Economic and Social Aspects," *Asian and African
Studies* 12 (1979):1-54. These last two articles are
excellent.
      Cf. Issawi, 417; Entner, 220.

419. Klein, Ira. "British Intervention in the Persian Rev-
         olution, 1905-9." *Historical Journal* 15 (1972):
         731-52.

      Gives a thorough account of the British role in the
      Persian revolution down to 1909, and attempts to explain
      the impact of the Anglo-Russian Convention on British
      policy and why that agreement did not put an end to
      Anglo-Russian rivalry. Maintains that the British took
      an active interest in promoting constitutionalism as a
      means of protecting their interests. Tends to confuse
      the fate of the Qajar dynasty with the fate of one mon-
      arch, Muhammad Ali Shah (1907-1909), and overstates
      Britain's role in the constitutional movement, which
      was less deliberate than Klein allows for. See Stephen
      Gwynn, editor, *The Letters and Friendships of Sir Cecil
      Spring-Rice* (London: Constable, 1929). Spring-Rice was
      ambassador to Persia and tried to get his government to
      take a more active stance. Useful conclusions. Curi-
      ously neglects to use Greaves, items 248 and 416. Con-
      trast with Keddie, item 512, and Kazemzadeh, item 251.
         Cf. Browne, 505; Lambton, 514; McLean, 421; Entner,
      220; McDaniel, 517.

420. Klein, Ira. "British Policy and the Iranian Constitu-
         tion, 1919-1920." *The Historian* 36 (1974):434-54.

      Did British policy after World War I help create a
      constitutional crisis in Iran that put a dictator into

power? Did British informal imperialism cause or facilitate the rise of Riza Khan? By aligning with conservative oligarchs and undermining the feeble reform efforts of constitutionally-minded reformers, the British helped promote a return of autocracy and non-parliamentary nationalism and government. This argument fails to consider the fragmented nature of Iran at the time, or that one of the individuals in the coup of 1921 was one of the constitutionally-minded reformers. Gives Britain too much credit.

Cf. Klein, 419; Stanwood, 428; McLean, 421; Olson, 424; Avery, 501; Cottam, 506.

421. McLean, David. *Britain and Her Buffer State: The Collapse of the Persian Empire, 1890-1914.* Royal Historical Society Studies, no. 14. London: Royal Historical Society, 1979. ix + 157 pp.

Examines the fate of "sick men"--nations suffering from internal decay and contact with Europe--in the geopolitical rivalries of the late 19th century. Discusses the variety of British interests in Persia, the importance of prestige in British thinking, the rivalry with Russia, and the difficulties of dealing with a weak and corrupt government. Argues that after 1890 and particularly after 1900 British policy towards Persia lost its former non-interference approach as the Foreign Office found more and more reason to become involved, especially to protect British interests in a situation where the Russians were showing every intention of absorbing as much of Persia as they could get. McLean overstates the break in continuity in British policy--the British had been willing to interfere in Persian affairs or to encourage commerce well before 1900--but he correctly shows that the major change in policy resulted from increasing foreign pressure that made a more definite arrangement necessary. The subtitle is misleading: the Persian Empire did not collapse.

Cf. Kent, 394; Busch, 352; Avery, 501; Curzon, 412; Gillard, 245.

Reviews: *AHR* 85 (1980):632-33, Lyle McGeoch.

422. McLean, David. "English Radicals, Russia, and the Fate of Persia, 1907-1913." *English Historical Review* 93 (1978):338-52.

Examines Radical criticism of Sir Edward Grey's foreign policy in Persia. In particular the Radicals were
outraged that Grey had concluded an agreement with the
reactionary Tsarist government. They also opposed his
commitment to the balance of power, with its concomi-
tant commitments. In 1911, linking with experts on
Persia such as E.G. Browne and old imperialists like
Curzon who opposed the 1907 Convention with Russia on
principle, they tried to force Grey from office and a
reversal of policy. They failed, though Russia's high-
handed actions in Persia gave them some momentum. On
the Radicals in general, see J.A. Morris, *Radicalism
Against War, 1906-1914* (London: Longmans, 1972); Howard
Weinroth, "Left-wing Opposition to Naval Armaments in
Britain before 1914," *Journal of Contemporary History*
6 (1971):93-120, and "The British Radicals and the Balance of Power, 1902-1914," *Historical Journal* 13 (1970):
653-82.
    Cf. Williams, 258; Klein, 419; Greaves, 248; McLean,
421.

423. Oberling, Pierre. "British Tribal Policy in Southern
      Persia, 1906-1911." *Journal of Asian History* 4
      (1970):50-79.

The tribal make-up of much of the Middle East, plus
the virtual autonomy of many of these groups even within formally-constituted nation-states, often lent a
peculiar feature to diplomatic relations between local
states and the European Powers. In southern Iran there
were a number of powerful tribes that, while nominally
loyal to the central government, enjoyed considerable
latitude. The British recognized this fact and negotiated separately or became entangled in the internal
affairs of some of these tribes in order to protect or
promote British interests. A similar pattern prevailed
in the Ottoman Empire, where the British maintained
close contact with the Arab tribal groups. These relations, pursued against the wishes of central authority, were often necessary to provide local security
for British interests, but they involved the British
in petty local squabbles and antagonized relations with
the central government and with local rival groups which
often exacerbated local problems, which, in turn, could
invite further involvement. Oberling studies one such
relationship, with the Qashqa'i, a study he expanded in
The Qashqa'i Nomads of Fars (Paris: Mouton, 1974).
    Cf. Garthwaite, 414; Busch, 352; Lorimer, 410; Sykes,
426.

424. Olson, William J. "The Genesis of the Anglo-Persian Agreement of 1919." *Towards a Modern Iran: Studies in Thought, Politics and Society.* Edited by Elie Kedourie and Sylvia Haim. London: Frank Cass, 1980.

Explores the attempts by Lord Curzon to convert Persia into a buffer state for the defence of India. Capitalizing on Britain's post-war position in Iran, Curzon forced the Persians to accept an agreement that would have enabled the British to restructure Persia's financial administration and armed forces. The attempt ran afoul of Persian nationalism and American and French hostility and came to nothing. Curzon overestimated his own understanding of Persia and underestimated his opposition.
Cf. Busch, 285 and 352; Graves, 159; Avery, 501; Ramazani, 425.

425. Ramazani, Rouhallah Karegar. *The Foreign Policy of Iran, 1500-1941: A Developing Nation in World Affairs.* Charlottesville: University Press of Virginia, 1966. xviii + 330 pp.

Examines the main components of Iran's foreign policy from the rise of the Safavis to Riza Shah's failure to protect the country from Anglo-Russian invasion in 1941. The majority of the study concentrates on the 19th and early 20th centuries, and is the best work on Iran's diplomatic response to the West.
Cf. Fatemi, 508; Lenczowski, 322; Cottam, 506; Avery, 501; Kazemzadeh, 251.
Reviews: *JP* 30 (1968):597; *MEJ* 24 (1970):383-4, Sepehr Zabih.

426. Sykes, Percy M. *A History of Persia.* 3rd edition. 2 volumes. 1921. Reprint. London: Routledge & Kegan Paul, 1969.

A survey of Persian history from ancient times to the end of World War I. There are not many such works in English on Persia and so this remains useful, though of limited value. Sykes was for many years a consul in Persia and played an active part in British military activities in Iran during the war. Those parts of his book based on personal experiences are of interest, though must be read with caution.
Cf. Moberly, 315; Skrine, 326; Wilson, 358; Busch, 285; Curzon, 412; Avery, 501; Browne, 505; Hardinge, 163.

427. Thornton, Archibald Paton. "British Policy in Persia,
      1858-1890." *English Historical Review* 70 (1954):
      554-79; 71 (1955):55-71.

      Examines British policy in Persia as influenced by
      the paramount concern for the defence of India. Dated
      and superseded by Greaves, item 416, but still useful.
          Cf. Avery, 501; Ramazani, 425; Keddie, 511; McLean,
      421.

428. Stanwood, Frederick. "Revolution and the 'Old Reac-
      tionary Policy': Britain in Persia, 1917." *Journal
      of Imperial and Commonwealth History* 7 (1978):144-65.

      The revolution in Russia jeopardized the Allied posi-
      tion in Iran, where local nationalists, Turkish forces,
      and German agents were trying to drag nominally neutral
      Iran into the war. Stanwood examines British attempts
      to deal with this crisis, most particularly with the
      debate over pursuit of the old policy or one that made
      concessions to legitimate Persian national claims. Un-
      fortunately the situation refused to respond to British
      ideas of concessions.
          Cf. Cottam, 506; Ullman, 328; Busch, 285; Olson, 424.

Westernization, Pan-Islam
and the Rise of Arab Nationalism

429. Allen, Richard H.S. *Imperialism and Nationalism in the
Fertile Crescent: Sources and Prospects of the Arab-
Israeli Conflict*. London: Oxford University Press,
1974. x + 686 pp.

The subtitle is more revealing of the contents than
the main title, but there is a useful background survey
on the origins of Arab nationalism and the rise of Zionism in the Middle East and the origins of the clash between the two. A survey that tries to speak reasonably
to the issues, with the aim of discovering a way to
peace.
    Cf. Sykes, 532; Marlowe, 528; Hurewitz, 523; Porath,
530; Tibawi, 533.
    Reviews: *MEJ* 28 (1974):466-7, Harry N. Howard.

430. Antonius, George. *The Arab Awakening: The Story of the
Arab Nationalist Movement*. London: Hamish Hamilton,
1938. 470 pp.

The classic study of the origins and development of
Arab nationalism. A Christian Arab and an official in
the British Palestine mandate, Antonius is not always
impartial, but he provides illuminating information on
the early development of Arab nationalism. Emphasizes
the role of Christian Arabs in promoting nationalism.
The first account to explore in detail the Husayn-
McMahon correspondence, and the chief Arab statement
about British perfidy. Must be read in conjunction
with Kedourie, item 346; Stein, item 531; Klieman, item
298; Friedman, item 521; Porath, item 530; Tibawi, item
533; Dawn, item 433; and Zeine, item 544.

For an examination of Antonius, see George Kirk, "The Arab Awakening Reconsidered," *Middle Eastern Studies* 13 (1962):162-73, which focuses on chapters 5 and 6 of the *Awakening*, casting serious doubts on the material and showing the work's main purpose as being Arab propaganda.

431.   Be'eri, Eliezer. *Army Officers in Arab Politics and Society*. London: Pall Mall Press, 1970. xii + 514 pp.

Concentrates on coup d'états since World War II but also has useful observations on the importance of the military in Islamic reform and the growth of nationalism which are applicable to World War I. Examines the role of the Arab officers in the Ottoman army who formed secret societies to promote Arab independence, a practice often resorted to by subsequent groups of army officers throughout the Middle East.
   Cf. Parry, 452; Hurewitz, 440; Polk, 453.
   Reviews: *PSQ* 87 (1972):484-6, Sydney N. Fisher.

432.   Cleveland, William Lee. *The Making of an Arab Nationalist: Ottomanism and Arabism in the Life and Thought of Sati' al-Husri, 1880-1968*. Princeton Studies on the Near East. Princeton, N.J.: Princeton University Press, 1971. xvi + 211 pp.

Studies the evolution of Arab nationalism from its origins in Ottomanism through the life of Sati' al-Husri, an Ottoman civil servant, confidant of King Faisal, and publicist for Arabism and Arab unity. A study of an individual, but also examines the environment that shaped him. Contains a useful bibliography on Arabism, Islamic reform and historical literature. Also see L.M. Kenny, "Sati' al-Husri's Views on Arab Nationalism," *Middle East Journal* 17 (1963):231-56. See Zeine, item 544; and Dawn, item 433; for the relation between Ottomanism and Arabism.
   Cf. Haim, 437; Khadduri, 445 and 447; Hourani, 439; Sharabi, 457; Clements, 004.
   Reviews: *AHR* 78 (1973):1105-6, James P. Jankowski; *BSOAS* 36 (1973):205-6, R. Michael Burrell; *MEJ* 27 (1973):77-8, Mejid Khadduri.

433.   Dawn, C. Ernest. *From Ottomanism to Arabism: Essays on the Origins of Arab Nationalism*. Urbana: University of Illinois Press, 1973. xi + 212 pp.

A collection of Dawn's essays on the common theme of
the origins of the Arab Revolt of 1917 and the rise of
Arab nationalism. The essays include: "The Amir of
Mecca al-Husayn ibn-'Ali and the Origins and the Arab
Revolt," 1-53, which appeared first in the *Proceedings
of the American Philosophical Society* 4 (1960):11-34;
"Abdullah ibn al-Husayn, Lord Kitchener, and the Idea
of an Arab Revolt," 54-68, which first appeared in
Italian in *Oriente Moderno* 37 (1957):1-12; "Ideological
Influences in the Arab Revolt," 69-86, which first appeared in *The World of Islam*, edited by James Kritzeck
and R. Bayly Winder (London: Macmillan, 1959), 233-48;
"From Ottomanism to Arabism: The Origins of an Ideology," item 434; and "The Rise of Arabism in Syria,"
item 435, both discussed below. There are also two interpretive essays, "Hashemite Aims and Policy in the
Light of Recent Scholarship on Anglo-Arab Relations
during World War I," 87-121, which is not contained
elsewhere; and "Ramifications and Reflections," 180-
206, which contains material drawn from "The Rise and
Progress of Middle Eastern Nationalism," *Social Education* 25 (1961):20-24, and "Arab Islam in the Modern
Age," *Middle East Journal* 19 (1965):435-46. All are
informative and interpretative accounts of the origins
of Arab nationalism.

Also see two essays by Rasheeduddin Khan, "The Rise
of Arab Nationalism and European Diplomacy, 1908-1916,"
Islamic Culture 26 (1962):196-206, 244-58; and "The
Arab Revolt of 1916-1918: Political Context and Historical Role," *Islamic Culture* 25 (1961):244-58.

Cf. Kedourie, 346; Antonius, 430; Klieman, 298;
Friedman, 344; Zeine, 544.

Reviews: *AHR* 79 (1974):1604-5, Briton C. Busch;
APSR 69 (1975):1470-1, William L. Cleveland; *MEJ* 28
(1974):203-4, Joseph Malone.

434.   Dawn, C. Ernest. "From Ottomanism to Arabism: The Ori-
       gins of an Ideology." *From Ottomanism to Arabism*,
       item 433, 122-47.

At the beginning of World War I very few Arabs considered the idea of a separate state, and most Arab
leaders were content to remain within the Ottoman Empire. The war and British encouragement, however,
stirred a latent urge for independence and in the course
of the war lone Arab intellectuals and small groups of
nationalists that had been underground emerged to clamor
for Arab independence. Dawn examines some of these

leading personalities in the underground revival of
Arabism, and the influences that shaped their ideas before World War I, noting that though Arabs and Turks
appealed to a common Islamic heritage, Arab intellectuals saw the Arab component as pre-eminent and thus
laid the foundations for an ethnic nationalism.
Cf. Hourani, 439; Sharabi, 457; Kedourie, 444;
Khadduri, 445-7.

435. Dawn, C. Ernest. "The Rise of Arabism in Syria." *From
      Ottomanism to Arabism*, item 433, 148-79.

Various centers of Arab nationalism during World War
I attempted to overthrow Ottoman authority, the most
familiar one being the revolt of the Sharif of Mecca in
1916. Others, however, were crushed, including Syrian
attempts. Dawn examines the leaders of the Syrian
movement, the underpinnings of local Arab nationalism,
the efforts to overthrow the Ottoman authority, and
the reasons for failure. Argues that most of the Syrian
Arab elite remained loyal to Ottomanism; they did not
desert the empire--it disintegrated around them. Also
see Robert Haddad, *Syrian Christians in Muslim Society:
An Interpretation* (Princeton, N.J.: Princeton University
Press, 1970), which examines the cultural role of Arab
Christians in translating Western learning into Islam,
and on their place in the formation of secular Arab
nationalism.
Cf. Hourani, 439; Zeine, 544; Antonius, 430.

436. Gabrieli, Francesco. *The Arab Revival*. The Great Rev-
      olutions Series. London: Thames & Hudson, 1976.
      178 pp.

Surveys the Arab experience from the spread of Islam
to modern times, concentrating on the emergence of Arab
nationalism after centuries of Turkish and Western do-
mination. An introductory study. In addition, see
Joel Carmichael, *The Shaping of the Arabs: A Study in
Ethnic Identity* (London: Allen & Unwin, 1969); and
Anthony Nutting, *The Arabs: A Narrative History from
Mohammed to the Present* (London: Hollis and Carter,
1964).
Cf. Fisher, 359; Polk, 453; Lewis, 449; Sharabi, 457;
Hourani, 439; Khadduri, 445 and 447.
Reviews: *CJH* 13 (1978):154-7, G.W. Egerton.

437. Haim, Sylvia G., editor. *Arab Nationalism: An Anthol-
      ogy*. Los Angeles: University of California Press,
      1962. 255 pp.

A collection of original articles or statements by leading figures in Arab nationalism from its origins to the 1950's. Haim's introductory essay discusses the basis of nationalism and the role and influence of the major figures, with much attention devoted to al-Afghani. Some of the principals whose works appear are Rashid Rida, Sharif Husayn, Sati' al-Husri, and al-Kawakibi. See the other works mentioned on Arab nationalism, particularly those by Keddie, item 442; Hourani, item 439; Sharabi, item 457; Antonius, item 430; Zeine, item 544; and Wendell, item 496.

Also see Kemal Karpat, editor, *Political and Social Thought in the Contemporary Middle East* (London: Pall Mall, 1968), which contains essays by Arab nationalists, as well as Turks and Persians, though most are contemporary figures.

Cf. Clements, 004.

Reviews: *MEJ* 16 (1962):538-9, Herbert Bodman, Jr.

438. Holt, Peter Malcolm; A.K.S. Lambton; and Bernard Lewis, editors. *The Cambridge History of Islam.* 2 volumes. London: Cambridge University Press, 1970.

A collection of essays by noted scholars on various aspects of Islamic life, political and social organization, and the arts. Volume 1, *The Central Islamic Lands*, covers Turkey, Persia, the Fertile Crescent, and Egypt from pre-Islamic to modern times, with essays on local government, the rise of the Ottomans, the concept of the caliphate, the coming of the West and the process of reform. Although generally good, the articles are of uneven quality and some tend to be rather obscure. Relevant essays include: P.M. Holt, "The Later Ottoman Empire in Egypt and the Fertile Crescent," 374-93; Ann Lambton, "Persia: The Breakdown of Society," 430-67; Kemal Karpat, "Modern Turkey," 527-65; Z.N. Zeine, "The Arab Lands," 566-94; Dankwart Rustow, "The Political Impact of the West," 673-97; and Monroe Berger, "Economic and Social Change," 698-730. For a comprehensive critique of the volume, see A.L. Tibawi's "The Cambridge History of Islam: A Critical Review," in his *Arabic and Islamic Themes: Historical, Educational and Literary Studies* (London: Luzacs, 1974).

Cf. Polk, 453; Haddad, 472; Baer, 487; Holt, 490; Shaw, 481; Lewis, 477; Salibi, 542; Avery, 501; Longrigg, 540.

439. Hourani, Albert H. *Arabic Thought in the Liberal Age, 1798-1939.* London: Oxford University Press, 1962. xi + 403 pp.

Examines the Islamic response to contact with Western
ideas and institutions; and how Arab intellectuals tried
to come to terms with Western power, Islamic decline and
the re-evaluation of values and ideas of political and
social organization. Discusses the main features of
the Islamic state in general and of the Ottoman Empire
in particular and then examines the ideas of significant figures--al-Afghani, Rashid Rida, Muhammad Abdu,
Sa'd Zaghlul, and others--in the development of Islamic
and Arab nationalism. Excellent study of the intellectual turmoil and ferment in the Islamic world in response to the West.
   Cf. Keddie, 442; Sharabi, 457; Kedourie, 444; Zeine,
544; Haim, 437; Wendell, 496; Antonius, 430.

440.   Hurewitz, Jacob Coleman. *Middle East Politics: The
       Military Dimension.* London: Pall Mall Press for the
       Council on Foreign Relations, 1969. xviii + 550 pp.

A comprehensive survey of the military in the Middle
East. After a brief introduction into the nature of
the military under early Islam, Hurewitz examines military modernization in response to the challenge of the
West in the Ottoman Empire, Egypt and Persia. Military
reform was the first avenue explored by Middle Eastern
and Asian states in an effort to discover a means of
combatting the West, whose power they believed was derived from its arms and armies. Unfortunately in many
cases reform ran counter to the interests of internal
political groups and thus military reform became a
source of division rather than strength. Even worse,
military reform often became the wedge for introducing
other Western ideas, a process that increased when the
efforts at military reform failed to fend off the West
and, as a result of failure, Western pressure increased.
Though the majority of the work deals with contemporary
aspects of military politics, it is a useful introduction to military reform.
   Cf. Shaw, 481; Parry, 452.

441.   Keddie, Nikki. "Pan-Islam as Proto-Nationalism." *Jour-
       nal of Modern History* 41 (1969):17-28.

Pan-Islam was a stepping stone on the way to more re-
gionally based national feelings, and its expression in
the late 19th and early 20th centuries was more than
traditional concepts of Islamic brotherhood, tapping
proto-nationalist sentiments brought on by contact with
the West. The Ottoman Sultan, as caliph, was the symbol

for worldwide Islamic loyalty--moral, not practical--
and this fact had to be considered by the Great Powers
that had Islamic populations, especially Britain, when
dealing with the Ottomans. Keddie examines the concept
and its importance. It might be added that one reason
pan-Islam failed to unite the Middle East was because
it proved impossible to organize such a diverse region
on the emotional but not very practical appeal of the
pan-Islamic ideologies; and activists were attracted
to more practical measures based on regional and ethnic
ties. See Arnold Toynbee, *A Study of History*, volume
8 (London: Oxford University Press, 1956), 692-5, for
a similar argument. Also see Bernard Lewis, "The Ottoman Empire in the Mid-Nineteenth Century: A Review,"
Middle Eastern Studies 1 (1965):291-4; and Dwight Lee,
"The Origins of Pan-Islamism," *American Historical Review* 36 (1942):278-87, who argues that Britain encouraged, if it did not create, the pan-Islamic movement.
 Cf. Keddie, 442; Kedourie, 444; Haim, 437; Dawn, 433.

442. Keddie, Nikki. *Sayyid Jamal ad-Din 'al-Afghani': A
  Political Biography.* Los Angeles: University of
  California Press, 1972. xvii + 479 pp.

Afghani was one of the most influential figures in
the revival of Islam and the Middle Eastern intellectual response to the West. He stressed a pragmatic assessment of traditionalism and modernism to decide on
the best features of each to rehabilitate the Middle
East in face of Western pressure. Afghani's ideas attracted numerous adherents throughout the Middle East,
the most important being Rashid Rida and the Egyptian
liberal religious leader Muhammad Abdu. Keddie examines Afghani's life, his works and the extent of his
influence on Middle Eastern nationalism, highlighting
Afghani's inconsistencies, his habit of concealing his
true beliefs and other deceptions that punctuated his
career. An exhaustive study. Compare with Elie
Kedourie, *Afghani and 'Abduh: An Essay on Religious
Unbelief and Political Activism in Modern Islam* (London:
Frank Cass, 1966), which takes a different view of
Afghani. Also see Malcolm Kerr, *Islamic Reform: The
Political Theories of Muhammad 'Abduh and Rashid Rida*
(Los Angeles: University of California Press, 1966).
An earlier work by Keddie on the same topic is *An Is-
lamic Response to Imperialism: Political and Religious
Writings of Sayyid Jamal ad-Din "Al-Afghani,"* Including
a Translation of the Refutation of the Materialists*
(Berkeley: University of California Press, 1968).

Cf. Hourani, 439; Khadduri, 445 and 447; Sharabi, 457; Haim, 437.

Reviews: *IJMES* 4 (1973):492-5, Albert Hourani; *MEJ* 27 (1973):402-4, Malcolm Kerr; *MES* 10 (1974):102-6, Elie Kedourie.

443. Keddie, Nikki, editor. *Scholars, Saints and Sufis: Muslim Religious Institutions in the Middle East Since 1500.* Los Angeles: University of California Press, 1972. xi + 401 pp.

Sixteen essays in two parts on the *ulama* and Islamic saints. The essays on the role of the religious hierarchy in various countries of the Middle East are valuable introductions, particularly Richard Repp, "Some Observations on the Development of the Ottoman Learned Hierarchy," 17-32; Richard Chambers, "The Ottoman Ulama and the Tanzimat," 33-46; Afaf Lutfi al-Sayyid-Marsot, "The Ulama of Cairo in the Eighteenth and Nineteenth Centuries," 149-66; Daniel Crecelius, "Nonideological Responses of the Egyptian Ulama to Modernization," 167-210; Keddie, "The Roots of the Ulama's Power in Modern Iran," 211-30; and Gustav Theiss, "Religious Symbolism and Social Change: The Drama of Husain," 349-67.

For another collection of essays on aspects of *ulama* power and its role in Islamic society, see Gabriel Baer, editor, *The "Ulama" in Modern History: Studies in Memory of Professor Uriel Heyd*, Asian and African Studies, no. 7 (Jerusalem: Israel Oriental Society, 1971).

Cf. Baer, 487; Holt, 490; Algar, 499; Lewis, 477.

Reviews: *AHR* 79 (1974):206-7, James Kritzeck; *CH* 42 (1973):149, Kenneth L. Crose; *MEJ* 27 (1973):518-9, Richard P. Mitchell.

444. Kedourie, Elie. *Arab Political Memoirs and Other Studies.* London: Frank Cass, 1974. viii + 327 pp.

Nineteen essays by Kedourie written and published in various journals. Many of the essays concern Arab nationalism, British policy, Arab and British personalities in Middle East politics, Arab-Jewish relations, and aspects of Turkish rule. Essays of interest include: "The Fate of Constitutionalism in the Middle East," 1-27; "Political Parties in the Arab World," 28-58, which surveys the formation of various groups to recent times; "The American University of Beirut," 59-72; "The Alliance Israélite Universelle, 1860-1960," 73-80; "The Impact of the Young Turk Revolution in the

Arabic-Speaking Provinces of the Ottoman Empire," 124-61; "Sir Mark Sykes and Palestine, 1915-16," 236-42; "Young Turks, Freemasons and Jews," 243-62; and "The Jews of Baghdad in 1910," 263-72. See *Chatham House Version*, item 363. Kedourie takes a more critical view of the origins, development and nature of Arab nationalism than do such scholars as A.L. Tibawi, item 533; Majid Khadduri, discussed below; and Hisham Sharabi, item 457, who take a more nationalistic stand.

445. Khadduri, Majid. *Arab Contemporaries: The Role of Personalities in Politics*. Baltimore, Maryland: Johns Hopkins University Press, 1973. x + 255 pp.

Continues themes developed in *Political Trends*, item 447, but concentrates on several political and intellectual figures that epitomized the development of Arab nationalism, and the struggle individuals faced in reconciling ideas, experiences and the demands of circumstances. Also describes their activities, the main features of their public careers and assesses their importance and influence. The subjects are discussed under three categories: military men; professional politicians; and intellectual politicians. Studies of interest focus on Aziz Ali al-Misri, discussed below, Nuri as-Sa'id, al-Hajj Amin al-Husayni, King Faisal, and Ahmad Lutfi al-Sayyid. For complementary studies, see Longrigg, item 540, Porath, item 530, and Wendell, item 496.
    Cf. Sharabi, 457; Zeine, 544; Haim, 437; Keddie, 442; Kedourie, 444; Hourani, 439; Safran, 495; Cleveland, 432.
    Reviews: *AAPSS-A* 410 (1973):179, Richard W. Mansbach; *AHR* 80 (1975):1016, Robert G. Landen; *APSR* 68 (1974): 1818-19, Iliya Harik; *MEJ* 29 (1975):349-50, John S. Badeau.

446. Khadduri, Majid. "'Aziz 'Ali al-Misri and the Arab Nationalist Movement." *Middle East Affairs*, no. 4, St. Antony's Papers, no. 17. Edited by Albert Hourani. London: Chatto & Windus, 1965, pp. 140-63.

Examines and evaluates the role of Aziz Ali al-Misri --an officer in the Turkish army--as the father of modern Arab nationalism. Aziz Ali's precise activities are unclear, but he was involved in secret societies encouraging Arab independence before 1914 and he worked during the war to promote Arab nationalism. At least

that is the impression—given in part by the best known
account of Arab nationalism, Antonius' *The Arab Awakening*, item 430.   But Aziz Ali was not a separatist,
rather a federalist who sought Arab autonomy within the
Ottoman framework and was thus not a significant contributor to the Arab revolt during World War I.   In the
interwar period he was unable to find employment for
his military skills and exercised little influence then
or during and after World War II.
    Cf. Ahmad, 485; Zeine, 544.

447.   Khadduri, Majid.   *Political Trends in the Arab World:*
       The Role of Ideas and Ideals in Politics.   Baltimore,
       Maryland: Johns Hopkins University Press, 1970.   xii
       + 297 pp.

       Studies main themes in the evolution of Arab-Islamic
       thought about nationalism, constitutionalism, Islam and
       revolution, and the best ways of reforming or rebuilding
       society to cope with the modern world.   Looks at indi-
       viduals and political movements and assesses their ideas,
       influence and results.   It also evaluates the impact of
       the West, both in stimulating ideas and as a source of
       political repression after World War I that stunted the
       growth of a healthy nationalism.   Whether or not remov-
       ing Western influence would have produced healthy gov-
       ernment and unified nationalism is open to debate.
       Chapters on the rise of nationalism, constitutionalism,
       and Islamic revival are most useful.   See Bernard Lewis,
       Islam in History: Ideas, Men and Events in the Middle
       East (London: Alcove Press, 1973), for an examination
       of some similar themes.   Contrast these views with those
       expressed by Elie Kedourie, items 346, 363, and 444.
          Cf. Dawn, 433; Sharabi, 457-8; Nuseibeh, 451;
       Antonius, 430.
          Reviews: *AAPSS-A* 394 (1971):155-6, Bernard Reich;
       AHR 76 (1971):811-2, Edmund Burke III; *MEJ* 27 (1973):
       227, Fiuzi Najjar.

448.   Lenczowski, George, editor.   *The Political Awakening of*
       the Middle East.   Englewood Cliffs, N.J.: Prentice-
       Hall, 1970.   ix + 180 pp.

       Collection of essays and primary sources on the ori-
       gins and development of nationalism within the succes-
       sor states to the Ottoman Empire.   Examines Islamic re-
       form ideas, both fundamentalism (as in the Wahhabis in
       Arabia) and modernist thought, and their impact on Arab

nationalism. Separate essays also deal with aspects
of Turkish and Arab nationalism.
  Cf. Antonius, 430; Zeine, 544; Sharabi, 457; Lewis,
477; Kushner, 476; Ahmad, 485.

449. Lewis, Bernard. *The Middle East and the West.* London:
    Weidenfeld & Nicolson, 1963. vii + 160 pp.

  A series of perspectives on the social, cultural,
economic, and political encounter between the West and
the Middle East and its impact on Middle Eastern ways
of life. Begins with a brief historical introduction
on the fundamental features of the Middle East and then
briefly examines how these were affected by Western
ideas: the rise of nationalism, the place of Islam in
Middle Eastern thinking, and the intellectual and political response to Western encroachment from the 16th
century to the post-World War II period. A handy,
brief survey of the major issues in Middle Eastern-
Western contact. For a similar brief survey, see Francesco Gabrieli, *The Arab Revival*, item 436.
  For a general study of the rise of nationalism and
the resurgence of Islam, see the useful, though dated,
A History of Nationalism in the Near East (New York:
Harcourt, Brace, 1929) by Hans Kohn. Also see Boyd
Shafer, *Nationalism: Myths and Reality* (New York:
Harcourt, Brace & World, 1955), for one of the best
studies on nationalism as an idea and its place in his-
tory; and Elie Kedourie, *Nationalism*, 3rd edition (Lon-
don: Hutchinson, 1966). See John J. Saunders, editor,
The Muslim World on the Eve of European Expansion
(Englewood, N.J.: Prentice-Hall, 1966), for a brief
survey of some of the major features of Middle Eastern
society before the Western onslaught. Also see Daniel,
item 199; and Polk, item 453. For a typology of non-
Western response to the West, see Dankwart Rustow,
"Politics and Westernization in the Near East," *The
Modern Middle East*, edited by Richard Nolte (New York:
Atherton Press, 1963); and Nabih Faris and Mohammed
Husayne, *The Crescent in Crisis: An Interpretive Study
of the Modern Arab World* (Lawrence: University of Kan-
sas Press, 1955).
  Cf. Khadduri, 445; Hourani, 439; Rosenthal, 456.
  Reviews: *PSQ* 80 (1965):469-70, Wayne Wilcox.

450. Lewis, Bernard, and P.M. Holt, editors. *Historians of
    the Middle East.* Historical Writings on the Peoples
    of Asia. London: Oxford University Press, 1962. xi
    + 519 pp.

A collection of 41 essays by various experts on aspects of Islamic historiography, either its nature and
development in the Middle East or as it has developed
in the West. Divided into three parts: Part 1 studies
Arabic, Persian and Turkish historiography from the
12th to the 19th centuries; Part 2 studies European
writings, including Russian, on the Middle East from
the Middle Ages to the 1960's; and Part 3 examines
19th- and 20th-century historiography. Provides an introduction to Middle Eastern historical literature.
Cf. Holt, 438.

451. Nuseibeh, Hazem Zaki. *The Ideas of Arab Nationalism.*
Ithaca, N.Y.: Cornell University Press, 1956. xiii
+ 227 pp.

A rather ambitious account of the origins and development of Arab nationalism from pre-Islamic times. While
some of the effort seems to overreach, it does provide
a study of how the heritage of Islamic civilization and
greatness affected the mind of modern Arab nationalists.
Identifies four major currents in the development of
nationalism: (1) impact of the West, which increased in
intensity throughout the 19th century and forced a re-
examination of Islamic values; (2) revival of Islam and
ideas of reform to cope with external pressure; (3) development of constitutionalism as a means of reform;
(4) the growth of a sense of nationalism based on race,
religion and culture as opposed to amorphous concepts
as Pan-Islamism or Pan-Ottomanism. Examines ideas and
idealists in the genesis of intellectual Arab nationalism, with special attention devoted to Abdul Rahman al-
Kawakabi, Rashid Rida, Shibli al-Shumayyil, and Mustafa
Kamil of Egypt. The study is carried down to the 1950's.
Cf. Antonius, 430; Zeine, 544; Haim, 437; Hourani,
439; Sharabi, 457; Dawn, 433; Keddie, 442; Wendell, 496.
Reviews: *AHR* 62 (1957):917-8, C. Ernest Dawn; *MEJ* 11
(1957):205-6, Farhat Ziadeh.

452. Parry, V.J., and Malcolm Yapp, editors. *War, Technology and Society in the Middle East.* London: Oxford
University Press, 1975. vi + 448 pp.

Examines the relationship between "developments in
war and technology and changes in forms of social organization." The twenty articles by a variety of experts cover aspects of military technology, tactics and
change from early Islam to modern times. Of particular

interest is the article by Yapp, "The Modernization of
Middle Eastern Armies in the Nineteenth Century: A Com-
parative view," 330–66, which looks at Ottoman, Egyp-
tian, Persian and Afghan armies in the light of develop-
ments in European armies and tactics; Glen Swanson,
"War, Technology, and Society in the Ottoman Empire from
the Reign of Abdulhamid II to 1913: Mahmud Şevket and
the German Military Mission," 367–85; and Dankwart
Rustow, "Political Ends and Military Means in the Late
Ottoman and Post-Ottoman Middle East," 386–99.
Cf. Hurewitz, 440; Shaw, 481; Polk, 453.
Reviews: *AHR* 81 (1976):788–99, Andrew C. Hess.

453. Polk, William Roe, and Richard Leon Chambers, editors.
*The Beginnings of Modernization in the Middle East:
The Nineteenth Century*. Publications of the Center
for Middle Eastern Studies, no. 1. Chicago: University of Chicago Press, 1968. v + 425 pp.

The result of a conference at the University of
Chicago Center for Middle Eastern Studies examining the
origins, meaning, and development of modernization in
the Middle East in the 19th century. Twenty-two contributors examined the influences of Western ideas on
Middle Easterners, their responses to the West, and the
consequences of their actions. Like most edited volumes resulting from conferences, there are many gaps
and a lack of cohesion, but this volume fares better
than most, and some of the individual essays are important contributions. Articles of note are: Roderic
Davison, "The Advent of the Principle of Representation
in the Government of the Ottoman Empire," 93–108; Hafez
Farman-Farmayan, item 507; Charles Issawi, "Asymetrical
Development and Transport in Egypt," 383–400; and P.M.
Holt, "Modernization and Reaction in the Nineteenth-
Century Sudan," 401–16.
On aspects of Islamic society and change, see the
works by Gustav von Grunebaum, particularly *Islam: Es-
says in the Nature and Growth of a Cultural Tradition*
(London: Routledge & Kegan Paul, 1955) and *Modern Islam:
The Search for Cultural Identity* (Los Angeles: Univer-
sity of California Press, 1962); and H.A.R. Gibb, *Stu-
dies in the Civilization of Islam* (London: Routledge &
Kegan Paul, 1962), and "Heritage of Islam in the Modern
World," *International Journal of Middle East Studies* 1
(1970):3–17, 221–37, and 2 (1971):129–47. Also see
Reuben Levy, *The Social Structure of Islam* (Cambridge:
Cambridge University Press, 1957).

Cf. Daniel, 199; Parry, 452; Haddad, 472; Lewis, 477;
Holt, 490; Ma'oz, 527.

Reviews: *AHR* 75 (1969):177-8, George Rentz; *MEJ* 24
(1970):91-2, Michael Hudson.

454. Proctor, Jesse Harris, editor. *Islam and International
      Relations*. New York: Praeger, 1965. viii + 221 pp.

A collection of 8 essays on aspects of Islamic nationalism and relations with the West. Although most
of the essays deal with contemporary events, all contain historical information and interpretations useful
in gaining some insight into the nature of the Islamic
response to the West. Of particular interest is Majid
Khadduri's "The Islamic Theory of International Relations and Its Contemporary Relevance," 24-39, which
examines the Islamic concept of international relations
and the consequences of being forced into a Western
system of diplomacy. Essays by Bayard Dodge, "The Significance of Religion in Arab Nationalism," 94-119;
P.J. Vatikiotis, "Islam and the Foreign Policy of Egypt,"
120-57; and T. Cuyler Young, "Pan-Islamism in the Modern
World: Solidarity and Conflict Among Muslim Countries,"
194-221, are also most useful.

Cf. Daniel, 199; Kedourie, 444; Zeine, 544; Lewis,
477; Polk, 453; Holt, 490; Haddad, 472.

Reviews: *MEJ* 20 (1966):114-5, Albert H. Hourani.

455. Rondot, Pierre. *The Changing Patterns of the Middle
      East*. Translated by Mary Dilke. New York: Praeger,
      1961. 196 pp.

Surveys the changing relationship between European
Powers and Middle Eastern countries, between Arabs and
Jews, and between the Powers themselves. Surveys the
area from 1914 to 1960, concentrating on Arab-Israeli
tensions, Arab nationalism and the nature of Great Power interest in the area. Though most attention concentrates on the 1930's to the 1960's, it is a useful survey of general themes.

Cf. Allen, 429; Polk, 543; Baer, 487; Holt, 490.

Reviews: *MEJ* 16 (1962):248-9, Fahim Qubain.

456. Rosenthal, Erwin I.J. *Islam in the Modern National
      State*. Cambridge: Cambridge University Press, 1965.
      xxii + 416 pp.

"The problem of adjusting a medieval culture and
civilization to the outlook and institutions moulded

in the West, which have come to influence and determine
contemporary state and society, is aggravated by the
deeply felt need of these states to preserve their Islamic identity, both as individuals and as nations."
Examines the confrontation in the Middle East between
spiritual values and the need for change, and the desire not to lose a personal and local sense of identity
and worth to foreign ideas and methods. A thorough,
scholarly study of the intellectual origins of Islamic,
Arab, and Turkish nationalism, as well as aspects of
nationalism in Pakistan, India and Malaya, in response
to Western ideas and methods.

Cf. Lewis, 449; Kushner, 476; Ahmad, 485; Dawn, 433;
Zeine, 544; Antonius, 430; Keddie, 442.

Reviews: *AAPSS-A* 368 (1966):202-3, Philip K. Hitti;
AHR 72 (1966):134-5, Majid Khadduri; *JR* 47 (1967):259-
60, Isma'il R. al-Faruqi; *PSQ* 81 (1966):489-91, G.E.
von Grunebaum.

457.   Sharabi, Hisham Bashir. *Arab Intellectuals and the
       West: The Formative Years, 1875-1914.* Baltimore,
       Maryland: Johns Hopkins University Press, 1970.   x
       + 139 pp.

Examines the origin and development of Arab nationalism in response to the impact of the West from the
1870's to 1914. Contends that this was the crucial formative phase of thought that influenced subsequent action. Concentrates on intellectuals, both Westernizers
and traditionalists, who grappled with Western ideas
and the need for reform. Looks at the role of the
ulama in spear-heading one aspect of the reaction to
the West, with a view of al-Afghani and Muhammad Abdu
that stresses their interest in preserving the essence
of Islam. A similar work that covers the period from
1798 to the 1870's, tracing the routes by which Western
ideas penetrated the Middle East and the intellectual
response to it, is Ibrahim Abu-Lughod's *Arab Rediscovery
of Europe: A Study in Cultural Encounters* (Princeton,
N.J.: Princeton University Press, 1963). Also see
Sharabi's *Nationalism and Revolution in the Arab World*
(London: Van Nostrand, 1966). Consult Keddie, item
442, for more details on the lives of al-Afghani and
Abdu. A useful, short introduction to the Islamic response to the West.

Cf. Safran, 495; Lewis, 449; Antonius, 430; Daniel,
199; Dawn, 433; Cleveland, 432.

Reviews: *AHR* 76 (1971):811-2, Edmund Burke III; *IJMES* 4 (1973):119-20, Caesar Farah; *PSQ* 87 (1972):687-92, Helen A.B. Rivlin.

458.   Sharabi, Hisham Bashir. *Governments and Politics of the Middle East in the Twentieth Century.* Princeton, N.J.: Van Nostrand, 1962. xiii + 296 pp.

Guide to the structure and functioning of the various states of the Middle East, emphasizing the development of local institutions, regional influences and international contacts that helped shape methods of government and attitudes towards politics. Most of the work covers the post-World War I period, but there is useful background material on Ottoman methods of government and their influence on the political order of its successor states. There is also information on Persia, and the various states of the Arabian Peninsula. Discusses why military, autocratic regimes, as opposed to democratic governments, are the prevailing pattern in the Middle East. Has informative footnotes and makes excellent use of local sources.
Cf. Lenczowski, 448; Holt, 490.

459.   Vatikiotis, P.J. *Conflict in the Middle East.* London: Allen & Unwin, 1971. xvi + 224 pp.

A brief survey of political conflict in the Middle East. Concentrates on inter-Arab relations, conflicting views of nationalism and differing ideas on priorities that have and continue to divide Middle Eastern societies. Stresses internal weaknesses in political institutions and in political community that reinforce suspicions and animosities between rulers and ruled and among social groups. Though most of the material concerns contemporary problems, the essay is a perceptive overview of a Middle Eastern crisis of morale that has roots in the advent of the West.
Cf. Lewis, 449; Rosenthal, 456; Polk, 453; Khadduri, 447.
Reviews: *AAPSS-A* 407 (1973):206-7, James A. Bill; *MEJ* 29 (1975):93-4, R.H. Dekmejian.

460.   Vatikiotis, P.J., editor. *Revolution in the Middle East: And Other Case Studies.* School of Oriental and African Studies of the University of London Studies on Modern Asia and Africa, no. 9. London: Allen & Unwin, 1972. 232 pp.

A collection of eleven essays on aspects of revolutions and revolutionary activity around the world. Many of the essays concern the period since World War II, but several essays discuss the Islamic background to revolution and the origins of Middle Eastern nationalism. Of interest are: Bernard Lewis, "Islamic Concepts of Revolution," 30-40; Albert Hourani, "Revolution in the Arab Middle East," 65-72; J.N.D. Anderson, "Law Reform in Egypt, 1850-1950," 146-72; and A.K.S. Lambton, "The Persian Constitutional Revolution of 1905-6," 173-82.

Cf. Sharabi, 457; Lewis, 477.

Reviews: *MEJ* 27 (1973):381-2, Manfred Halpern; *PSQ* 88 (1973):335-6, Charles Issawi.

*   Zeine, Zeine. *The Emergence of Arab Nationalism*. Cited as item 544.

The Rise of Turkish Nationalism

461.   Ahmad, Feroz. *The Young Turks: The Committee of Union and Progress in Turkish Politics, 1908-1914*. Oxford: Clarendon Press, 1969. xiii + 205 pp.

Studies the emergence of the Committee of Union and Progress from a secret society to the leading political organization in the pre-World War I Ottoman Empire. The Committee reflected reformist tendencies, but in the process of disintegration going on within the Ottoman Empire it came to represent Turkish as opposed to Ottoman nationalism; the Committee of Union and Progress also became more exclusively political, vying for control of the government, and it was not until just before World War I that the Committee emerged as the dominant political force. Ahmad picks up where Ramsaur, item 479, concludes. Has a useful bibliography of Turkish and European sources and a biographical appendix on the main political figures in the Committee.

For a brief account of the Young Turk revolution, see Ahmad's "The Young Turk Revolution," *Journal of Contemporary History* 3 (1968):19-36; for a comparison, see Andrew Mango, "The Young Turks," *Middle Eastern Studies* 8 (1972):107-17. On aspects of the Young Turk group and of the early activities of Mustafa Kemal, see

Gwynne Dyer, "The Origins of the 'Nationalist' Group
of Officers in Turkey, 1908-18," *Journal of Contemporary History* 8 (1973):121-64. For a study of Committee
relations with the Arabs that helped push the Arabs
toward independence, see Tag Elsir Ahmad Hassan, "The
Young Turks and the Arabs, 1909-1912," *Arabic and Islamic Garland: Historical, Educational and Literary
Papers Presented to Abdul Latif Tibawi by Colleagues,
Friends and Students* (London: Islamic Cultural Centre,
1977).

Cf. Lewis, 477; Davison, 466; Devereaux, 468; Shaw,
481; Berkes, 465; Findley, 470; Kushner, 476; Dawn, 433;
Trumpener, 340.

Reviews: *AAPSS-A* 398 (1971):143-5, A.A. Cruikshank;
AHR 75 (1970):1750, Kerim Key; *BSOAS* 33 (1970):394-5,
C.H. Dodd; *IJMES* 2 (1971):287-9, Victor Swenson; *MEJ*
25 (1971):541-2, Glen Swanson.

462.   Alderson, Anthony Dolphin. *The Structure of the Ottoman Dynasty.* Oxford: Clarendon Press, 1956. xvi +
186 pp.

A general survey; competent but limited, dealing
mostly with genealogy.
Cf. Lewis, 477; Shaw, 481.
Reviews: *JMH* 29 (1957):117-8, A.L. Horniker.

463.   Balfour, J.P.D., Baron Kinross. *Atatürk: The Rebirth
of a Nation.* London: Weidenfeld & Nicolson, 1964.
xviii + 542 pp.

An admiring but good, perhaps the best, biography of
Mustafa Kemal, the founder of modern Turkey. Atatürk
was a phenomenal figure whose force of personality can
still be seen in Turkey. For a less sophisticated
study, see H.C. Armstrong, *Grey Wolf, Mustafa Kemal:
An Intimate Study of a Dictator* (London: Arthur Barker,
1932). For a very human view of Atatürk and of Reza
Shah of Persia, see Gordon Waterfield, *Professional
Diplomat: Sir Percy Loraine of Kirkhale, Bt., 1880-
1961* (London: Murray, 1973). For a study of the Turkish Republic, see Richard Robinson, *The First Turkish
Republic: A Case Study in National Development* (Cambridge: Harvard University Press, 1963); Eleanor Bisbee,
The New Turks: Pioneers of the Republic, 1920-1950
Philadelphia: University of Pennsylvania Press, 1951);
and Elaine Smith, *Turkey: Origins of the Kemalist Movement and the Government of the Grand National Assembly,*

1919-1923 (Washington, D.C.: Judd & Detweiler, 1959). Other, less satisfactory, studies include Dagobert von Mikusch, *Mustafa Kemal: Between Europe and Asia*, translated by John Linton (London: Heinemann, 1939); and, on Mustafa Kemal's military career, Hanns Froembgen, *Kemal Atatürk: A Biography* (London: Jarrolds, 1938).

Cf. Shaw, 481; Busch, 285; Sonyel, 482; Lewis, 477; Walder, 316.

Reviews: *AHR* 71 (1966):631-2, Norman Itzkowitz; *MEJ* 19 (1965):532-4, Walter F. Weiker; *PSQ* 82 (1967):289-91, J.C. Hurewitz.

464. Balfour, J.P.D., Baron Kinross. *The Ottoman Centuries: The Rise and Fall of the Turkish Empire*. London: Jonathan Cape, 1977. 638 pp.

Surveys the history of the Ottoman Empire from its origins to the end of World War I. Kinross examines the strengths and weaknesses of the Ottoman state; its social, political and economic institutions and practices; and the consequence for Ottoman state and society of intimate contact with the West. While it does not gloss over Ottoman faults, it puts them into perspective, giving a balanced view of the Ottoman achievement.

Cf. Haddad, 472; Ma'oz, 527; Lewis, 477; Shaw, 481.

465. Berkes, Niyazi. *The Development of Secularization in Turkey*. Montreal: McGill University Press, 1964. xiii + 537 pp.

Details the features of Ottoman decline and the attempts by the ruling elite to introduce reforms, both to strengthen the state against the Europeans and to placate them with a show of reform. Covers aspects of reform from 1718 through the Tanzimat (1826-1878) to the period of Abdul Hamid II (1878-1908) through the Young Turks and the emergence of the Republic, 1908-1939. An excellent overview of the personalities, ideas and achievements of the reformers and the domestic and international systems in which they functioned.

Cf. Lewis, 477; Shaw, 481; Karpat, 475; Mardin, 478; Kushner, 476.

Reviews: *AAPSS-A* 359 (1965):234-5, Harry N. Howard; *AHR* 71 (1965):265-6, Roderic Davison; *JMH* 37 (1965): 481-2, William McNeill.

466. Davison, Roderic H. *Reform in the Ottoman Empire, 1856-1876*. Princeton, N.J.: Princeton University Press, 1963. xiii + 479 pp.

Examines the Tanzimat period, Ottoman attempts to reform the empire as a means of preserving it against
Western encroachment. Ottoman statesmen were caught
in the paradox of trying to adopt Western institutions
and ideas of organization to the Ottoman state as a
means of combatting the West--efforts which often aggravated internal problems and increased separatism
among the minorities. Excellent study of reform and
reformers, the problems of modernization, and the disintegration of traditional society. Good, annotated
bibliography.
Cf. Lewis, 477; Karpat, 475; Shaw, 481.
Reviews: *AHR* 70 (1964):163-4, C. Ernest Dawn; *JMH* 36
(1964):465-6, A.O. Sarkissian; *MEJ* 18 (1964):378-80,
Kerim K. Key; *PSQ* 81 (1966):160-2, Şerif Mardin.

467.   Davison, Roderic H. "Turkish Diplomacy from Mudros to
       Lausanne." *The Diplomats, 1919-1939.* Edited by
       Gordon A. Craig and Felix Gilbert. 2 volumes.
       Princeton, N.J.: Princeton University Press, 1953,
       pp. 172-209.

Turkey lay defeated at the end of World War I and
faced partition by the Allies into numerous petty states.
Even Asia Minor, the Turkish center to the Ottoman Empire, was to be divided into Armenian, Greek, Italian,
French and British territories. The rise of Turkish
nationalism under the forceful leadership of Kemal
Atatürk prevented this dismemberment. Davison highlights Turkish efforts to preserve their state.
Cf. Balfour, 463; Lewis, 477; Busch, 285; Walder,
316.

468.   Devereaux, Robert Essex. *The First Ottoman Constitu-
       tional Period: A Study of the Midhat Constitution and
       Parliament.* Johns Hopkins Studies in Historical and
       Political Science, series 81, no. 1. Baltimore,
       Maryland: Johns Hopkins University Press, 1963.
       310 pp.

Examines the development of constitutionalism in
Turkey in the mid-1870's. A thoroughly researched work
relying on Ottoman sources as well as a review of
available Western diplomatic material and a review of
the monographic and periodical sources, providing an
important corrective to the mis-information accumulated
there. Although largely narrative, it shows that the
constitutional movement was more than just an attempt

to placate Western pressure for reform, but reflected sentiments within Ottoman society. Examines in detail the constitution, the Chamber of Deputies and the political climate.

Cf. Lewis, 477; Davison, 466; Karpat, 475; Shaw, 481; Kushner, 476; Mardin, 478; Berkes, 465.

Reviews: *AHR* 69 (1963):139, Robert Delk; *EHR* 80 (1965):425-6, J.R. Walsh; *H* 49 (1964):251-3, Bernard Lewis; *JMH* 35 (1963):436-7, Richard Chambers; *MEJ* 17 (1963):179-80, Norman Itzkowitz.

469. Dyer, Gwynne. "The Turkish Armistice of 1918: 1--The Turkish Decision for a Separate Peace, Autumn 1918"; "2--A Lost Opportunity: The Armistice Negotiations of Mudros." *Middle Eastern Studies* 8 (1972):143-78; 313-48.

A detailed study of the Turkish background to the Mudros Armistice that ended hostilities in the Middle East.

Cf. Guinn, 291; Kedourie, 333; Busch, 352 and 285.

470. Findley, Carter. *Bureaucratic Reform in the Ottoman Empire: The Sublime Porte, 1789-1922.* Princeton Studies in the Near East. Princeton, N.J.: Princeton University Press, 1980. 450 pp.

Examines Ottoman efforts to restructure the civil administration in response to Western demands for reform, as well as a means to strengthen the state in order to resist the West. Gives an overview of the process of Ottoman reform, and shows that it promoted centralization and Turkification of the administration that reflected Turkish nationalism and Ottoman reaction to the revolt of the minorities, resulting in the formation of a secular Turkish national state by 1922. Complements Lewis, item 477, and Shaw, item 481.

Cf. Ramsaur, 479; Ahmad, 461; Hurewitz, 473.

471. Gökalp, Ziya. *Turkish Nationalism and Western Civilization: Selected Essays of Ziya Gökalp.* Translated and edited by Niyazi Berkes. New York: Columbia University Press, 1959. 336 pp.

Gökalp (1876-1924) was the chief philosopher of Turkish nationalism. A prolific writer, he re-interpreted the Ottoman-Turkish-Islamic past in order to derive the essence of Turkishness and religion that could be used as guiding principles in restoring national glory and

self-esteem while accommodating the need for Westerni-
zation. Berkes has selected essays that reflect
Gökalp's search for a way of reconciling the past and
the present. His introductory essay is a valuable sum-
mary of Gökalp's ideas and their place in the develop-
ment of modern Turkish nationalism. Also see Berkes'
"Ziya Gökalp: His Contribution to Turkish Nationalism,"
Middle East Journal 8 (1954):375-90.
   Cf. Heyd, 474; Lewis, 477; Shaw, 481; Kinross, 464.
Reviews: *MEJ* 14 (1960):224-5, Roderic Davison.

472. Haddad, William, and William Ochsenwald, editors. *Na-
      tionalism in a Non-National State: The Dissolution
      of the Ottoman Empire*. Columbus: Ohio State Univer-
      sity Press, 1977. x + 297 pp.

A collection of eleven essays on nationalism in various provinces of the Ottoman Empire, concentrating,
however, on the Middle East in the 19th and 20th centuries. Of particular interest are: William Haddad,
"Nationalism in the Ottoman Empire," 3-24, which gives
an overview of the growth of nationalist aspirations
among the minorities within the Empire; Roderic Davison,
"Nationalism as an Ottoman Problem and the Ottoman Re-
sponse," 25-56, which examines how Ottoman officialdom
tried to cope with the disruptive forces of nationalism;
Russel Smith, "The British and Sa'd Zaghlul, 1906-1912,"
195-206, which looks at Egyptian nationalism before
World War I; Rashif Khalidi, "Arab Nationalism in Syria:
The Formative Years, 1908-1914," 207-38; Suleiman Mousa,
"The Rise of Arab Nationalism and the Emergence of
Transjordan," 239-64; and Ann Lesch, "The Origins of
Palestine Arab Nationalism," 265-90. Also see William
Ochsenwald, "The Financial Basis of Ottoman Rule in the
Hijaz, 1840-1877," 129-49; and along with this, see
Jacob Landau, *The Hejaz Railway and the Muslim Pilgrim-
age: A Case of Ottoman Political Propaganda* (Detroit,
Michigan: Wayne State University Press, 1971), which
studies Ottoman efforts to use pilgrimage to promote
local control. Each article provides useful biblio-
graphic information. A valuable study using primary
material. Compare the article by Khalidi with C.
Ernest Dawn, item 433, and Antonius, item 430.
   For a further study, though loosely constructed, of
Arab nationalism, see Hassan Saab, *The Arab Federalists
of the Ottoman Empire* (Amsterdam: Djambatan, 1958).
   Cf. Ma'oz, 527; Polk, 453; Cleveland, 432; Zeine,
544; Hourani, 439; Kushner, 476.

Reviews: *AHR* 83 (1978):493-4, Gale Stokes; *MEJ* 32 (1978):224-5, William Cleveland.

473. Hurewitz, Jacob Coleman. "Ottoman Diplomacy and the European State System." *Middle East Journal* 15 (1961): 141-52.

The methods of modern diplomacy developed from a variety of European practices that gradually became a system. The Europeans then exported this system to the rest of the world, which accepted--willingly or not--the benefits of international relations on a European pattern. The Ottomans were the first non-European, non-Christian state to enter this system and by accepting it, helped transform it into an international norm. Hurewitz examines how the Ottomans viewed their participation and how they functioned in the system. For a more detailed study of the reform of Ottoman diplomacy, see Carter Findley, "The Legacy of Tradition to Reform: Origins of the Ottoman Foreign Ministry," *International Journal of Middle East Studies* 1 (1970):334-57. On the evolution of the capitulatory regime that formed the basis for much of Middle Eastern-European contact, see the somewhat muddled account by Nasim Sousa, *The Capitulatory Regime of Turkey: Its History, Origin and Nature* (Baltimore, Maryland: Johns Hopkins University Press, 1933).
      Cf. Findley, 470.

474. Heyd, Uriel. *Foundations of Turkish Nationalism: The Life and Teachings of Ziya Gökalp.* London: Luzac, Harvill Press, 1950. 174 pp.

Studies the life and works of the father of modern Turkish nationalism. Though not an original thinker, Gökalp was a synthesizer and was able to bridge the gap between the demands of a modern society and the need for a Turkish secular identity apart from but not hostile to Islam and the Ottoman background. Heyd examines the influences that shaped Gökalp's thought, how they were expressed in his major works, and the impact of his ideas on the subsequent leaders of Republican Turkey. Complement with Gökalp's essays, item 471.
      Cf. Lewis, 477; Mardin, 478; Kushner, 476.

475. Karpat, Kemal. "The Transformation of the Ottoman State, 1789-1908." *International Journal of Middle East Studies* 3 (1972):243-81.

It is often assumed that the Western impact on traditional societies was the source or stimulus for all
subsequent transformations--economic, political, or social. This ignores important internal, local forces
that produced changes. Karpat examines these, but does
not explain adequately why reforms were felt to be necessary or took the shape they did without Europe acting
as a threat or model. Valuable information on Turkish
nationalism and the process of cultural change.
Cf. Lewis, 477; Shaw, 481; Carter, 470; Davison, 466;
Mardin, 478; Berkes, 465.

476.   Kushner, David. *The Rise of Turkish Nationalism, 1876-*
       1908. London: Frank Cass, 1977. x + 126 pp.

Explores the intellectual antecedents of Turkish nationalism that shaped the ideas of Gökalp, the main
propagandist of Turkish nationalism, and his countrymen. Examines the role of Islam in Ottoman society,
the impact of the West on methods of organization and
habits of life and thought, and the evolution of a concept of secular nationalism in the age of Abdul Hamid
II. The trauma of decline that the Ottoman Empire
faced was a combination of Western pressure, the
struggle for independence by minorities within the empire, and a decline in ability to govern effectively.
These factors forced a reconsideration of the rationale
of empire in which "Turkism" emerged as the core of a
new sense of pride. Kushner explores these themes by
surveying the Ottoman press in Constantinople. Thoughtful, but narrow and too brief.
Cf. Berkes, 464; Davison, 465.
Reviews: *AHR* 83 (1978):1065, Richard Chambers; *MEJ* 32
(1978):96-7, Sydney N. Fisher.

477.   Lewis, Bernard. *The Emergence of Modern Turkey.* Royal
       Institute of International Affairs. London: Oxford
       University Press, 1961. xv + 511 pp.

The standard work on the development of modern Turkey
and the impact of the West from 1800 to 1950. Delineates the character of Ottoman government and society,
and the response to economic and political decline.
Societies that came into contact with the West and were
unable to maintain parity were forced to accept a measure of foreign interference in every aspect of national life that disturbed local patterns of thought and
organization; and forced a broad-ranging re-evaluation

of political, economic and social values. This process
was never even, never occurring at the same time or in
the same way to different groups within a given society;
as a result there was a multiplicity of responses that
further confused the system's response to external pressure. Lewis traces the responses from reform to revolution. Compare with Devereaux, item 467; Davison,
item 465; and Berkes, item 464; who have different
views on the sincerity of Ottoman reform efforts in the
1870's. Also see Kemal Karpat, editor, *The Ottoman
State and Its Place in World History* (Leiden: Brill,
1974), for a collection of eight thoughtful essays by
Karpat, Albert Hourani, Charles Issawi, and others on
the structure and nature of the Ottoman state and its
place in Middle Eastern history. For a study of the
ruling elite, with genealogical charts, see A.D. Alderson, *The Structure of the Ottoman Dynasty*, item 462.
Cf. Shaw, 481.
Reviews: *AHR* 67 (1962):727-8, Kerim Key; *JMH* 34
(1962):446-7, Roderic Davison; *MEJ* 16 (1962):256-7,
Stanford Shaw.

478. Mardin, Şerif. *The Genesis of Young Ottoman Thought:
      A Study in the Modernization of Turkish Political
      Ideas.* Princeton Oriental Studies, no. 21. Prince-
      ton, N.J.: Princeton University Press, 1962. viii
      + 456 pp.

      The Young Ottomans represented one response of the
      West. A group of liberal patriots who sought to
      strengthen the Empire on the basis of constitutional
      reform, they saw the Ottoman state as a multinational
      one and did not conceive of nationalism on the basis
      of Turkishness. Mardin traces the development of their
      ideas, the influence of Islam and the West, and then
      examines key individuals in the movement for reform
      that produced the Tanzimat. Rather turgid but useful.
      Reviews: *H* 49 (1964):251-3, Bernard Lewis; *JMH* 36
      (1964):86-7, Sydney Fisher; *MEJ* 17 (1963):180-1, Harry
      Howard.

479. Ramsaur, Ernest Edmondson. *The Young Turks: Prelude
      to the Revolution of 1908.* Princeton Oriental Stu-
      dies, Social Science, no. 2. Princeton, N.J.: Prince-
      ton University Press, 1957. xii + 180 pp.

      Studies the activities of the small groups of liberal
      reformers who tried to modernize the Ottoman Empire and

make it strong enough to resist the Europeans. Examines
the individuals and forces that shaped the ideas of the
Committee of Union and Progress, the leading element in
Turkish reform.

Cf. Ahmad, 460.

Reviews: *H* 43 (1958):262, V.J. Parry; *JMH* 29 (1957):
427–8, R.S. Rodkey; *MEJ* 14 (1958):345–6, Howard Reed.

480. Sachar, Howard. *The Emergence of the Middle East, 1914–
        1924.* New York: Knopf, 1969. xiii + 518 + xxix pp.

Examines the Ottoman Empire's last attempt to assert
its independence during World War I. The title is misleading in that the work's main concern is not with the
whole Middle East but with the fall of the Ottoman Empire and the origins of its successor states. Surveys
Ottoman entrance into World War I, the origins of the
Arab revolt, the post-war partitions, and the Arab and
Turkish nationalist reaction to being parcelled out
into European-controlled mandates or possessions. A
general survey. Compare the views of Ottoman entrance
into the war with those expressed by Trumpener, item
340.

Cf. Monroe, 304; Klieman, 298; Rothwell, 306; Gottlieb, 290; Kedourie, 346; Nevakivi, 324; Zeine, 545;
Porath, 530; Sluglett, 357; Fisher, 359.

Reviews: *AHR* 75 (1970):2096, Norman Itzkowitz; *MEJ*
25 (1971):410–11, Sydney N. Fisher.

481. Shaw, Stanford, and Ezel Kural Shaw. *Reform, Revolu-
        tion and Republic, 1808–1975. History of the Otto-
        man Empire and Modern Turkey*, vol. 2. London: Cam-
        bridge University Press, 1977. xxiv + 518 pp.

A comprehensive survey of the development of modern
Turkey from the reforms of Mahmut II to 1975. The work
examines Ottoman response to Western ideas and methods
of political, military and social organization and
traces the attempts of Ottoman, and later Turkish, nationalists to revitalize the state and resist Western
encroachment. Examines the Tanzimat Period, the Young
Ottomans, and the Young Turks, World War I, the Kemalist movement, and the major features of the history of
the Turkish Republic. The work is useful but plagued
by inaccuracies. See P. Hidiroglou, "Political Expe-
diency and Historical Scholarship: Some Remarks on
Stanford and Ezel Kural Shaw's *History of the Ottoman
Empire and Turkey*, Vol. II," *Balkan Studies* 19 (1978):

427-35, for a critical review. Compare the Shaws' views with those of Berkes, item 465; Davison, item 466; Devereaux, item 468; and Lewis, item 477.

An earlier study of Turkish reform is Shaw's *Between Old and New: The Ottoman Empire under Sultan Selim III, 1798-1807*, Harvard Middle Eastern Studies, no. 15 (Cambridge: Harvard University Press, 1971).

Cf. Kushner, 476; Mardin, 478; Sonyel, 482.

Reviews: *AHR* 83 (1978):242-3, Kemal H. Karpat; *MEJ* 31 (1971):491-2, George S. Harris.

482. Sonyel, Salahi Ramsdan. *Turkish Diplomacy, 1918-1923: Mustafa Kemal and the Turkish National Movement.* Sage Studies in 20th-Century History, no. 3. London: Sage, 1975. xv + 267 pp.

Studies the Turkish reaction to Allied plans for the dismemberment of the Ottoman Empire and the surge of Turkish nationalism, led by Mustafa Kemal, to prevent the Allied partition of Anatolia. Sonyel examines the basis for Turkish nationalism; the relations of the nationalists with Ottoman authorities and with the Allies, and their policies towards the minorities; the resort to war; and the settlement at Lausanne where the Allies recognized the impossibility of partitioning Anatolia in the face of Turkish nationalism.

Cf. Kinross, 464; Walder, 316; Busch, 285; Sachar, 480; Davison, 467; Dyer, 469.

Reviews: *AHR* 82 (1977):153-4, Roderic H. Davison; *MEJ* 34 (1980):242-3, Laurence Evans.

483. Swenson, Victor. "The Military Rising in Istanbul, 1909." *Journal of Contemporary History* 5 (1970): 171-84.

Argues that the customary view of the military uprising against the Young Turks in April 1909 as a carefully orchestrated counter-revolution by conservative forces is not accurate, but that the revolt resulted from discontent among the rank and file soldiers over being neglected and discriminated against by their Young Turk officers. This discontent was fertile soil for anti-government agitation, but the resulting insurrection was not the result of a conspiracy, though the Young Turks presented it in this light afterwards to cover up their mismanagement.

Cf. Ahmad, 461; Lewis, 477; Shaw, 481.

Egypt and the Sudan

484. Abd al-Rahim, Muddathir. *Imperialism and Nationalism
      in the Sudan: A Study in Constitutional and Political
      Development, 1899-1956.* Oxford: Clarendon University
      Press, 1969. xv + 275 pp.

      Traces the evolution of Sudanese nationalism and the
      role of British policy, Egyptian involvement in and at-
      titudes towards the Sudan in shaping that development.
      Thorough, well-researched account. For a study of
      Anglo-Egyptian relations in the Sudan, see Fabunmi,
      item 376, and Holt, item 379.
         Cf. Warburg, 392; Wingate, 393.
         Reviews: *AAPSS-A* 389 (1970):158-9, Kenneth D.D.
      Henderson; *MEJ* 25 (1971):251-2, Robert L. Tignor; *MES*
      10 (1974):93-5, Gabriel Warburg.

485. Ahmed, Jamal Muhammad. *The Intellectual Origins of
      Egyptian Nationalism.* Middle East Monographs, no.
      3. London: Oxford University Press, 1960. xi +
      135 pp.

      A brief but informative account, providing a summary
      of the influences and individuals that shaped Egyptian
      nationalism. Important for what it shows about the de-
      velopment of Egyptian intellectuals and national senti-
      ment before the British occupation of 1882, and the
      course of Egyptian thinking after the occupation down
      to World War I. Compare the views on Ahmad Lufti al-
      Sayyid expressed here with those of Wendell, item 496.
         Cf. Holt, 490; Vatikiotis, 391; Sharabi, 456; Hourani,
      439; Nuseibeh, 451.
         Reviews: *MEJ* 15 (1961):221-3, Helen A.B. Rivlin.

486. Baer, Gabriel. "Social Change in Egypt, 1800-1914."
      Political and Social Change in Modern Egypt, item
      490, 135-61.

      Surveys the changes in Egyptian social life in re-
      sponse to European pressures and to internal forces,
      describing the impact of Muhammad Ali's modernizing
      programs in the first decades of the 19th century, and
      discusses the declining economic power of the *ulama*
      and the traditional Turkish political elite. Looking
      at the impact of British rule on political and economic
      patterns of Egyptian life, Baer shows that a separate,
      "westernized" class developed that was isolated from

the mainstream of society. At the same time modern
economic practices increased social mobility, though
it did little to alter the status of women.
   Cf. Vatikiotis, 391; Tignor, 390.

487. Baer, Gabriel. *Studies in the Social History of Egypt*.
     University of Chicago. Publications for the Center
     for Middle East Studies, no. 4. Chicago: University
     of Chicago Press, 1969. xx + 259 pp.

     A collection of essays with the common theme of
     Egypt's gradual evolution to a modern society. Examines
     the role of the bedouins, the nature of land holding and
     the social attitudes of the peasants, the beginnings of
     urbanization and municipal government, and an overview
     of social change in Egypt from 1800 to 1914. Useful
     information on Egyptian social development as a back-
     ground to nationalism. This book is complemented by
     Baer's *Population and Society in the East*, translated
     by Hanna Szoke (London: Routledge & Kegan Paul, 1964);
     and by David Lerner, *The Passing of Traditional Society:
     Modernizing the Middle East* (New York: Free Press of
     Glencoe, 1963).
        Cf. Holt, 490; Cook, 218; Issawi, 227.
        Reviews: *H* 56 (1971):313-5, M.A. Cook; *MEJ* 24 (1970):
     243-4, P.J. Vatikiotis.

488. Deeb, Marius. *Party Politics in Egypt: The Wafd and
     Its Rivals, 1919-1939*. St. Antony's Middle East Mono-
     graphs, no. 9. London: Ithaca Press for the Middle
     East Centre, St. Antony's College, Oxford, 1979. vii
     + 451 pp.

     The period 1919-1939 was one of intense political-
     nationalist activity in Egypt, when political factions
     and parties flourished and competed with one another,
     with the Sultan and with the British for leadership.
     Deeb begins with the social upheavals of 1919 and the
     mass popular support for Sa'd Zaghlul and the Wafd.
     He examines the socioeconomic base of the parties' sup-
     port, their class backgrounds, their programs, and suc-
     cesses. Looks at the role of nationalism in their ap-
     peal and in inter-party rivalry. Also see Afaf Lutfi
     al-Sayyid-Marsot, *Egypt's Liberal Experiment: 1922-
     1936* (Los Angeles: University of California Press,
     1977).
        Cf. Richmond, 494; Marlowe, 383.
        Reviews: *AHR* 85 (1980):689, Charles Smith.

489. Goldschmidt, Arthur. "The Egyptian Nationalist Party: 1892-1919." *Political and Social Change in Modern Egypt*, item 490, 308-33.

Reveals the role of the Nationalist Party of Mustafa Kamil (1874-1908) and Muhammad Farid (1868-1919) in disseminating early ideas of nationalism and in providing a prototype for later political organization. The Nationalist Party was the chief source of opposition to Britain before the Wafd Party and the riots of 1919. Nationalist Party support came mainly from the middle classes and the educated Egyptian elite who resented the extended period of tutelage Britain considered necessary before Egyptians were to be allowed to govern themselves. Unable to achieve a popular base, the Nationalist Party remained small, and internal differences and habits of secrecy undermined its limited effectiveness.
Cf. Holt, 378; Kedourie, 444; Vatikiotis, 391.

490. Holt, Peter Malcolm, editor. *Political and Social Change in Modern Egypt: Historical Studies from the Ottoman Conquest to the United Arab Republic.* London: Oxford University Press, 1968. xx + 400 pp.

Twenty-four articles by nineteen specialists, including Gabriel Baer, P.J. Vatikiotis and Elie Kedourie, examine aspects of Egyptian political, intellectual and social development. The articles are divided into three major sections. The first, "Studies in Source-Materials," contains seven short articles on documentary collections or source materials in Turkey, Egypt and Britain, and is an invaluable guide. See especially Holt's "Ottoman Egypt (1517-1798): An Account of Arabic Historical Sources," 3-12; Stanford J. Shaw's "Turkish Source Materials for Egyptian History," 28-48; and Şinasi Altundağ's "Ottoman Archival Materials on Nineteenth-Century History," 49-71. The remaining two sections cover 1517-1798 and the 19th and 20th centuries respectively. Articles of particular note are: Gabriel Baer, "Social Change in Egypt: 1800-1914," item 486; H.S. Deighton, "The Impact of Egypt on Britain: A Study in Public Opinion," 231-48; Arthur Goldschmidt, "The Egyptian Nationalist Party: 1892-1919," item 489; and Elie Kedourie, "The Genesis of the Egyptian Constitution of 1923," 347-61.
Cf. Baer, 487; Safran, 495; Vatikiotis, 391.
Reviews: *EHR* 84 (1969):865-6, Albert Hourani.

491. Kedourie, Elie. "Sa'ad Zaghlul and the British."
   Middle Eastern Affairs, no. 2, St. Antony's Papers,
   no. 11. Edited by Albert Hourani. London: Chatto
   & Windus, 1961, pp. 139-60.

   Describes the career of Sa'd Zaghlul, one of Egypt's
   most influential nationalist leaders, between 1918 and
   1924--the most crucial period in Anglo-Egyptian relations when, by a painful process of confrontation and
   negotiation, Egypt passed from a Protectorate to a
   constitutional monarchy. Britain's declining nerve or
   willingness to rule an empire, plus nationalist sentiments led and represented by inflexible figures such as
   Sa'd Zaghlul, eroded Britain's position in Egypt.
      Cf. Holt, 378; Ahmad, 485; Vatikiotis, 391; Hourani,
   439; Tignor, 390; Deeb, 488; Kedourie, 444.

492. Little, Tom. *Modern Egypt*. Nations of the Modern
   World Series. 1958. Reprint. London: Ernest Benn,
   1967. xiii + 300 pp.

   A survey of Egypt's land, people and history from before Islam to the 1950's, concentrating on the last 25
   years. Of limited use.
      Cf. Vatikiotis, 391; Holt, 378; Richmond, 494.

493. Mahmud, Zayid. "The Origins of the Liberal Constitutional Party in Egypt." *Political and Social Change
   in Modern Egypt*, item 490, 334-46.

   Studies the contributions of the Hizb al-Umma (Party
   of the Nation) in providing a forum for the political
   education of Egyptian nationalists such as Sa'd Zaghlul
   and Lutfi al-Sayyid. It was a moderate party that ad-
   vocated cooperation with the British, an aspect that
   later nationalists would drop.
      Cf. Holt, 378; Wendell, 496; Safran, 495; al-Sayyid,
   387; Kedourie, 444.

494. Richmond, John C.B. *Egypt, 1798-1952: Her Advance Toward a Modern Identity*. New York: Columbia University Press, 1977. xii + 243 pp.

   A survey of Egyptian history from Napoleon to Nassar,
   concentrating on the clash of cultures, the difficulties and traumas of integrating a traditional, Islamic
   society into Western economic and political patterns.
   A good, brief introduction. A similar book, though
   not as useful, is Raymond Flower's *Napoleon to Nassar:*

The Story of Modern Egypt (London: Tom Stacey, 1972).
The best survey is still P.J. Vatikiotis' *Modern History of Egypt*, item 391.

For two studies, though now outdated, on the rise of
Egypt's first modernizer, see Henry H. Dodwell, *The Founder of Modern Egypt: A Study of Muhammad Ali* (Cambridge: Cambridge University Press, 1931); and Shafiq
Ghurbal, *The Beginnings of the Egyptian Question and the Rise of Mehmet Ali* (London: Routledge and Sons,
1928).

Cf. Holt, 378; Marlowe, 383; Issawi, 380; Cromer,
147.

Reviews: *GJ* 144 (1978):145; *IJMES* 11 (1980):279,
Robert Tignor; *MEJ* 33 (1979):369-70, Lorne M. Kenny.

495. Safran, Nadav. *Egypt in Search of Political Community:
An Analysis of the Intellectual Evolution of Egypt,
1804-1952.* Harvard Middle Eastern Studies, no. 5.
Cambridge: Harvard University Press, 1961.   298 pp.

Analyzes the evolution of ideas in Egypt in response
to contact with the West. This contact affected the
Egyptians' view of themselves, throwing into doubt
their values and methods of organization and forcing
them to re-examine their lives. But material reality
changed faster than this transvaluation of traditional
ideas and thus introduced tension and conflict into the
society as it struggled for solutions to dealing with
the West. The first half of the book is most relevant
and examines the rise of Egyptian nationalism and the
impact of the ideas of such intellectuals as Muhammad
Abduh, Rashid Rida, Lutfi al-Sayyid and Mustafa Kamil.

Cf. Vatikiotis, 391; Ahmad, 485; Wendell, 496; Holt,
378; al-Sayyid, 387; Hourani, 439.

*   Vatikiotis, P.J. *The Modern History of Egypt.* Cited
as item 391.

496. Wendell, Charles. *The Evolution of the Egyptian National Image, From Its Origins to Ahmad Lutfi al-Sayyid.* Berkeley: University of California Press,
1972. xvii + 329 pp.

Explores the various interpretations of *umma*, the
Arabic word meaning "community" or "nation," and how
19th-century Egyptian intellectuals defined the term
and tried to develop a modern concept of nationalism
from a traditional concept that referred to the com-

munity of believers of Muhammad's revelations. The development of nationalism has everywhere caused trauma,
dividing as many people one from another as it has
united others. The coming of the West forced Middle
Easterners to re-evaluate their ethics and assumptions
and gradually led them to formulate indigenous ideas of
nationalism as opposed to pan-Islamic feelings. The
process involved psychological difficulties because the
umma was a community of Muslims, whereas nationalism,
especially for Egyptians, began to reinforce divisions
between various Muslims. The dichotomy thus engendered
in the Middle Eastern personality remains today. The
process of contact with the West also prompted not only
the desire for liberal reform, but a simultaneous desire
not abandon a rich tradition as well. Wendell examines
how Egyptian intellectuals, particularly Lutfi al-
Sayyid, tried to reconcile these conflicting motivations.
    Cf. Vatikiotis, 391; Hourani, 439; Keddie, 443;
Kedourie, 444; Nuseibeh, 451; Sharabi, 457; Khadduri,
445.
    Reviews: *APSR* 69 (1975):353-4, Majid Khadduri; *BSOAS*
38 (1975):156-7, Fritz Steppat; *IJMES* 7 (1976):459-60,
al-Sayyid-Marsot.

Iran

497. Abrahamian, Ervand. "The Cause of the Constitutional
        Revolution in Iran." *International Journal of Middle
        East Studies* 10 (1979):381-414.

    Examines the revolution within a mildly neo-Marxist-
Weberian framework and concludes that the socioeconomic
impact of the West on Iran--by integrating the diverse
regional economies that in turn reduced commercial division and prompted the development of a middle class
which then fought to protect its gains--was the major
determining factor in the revolution of 1906. Overlooks the fact that the main economic class in the revolution was the traditional merchants, not an aspiring
bourgeoisie, and that the revolution did not result from
class struggle and was not aimed at social reconstitu-
tion, but political redress. Also see Ahmad Ashraf,
"Historical Obstacles to the Development of a Bourgeoisie in Iran," *Economic History of the Middle East,* item
218.
    Cf. Keddie, 512; Lambton, 514; Browne, 505.

498. Algar, Hamid. *Mirza Malkum Khan: A Study in the History
      of Iranian Modernism.* Berkeley: University of Cali-
      fornia Press, 1973. x + 327 pp.

      An unsympathetic view of a Persian statesman who was
      a prime influence, despite personal peccadilloes, in
      Persian nationalism in the late 19th century. An es-
      sential study, especially since so little has been done
      on the development of Persian nationalism and the in-
      dividuals that helped direct it. In addition to the
      works cited in this section on Persian nationalism and
      the revolution of 1906, see Ervand Abrahamian, "The
      Crowd in the Persian Revolution," *Iranian Studies* 2
      (1969):128-50; "Oriental Despotism: The Case of Qajar
      Iran," *International Journal of Middle East Studies* 5
      (1974):3-31; Homayoun Katouzian, "Nationalist Trends
      in Iran, 1921-1926," *International Journal of Middle
      East Studies* 10 (1979):523-51; Gholam Hoseyn Yousafi,
      "Dekhoda's Place in the Iranian Constitutional Move-
      ment," *Zeitschrift der deutschen morgenländischen Ge-
      sellschaft* 125 (1975):117-32; Asghar Fathi, "The Role
      of the 'Rebels' in the Constitutional Movement in Iran,"
      International Journal of Middle East Studies 10 (1979):
      55-66; George Haddad, "The Persian Revolution of 1906:
      Comparisons and Comments," *Persica* 2 (1966):73-79;
      Pierre Oberling, "The Role of the Religious Minorities
      in the Persian Revolution, 1906-1912," *Journal of Asian
      History* 12 (1978):1-29; F.R.C. Bagley, "Religion and
      State in Modern Iran," *Islamic Studies* 10 (1971):1-22;
      "Religion and State in Modern Iran," *Proceedings of the
      VIth Congress of Arabic and Islamic Studies* (Leiden:
      Brill, 1975); and Mangol Philipp, "Mirza Aga Khan
      Kirmani: A Nineteenth Century Persian Nationalist,"
      Middle Eastern Studies 10 (1974):36-59.
        Cf. Kazemzadeh, 251; Cottam, 506.
        Reviews: *BSOAS* 38 (1975):167, R. Michael Burrell;
      MEJ 27 (1973):505-6, James A. Bill.

499. Algar, Hamid. *Religion and State in Iran, 1785-1906:
      The Role of the Ulama in the Qajar Period.* Berkeley:
      University of California Press, 1969. xviii +
      286 pp.

      Delves into the intricacies of the political, social
      and intellectual relationship between "church" and
      state in Iran during the 19th century and what conse-
      quences this had for religion and political order.
      Examines the theological niceties of Shi'a thought in-

fluential in the 19th century and the tension between religious authorities and government officials who sparred with one another for the leadership of the nation. The religious leaders, traditionally the guardians of the people against government injustice, became the chief opposition to the government during the 19th century and afterwards, especially as the government proved itself incapable of providing orderly government or of protecting the nation from external--i.e., European--interference. An essential work.

On the *ulama* in other societies, see Nikki Keddie, editor, *Scholars, Saints and Sufis*, item 443; and Asghar Fathi, "Role of the Traditional Leader in [the] Modernization of Iran," *International Journal of Middle East Studies* 11 (1980):87-98.

Cf. Keddie, 512; Browne, 505.

Reviews: *AAPSS-A* 390 (1970):160-1, Edwin M. Wright; *AHR* 76 (1971):176-7, T. Cuyler Young; *BSOAS* 34 (1971): 610-11, A.K.S. Lambton; *MEJ* 25 (1971):413-5, Hafez F. Farmayan.

500. Amirsadeghi, Hossein, editor, with Ronald Ferrier.
    Twentieth Century Iran. Introduction by Denis Wright.
    London: Heinemann, 1977. xv + 299 pp.

A collection of eight essays covering aspects of contemporary Iranian history from 1900 to 1976. Of particular note are the chapters by Malcolm Yapp, "1900-1921: The Last Years of the Qajar Dynasty," 1-22; Wilfred Knopp, "1921-1941: The Period of Reza Shah," 23-52; and Ronald Ferrier, "The Development of the Iranian Oil Industry," 93-128.

Cf. Lenczowski, 322; Greaves, 248; Keddie, 511; Avery, 501.

Reviews: *AHR* 83 (1978):1309-10, Thomas Ricks; *GJ* 144 (1978):488; *MEJ* 33 (1979):64-5, Hafez F. Farmayan.

501. Avery, Peter W. *Modern Iran.* London: Ernest Benn, 1965. xvi + 527 pp.

A general history from the 1840's to the 1960's that is rather garbled and difficult to use. For a complementary study, see Joseph Upton, *The History of Modern Iran: An Interpretation* (Cambridge: Harvard University Press, 1960). For a brief overview of Anglo-Persian encounters in the 19th and 20th centuries, see Denis Wright, *The English Amongst the Persians* (London: Heinemann, 1978). On aspects of relations in the 19th

century, see Barbara English, *John Company's Last War*
[published in the United States as *War for a Persian
Lady*] (London: Collins, 1971). See also J.F. Standish,
"British Maritime Policy in the Persian Gulf," *Middle
Eastern Studies* 3 (1967):324-54, and "The Persian War
of 1856-1857," *Middle Eastern Studies* 3 (1966):18-45.
     Reviews: *AAPSS-A* 364 (1966):198-9, Paul L. Beckett;
AHR 71 (1966):1395, F. Kazemzadeh; *MEJ* 20 (1966):121-2,
Rouhollah K. Ramazani.

502. Bakhash, Shaul. *Iran: Monarchy, Bureaucracy and Reform
      under the Qajars: 1858-1896.* St. Antony's Middle East
      Monographs, no. 8. London: Ithaca Press for the
      Middle East Centre, St. Antony's College, Oxford,
      1978. ix + 444 pp.

      A detailed examination of reform efforts in Persia in
      response to the West. Bakhash studies the principal
      reformers, their programs, the difficulties they en-
      countered, and the success and failure of their efforts.
      Focuses on the reign of Nasir ad-Din Shah and the at-
      tempts to introduce Cabinet-style government and stream-
      line the bureaucracy. One of the few studies of Persian
      governmental attempts to cope with modernization. A
      summary of many of the elements in this monograph is
      contained in Bakhash's "The Evolution of Qajar Bureau-
      cracy, 1779-1877," *Middle Eastern Studies* 7 (1971):
      139-68.
          In addition, see the collection of articles in *Iranian
      Studies* 4 (1971): Collin Meredith, "Early Qajar Admini-
      stration: An Analysis of Its Development and Function,"
      59-84; John Lorentz, "Iran's Great Reformer of the Nine-
      teenth Century: An Analysis of Amir Kabir's Reforms,"
      85-103; A. Reza Sheikholeslami, "The Sale of Offices in
      Qajar Iran, 1858-1896," 104-19, and "The Patrimonial
      Structure of Iranian Bureaucracy in the Late Nineteenth
      Century," *Iranian Studies* 11 (1978):199-258; and Ann
      K.S. Lambton, "Quis Custodiet Custodes: Some Reflections
      on the Persian Theory of Government," *Studia Islamica*
      5 (1956):125-48, concluded in 6 (1956):125-46.
          Cf. Algar, 499; Avery, 501; McDaniel, 517.

503. Bill, James A. *The Politics of Iran: Groups, Classes
      and Modernization.* Columbus, Ohio: Charles Merrill,
      1972. ix + 174 pp.

      Although Bill examines the main features of political
      environment of the post-war Muhammad Riza Shah era, it

is useful in understanding one view of the intricacies of Persian politics.

Cf. Cottam, 506; Keddie, 514; Bakhash, 502.

Reviews: *APSR* 68 (1974):1793-4, Sepehr Zabih; *JP* 35 (1973):768-71, Nikki R. Keddie; *MEJ* 27 (1973):504-5, William Miller.

504. Browne, Edward Granville. *A Literary History of Persia, 1500-1924*. Volume 4. Cambridge: Cambridge University Press, 1930. xvi + 530 pp.

A comprehensive survey of Persian literature, its forms, major trends and literary figures. Volume 4 covers the impact of nationalism on Persia's belles lettres, how Persians responded to their condition, and the role of literature in the Persian Revolution.

505. Browne, Edward Granville. *The Persian Revolution of 1905-1909*. 1910. Reprint. London: Frank Cass, 1966. xxvi + 470 pp.

The standard work on the Persian revolution by one of Britain's chief experts on Iran in the late 19th and early 20th centuries. Browne was sympathetic to Iranian nationalism and, like Wilfred Scawen Blunt, he criticized the exercise of British policy in the Middle East. A modern, comprehensive study of the Persian revolution remains to be done.

Cf. Keddie, 512-3; Lambton, 514; Abrahamian, 497; Algar, 499; Bakhash, 502; Cottam, 506.

506. Cottam, Richard. *Nationalism in Iran*. Pittsburgh: University of Pittsburgh Press, 1964. ix + 332 pp.

Surveys Iranian nationalism from its origins in the middle of the 19th century to the 1960's. Topically arranged, it details the various elements composing Iranian society—ethnic, social and political—and how they combine to shape nationalism. One of the few general works on Iranian nationalism and, although Cottam tends to over-generalize, still essential. See the other works on Iran in this section. Also see Homayoun Katouzian, "Nationalist Trends in Iran, 1921-1926," *International Journal of Middle East Studies* 10 (1979): 533-51.

Cf. Kazemzadeh, 251; Ramazani, 425.

Reviews: *AAPSS-A* 357 (1965):193-4, Edwin M. Wright; *AHR* 71 (1965):266-7, Peter Avery; *APSR* 59 (1965):702-3, Frederick W. Debate; *JP* 28 (1966):223-5, Manfred Halpern; *MEJ* 19 (1965):232-4, Rouhollah Ramazani.

507.   Farmayan, Hafez F.   "The Forces of Modernization in
        Nineteenth Century Iran: A Historical Survey." *Be-
        ginnings of Modernization in the Middle East*, item
        453, 119-51.

        A basic and essential survey of the forces behind mo-
        dernization in Iran. Shows that many of these changes
        stemmed from an awareness among Iranians of the dis-
        parity in material and institutional power between Iran
        and Europe and the determination to rectify that dis-
        parity by adopting European models to strengthen local
        patterns. Studies the main personalities involved,
        what they attempted, and how much they accomplished.
        Along with the other contributions to the Polk and
        Chambers volume, it makes an excellent historical in-
        troduction to the problems of modernization. A more
        detailed study of Persian reform efforts is Shaul
        Bakhash, item 502.

508.   Fatemi, Nasrollah Saifpour. *Diplomatic History of
        Persia, 1917-23: Anglo-Russian Power Politics in Iran.*
        New York: R.F. Moore, 1952. xiii + 331 pp.

        Examines the role of a small power caught between the
        interests of Great Powers. A somewhat partisan account,
        but a useful survey, that suffers from limited source
        material, particularly the newly-available documentary
        materials. One interesting note--Fatemi includes a
        lengthy quote from James Balfour's *Recent Happenings in
        Persia* (London: Blackwood, 1922). Balfour was part of
        a financial mission to Iran in 1919 and, in the para-
        graph quoted, he accused the Persian Prime Minister of
        taking a bribe to conclude the Anglo-Persian Agreement
        of 1919. No such paragraph will be found in Balfour's
        book, because the Persian Prime Minister took Balfour
        to court in Britain, won his case, and the work was re-
        called and the offending remarks were expunged. Fatemi's
        book contains no index, no bibliography and poor foot-
        notes. It is still useful if used judiciously.
            Cf. Avery, 501; Kazemzadeh, 251; Ramazani, 425; Olson,
        424; Hurewitz, 048.
            Reviews: *MEJ* 7 (1953):249-50, Cornelius Engert.

509.   Gilbar, Gad. "The Big Merchants (*tujjar*) and the Per-
        sian Constitutional Revolution of 1906." *Asian and
        African Studies* 2 (1976):275-304.

        The large merchants, frustrated by irrational govern-
        ment practices, helped organize and finance opposition

and joined with other groups to effect a change. The merchants were also reacting to the government's inability to halt the encroachment of foreign capital and enterprise on traditional areas of income, and to the increase in arbitrary exactions from merchants by government officials. The introduction of Western concepts of political organization suggested alternatives, and the merchants, together with clerics and a small elite of Westernizers, were willing to explore the advantages of constitutionalism.
Cf. Browne, 505; Abrahamian, 497.

510. Hairi, Abdul-Hadi. "European and Asian Influences on the Persian Revolution of 1906." *Asian Affairs* 6 (1975):155-64.

Endeavors to show that the Persian Revolution was an extension of constitutional movements throughout Asia that were influenced by European political concepts. This is doubtless true.
Cf. Browne, 505; Keddie, 512.

* Kazemzadeh, Firuz. *Russia and Britain in Persia, 1864-1914.* Cited as item 251.

511. Keddie, Nikki. "British Policy and the Iranian Opposition: 1901-1907." *Journal of Modern History* 39 (1967): 266-82.

Long a supporter of liberal elements in Persia, Britain was reluctant to support the constitutionally-minded Iranian opposition because it did not want to jeopardize chances of a settlement with Russia. Contrast with Klein, item 419, and Kazemzadeh, item 251.
Cf. McDaniels, 517; McLean, 421-2.

512. Keddie, Nikki. "Iranian Politics, 1900-1905: Background to Revolution." *Middle Eastern Studies* 5 (1969):3-31, 153-67, 234-50.

A comprehensive study of the origins of the Persian Revolution of 1906. Examines the impact of foreign loans that increased foreign meddling in Iran's internal affairs while simultaneously antagonizing internal elements opposed to foreign involvement and upset over government weakness. These internal elements--religious leaders, Westernized intellectuals, and businessmen--were united only in their opposition to the government and a loose commitment to constitutionalism.

This opposition worked through secret societies and was abetted by government mismanagement that eventually generated the political crisis that produced the revolution. The best single overview of the revolution's background.

For more background information on growing nationalist sentiment in Iran, see Keddie's *Religion and Rebellion in Iran: The Iranian Tobacco Protest of 1891-1892* (London: Frank Cass, 1966); and A.K.S. Lambton, "The Tobacco Regie: Prelude to Revolution," *Studia Islamica* 22 (1965):119-57, and 23 (1966):71-96; and Keddie's "The Origins of the Religious-Radical Alliance in Iran," *Past and Present* 34 (1966):70-80; all of which look at the misalliance of convenience of Iran's Western-directed reformers and the religious leaders. The various works by Lambton, Keddie and Algar give the best introduction to Persian political movements.

Cf. Cottam, 506; Avery; 501; Browne, 505; Bakhash, 502.

513.   Keddie, Nikki. "The Iranian Power Structure and Social Change, 1800-1969: An Overview." *International Journal of Middle East Studies* 2 (1971):3-20.

Traces change, as opposed to continuity, in the nature and structure of power in Iran. Keddie examines the traditional aspects of power, the role of the monarchy, the bureaucracy, and the religious classes or *ulama*, and then follows the various changes in their position and relationship to one another. Contrast with James Bill, "The Plasticity of Informal Politics: The Case of Iran," *Middle East Journal* 27 (1973):131-51, who argues a case for continuity.

Cf. Bill, 503; Bakhash, 499.

514.   Lambton, A.K.S. "Persian Political Societies, 1906-1911." *Middle Eastern Affairs*, no. 3, St. Antony's Papers, no. 16. Edited by Albert Hourani. London: Oxford University Press, 1963, pp. 41-89.

The secret societies that prepared the intellectual ground for constitutionalism in Persia emerged into the open with the revolution in 1906 and became semi-official bodies—not quite political parties, but more than mere lobbying groups and factions. They disseminated knowledge about constitutional government, advised the government on policies, and served as rallying points for patriotism and the defence of the revolution.

They also became obstructionists by constantly interfering with government business; and many individuals
used the societies to enhance their own personal power
rather than strengthen the spirit of constitutionalism.

515. Lambton, A.K.S. "Secret Societies and the Persian Re-
   volution of 1905-6." *Middle Eastern Affairs*, no. 1,
   St. Antony's Papers, no. 4. Edited by Albert Hourani.
   London: Oxford University Press, 1958, pp. 43-60.

   One of the major studies on the origins of the Iranian revolution, exploring the role of underground study
   and discussion groups that met to discuss Western theories of government and to voice discontent with government policies. These discussion groups evolved slowly
   into action groups and formed the nucleus for the spread
   of the ideas of constitutionalism and revolution.

516. Lorraine, Michael B. "A Memoir on the Life and Poetical
   Works of Maliku 'al-Shu'ara Bahar." *International
   Journal of Middle East Studies* 3 (1972):140-68.

   Bahar was an influential Iranian poet and editor who
   became active in Iran's constitutional movement in the
   early 1900's. Lorraine traces his career, examines his
   literary output for the evolution of his political
   ideas, and assesses his influence. Useful as a study
   in the intellectual development of Iranian nationalism.
   Also see Lorraine's "Bahar in the Context of [the] Persian Constitutional Revolution," *International Journal
   of Middle East Studies* 5 (1972):79-87.
      Cf. Browne, 504.

517. McDaniel, Robert A. *The Shuster Mission and the Persian Constitutional Revolution*. Studies in Middle
   Eastern History, no. 1. Minneapolis, Minn.: Biblio-
   teca Islamica, 1974. ix + 259 pp.

   Morgan Shuster, an American, went to Iran in 1910 at
   the invitation of the new constitutional government to
   reorganize the financial administration and help the
   Persians operate their government on a more rational
   basis and restore a measure of financial solvency.
   Shuster began his work but refused to give proper heed
   to Russian sensibilities or interests. The Russians,
   happy with their predominant influence in Iran, were
   loath to see a non-Russian exercise the type of far-
   reaching authority enjoyed by Shuster; and they were
   not keen on seeing him succeed, lest reforming Persian

finances strengthen the nation's ability to resist the
steady encroachment of Russian interests. Eventually
the Russians invaded Iran to force Shuster's dismissal.
McDaniel examines Shuster's personality, his activities
in Iran, the Russian reaction, the British attitude to
the situation, Persian motives for hiring Shuster--they
hoped to counter-balance Anglo-Russian influences by
involving a third Power--and the dismal outcome. Mc-
Daniel's contention that the Anglo-Russian Convention
of 1907 restrained Russian activities seems strained.
This is the only in-depth study of this crucial period
since Shuster's own account, *The Strangling of Persia*
(New York: Century, 1912). Useful.

Cf. Browne, 505; Avery, 501; Cottam, 506; Greaves,
248; Issawi, 417; Keddie, 418; McLean, 421.

Palestine

518. Abu-Lughod, Ibrahim, editor. *The Transformation of
Palestine: Essays on the Origin and Development of
the Arab-Israeli Conflict*. Evanston, Illinois: North-
western University Press, 1971. xv + 522 pp.

Sixteen essays outlining the Arab case for Palestine
vis-a-vis Israeli claims. Of particular interest are
the articles by Alan Taylor, "Vision and Intent in
Zionist Thought," 9-26, which examines the intellectual
and cultural origins of Zionism; David Waines, "The
Failure of the National Resistance," 207-35, which examines the failure of the Arab anti-Zionist movement
down to 1948; and Richard Verdery, "Arab 'Disturbances'
and the Commissions of Inquiry," 275-303, which looks
at the outbreaks of violence and the official response
to them. All of the essays are general and share a
pro-Palestinian bias, not as a simple polemic but as
reflecting an awareness that the Arabs have a case. Of
all the areas in the Middle East, Palestine has received the most thorough treatment from recent scholarship. See the section on Arab nationalism.

Cf. Kedourie, 346; Stein, 531; Lesch, 524; Porath,
530; Klieman, 298; Friedman, 521.

Reviews: *APSR* 66 (1972):1370; *MEJ* 26 (1972):218-9,
Emile A. Nakhleh.

519. Caplan, Neil. "Arab-Jewish Contacts in Palestine After the First World War." *Journal of Contemporary History* 12 (1977):635–668.

Examines the attempts by some Zionists to establish links with the Arab community. There was considerable distance between the two and official Zionist policy favored avoiding relations with the Arab community and concentrating on winning ground with the major Powers. However, there were individual and grassroots efforts at contact, although these never overcame the suspicion and hostility, and in some cases, contempt between the two communities.

Cf. Mandel, 526; Mossek, 529; Ma'oz, 527; Haddad, 472; Sykes, 532.

520. Caplan, Neil. *Palestine Jewry and the Arab Question, 1917-1925.* London: Frank Cass, 1978. xiv + 268 pp.

Studies the Palestine Jewish–Zionist community's view of the Arabs and shows that from an early period the Zionist community was aware of the basic differences between the Arab and Zionist positions. There were two major views among Zionists for coping with these differences. The minority sought a rapprochement with the Arab community, while the majority believed rapprochement was impossible and concentrated on relations with the British and on building up the Zionist organization in Palestine for achieving an independent Jewish state. A valuable study and—in conjunction with the recent works by Lesch, item 524; Porath, item 530; Tibawi, item 533 —casts new light on the nature of Zionist-Arab relations. The book deals well with primary material in Israel and Britain and has a useful biographical section on the major individuals involved. Also see Yaacov Ro'i, "The Zionist Attitude to the Arabs, 1908–1914," *Middle Eastern Studies* 4 (1968):198–242.

Cf. Mossek, 529; Mandel, 526; Antonius, 430; Wasserstein, 535.

Reviews: *AHR* 84 (1979):1440-1, Bernard Wasserstein; *MEJ* 33 (1979):382-3, Scott Johnston.

521. Friedman, Isaiah. *The Question of Palestine, 1914-1918: British-Jewish-Arab Relations.* New York: Schocken, 1973. xiii + 433 pp.

Examines the evolution of the Arab–Jewish-British triangle in Palestine during World War I. Recent schol-

arship has shown that there was a developing Palestinian
nationalism or self-awareness before World War I, and
much attention has been devoted to Palestine after the
war.   Until the war the British had had little direct
concern with either Zionism or Arab nationalism, but
the war forced them to consider these as a means of
winning support for the war effort.   The result was conflicting promises and post-war tensions resulting from
trying to reconcile them.   Friedman examines the rationale behind the Sykes-Picot Agreement, the Husayn-
McMahon correspondence and the Balfour Declaration,
studying the impact of personalities and events.   Argues that Sykes-Picot was the result of inter-Allied
efforts to involve the Arabs in the war and not designed as an instrument to divide the spoils; that British policy was anti-annexationist at least before 1917;
and that the Balfour Declaration was made to preclude a
similar Turko-German move, but that the British knew
what they meant by "national home" over such possible
alternatives as "refuge" or "asylum."   While a useful
study, well-documented and providing a guide to primary
and secondary materials, the work tends to see a
straightforwardness in policy formation that did not
exist.   There is also a pro-Zionist undercurrent; and
despite the fact that the war influenced decisions,
Friedman does not take this into full account.   On the
randomness of British policy, see Kedourie, item 346.
Also see Rothwell, item 306; Busch, item 352; and Guinn,
item 291.   For a documentary record that supplements
this study, see Ingrams, item 049.
    Cf. Mossek, 529; Wasserstein, 535; Klieman, 298;
Stein, 531; Porath, 530; Tibawi, 533.
    Reviews: *AHR* 79 (1974):1226-7, William Polk; *APSR* 70
(1976):676-7, Aaron S. Klieman.

522. Halpern, Ben.   *The Idea of the Jewish State.*   Cambridge:
      Harvard University Press, 1961.   xvii + 492 pp.

      A somewhat partisan account of the origins of polit-
      ical Zionism and the movement to establish a state in
      Palestine.   Traces the European background to Zionism;
      the activities of Herzl, Jabotinsky, Weizmann, and
      others; the growth of Jewish settlements; and Zionist
      relations with Britain and the Arabs from World War I
      to 1947.
          Cf. Sykes, 532; Marlowe, 528; Hurewitz, 523; Laquer,
      554.
          Reviews: *MEJ* 16 (1962):253-4, Harry N. Howard.

523. Hurewitz, Jacob Coleman. *The Struggle for Palestine*. New York: Norton, 1950. 404 pp.

Although it deals basically with the period from the 1930's to the founding of Israel, the first section contains useful background material on the mandate, on demographic features, and on political activities of the Zionists, the British and the Arabs.
Cf. Klieman, 298; Kedourie, 346; Sykes, 532.

524. Lesch, Ann Mosely. "The Palestine Arab Nationalist Movement Under the Mandate." *The Politics of Palestinian Nationalism*. Edited by William Quandt, et al. Berkeley: University of California Press, 1973, pp. 5-42.

Examines the growth of Arab opposition to British rule and to the influx of Jews into Palestine before World War II. Concentrates on inter-group relations within the Arab nationalist movement, analyzes the ideology of opposition, the organization of resistance, and the failure of the Arabs to achieve their aims. One of the principal problems the Arabs had was their inability to resolve factional differences or to establish institutions recognized by the British that could effectively represent the Arab case. Unable to negotiate effectively, they resorted to violence, which received attention but achieved little. Lesch also explores "The Origins of Palestinian Arab Nationalism" in William Haddad, editor, *Nationalism in a Non-National State*, item 472, 265-90; and in depth in her book, *Arab Politics in Palestine, 1917-1939: The Frustration of a Nationalist Movement* (Ithaca, N.Y.: Cornell University Press, 1979).
Cf. Porath, 530; Tibawi, 533; Abu-Lughod, 518; Klieman, 298.

525. Mandel, Neville. *The Arabs and Zionism Before World War I*. Berkeley: University of California Press, 1976. xxiv + 258 pp.

Explores the origins of Arab-Israeli antagonism. A number of recent studies have revised ideas about the origins, or rather the timing, of Arab nationalism and its response to Jewish immigration, Zionism and the idea of a Jewish state. Mandel examines Arab attitudes and Turkish policy towards Jewish immigration, arguing convincingly that almost from the beginning of significant Jewish immigration into Palestine in 1882, there

was a hostile response among the Arab political elite
that grew more intense and coordinated before World War
I and the Balfour Declaration. He points out that there
was, however, some spirit of compromise and accommodation, and that Palestinian nationalism grew out of the
particularism of various minorities following the collapse of the Ottoman Empire. An excellent study with
the very useful survey of relevant archival sources in
Britain, France, Germany, and Israel. Part of this
study was published in *Middle Eastern Studies* 1 (1964):
238-67, under the title "Attempts at an Arab-Zionist
Entente, 1913-1914."

Recently awareness of Palestinian nationalism has received more attention, reflected in part by the existence now of the scholarly, but politically biased,
Journal for Palestinian Studies. There have also been
a variety of new studies exploring Palestinian, as opposed to Arab, nationalism. One of these is William
Quandt, et al., *The Politics of Palestinian Nationalism*
(Los Angeles: University of California Press, 1973),
see item 524.

Cf. Haddad, 472; Ma'oz, 527.

Reviews: *AAPSS-A* 436 (1978):161-3, Julius Weinberg;
AHR 82 (1977):1031-2, Briton C. Busch; *MEJ* 33 (1979):
61, C. Ernest Dawn.

526. Mandel, Neville. "Turks, Arabs and Jewish Immigration
      into Palestine, 1882-1914." *Middle Eastern Affairs*,
      no. 4, St. Antony's Papers, no. 17. London: Oxford
      University Press, 1965, pp. 77-108.

      Studies Arab and Ottoman response to Jewish immigra-
      tion and argues that a negative response to that immi-
      gration did not develop suddenly after World War I,
      but began earlier. The period 1882-1914 is important
      as a formative period in anti-Zionism in Palestine.
      Examines the development and motives for Jewish migra-
      tion and official Ottoman responses to the influx of
      foreigners and the animosities that developed between
      Arabs and Jews as the result of contact and growing
      Arab nationalism. Mandel also deals with this topic
      and official Ottoman policy in "Ottoman Practice as
      Regards Jewish Settlement in Palestine: 1881-1908,"
      Middle Eastern Studies 11 (1975):33-46. These studies
      represent sections of his monograph *Arabs and Zionism*,
      discussed above.

      Cf. Antonius, 430; Haddad, 472; Porath, 530; Ma'oz,
      527; Wasserstein, 535.

527. Ma'oz, Moshe, editor. *Studies on Palestine During the Ottoman Period.* Jerusalem: Magnes Press, 1975. xix + 582 pp.

A collection of 40 articles largely by Israeli scholars on 19th-century Palestine. A generous attempt has
been made to make the collection more than disparate
articles cobbled together. There are six parts: (1)
geography and population, discussing urban life, settlement patterns, various minorities; (2) the Jewish communities; (3) the Central Government and political
change; (4) foreign activities; (5) the impact of the
West; and (6) archival sources. The articles are relatively short and impressionistic, providing useful
information on sources and an introduction to some of
the major issues and problems in the last years of Ottoman rule. See particularly the articles by Paul
Alsberg, "The Israel State Archives as a Source for the
History of Palestine during the Period of Ottoman Rule,"
533-44; Michael Heymann, "Material in the Central Zionist Archives Concerning the History of Palestine during
the Ottoman Period," 545-47; and Alex Carmel, "Documentary Material in Austrian and German Archives Relating
to Palestine during the Period of Ottoman Rule," 568-
77. Lacks an index or bibliography.

For an excellent study of Ottoman administration in
Syria and Palestine and its influence on local society,
see Moshe Ma'oz's earlier *Ottoman Reform in Syria and
Palestine, 1840-1861: The Impact of the Tanzimat on
Politics and Society* (Oxford: Clarendon Press, 1968);
and Amnon Cohen's *Palestine in the Eighteenth Century:
Patterns of Government and Administration* (Jerusalem:
Magnes Press, 1973).

Cf. Haddad, 472; Polk, 453.

Reviews: *MEJ* 32 (1978):226-7, William Ochsenwald.

528. Marlowe, John. *The Seat of Pilate: An Account of the
Palestine Mandate.* London: Cresset Press, 1959. xi + 289 pp.

Examines the background to and history of the British
occupation and control of Palestine from the Balfour
Declaration to the creation of Israel. A balanced and
useful general study of Anglo-Arab-Zionist relations,
motives and activities.

Cf. Stein, 531; Klieman, 298; Antonius, 430; Porath,
530; Sykes, 532; Hurewitz, 523.

Reviews: *MEJ* 15 (1961):101-2, Fred J. Khouri.

529.   Mossek, M. *Palestine Immigration Policy under Sir*
       Herbert Samuel: British, Zionist and Arab Attitudes.
       London: Frank Cass, 1978. xiii + 179 pp.

       Examines the relationship between the British and the
       Zionists over the question of immigration into Pales-
       tine. Sir Herbert Samuel (first British High Commis-
       sioner to Palestine, and a Jew) was sympathetic to the
       Zionist cause and in his five years in Palestine, from
       1920-1925, promoted Jewish immigration; but his even-
       handedness and concern for measured immigration pro-
       duced a clash with the Zionist Organization. Samuel
       was a gradualist who favored immigration that could be
       absorbed economically by the Jewish community in Pales-
       tine. When it became clear that the influx of Jews ex-
       ceeded Palestine's absorptive capacity, he moved to
       slow the pace and as a result came into conflict with
       the Zionists. A solid, well-researched piece, if pon-
       derous. For a shorter account of Samuel's policy, see
       Elie Kedourie, "Sir Herbert Samuel and the Government
       of Palestine," *Middle Eastern Studies* 5 (1969):44-68,
       which is also contained in item 363.
          Cf. Caplan, 520; Wasserstein, 535; Lesch, 534; Mar-
       lowe, 528; Porath, 530; Mandel, 525.
          Reviews: *AHR* 84 (1979):1440-1, Bernard Wasserstein;
       MEJ 33 (1979):382-3, Scott Johnston.

530.   Porath, Yehoshua. *The Emergence of the Palestinian-*
       Arab National Movement, 1918-1929. London: Frank
       Cass, 1974. ix + 406 pp.

       Traces the origins of Palestinian nationalism and
       anti-Zionist sentiments, showing that opposition de-
       veloped very early, though it was not always well-
       organized or articulated; and that inter-family rivalry
       and struggle for influence were important elements in
       the development of the Palestinian movement. A tho-
       rough study of the ideological, political and social
       background of the movement and its leadership, most
       particularly of al-Hajj Amin al-Husayni, the Grand
       Mufti. One of the first and the best of the major stu-
       dies on Palestinian nationalism. A follow-up work,
       The Palestinian Arab National Movement: From Politics
       to Rebellion, 1929-1939 (London: Frank Cass, 1977),
       completes this well-documented, well-written study.
       Compare with Ann Lesch, *Arab Politics in Palestine,*
       1917-1939: The Frustration of a National Movement
       (Ithaca, N.Y.: Cornell University Press, 1979); and

A.L. Tibawi, item 533. Also see Neville Mandel, *Arabs and Zionism*, item 525.

Cf. Caplan, 520; Haddad, 472; Ma'oz, 527; Stein, 531; Klieman, 298; Dawn, 433; Antonius, 430.

Review: *MES* 13 (1977):156-9, Bernard Wasserstein.

531. Stein, Leonard. *The Balfour Declaration*. New York: Simon & Schuster, 1961. xiv + 681 pp.

The major study of the political background to the declaration given by British Foreign Secretary A.J. Balfour to Baron Rothschild recognizing the right of the Jews to a national home in Palestine. Stein examines the rise of Zionism in the anti-semitic climate of 19th-century Europe and Theodor Herzl's moves to create the Zionist organization. He then concentrates on Zionist activities, led by Chaim Weizmann, during World War I in Britain and America to secure Allied recognition of and support for a home for the Jews in Palestine. Stein looks at the personalities of the major figures (Balfour, Herbert Samuel, Mark Sykes, Chaim Weizmann, Jan Smuts, etc.) and the political atmosphere (i.e., Anglo-French rivalry for control of post-war Palestine) that surrounded Zionist lobbying for Allied support. An excellent study. Also see D.Z. Gillon, "The Antecedents of the Balfour Declaration," *Middle Eastern Studies* 5 (1969):131-50; Carrol Quigley, "Documents: Lord Balfour's Personal Position on the Balfour Declaration," *Middle Eastern Studies* 22 (1968): 340-5; and Christopher Sykes, "The Prosperity of His Servant: A Study of the Origins of the Balfour Declaration of 1917," *Two Studies in Virtue* (New York: Knopf, 1953), 107-235.

The Balfour Declaration and the subsequent history of Palestine down to the formation of the state of Israel are, of course, a fertile field of controversy and recrimination. Literature praising or excoriating the decisions and intentions of the British, the Jews, the Arabs, or anyone else foolish enough to get involved is legion. For a general history of Zionism and of Israel, see Howard Sachar, *A History of Israel: From the Rise of Zionism to Our Time* (New York: Knopf, 1976), which is one of the few overall studies and useful despite its biases and minor errors. For a pro-Arab general history of Palestine, Zionism and Western imperialism, see Robert John and Sami Hadawi, *The Palestine Diary*, 3 vols. (New York: New World Press, 1970), especially volume 1, which covers the period 1914-1945.

For a pro-Jewish account of Zionism, the Balfour Declaration, Arab nationalism, and the Mandate, see *Palestine: A Study of Jewish, Arab and British Policies*, 2 vols., (1947; reprint. New York: Kraus, 1970), a collection of commissioned essays published by the Esco Foundation for Palestine. For a collection of assorted documents, essays and pamphlets in French, English and German on the background to the question of Palestine, concentrating on Zionist and Jewish activities or attitudes to such activities, see *Seeds of Conflict*, Series 2, *Palestine, Zionism and the Levant, 1912-1946*, 6 parts in 9 volumes (Nendeln, Liechtenstein: Kraus Reprint, 1974). For a brief collection of documents on the origins of the Palestine problem, see Doreen Ingrams, compiler, *Palestine Papers, 1917-1922: Seeds of Conflict*, item 049.

Also see Chaim Weizmann's autobiography, *Trial and Error* (London: Hamish Hamilton, 1949); and Series A, volume 7 of *The Letters and Papers of Chaim Weizmann*, edited by Leonard Stein (London: Oxford University Press, 1975).

Cf. Kedourie, 333; Klieman, 298; Hancock, 161; Judd, 167; Adelson, 143; Vereté, 534; Sykes, 532.

Reviews: *AHR* 67 (1962):396-8, Hans Kohn; *MEJ* 17 (1963):176-7, Fred Khouri.

532.   Sykes, Christopher H. *Cross Roads to Israel*. London: Collins, 1965. xii + 404 pp.

Studies political Zionism and the effort to create a Jewish state in Palestine after World War I. One of the most balanced studies of the conflicting Arab-Jewish-British efforts to get their way in Palestine. Excellent. For a more general introduction, also see William Polk, et al., *Backdrop to Tragedy: The Struggle for Palestine* (Boston: Beacon Hill Press, 1957).

Cf. Hurewitz, 523; Marlowe, 528; Klieman, 298; Porath, 530; Tibawi, 533; Lesch, 524; Mossek, 529; Wasserstein, 535; Friedman, 521; Mandel, 525; Stein, 531; Antonius, 430.

533.   Tibawi, Abdul Latif. *Anglo-Arab Relations and the Question of Palestine, 1914-1921*. London: Luzac, 1977. xxvii + 523 pp.

Examines the intricacies of Anglo-Arab relations focusing on the frustration of Arab nationalism by British policies in Palestine during and after World War I.

Recent scholarship argues that Palestinian nationalism was not a late development derivative of the Zionist-Arab tensions of the inter-war years, but began developing earlier and was ignored or suppressed by the British in pursuit of imperial policy. Tied up in this is the question of whether or not the British promised the Arabs of the Middle East, including Palestine, full independence for help in fighting the Turks during World War I. Tibawi is in the "perfidious Albion" ranks and documents a history of broken promises, misrepresentations and obfuscations. Similar themes may be found in articles by Tibawi in a volume of his collected essays entitled *Arabic and Islamic Themes: Historical, Educational and Literary Studies* (London: Luzacs, 1974). Also see his *Arab Education in Mandatory Palestine: A Study of Three Decades of British Administration* (London: Luzacs, 1956).

Contrast with Kedourie, item 346, who argues a different line, showing that confusion, disingenuousness and mistakes by both the British and the Arabs were more influential in shaping events than perfidious intent; and with Porath, item 530. In addition, see Tibawi's "T.E. Lawrence, Faisal and Weizmann: The 1919 Attempt to Secure an Arab Balfour Declaration," *Journal of the Royal Central Asian Society* 56 (1969):156-63, which studies the meetings between Weizmann and Faysal to effect some mutually acceptable compromise on Arab-Jewish relations in Palestine.

Cf. Klieman, 298.

Reviews: *MEJ* 32 (1978):87.

534. Vereté, Mayir. "The Balfour Declaration and Its Makers." *Middle Eastern Studies* 6 (1970):48-76.

Studies the evolution in British thought of the idea of a Jewish homeland in Palestine. There had been earlier support for such a home in Africa, but the war and the prospect of Ottoman defeat offered an opportunity to realize a Zionist goal of returning to Palestine. Vereté examines the roles of various individuals involved in shaping British policy in the Middle East (Kitchener, Grey, Weizmann, Mark Sykes, and of course, Balfour) tracing the development of the particular form the Declaration took--a vague statement that kept actual control in British hands. Also see Vereté's "Kitchener, Grey and the Question of Palestine in 1915-1916: A Note," *Middle Eastern Studies* 9 (1973):223-7, in which he responds to a criticism by Keith Robbins,

item 184, that Vereté, in his article on the Balfour
Declaration, misconstrued Kitchener's position on Britain's securing Palestine in 1916. Robbins adduces a
remark that shows Kitchener was against it. Vereté
shows the remark was made in a particular context and
that Kitchener was posturing for personal reasons and
was not opposed to securing Palestine. Shows the type
of considerations one must keep in mind when evaluating
expressed opinions, and the influence of personalities
on the formation of policy. See Joll, "Unspoken Assumptions," item 297.
 Cf. Busch, 352; Klieman, 298; Kedourie, 346.

535. Wasserstein, Bernard. *The British in Palestine: The
     Mandatory Government and the Arab-Jewish Conflict,
     1917-1929.* London: Royal Historical Society, 1978.
     xii + 278 pp.

Delineates the crucial decisions of the years between
1917, when the British occupied Palestine, and 1929,
when bloody riots broke out, that determined the institutional and psychological habits that became charac-
teristic of the Arab-Jewish-British impasse. Concentrates on the conflict of opinion between British officials in Palestine and those in London that created
tension in policy-making which in turn exacerbated
Arab-Jewish relations. A thoughtful study that demonstrates the importance of personalities and intragroup
conflicts in the formation of policy. Part of this
study, "Herbert Samuel and the Palestine Problem," appeared in the *English Historical Review* 91 (1976):753-
75.
 Cf. Klieman, 298; Porath, 530; Tibawi, 533; Sykes,
532; Stein, 531; Hurewitz, 523.
 Reviews: *AHR* 84 (1979):1439-40, Briton Busch.

Syria, Mesopotamia and the Arabian Peninsula

536. Dickson, Harold R.P. *Kuwait and Her Neighbors.* 1956.
     Reprint. London: Allen & Unwin, 1968. 627 pp.

Harold Dickson served in the Middle East during World
War I, working in the Political Department under Sir
Percy Cox. In the interwar years he served in the Civil
Administration in Iraq and as Britain's Political Agent

to Kuwait; later he remained in Kuwait as the chief local representative of the Kuwait Oil Company. In this
work he gives a general history of Kuwait, its rulers,
its origins and its relations with Britain and its Arab
neighbors. Provides information on local customs, the
main personages and the nature of local and international rivalries that attracted British solicitude for the
fate and condition of Kuwait.

Cf. Kelly, 407; Busch, 404; Kumar, 409; Hopwood, 406;
Monroe, 304.

537.   Edens, David. "The Anatomy of the Saudi Revolution."
       International Journal of Middle East Studies 5
       (1974):50-64.

Examines the rise of Wahhabism in Arabia and the
emergence of Abd al-Aziz ibn Saud, comparing the Saudi
Revolution with Western revolutions (in America, France,
Britain and Russia as studied by Crane Briton) and
finds a surprising degree of similarity. The similari-
ties, however, seem strained and a case could be made
for the dissimilarities; for example, the fact that in
the Western cases it was established, articulated governments being toppled and not one tribal hierarchy replacing another (though this says nothing about the
"fever of revolution"). For more detailed information
on the background of Wahhabism, see R.B. Winder, *Saudi
Arabia in the Nineteenth Century* (New York: St. Martin's
Press, 1965); and the somewhat evasive H.St. J.B.
Philby, *Sa'udi Arabia* (London: Benn, 1955).

Cf. Troeller, 411; Kelly, 408.

538.   Howard, Harry N. *The King-Crane Commission*. Beirut:
       Khayats 1963. xiv + 369 pp.

Studies the King-Crane fact-finding mission to the
Arab Middle East after World War I. Originally designed as a commission representing the four major powers at the Peace Conference to institute a local en-
quiry concerning sentiments for self-determination in
the Arab Middle East, only the American delegates went,
interviewing Arabs in Syria and Palestine, getting
their views on Zionism and self-government. Howard
examines the Paris background to the origins of the
commission, which was envisioned as a means of reconciling the secret treaties and conflicting promises.
Britain and France backed out of the commission, fear-
ing its findings would go against them, and the French

repudiated its findings when the commission found little sympathy for the French mandate. The majority of this study concentrates on the commission's work in Syria, though attention is also given to the development of American policy in the Middle East and to the Treaty of Lausanne. An excellent, essential study. Also see Howard's earlier, "An American Experiment in Peacemaking: The King-Crane Commission," *The Moslem World* 32 (1942):122-8.

    Cf. Sachar, 480; Nevakivi, 324; Porath, 530.
    Reviews: *JMH* 37 (1965):114, Roderic H. Davison.

539.   Landen, Robert Geran. *Oman Since 1856: Disruptive Modernization in a Traditional Arab Society*. Princeton, N.J.: Princeton University Press, 1967. xv + 488 pp.

Studies the impact of the West on a traditional society, but also looks at Anglo-French rivalry in the area, the nature of British indirect rule, and the Omani response. Oman remains one of the step-children in historical studies. For a general history, see Wendell Phillips, *Oman: A History* (London: Longmans, 1967). For a detailed, but dated, study of the area, see S.B. Miles, *The Countries and Tribes of the Persian Gulf* (1919; reprint. London: Frank Cass, 1966).
    Cf. Kelly, 407; Hopwood, 406; Lorimer, 410; Busch, 404.
    Reviews: *AAPSS-A* 377 (1968):188-9, Majid Khadduri; *AHR* 73 (1968):1588, Sydney N. Fisher; *JEH* 29 (1969): 368-9, Nikki R. Keddie.

540.   Longrigg, Stephen Hemsley. *Iraq, 1900-1950: A Political, Social and Economic History*. Royal Institute for International Affairs. London: Oxford University Press, 1953. x + 436 pp.

A detailed survey of the rise of modern Iraq from a Turkish province to a British mandate to independence and the post-World War II period. Discusses aspects of local life, religious and tribal groups, the development of nationalism, aspects of World War I and Turkish and British administration, as well as weaving together a picture of social and economic life in a fluid narrative. More recent scholarship capitalizes on newly-available documents, and since Longrigg served in the British administration in Iraq his book has hints of his personal reactions, but his handling of the complexities of local history remains useful. Longrigg's earlier *Four Centuries of Modern Iraq* (1925; reprint. Beirut: Librairie du Liban, 1968), gives a background history of Mesopotamia before 1900.

Aspects of Iraqi history, information on elections, minorities, the army and politics from 1919-1970 can be found in Abbas Kelidar, editor, *The Integration of Modern Iraq* (London: Croom Helm, 1979). Lord Birdwood, *Nuri as-Said: A Study in Arab Leadership* (London: Cassell, 1959), provides an intimate view of one of Iraq's early leaders. A dated account of British involvement in Iraq from World War I to independence in the 1930's is Philip Ireland, *Iraq: A Study in Political Development* (London: Jonathan Cape, 1939). See the section on "Britain in Mesopotamia."

Cf. Sluglett, 357; Cohen, 394; Wilson, 358; Busch, 285 and 352; Penrose, 541; Edmonds, 550.

Reviews: *JMH* 28 (1956):73, T.H. Vail Motter; *MEJ* 8 (1954):431-2, Albert Hourani.

541. Penrose, Edith, and E.F. Penrose. *Iraq: International Relations and National Development*. London: Benn, 1978. xviii + 569 pp.

Surveys the development of modern Iraq from a Turkish province in the early 1900's to independence and down to the 1970's. Chapters 1 and 2 cover the Turkish administration, local groups, the rise of nationalism, the development of British interests, the growth of the oil industry, the outcome of World War I, and the course of the Mandate down to 1932. Argues that the development of the mandate concept was a step towards decolonialization, progress away from direct annexation. Useful survey.

Cf. Cohen, 394; Sluglett, 357; Busch, 352.

Reviews: *JEL* 17 (1979):557-9, Majid Khadduri.

542. Salibi, Kamal Sulayman. *The Modern History of Lebanon*. Asia-Africa Series of Modern Histories. Edited by Bernard Lewis. London: Weidenfeld & Nicolson, 1965. xxvii + 227 pp.

A brief survey of Lebanon's history from the 18th century to the 1950's. Important background information on the minorities (Marionites, Shi'ites, Druzes, etc.), intercommunity relations, local patterns of government, Ottoman administration, the development of foreign interests (mainly French), the development of

nationalism and the experiences during World War I,
under the French Mandate and after. Useful.

For more information on the impact of the West, see
William Polk, *The Opening of South Lebanon, 1788-1840:
A Study of the Impact of the West on the Middle East*
(Cambridge: Harvard University Press, 1963); on the
French Mandate, see Stephen Longrigg, *Syria and Lebanon
under French Mandate* (London: Oxford University Press,
1958); also see Albert Hourani, *Syria and Lebanon: A
Political Essay* (London: Oxford University Press, 1946).
On aspects of Lebanese and Arab nationalism, see Pierre
Rondot, "Lebanese Institutions and Arab Nationalism,"
Journal of Contemporary History 3 (1968):37-52; and
Salibi's "The Lebanese Identity," *Journal of Contemporary History* 6 (1971):76-86.

Cf. Hitti, 396; Nevakivi, 324; Shorrock, 266; Spagnolo,
268.

Reviews: *AAPSS-A* 366 (1966):186, Don Peretz; *AHR* 72
(1966):251-2, Sydney N. Fisher; *JP* 28 (1966):697-8,
Rouhollah K. Ramazani; *MEJ* 20 (1966):237-8, Kamel S.
Abu Jaber.

*   Sluglett, Peter. *Britain in Iraq, 1914-1932.* Cited
        as item 357.

*   Troeller, Gary. *The Birth of Saudi Arabia: Britain and
        the Rise of the House of Sa'ud.* Cited as item 411.

543.   Vinogradov, Amal. "The 1920 Revolt in Iraq Reconsidered:
       The Role of Tribes in National Politics." *International Journal of Middle East Studies* 3 (1972):123-
       39.

       Maintains that the Iraqi revolt was "a 'primitive,'
       but genuine, national response to fundamental dislocations in the political and socio-economic adaptation of
       the tribally organized rural Iraqis." The dislocations
       were the result of direct and indirect Western encroachment, particularly British, which produced a reaction
       that indicated a nascent nationalism. While there is
       much point in this, it would seem that features of Ottoman rule and the dislocations of World War I were
       significant contributions to the climate of confusion
       that helped to nourish the revolt.

       Cf. Longrigg, 540; Ireland, 397; Penrose, 541; Khan,
       399; Sluglett, 357; Busch, 352; Wilson, 358.

544. Zeine, Zeine N. *The Emergence of Arab Nationalism:*
With a Background Study of Arab-Turkish Relations in
the Near East [first published in 1958 as *Arab-Turkish*
Relations and the Emergence of Arab Nationalism]. 3rd
edition. Delmar, N.Y.: Caravan Books, 1973. xiii +
297 pp.

One of the best short studies of the origins of Arab
nationalism in an Ottoman context, studying its intellectual features and political activities before, during
and immediately after World War I, stressing the central
role of Syrian and Lebanese political, intellectual and
military figures in developing Arab nationalism. Examines the interests of the Great Powers in the area and
how they supported and used Arab nationalism in World
War I and how they tried to reconcile Arab nationalism
with imperial interests in the post-war settlements.
Argues that promises to the Arabs were broken by the
British, but that this must be interpreted in the context of Anglo-French rivalry and the fact that the
French forced the British to live up to the Sykes-Picot
Agreement, an event unwelcome to the British and unan-
ticipated by the Arabs.

Cf. Antonius, 430; Dawn, 433; Kedourie, 333; Busch,
352; Klieman, 298; Nevakivi, 324.

Reviews: (1st ed.) *AHR* 66 (1961):1042-3, Stanford
Shaw; *JMH* 33 (1961):467-8, George Kirk; *MEJ* 12 (1958):
346-7, Harry N. Howard; (2nd ed.) *MEJ* 20 (1966):556,
Harry N. Howard.

545. Zeine, Zeine N. *The Struggle for Arab Independence:*
Western Diplomacy and the Rise and Fall of Faisal's
Kingdom in Syria. Beirut: Khayats, 1960. xiii +
297 pp.

Details the development of Anglo-French policies towards one another and to the Arabs during and just after World War I. Examines the Sykes-Picot Agreement,
the Husayn-McMahon correspondence, the clash of Anglo-
French interests at the conclusion of the war at the
Paris Peace Conference, Faysal's attempts to sail between those tensions and secure independence for Syria,
and the French invasion of Syria that put the question
of independence to rest. An evenhanded study that illustrates the "fog" of war--the pressures that led the
Allied Powers to make vague or conflicting promises to
each other and to the Arabs, the Arab misunderstanding

of what was promised and reaction to the post-war set-
tlements, and the struggles to end Western dominance.
Follows on from Zeine's *Emergence of Arab Nationalism*,
item 544.   Compare with Elie Kedourie, *Anglo-Arab Lab-
yrinthe*, item 346, who makes many of the same points.
Has a useful bibliography.
  Cf. Antonius, 430; Klieman, 298; Nevakivi, 324;
Busch, 352.

Minorities

546.   Arberry, A.J., editor.   *Religion in the Middle East:*
       Three Religions in Concord and Conflict.   2 volumes.
       Cambridge: Cambridge University Press, 1969.

       Volume 1, *Judaism and Christianity*, contains 13 es-
       says on Jews and Christian groups in the Middle East,
       usually by religious scholars.   Volume 2, *Islam*, has
       24 essays on aspects of Islam--schisms, sufism, and
       Islamic tenets--in the different countries of the
       Middle East.   In particular, see Richard Hill, "Islam
       in the Sudan," 187-202; Jacques Jamier, "Islam in
       Egypt," 31-47; Annemarie Schimmel, "Islam in Turkey,"
       68-95; Seyyid Hossein Nasr, "Ithna'Ashari Shi'ism and
       Iranian Islam," 96-118; and the Rev. Eric Bishop, "Is-
       lam in the Countries of the Fertile Crescent," 48-67.
         Cf. Rosenthal, 456; Sharibi, 457; Keddie, 443;
       Grabill, 282.
         Reviews: *CH* 39 (1970):569-70, Alford Carleton; *MEJ*
       24 (1970):252-3, Majid Khadduri.

547.   Atiyah, Aziz Suryal.   *A History of Eastern Christianity.*
       London: Methuen, 1968.   xiv + 486 pp.

       Surveys the Christian experience in the East, par-
       ticularly the Coptic, Nestorian, Armenian and Marionite
       churches.   Gives historical background, main features,
       experience of Islam and modern trends.   Useful as a
       brief introduction.   Also see Robert Brenton Betts,
       Christians in the Arab East: A Political Study (London:
       SPCK, 1979), which surveys the influence of Christian
       groups and their fate in recent times.
         Cf. Grabill, 282.
         Reviews: *EHR* 84 (1969):788-90, S.L. Greenslade; *H* 54
       (1969):475-6, D.M. Lang; *MEJ* 23 (1969):552-4, John
       Joseph.

548. Cohen, Hayyim J. *The Jews of the Middle East, 1860-1972.* New York: John Wiley, 1973. viii + 213 pp.

   Examines the social conditions, way of life and experiences of Oriental Jews. Begins with historical background and then looks more closely at the Jewish communities in Iran, Iraq, Turkey, Syria, the Yemen and Egypt, examining education, demographic features, political activities, social change and economic development. For other material, see the *Jewish Journal of Sociology.*
   Cf. Hourani, 551; Landau, 555; Haddad, 472; Mandel, 525.
   Reviews: *MEJ* 28 (1974):349-50, Jacob Landau.

549. Edmonds, Cecil John. "Kurdish Nationalism." *Journal of Contemporary History* 6 (1971):87-107.

   A brief account of the origins of the Kurds and the development of their national consciousness, dealing mostly with the period from 1920-1960.

550. Edmonds, Cecil John. *Kurds, Turks and Arabs: Politics, Travel and Research in Northeastern Iraq, 1919-1925.* London: Oxford University Press, 1957. xiii + 457 pp.

   Edmonds' memoirs of his experiences as a political officer in the Middle East. The bulk of the work deals with Anglo-Turkish hostilities over the disposition of Mosul, but there is much information on local affairs in Kurdistan. Edmonds worked under Sir Percy Cox (see item 159), and his account of the Persian-Mesopotamia border areas both before and after World War I is still a useful account both of British policy and the social life of the Kurds. For a short bibliographical guide on the Kurds, see Wolfgang Behn, *The Kurds of Iran: A Selected and Annotated Bibliography* (London: Mansell, 1977). For a general history of the Kurds, concentrating on the period 1900-1947, see Hassan Arfa, *The Kurds: An Historical and Political Study* (London: Oxford University Press, 1966).
   Cf. Sluglett, 357; Ireland, 397; Longrigg, 540.
   Reviews: *JMH* 30 (1958):377-8, Sydney N. Fisher; *MEJ* 12 (1958):469-70, Majid Khadduri.

551. Hourani, Albert. *Minorities in the Arab World.* London: Oxford University Press, under the auspices of the Royal Institute of International Affairs, 1947. viii + 140 pp.

Studies ethnic and religious minorities in Egypt,
Syria, Iraq, Palestine and Jordan. Describes the *millet*
system and the status of minorities under the Ottomans,
under the mandate, and under Arab national governments.
Dated, but useful; gives breakdowns of populations and
social roles of various groups, including Armenians,
Kurds, Jews, the Druze, and others. For a study of
minorities and social classes, including merchants,
military officers, the clergy, etc., see the essays in
Sydney N. Fisher, editor, *Social Forces in the Middle
East* (Ithaca, N.Y.: Cornell University Press, 1955),
which has a useful, though dated, annotated bibliography.
    Cf. Weekes, 558; Arberry, 546.

552.   Hovannisian, Richard G. *Armenia on the Road to Inde-
           pendence, 1918.* Los Angeles: University of Califor-
           nia Press, 1967. viii + 364 pp.

Examines the Armenians' attempts to establish their
independence after World War I. The Armenians had been
divided between the Ottoman and Russian empires for centuries, and with the disintegration of those two states
after World War I, they tried to create a unified, independent state from the chaos. With care and objec-
tivity, Hovannisian examines the background to Armenian
nationalism and details the efforts to erect an Armenian
Republic, one the Allies agreed to support and in a limited way tried to bring into existence. The story is
continued in *The Republic of Armenia*, item 553.
    See Hovannisian's "The Ebb and Flow of the Armenian
Minority," *Middle East Journal* 28 (1974):19-34, for a
brief account of the distribution of Armenians in the
Middle East. For a background on Armenian political
activity, see Louise Nalbandian, *The Armenian Revolutionary Movement: The Development of Armenian Political
Parties through the Nineteenth Century* (Los Angeles:
University of California Press, 1963). Hovannisian explores various aspects of Armenian nationalism and relations with the Allies in "Simon Vratzion and Armenian
Nationalism," *Middle Eastern Studies* 5 (1969):192-220;
and "The Allies and Armenia, 1915-1918," *Journal of
Contemporary History* 3 (1968):145-68. Also see Arten
Arslanian, "British Wartime Pledges, 1917-18: The Armenian Case," *Journal of Contemporary History* 13 (1978):
517-30. Relations between Armenians in the Ottoman
bureaucracy and the Armenian community in Syria are
studied in Mesrob Krikorian, *Armenians in the Service
of the Ottoman Empire, 1860-1908* (London: Routledge and

Kegan Paul, 1977); and Avedis Sanjian, *The Armenian Community in Syria under Ottoman Domination*, Harvard Middle Eastern Studies, no. 10 (Cambridge, Mass.: Harvard University Press, 1965). Also see "The Armenian Question-- A Forum" in *International Journal of Middle East Studies* 9 (1978), for a debate on the fate of Armenians in the Ottoman Empire by Stanford Shaw and Hovannisian. For an older, more general study, see Sarkis Atamian, *The Armenian Community: The Historical Development of a Social and Ideological Conflict* (New York: Philosophical Library, 1955).

Cf. Grabill, 282; Kazemzadeh, 251; Shaw, 481; Heller, 368.

Reviews: *AAPSS-A* 377 (1968):189-90, A.O. Sarkissian; *AHR* 73 (1968):1211, James Gidney; *MEJ* 23 (1969):87-9, Lawrence H. de Bivort; *MES* 5 (1969):269-71, M.S. Anderson.

553. Hovannisian, Richard G. *The First Year, 1918-1919. The Republic of Armenia*, volume 1. Los Angeles: University of California Press, 1971. xxiii + 547 pp.

Examines the brief life of the Armenian attempt to erect an independent state after World War I. Part of a two-volume work, of which only volume 1 is known to me, it is an exhaustive study and virtually alone in the field, except for Firuz Kazemzadeh's *The Struggle for Transcaucasia, 1917-1921*, item 320. While not a dispassionate study, it is supported by extensive research and backed-up by a lengthy bibliography. It examines the leadership and the ideology of the Republic, the internal politics, the struggles with other groups, the effort at the Paris Conference to secure Allied recognition and support, and the war with the Bolsheviks and a resurgent Turkey.

Cf. Sarkissian, 557; DeNovo, 281; Shaw, 481.

Reviews: *AHR* 77 (1972):1488-9, Thomas Bryson; *APSR* 69 (1975):315-6, Robert L. Daniel; *IJMES* 7 (1976):308-9, Firuz Kazemzadeh; *MEJ* 26 (1972):204-5, David Long.

554. Laquer, Walter Ze'ev. *A History of Zionism*. New York: Holt, Rinehart & Winston, 1972. xvi + 640 pp.

A comprehensive survey of the development of Zionism as an ideology, as an expression of Jewish nationalism, and as a political movement. Examines the background to the Jewish experience in Europe in the 19th century, especially the pogroms in eastern Europe and the anti-semitism exposed by the Dreyfus case in France, and how

this affected Theodor Herzl and those Jews who took up his efforts to form a Zionist organization. Laquer, not without sympathy for Zionism, traces the efforts of Weizmann and others during World War I to gain international recognition of Zionist goals and then briefly recounts the major events leading to the founding of Israel. A thorough study with a useful bibliography.
Cf. Hurewitz, 523; Halpern, 522.
Reviews: *JMH* 47 (1975):152-3, Léon Poliakov; *MEJ* 27 (1973):514-6, Aaron S. Klieman.

555. Landau, Jacob M. *Jews in Nineteenth-Century Egypt.* New York University. Studies in Near Eastern Civilization, no. 2. New York: New York University Press, 1969. xvii + 354 pp.

Studies the Jewish community in Egypt, concentrating on the late 19th century to World War I. Examines aspects of community organization, education, the rise of Zionism and intellectual pursuits. The second half of the book is a collection of documents in Hebrew, Arabic, French and English that support the text and indicate the types of material available in various archives, such as the Central Zionist Archives in Jerusalem, the Public Record Office in London, the archives of the Alliance Israélite Universalle in Paris (see Kedourie, item 444), and the French and Italian state archives. Also see Solomon Goitein, *Jews and Arabs: Their Contact through the Ages*, 3rd ed. (New York: Schocken Books, 1974).
Cf. Holt, 490; Baer, 487; Cohen, 549.
Reviews: *AHR* 75 (1970):2097, Oscar I. Jankowsky; *IJMES* 2 (1971):93-5, Helen A.B. Rivlin; *MEJ* 24 (1970): 538-9, David Kimche.

556. Naby, Eden. "The Assyrians of Iran: Reunification of a 'Millat,' 1906-1914." *International Journal of Middle East Studies* 8 (1977):237-49.

Study of the Assyrian community, a Christian minority group, in Iran and eastern Turkey. Concerns both Assyrian relations with Islamic neighbors and relations with other Christian groups, and the fate of the community. One of the few histories of the Assyrians, now dated, is W.A. Wigram, *The Assyrians and Their Neighbors* (London: Bell, 1929).
Cf. Grabill, 282.

557. Sarkissian, Arshag O. "Concert Diplomacy and the Armenians, 1890-1897." *Studies in Diplomatic History
and Historiography in Honour of G.P. Gooch*. Edited
by A.O. Sarkissian. London: Longmans, 1966, pp. 48-
75.

European concern for the Armenians and for the preservation (or division) of the Ottoman Empire often became confused. Sarkissian examines the origins and
rise of Armenian nationalism and Armenian attempts to
arouse European support for their cause, factors which,
in the troubled state of 19th-century Turkey, generated
tensions that led to horrible outrages and communal
violence. A similar study is Robert Zeidner's "Britain
and the Launching of the Armenian Question," item 559.
For background on the diplomatic history of the "Armenian Question," and Armenian relations with the Ottoman
Government and the European Powers, see Sarkissian,
History of the Armenian Question to 1885 (Champaign-
Urbana: University of Illinois Press, 1938); and on
British and Great Power interest in Ottoman reform and
minorities, see R.W. Seton-Watson, *Disraeli, Gladstone
and the Eastern Question* (London: Macmillan, 1935), as
well as Jelavich, item 206.
    Cf. Hovanissian, 551; Millman, 207; Shaw, 481; Lewis,
477; Anderson, 212; Busch, 285.

558. Weekes, Richard V., editor-in-chief. *Muslim Peoples:
A World Ethnographic Survey*. Westport, Conn.: Green-
wood Press, 1978. xxxv + 546 pp.

Contains essays by a number of experts on virtually
every Muslim group in the Middle East and Central Asia,
and elsewhere. Since the essays are by different contributors, their quality and depth vary, but as a quick
guide to the minorities as well as a list of relevant
sources on each group mentioned, it is an invaluable
aid.
    Cf. Hourani, 551.
    Reviews: *ARBA* 10 (1979):377; *CRL* 40 (1979):53.

559. Zeidner, Robert. "Britain and the Launching of the Armenian Question." *International Journal of Middle
East Studies* 7 (1976):465-83.

Studies the development of the Armenian Question as
an international issue between 1877-1890, and most particularly Britain's attitude toward Armenian nationalism and the atrocities in the late 19th century.
    Cf. Shaw, 481; Sarkissian, 557; Heller, 368; Taylor,
209.

CHAPTER 6
RECENT DOCTORAL THESES AND DISSERTATIONS
ON THE MIDDLE EAST

Arabia

560. al-Amr, S.M. "The Hijaz under Ottoman Rule, 1869-1914:
The Ottoman Vali, the Sharif of Mecca and the Growth
of British Influence." Leeds University, 1974.

561. Goldberg, David. "The Foreign Policy of the Third
Saudi State, 1902-1918." Harvard University, 1978.

562. Goldrup, Lawrence Paul. "Saudi Arabia: 1902-1932: The
Development of a Wahhabi Society." University of
California, Los Angeles, 1971.

563. El-Kurd, Abbas Ahmad. "The Hashemites' Role in the
Arab Independence Movement Against the Turks." New
York University, 1963.

564. Large, R.W.C. "The Extention of British Influence in
and around the Gulf of Aden, 1865-1905." School of
Oriental and African Studies, University of London,
1975.

565. Linabury, George Ogden. "Sa'udi Arab Relations, 1902-
1927: A Revisionist Interpretation." Columbia University, 1970.

566. Silverfarb, Daniel Nola. "British Relations with Ibn
Saud of Najd, 1914-1919." University of Wisconsin,
1972.

Egypt

567. Altman, Israel. "The Political Thought of Refa'ah Rafi' al-Tahtawi, A Nineteenth Century Egyptian Reformer." University of California, Los Angeles, 1976.

568. Atkins, Richard A. "British Policy Towards Egypt: 1864 to 1882." University of California, Berkeley, 1968.

569. Bradshaw, Dan Fred. "A Decade of British Opposition to the Suez Canal Project, 1854-1864." University of Oklahoma, 1973.

570. Cannon, Byron David. "The Politics of Judicial Reform: Egypt, 1876-1891." Columbia University, 1970.

571. Crabbs, Jack A. "The Historians of Egypt, 1798-1922." University of Chicago, 1972.

572. Crowther, D.R.F. "British Military Policy and the Defence of Egypt, 1882-1914." King's College, University of London, 1970.

573. Dessuuki, Ali E.H. "The Origins of Socialist Thought in Egypt, 1882-1922." McGill University, 1972.

574. Fakhrel-Deen, Tarek A.J. "Abd al-Rahman Shukir (1886-1958), an Egyptian Writer in the Age of Imperialism and Nationalism: A Study in the Influence of European Thought on Modern Arabic Literature." New York University, 1977.

575. Horn, Michael Serge. "The 'Urabi Revolution: Convergent Crises in Nineteenth Century Egypt." Harvard University, 1973.

576. Kazziha, W. "The Evolution of the Egyptian Political Elite, 1907-1921: A Case Study of the Role of the Large Landowners in Politics." School of Oriental and African Studies, University of London, 1970.

577. Kinsey, David C. "Egyptian Education under Cromer: A Study of East-West Encounter in Educational Administration and Policy, 1883-1907." Harvard University, 1965.

578. Lissauer, F. "British Policy Towards Egypt, 1914-1922."
      London School of Economics, 1975.

579. Mayer, Ann Elizabeth. "Abbas Helmi II: The Khedive and
      Egypt's Struggle for Independence." University of
      Michigan, 1978.

580. Meszaros, Paul Frank. "The Corporation of British Bond-
      holders and British Diplomacy in Egypt 1876 to 1882:
      The Efforts of an Interest Group in Policymaking."
      Loyola University (Chicago), 1973.

581. Mowat, R.C. "Lord Cromer and His Successors in Egypt."
      Oxford University, 1970.

582. Philipp, Thomas. "The Role of Jurji Zaidan in the In-
      tellectual Development of the Arab Nahda from the
      Beginning of the British Occupation of Egypt to the
      Outbreak of World War I." University of California,
      Los Angeles, 1971.

583. Platt, Wilfred Carlton, Jr. "Egypt on the Eve of the
      Great War." University of Georgia, 1966.

584. Rafuse, John Laurence. "Egypt and the British Parlia-
      ment, 1882-1918." Notre Dame University, 1972.

585. Roberts, Calvin Alexander. "The Egyptian Question and
      the Triple Alliance, 1884-1904." University of New
      Mexico, 1973.

586. Sevier, Candida Elizabeth. "The Anglo-Egyptian Con-
      dominium in the Southern Sudan, 1918-1939." Prince-
      ton University, 1975.

587. Smith, Rusnel Yales. "The Making of an Egyptian Na-
      tionalist: The Political Career of Saad Zaghlul Pasha
      Prior to 1919." Ohio State University, 1972.

588. Talhami, Ghada Haslem. "Egypt's 'Civilizing Mission':
      Khedive Isma'il's Red Sea Province, 1865-1885." Uni-
      versity of Illinois at Chicago Circle, 1975.

589. Ufford, Letitia W. "The Milner Mission to Egypt, 1919-
      1921: The Search for A Cooperative Class." Columbia
      University, 1977.

Iran

590. Garthwaite, Gene. "The Bakhtiyari Khans: Tribal Unity in Iran, 1880-1915." University of California, Los Angeles, 1969.

591. Karny, Azriel. "Mirza Hosein Khan Moshir od-Dowle and His Attempts at Reform in Iran, 1871-1873." University of California, Los Angeles, 1973.

592. Lorenz, John H. "Modernization and Political Change in Nineteenth-Century Iran: The Role of Amir Kabir." Princeton University, 1974.

593. Mangeneh-Nourai, Fereshteh. "The Life and Thought of Mirza Malkam Khan, 1833/4-1908: A Contribution to the History of Iranian Liberal Ideas." University of Colorado, 1970.

594. Nashat-Mudamad, Guity. "The Beginnings of Modernizing Reform in Iran, 1870-1880." University of Chicago, 1973.

595. Olson, William J. "Some Aspects of Anglo-Iranian Relations 1914-1919: A Study in Great Power Politics in Regional Affairs." University of Texas at Austin, 1977.

596. Philipp, Mangol Bayat. "Mirza Aga Khan Kirmani: Nineteenth Century Persian Revolutionary Thinker." University of California, Los Angeles, 1971.

597. Safiri, Floreeda. "A History of the South Persia Rifles: 1918-1921." University of Edinburgh, 1976.

598. Saleh, Jahangier. "Social Formations in Iran, 750-1914." University of Massachusetts, 1978.

599. Silberman, G.G. "The Persian Constitutional Revolution: The Economic Background, 1870-1906." School of Oriental and African Studies, University of London, 1975.

600. Strunk, William T. "The Reign of Shaykh Khaz'al ibn Jabir and the Suppression of the Principality of

'Arabistan: A Study in British Imperialism in Southwestern Iran, 1897-1925." University of Indiana,
1977.

601. Vatandoust, Gholamreza. "Sayyid Hasan Tagizadeh and
'Kaveh': Modernism in Post-Constitutional Iran (1916-
1921)." University of Washington, 1977.

Iraq

602. Atlar, Kerim A. "The Minorities of Iraq During the
Period of the Mandate, 1920-1932." Columbia University, 1967.

603. Fuleihan, D.E.B. "The Development of British Policy
in Iraq from 1914-1926." London School of Economics,
1970.

604. Marr, Phebe Ann. "Yasir al-Hashimi, the Rise and Fall
of a Nationalist (A Study of the Nationalist Leadership in Iraq, 1920-1936)." Harvard University, 1967.

605. Niama, K.H. "Anglo-Iraqi Relations During the Mandate."
University of Wales, Aberystwyth, 1975.

606. Stevens, William A. "The Mastery of Iraq: Anglo-
American Politics of Primacy and Oil, 1918-1930."
Johns Hopkins University, 1978.

607. Yaphe, Judith Share. "The Arab Revolt in Iraq of 1920."
University of Illinois at Champaign-Urbana, 1972.

Jordan

608. Mahmoud, Amir Abdullah. "King Abdullah and Palestine:
An Historical Study of His Role in the Palestine Problem from the Creation of Transjordan to the Annexation of the West Bank, 1921-1950." Georgetown University, 1972.

Lebanon

609. Abraham, Antoine. "Maronite-Druze Relations in Lebanon,
      1840-1960: A Prelude to Arab Nationalism." New York
      University, 1975.

610. Ajay, Nicholas, Jr. "Mount Lebanon and the Wilayah of
      Beirut, 1914-1918: The War Years." Georgetown Uni-
      versity, 1973.

611. Baaklini, Abdo Iskandar. "Legislatures and Political
      Development: Lebanon: 1840-1970." State University
      of New York at Albany, 1972.

Middle East

612. Adelson, Roger Dean. "The Formation of British Policy
      Towards the Middle East, 1914-1918." Columbia Uni-
      versity, 1976.

613. Darwin, G.J. "The Lloyd George Coalition Government
      and Britain's Imperial Policy in Egypt and the Middle
      East, 1918-22." Oxford University, 1976.

614. Davies, C. "British Oil Policy in the Middle East,
      1919-1932." University of Edinburgh, 1976.

615. Kearney, Helen McCready. "American Images of the Middle
      East, 1824-1924: A Century of Antipathy." University
      of Rochester (New York), 1976.

616. Khoury, Nabil A. "Islam and Modernization in the Middle
      East: Muhammad Abduh, An Ideology of Development."
      State University of New York at Albany, 1976.

617. Klein, Ira. "British Imperialism in Conflict and Al-
      liance: Anglo-French and Anglo-Russian Relations,
      1885-1914." Columbia University, 1968.

618. Louis, M.C. "Some British Attitudes to Islamic Aspira-
      tions, 1878-1914." University of Manchester, 1971.

619. Marshall, Caroline Terrell. "Gertrude Bell: Her Work and Influence in the Near East, 1914-1926." University of Virginia, 1968.

620. Reguer, Sara. "Winston Churchill and the Shaping of the Middle East, 1919-1922." Columbia University, 1976.

621. Rose, Linda Carol. "Britain in the Middle East, 1914-1918: Design or Accident." Columbia University, 1969.

622. Stanwood, Frederick Julian. "Britain in Central Asia, 1917-1919: A Study of the Empire's Response to Nationalism, Bolshevism and Idealism." University of California, San Diego, 1969.

623. Thomas, James Paul. "The Sykes-Picot Agreement of 1916: Its Genesis in British Policy." Johns Hopkins University, 1971.

Palestine

624. Bensinger, Gad J. "Palestine in German Thought and Action, 1871-1914." Loyola University, 1971.

625. Doxsee, Gifford. "British Policy Towards Palestine, 1914-1939." Harvard University, 1966.

626. Herrman, I.R. "Arab-Zionist Relations from Herzl to the Balfour Declaration." Oxford University, 1971.

627. Knox, Dennis Edward. "The Development of British Policy in Palestine, 1907-1915: Sir Gilbert Clayton and the 'Near Eastern Question.'" Michigan State University, 1971.

628. McTague, John. "British Policy in Palestine, 1917-1922." State University of New York at Buffalo, 1974.

629. Marom, Ran. "Soviet Russia and the Jewish Communists of Palestine: 1917-1921." Georgetown University, 1975.

630. Miller, Ryana Nolmie. "From Village to Nation: Govern-ment and Society in Rural Palestine, 1920-1948." University of California, Berkeley, 1975.

631. Nashif, Taisir N. "A Quantitative Comparative Study of the Jewish and Palestine Arab Political Elite (1920-48)." State University of New York at Bing-hamton, 1974.

632. Pick, Walter Pinha S. "The Development and History of Railways in Palestine, Israel, and Adjoining Areas from 1838." Dropsie University, 1976.

633. Schoenberg, Philip Ernest. "Palestine in the Year 1914." New York University, 1978.

634. Silverberg, Sanford Robert. "Organization and Violence: The Palestinian Arab Nationalistic Response, 1920-1948." American University, 1973.

635. Taqqu, Rachelle Leah. "Arab Labor in Mandatory Pales-tine, 1920-1948." Columbia University, 1977.

636. Tsimhosi, D. "The British Mandate and the Arab Chris-tians in Palestine, 1920-1925." School of Oriental and African Studies, University of London, 1976.

Persian Gulf

637. Morsy, 'Abdullah M. "Britain and the Trucial States between 1892 and 1939." Cambridge University, 1975.

638. al-Ramaihi, M.G. "Social and Political Change in Bahrain Since World War I." Durham University, 1972.

Sudan

639. Bukhari, S.A.R. "Military Aspects on Internal Security in the Anglo-Egyptian Sudan, 1898-1925, with Special Reference to the Northern Sudan." Master's thesis, Royal Holloway College, University of London, 1971.

640. Goode, James Hubbard. "The Fashoda Crisis: A Survey of
      Anglo-French Imperial Policy in the Upper Nile Ques-
      tion, 1882-1899." North Texas State University, 1971.

641. Mohammed, Hassan Abdin. "The Growth of Nationalist
      Movements in the Sudan, 1919-1925." University of
      Wisconsin, 1971.

                              Syria

642. Abu Manneh, B. "Some Aspects of Ottoman Rule in Syria
      in the Second Half of the Nineteenth Century: Reforms,
      Islam and Caliphate." Oxford University, 1971.

643. Hreib, Alaeddin Saleh. "The Influence of Sub-Regional-
      ism (Rural Areas) on the Structure of Syrian Politics."
      Georgetown University, 1976.

644. Kalla, Mohammad. "The Role of Foreign Trade in the
      Economic Development of Syria, 1831-1914." American
      University, 1969.

645. Miller, Joyce Laverty. "Henry de Jouvenel and the
      Syrian Mandate." Bryn Mawr College, 1970.

646. Russell, Malcolm Bruce. "The Birth of Modern Syria:
      Amir Faysal's Government in Damascus, 1918-1920."
      Johns Hopkins University, 1977.

647. Saliba, Najib. "Wilayat Suriyya, 1876-1909." Univer-
      sity of Michigan, 1971.

                             Turkey

648. Akarli, Ergin Deniz. "Ottoman Politics under Abdul-
      hamid II (1876-1908): Origins and Solutions." Prince-
      ton University, 1976.

649. Arslanian, Artin. "The British Military Involvement in
      Transcaucasia, 1917-1919." University of California,
      Los Angeles, 1974.

650. Attrep, Abraham. "The Road to the Empty Peace: Anglo-
Turkish Relations, 1918-1920." University of Georgia,
1972.

651. De Luca, Anthony Rocco. "The Turkish Straits." Stanford University, 1974.

652. Devore, Ronald Marvin. "British Military Consuls in
Asia Minor, 1878-1882." Indiana University, 1973.

653. Heller, Joseph. "British Policy Towards the Ottoman
Empire, 1908-1914." London School of Economics,
1970.

654. Macfie, A.L. "The Straits Question, 1908-1936."
Birkbeck College, University of London, 1973.

655. Milgrim, Michael. "The 1878 War Indemnity: A Neglected
Problem in Russo-Turkish Relations." University of
Pennsylvania, 1974.

656. Montgomery, A.E. "Allied Policy in Turkey from the
Armistice of Mudros, 30 October, 1918, to the Treaty
of Lausanne, 24 July 1923." Birkbeck College, London
University, 1970.

657. Ochsenwald, William. "The Hijaz Railroad: A Study in
Ottoman Political Capacity and Autonomy." Chicago
University, 1972.

658. Quataert, Donald. "Ottoman Reform and Agriculture in
Anatolia, 1876-1908." University of California, Los
Angeles, 1973.

659. Rice, Eber Harold. "British Policy in Turkey: 1908-
1914." University of Toronto, 1974.

660. Skaggs, Glenn Eugene. "Britain at the Straits: A Study
of British Diplomacy Toward the Turkish Straits,
1900-1923." Georgetown University, 1977.

661. Snodgrass, Nancy. "The Chanak Crisis: A Study in British Diplomacy." University of Illinois at Champaign-
Urbana, 1971.

662. Sullivan, Charles Donald. "Stamboul Crossings: German
Diplomacy in Turkey, 1908 to 1914." Vanderbilt University, 1977.

663.   Swanson, Glen W.   "Mahmud Şevket Paşa and the Defense
       of the Ottoman Empire: A Study of War and Revolution
       During the Young Turk Period."   Indiana University,
       1970.

664.   Woods, J.F.   "British Railway Investment in Turkey,
       with Special Reference to the Imperial Ottoman Rail-
       way from Smyrna to Aidin, 1856-1935."   Master's thesis,
       Birkbeck College, University of London, 1979.

INDEX

All numbers refer to item numbers. Underlined numbers refer to authors or subjects of annotated main
entries; other numbers, preceded by "in," refer to
authors or subjects mentioned within an annotated
main entry. Arabic and Persian names of authors are
treated differently than those of subjects--authors'
names are inverted (i.e., the final portion of the
name is treated as a surname and placed ahead of
the first portions of the name), but subjects' names
are not inverted (although an initial article "al-"
is not used for alphabetizing).